The Arms Trade and International Systems

The Arms Trade and International Systems

Robert E. Harkavy
Kalamazoo College

Ballinger Publishing Company ● Cambridge, Mass.
A Subsidiary of J.B. Lippincott Company

International Standard Book Number: 0-88410-021-9

Library of Congress Catalog Card Number: 74-14844

Printed in the United States of America

Library of Congress Cataloging in Publication Data

Harkavy, Robert E
   The arms trade and international systems.

   Includes bibliographical references.
   1. Munitions. 2. Weapons systems. 3. International relations. I. Title.
HD9743.A2H37   382'.45'6234   74-14844
ISBN 0-88410-021-9

To Jane, Michael,
my Mother and Father,
with Gratitude.

Contents

List of Tables

Foreword

This work on the arms trade originated in 1969, at a time when little of even a descriptive or fact-finding nature, much less something with any analytical or theoretical content, had heretofore been assayed on a subject of rather obvious global import. However, during the course of my research and writing, studies made by teams at the MIT Center for International Studies, the London Institute for Strategic Studies and the Stockholm International Peace Research Institute have resulted in a wealth of information on arms transfers in the contemporary period and have provided some useful, applicable modes of analysis.

Still, nothing of broad theoretical thrust nor anything with an historical, systemic dimension had emerged. Thus, it is hoped that this work, with all of its obvious limitations, including sins of commission as well as of omission, may serve as a halting step in that direction, perhaps, if nothing else, providing some inspiration for others who might wish to pursue the subject either more deeply or broadly.

Concerning sins of omission, it will be apparent to the reader that large, important dimensions of the subject of the arms trade, and some regions around its periphery, are touched upon only lightly here. Among these are the comparative behavior and decision-making structures of arms supplier nations, the distribution of economic and political motivations for arms-selling, the motives or imperatives of the acquirers of arms, the economic costs or trade-offs incurred by purchasers of arms—particularly those in the emergent nations category—and the extent to which arms suppliers are able to achieve broad political and economic influence through these activities. Each of these subjects could by itself serve as a focus for a major work. None has yet been attempted in any of these areas. The author, with the simple excuse that one must establish priorities and boundaries somewhere, makes no apologies for giving them short shrift.

In revising this work for publication, I became painfully aware of just how quickly the onrush of events can outrun research, the basic framework for which seemed essentially durable only a few years ago. Among other things, the events in the Middle East in October, 1973 strongly indicated that a new era of conventional warfare and weaponry had dawned, and concomitantly, that the basic nature of the arms trade had also been altered. No longer could it so simply be measured and categorized by movements of aircraft, tanks and ships, when a perusal of military journals indicated that transactions in electronic counter-measure equipment, complex radars and computers, pilotless drones, laser- and television-guided stand-off bombs and missiles, and surprisingly effective new antitank weapons had become central to relations between major and minor powers and to power balances between nations in both categories. The nature of the diplomacy of the arms trade remained essentially intact, although growing world resource problems seemed to augur trends toward barter arrangements involving arms transfers for some developing nations in exchange for scarce raw materials. These matters will be subjects of concern for future writers.

Acknowledgements

I owe a debt of gratitude to a number of people who have aided me in this enterprise. First, to Professors Bruce M. Russett—a particularly effective and helpful advisor—John D. Sullivan, H. Bradford Westerfield, William Foltz and Paul Wolfowitz of the Yale Political Science Department, who all were generous with advice and comments at various stages of my work. Then, to Amelia C. Leiss of the arms control project at the MIT Center for International Studies, who very generously provided assistance and, with the consent of the United States Arms Control and Disarmament Agency, granted me the use of data for the postwar period. Without her aid, I could not have gotten to first base. Geoffrey Kemp, also of the MIT arms control project, provided additional advice. Michael Mihalka, formerly an MIT undergraduate, was invaluable in carrying out the computer programming and in providing additional assistance in processing the data.

John Taylor and the other members of the staff of the Modern Military Division, National Archives, in Washington, D.C. spent many long hours helping me cope with the arcana of the filing system of that great depository of historical materials. I apologize belatedly for having set what they claimed was a modern record for the number of documents pulled from the files.

The author received financial support for this project from the following sources: the de Karman Scholarship Fund (administered by the Aerojet-General Corporation); the United States Arms Control and Disarmament Agency Fellowship Program—Grant ACDA/E-158 (administered by the National Academy of Sciences); the Kalamazoo College Faculty Development Committee; and the Advanced Research Projects Agency, Contract N0014-67-A-0097-007, monitored by the Office of Naval Research.

Anthony Chipello of New Haven is owed a special debt for innumerable kindnesses rendered over a number of years during my period of graduate work and beyond. Mrs. Dorothy Bauckham did an excellent job of typing and editing the draft manuscript, and is accordingly heartily thanked.

Most of all I wish to thank my beloved wife, Jane, for having forborne with grace a seemingly interminable period of work on this book and for valuable assistance in the editing of it.

The Arms Trade and International Systems

Chapter One

The International Arms Trade

Until recently in the postwar period, the subject of the international trade in arms has received surprisingly scant attention from specialists or theorists in international relations despite its persistent and sometimes overriding importance in the affairs of nations. This has been the case despite the obvious fact that sales, loans and gifts of weapons have become a huge global business and a veritable hinge of global politics. One might indeed be tempted to claim that the international trade in arms—in all its aspects, from the smuggling of a crate of small arms to a clandestine revolutionary movement, to the transfer of a Phantom, Mirage or MIG jet to governmental clients of major powers—has become the weightiest and most important instrument of international power and diplomacy.

The lack of emphasis in the scholarly literature of international relations is particularly striking with respect to general, theoretical or macrolevel analyses which might serve to relate the patterns of arms flows to some of the other traditional staple concerns of the discipline: alliance patterns, the extent and rigidity of bloc polarization, the ideological content of international rivalries, the distribution of power among leading nations of a period and the mood or zeitgeist of an epoch as reflective of varying emphasis on totality of conflict. Further, the few recent studies made of the arms trade in the postwar period have been altogether lacking in historical perspective, paying little heed to long-range trends or to the interrelation of arms flow patterns with some of the above enumerated systems characteristics.

A review of the general literature on military history reveals almost nothing about the process of weapons acquisition on the part of the protagonists of man's countless and unceasing violent conflicts. Military histories such as those by B. Liddell-Hart and J. F. C. Fuller, while quite detailed on the ebbs and flows of weapons developments and innovations and corresponding tactics and strategies, reveal little about where the weapons have come from, whether from external sources or through various possible types of internal acquisition.[1] Some military histories, Fuller's in particular, contain implicit theories about the reciprocal relationship between social structures and values on the one hand, and the use of weapons and receptivity to innovation in weaponry on the other.[2] But there is little concrete information at hand concerning the capability of various nations in different periods to make their own weapons, the extent of their dependence on others or the mechanisms by which such dependence has been overcome.[3] As we shall see, the reciprocal relationship between weapons dependence and independence (autarky) is critical to an explanation of the patterns of weapons transfers.

If the recent historical literature of the Western world contains such lacunae, the omissions are even greater for nonwestern societies of the past, in periods before the present truly interrelated international system had taken shape.[4] Further, the extent and modes of the diffusion of weapons technology between earlier subsystems, existing in quasi-isolation, remain obscure. For it is only in the past few centuries, with the advent of increased global interaction and the gradual blurring of previously more distinct geographical subsystem boundaries, that one can truly speak of an international arms market qua market.

An investigation of premodern patterns of the arms trade as applied to theorizing on this subject for this century is not merely a matter of idle curiosity. As an example, one of the initial central assumptions in the writing of this book was that there must have been a long-term secular trend toward increasing dependency on the part of a larger number of nations or entities, in line with increasing technological change and greater international interaction. Conversely, the assumption was that the number of nations capable of achieving autarky in weapons production has gradually been diminished. This ought, I had speculated, to have been the case as one moved from a system composed of more primitive to relatively advanced nations, and from limited subsystems to a relatively global system. That is, an inexorable trend was hypothesized in the direction of more and more of the world's nations becoming weapons-dependent, which if it were and is the case would have very critical diplomatic implications. As we shall see, however, there are both cyclical and linear trends at work, due to the ebbs and flows of various factors, which confound any easy generalizations.

Needless to say, an extensive long-range historical analysis of these problems would be beyond the possible scope of this book. As a step in this direction, however, this inquiry consists of a comparative analysis of the worldwide arms trade for major weapons systems in what are normally considered two distinct diplomatic periods: the period between the world wars (hereafter referred to as the interwar period), and the present post-World War II period. Some scattered materials from prior eras will be discussed briefly in order to gain some perspective on the modern era and to question, tentatively, whether long-range trends may be adduced on the basis of limited information.

THEORETICAL THRUST OF THIS STUDY

To the extent that this study purports to be a contribution to the corpus of international relations theory, beyond a mere description of the patterns of the arms trade in two periods, its inspiration is derived from some recent attempts at applying general systems analysis to the study of international politics. However, a really adequate discussion of my intention to tie this study to this recent intellectual trend would involve a lengthy analysis of a whole range of epistemological problems.

Systems Analysis and Theory

Over a decade ago, in a cogent critique of then extant and dominant theories of international relations, Stanley Hoffmann made a plea for an effort toward developing what he referred to as, borrowing a term from Raymond Aron, a "sociology of international relations." After critically dismembering a number of previously elaborated general theories of international relations centered on such concepts as equilibrium, balance and power, he urged the use of inductive methods, utilizing the materials of diplomatic history to supersede a prior tendency toward allegedly simplistic and deductive theorizing.[5]

Since Hoffmann's work, efforts at theorizing in international relations along these lines have not been altogether lacking. Building upon Morton Kaplan's pioneering work on identification and analysis of international systems, which essentially utilized ideal-type systems, Richard Rosecrance made an important attempt at an inductively based framework for the study of successive diplomatic systems or constellations.[6] Using such key characteristics as what he termed the "regulator" of the system and the "ethos of elites," he focused on a description of the systems themselves rather than on the impact of systems characteristics upon aspects of international politics such as the arms trade.

More recently, under the aegis of J. David Singer and Melvin Small, a group of scholars at the University of Michigan has undertaken a "Correlates of War" project which is in many ways an attempt at following up on Hoffmann's strictures about the necessity for an inductive approach utilizing the materials of diplomatic history. Here, data have been collected on alliances, wars, national capabilities, trade patterns, intergovernmental organizations, national attributes and a plethora of other variables for the whole period since the Congress of Vienna in 1815. These characteristics have been interrelated within what is at least implicitly a systems approach.[7]

This study is an effort at building upon this intellectual trend, using various aspects of the arms trade as dependent variables which are in turn acted upon by those systems characteristics deemed most critical in their determination. Given the difference in purpose here from Rosecrance's general theoretical work, the systems variables used will be chosen at a lower level of abstraction, to allow for some meaningful discussion of cause and effect relationships.

The use of the terms "dependent" and "independent" variables is somewhat hazardous in this type of analysis, for what is really involved is a complicated web of reciprocity. One can, on the one hand, analyze aspects of the arms trade as functions of various general systems characteristics, while simultaneously realizing that the nature of the arms trade itself is an important characteristic of a given system, itself impinging causally on a host of other variables such as the distribution of power among nations, alliances and overall trade patterns.

Given some of these difficulties, what is assayed here is a step toward a model in which the basic lines of influence are delineated between aspects of the arms trade and some of the aforementioned variable characteristics which describe any diplomatic epoch.

Extrapolation to Future

Another rationale for a combined historical and systems approach to the study of the arms trade is that of using the past in conjunction with the present to anticipate the future. One of the primary theses of this work is that an analysis of the past patterns of the arms trade may aid in understanding emerging present patterns—and by extrapolation what may be expected in the future—for the very reason that present trends in this area appear to be somewhat reminiscent of the past. The basic point here, to be developed more fully later, is the seeming movement from a bipolar to a multipolar or balance of power international system in which ideological ties appear to be waning.[8] The basic structure of the international system, that is, seems to be moving towards a partial return to that of the pre-World War II period.

As we shall see, however, the factors of polarity, alliances and ideology are only a few of the variables impinging upon the patterns of the arms trade. Also, one must resort at some point to the truism that each epoch is unique. Thus, the advent of nuclear weapons has introduced a new factor to be considered in judging the relative power of nations, or degrees of polarity, even though the structure of the nuclear supplier market may be viewed as an extension of that for "conventional" weapons.

FRAMEWORK FOR ANALYSIS

We may now proceed to outline the basic framework for analysis, indicating some of the variables, categories and typologies to be used in subsequent chapters. First we shall define and explain those aspects of the arms trade to be used as dependent variables in a loose sense. Then, briefly, we shall indicate those characteristics, varying between diplomatic eras, which shall be used as independent variables. In the following chapter, these systems variables will be examined in greater detail in terms of their assumed or predicted impact upon the arms trade in different periods. Finally, we shall set up a diagrammatic model describing the essential relationships under investigation and stating some of the basic hypotheses of this study.

Dependent Variables

Four separate through interconnected areas of concern will serve as categories for analyzing the various aspects of the arms trade. These are broadly designated as follows: (1) the structure of the supplier market and the "behavior" of various suppliers; (2) donor-recipient patterns and their juxtaposition upon other types of internation association; (3) the distribution of transfer modes or methods, according to type; and (4) the reciprocal extent of dependency and autarky exhibited in weapons acquisition or production by nations at various levels of economic development.[9]

Supplier Markets and the Behavior of Suppliers. There are a number of interconnected questions regarding the structure of the supplier markets and the differential behavior of various factors in those markets. Concerning market structures, analysis may be conducted by analogy with the traditional method for examining corporate market shares, centering on questions such as the number of factors in the market, changes in market shares over time and analysis of various products (weapons types) according to differing levels of oligopoly prevailing in different periods.[10]

The most critical question here, and one with significant implications for controls, is that of the number of suppliers of given weapons types existing at any given time. This is virtually, but not quite, the same as the number of nations capable of producing the various types of weapons, or how many are actually engaged in production.

There will be, at times, anomalous cases, such as Sweden in the postwar period, where a nation producing various types of weapons systems will not be a significant factor in the supplier markets for policy reasons such as that of maintaining a neutralist posture in world affairs.[11] In most cases, however, smaller factors in the market will not produce merely for internal consumption, as the necessity for achieving economies of scale will in effect require export of a significant percentage of production.

The number of extant suppliers and the breakdown of market shares will, of course, vary by weapons system. One would expect a smaller number of suppliers for the more technologically sophisticated and expensive weapons systems and a larger number for more prosaic and inexpensive ones. Hence, the market would naturally be expected to narrow as one moves from small arms to jet aircraft or to nuclear weapons.

One question is whether there appears to be a long-term secular trend toward a lesser number of nations being able to produce the "state of the art" weapons systems of a period, and hence a lesser number of factors in the supplier markets. As previously noted, this appears to be almost intuitively obvious in long-range historical perspective. But the number of producers and suppliers of weapons systems will depend on the structure of the international system itself, as well as on technological and cost factors. Concerning controls, it is clear that, other things being equal, they should be more easily afforded where there are a small number of supplier factors.

Besides the basic structure of the supplier market, we will also look at some aspects of the "behavior" of various types of suppliers. The behavior of arms suppliers, in some contrast to behavior in "normal" competitive economic markets, is not limited to price considerations, although one possible hypothesis is that this disparity is heightened in primarily ideological systems or where stringent governmental controls are being applied.

There will be varying propensities by different suppliers to transfer arms of varying modernity or quality.[12] There will also be varying tendencies toward limiting transfers to a small number of nations, or, alternately, toward spreading transfers among a larger number of recipient nations. The latter tendencies will also be affected by the amount of arms which can be diverted from internal use, and ultimately by the amount of a certain type produced. Such calculations have affected, for instance, United States aircraft supplies to Israel, in the light of earlier Vietnam requirements among other things and, more recently, American tank supplies to Israel.[13] In the interwar period an example was the Soviet Union's dilemma in 1936-1937 over allocation of a limited supply of planes and tanks between Loyalist Spain and the Kuomintang in China, with its own forces a rival claimant for scarce materiel.[14]

Finally, with regard to supplier behavior, one can test hypotheses on the respective behavior of revisionist or expansionist nations or blocs and defensive or conservative ones insofar as one can make such easy dichotomous designations. One would expect, over time, that expansionist nations or blocs would have less interest in controls and would be more willing to use arms shipments to expand influence and perhaps to stir up trouble out of which gains of various kinds might be made. As we shall see, the parallel between the Axis powers in the interwar period and the Soviet bloc in the postwar one is rather striking.[15]

Donor-Recipient Patterns and Relationships.   Basically, this central dimension of the arms trade involves questions of who supplies arms to whom, in what amounts, when and in what aggregate patterns. Going beyond a mere description of these patterns, what is involved is an attempt at analyzing client ties in terms of alliance patterns, ideological cohesion and other types of internation association.

A key question here is that of the propensity of various recipient nations to acquire their weapons over time either primarily from one supplier (single client relationship) or from several (multiple client relationship). The stability of such relationships over time is an additional important question.

With regard to juxtaposition of arms trade patterns upon alliance networks, a key question is whether multiple client relationships involve suppliers within alliance blocs, across blocs or in a mixture of bloc ties and relationships with neutrals. These questions, like those pertaining to the size and structure of the supplier market, will have important implications for the possibility of controls.[16] Multiple client relationships, particularly those running across ideologically based alliance blocs, may be more conducive to bargaining on the part of dependent nations which can play off one side against the other to the extent that their economic and diplomatic leverage may allow for such a strategy. As we shall see, recent trends towards an increase in multiple, cross-bloc client relationships are reminiscent of conditions which obtained during the interwar years and would seem to indicate in themselves some movement towards multipolarity in the system.

Transfer Modes.   The third general aspect of the arms trade to be analyzed in comparative focus is that of the varying distribution of the use of different transfer modes. In addition to the most prevalent modes—outright sale or military assistance (including long-term loans or barter)—use has been made in both periods of licensing, assembly abroad, coproduction, codevelopment, capture in the aftermath of or during wars and copying.[17]

In previous centuries, particularly during the Renaissance but also through the 19th century, labor mobility constituted an additional type of transfer mode, with the relatively free movement of weapons specialists for hire across borders. The present virtual absence of this transfer mode is one illustration of long-range changes created by increasing emphasis on the totality of diplomacy and warfare, by broad changes in economic practices and by decreased movements of populations in an era where nationalism holds increasing sway.

Also, before current restrictions were placed on arms manufacture in capitalist countries, large international armaments corporations were able to operate abroad with virtual impunity in setting up subsidiaries which, in turn, could sell weapons without the hindrance of end-use restrictions. The previously far greater internationalization of the worldwide munitions industry had important implications for the mechanisms by which weaponry was formerly diffused since few, if any, controls were applied to the foreign subsidiaries of these companies.

The frequency of the use of different transfer modes may, therefore, vary with the practices of diplomatic eras. Further, the extensive use of licensing and assembly may, in the absence of end-use restrictions, greatly increase the available number of suppliers for dependent countries, constituting thereby an additional problem for controls. That is, nations not capable of independent design and development of weapons systems may, nevertheless, become important, though indirect, factors of supply and develop capability for an independent arms base in the process.

Dependence and Autarky.   The final aspect of arms trade patterns to be examined involves the reciprocal notions of dependence and autarky, that is, degrees of weapons-producing independence. Here one is reversing the analysis of the supplier market and examining the dependence of given nations in each weapons category, ranging from total dependence to complete independence. Clearly, the context is broader here than with analysis of supplier markets as it entails examination of efforts at low-level weapons production by many smaller nations which are not significant factors in the supplier markets. The subject is rendered more complex in that the use of some transfer modes, such as licensing and assembly, can represent intermediate forms of dependence or independence.

In historical context, an important question here, again, is whether a larger number of countries are becoming dependent for their weapons upon a smaller number of suppliers, which in turn raises questions of why this may be the case. Another critical question is whether various unilateral and multilateral efforts at controls will push normally dependent nations toward attempting to achieve higher degrees of autarky. Israel and South Africa are present examples.

Finally, if arms production data can be related to those on economic capacity and development (measured in GNP or per capita GNP), analysis can be made of the constraints imposed on efforts toward autarky by basic economic capability, although again the impact of these factors will be mitigated by others deriving from the overall structure of the international system.

Independent Variables

In the next chapter we shall examine in detail each of a number of characteristics of diplomatic eras in terms of their differential impact on the aforementioned aspects of the arms trade. At this point, and before examining a basic model indicating the basic relationships involved, let us briefly list and define those systems characteristics which will be used.

The identification of diplomatic or epochal systems is itself an arguable matter. The very notion of "system" is a mere reification, and particularly problematic in terms of temporal boundaries, even in a case such as the one under study where the dividing line between the interwar and postwar periods presents a rather clear juncture. As we shall see, however, the dividing lines between diplomatic eras do not necessarily coincide with dividing lines or watersheds for specific aspects of the arms trade. An example is the basic change in the nature of the arms trade caused by the imposition of licensing controls by many Western nations in the mid-1930s. Also, some of the characteristics associated with given periods (such as types of alliance systems, bipolarity, etc.) need not be altogether consistent throughout a period.

At any rate, the first set of important systemic factors impinging upon the arms trade includes alliance systems, polarity, the extent to which ideology is the basis of conflict between the major powers and the distribution or gradient of power among the major nations of a period. These factors, in combination, aggregate to a structural picture of the international system at any given time or for any given period.

Perhaps the most basic distinguishing structural characteristic of a system is that set of factors which defines a diplomatic constellation along a continuum from bipolar to multipolar. In terms of both senses of the latter concepts—that having to do with bloc structure and that with the distribution of power among major nations—there are important implications for the arms trade. Likewise, the varying degrees to which international systems can be characterized in terms of ideological locus of conflict as opposed to primarily balance of power considerations are also crucial to arms trade patterns. Ideological periods of diplomacy tend to be characterized by predictable patterns of arms flows within allegiant bloc relationships.

Other variables affecting the patterns of the arms trade differentially between periods are: the extent of governmental controls or licensing as opposed to private decision making in a laissez faire context, the degree of emphasis on totality in diplomacy and warfare and the rate of technological change in weaponry. The problem of totality is closely linked to that of ideological conflict, while the distribution of governmental and private controls over decision making with respect to arms sales has historically been determined by the overall context of modes of economic intercourse prevailing in a given period, be it mercantilism, laissez faire or state capitalism and socialism. As we shall see, the advent of substantial governmental controls in most nations in the 1930s may perhaps be viewed, retrospectively, as signaling the end of an anachronism based on the economic theories and practices of an earlier era.[18]

These systems variables will be discussed in greater detail in the next chapter. The foregoing brief identification of the most important period characteristics impinging on aspects of the arms trade should enable us, at this point, to set out the basic relationships which underpin this study.

BASIC MODEL OF THE RELATIONSHIP BETWEEN ASPECTS OF THE ARMS TRADE AND SYSTEMIC CHARACTERISTICS

In Figure 1-1 the basic lines of relationship between the most important systems characteristics and the four aforementioned aspects of the arms trade are indicated. The diagram depicts these relationships in a somewhat oversimplified

Figure 1-1. Comparison of Postwar and Interwar Arms Trade Relationships (Diagrammatic Model)

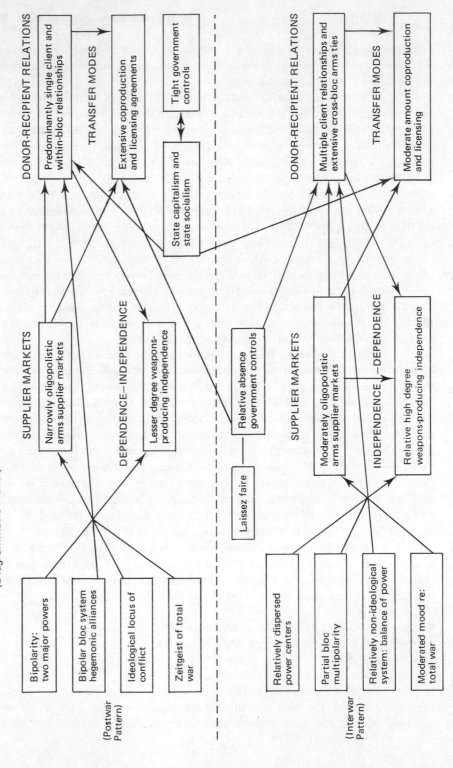

schematic way and may ignore some important feedback mechanisms. In subsequent discussion of these relationships we shall attempt to analyze some qualifications, paradoxes and nuances.

The diagram is divided horizontally into models depicting the essentials of the postwar and interwar relationships governing the patterns of the arms trade. These relationships give rise to a number of basic hypotheses which can be stated in terms of opposite pairs pertaining respectively to the two periods. These hypotheses are based on what ought to be the "logical" outcomes of these relationships and do not necessarily anticipate actual research results, although they were derived from exploratory scanning of historical materials. The initial inspiration for the model was, in fact, drawn from what appeared to have been some rather peculiar patterns of arms trading in the 1930s, of which more later.

Hypotheses

In the postwar period that concatenation of factors involving bipolarity, stable hegemonic alliances under the leadership of the two major powers, an ideological locus of conflict and a zeitgeist of total war has given rise to: (1) narrowly oligopolistic supplier markets, both in terms of the absolute number of suppliers and of the dominance of the market by two major powers; (2) the relative predominance of single client donor-recipient relationships and within-bloc acquisition patterns both for members of the major alliance blocs and for peripheral or nominally neutral nations; (3) extensive coproduction and licensing agreements based on expectations of the stability of client ties and alliances by supplier nations; and (4) a generally lesser degree of striving for weapons-producing autarky by small and medium-range powers based on expectations of stable relationships with long-term suppliers as well as on cost and technological factors.

In the interwar period a different constellation of factors, involving relatively dispersed centers of power among major nations, fragmented bloc multipolarity, shifting alliances and the relative absence of ideological conflict in conjunction with a more moderate mood of totality, gave rise to: (1) only moderately oligopolistic supplier markets in most major weapons categories, due both to factors of technological capability and of the contingent nature of supply sources; (2) a relatively greater number of multiple client relationships and extensive arms acquisitions across the lines of alliance blocs on the part of peripheral nations; (3) only moderate numbers of licensing and coproduction agreements due to the instability of relationships; and (4) a relatively high degree of striving for arms production capability by middle-range and small powers whose supplier sources were somewhat unsure, thus in turn broadening the supplier markets.

As the diagram indicates, however, the overall model for the two periods is complicated by the factor of governmental controls and licensing. For, paradoxically, this factor has usually tended to operate in the opposite direction from the combination of variables which describes the essential structure of either period. Thus, the laissez faire mood of the interwar period should have resulted in more promiscuous dispensing of licensing agreements, even though the rapidly shifting diplomatic patterns of that time would not appear to have militated in that direction. Today's ally, given modern weapons technology, could easily become tomorrow's enemy and, hence, the resupplier of that technology to other enemies.

This factor also mitigates some assumptions that the latter part of the postwar period evidences some trends reminiscent of interwar patterns. As bipolarity gives way to multipolarity, as the ideological content of international conflict subsides or gives way to traditional balance of power considerations, the fact of strict governmental controls remains. For this reason, a return to the somewhat random and often surprising patterns of the interwar arms trade would clearly not be predicted for the near future, although there are strong trends toward cross-bloc acquisition patterns for many of the nations of the Third World and even for some normally considered somewhat aligned with one bloc or another.

The Arms Trade Literature

In reviewing the scholarly literature on the arms trade in the whole of the 20th century, it is apparent that interest in the subject has been narrowly concentrated in three specific periods. These spurts of interest are easily related to the events of the time. During and immediately after World War I there was a flurry of writings in which questions were posed about the role of munitions makers in causing the arms races which had preceded that conflict.[19] The machinations of the "arms international" were considered by some a prime cause of the war. In the mid-1930s there was a prolific outpouring of writing on the arms trade, much of it of the muckraking or exposé variety.[20] Its immediate impetus arose from the furor over the conflict situations in China, the Chaco, Ethiopia and Spain. This was the period of the Nye Committee hearings and the neutrality laws (and their equivalents in Great Britain, France and elsewhere) and the result was a tightening of controls on arms exports by the several Western powers. The mood of pacifism and isolationism then prevalent among segments of the population in those countries, the Great Depression and the impact of revisionist theories about the causes of the First World War also played important roles.

Aside from the efforts of muckraking publicists, evidence of considerable interest in the interwar arms trade is found in the international legal journals.[21] No doubt this is generally reflective of the legalistic approach to the study of international relations which then prevailed. The complicated legal issues surrounding transfers under the neutrality laws gave further impetus in this direction, at least for the United States.

An additional important source of information and forum for discussion on the interwar arms trade was the League of Nations' *Armaments Yearbook*, published annually. Here an attempt was made to quantify, on a cost basis, all of the arms transfers of the period, an effort flawed by the reluctance of some nations, particularly the Axis powers, to divulge the full extent of their arms-trading operations. On this basis, however, Nokhim Sloutzki, in 1941, did publish a short summary of the league data which represented the sole real attempt at a general study of the arms flow patterns of that period.[22] It is valuable in allowing for an approximate overview of the arms trade of that period, particularly with respect to the relative roles of various suppliers.

For the first 20-odd years of the postwar period little was written on the arms trade save for the annual compilations—since 1959—of the Institute for Strategic Studies and a number of associated monographs published by that organization, most notably that by Sutton and Kemp.[23] Additionally, of course, the subject was sometimes cursorily covered in works on the military in developing nations and on American and other nations' military aid abroad.[24]

In the past several years, there has been a growing resurgence of interest in problems of the arms trade. Partly, this would appear to have been the result of a realization by some scholars that they had been given short shrift in the arms control literature, shaded by the dominant interest in nuclear strategy. But the growing interest in conventional arms control problems appears to have been fueled by the events surrounding the crises in the Middle East and the Indian subcontinent. Further, the wave of antiwar and antimilitary sentiment engendered in the United States by the Vietnam War brought in its train a series of congressional hearings which served to highlight the United States' role as an arms supplier.

In the past few years, full length books have been published on the postwar arms trade by George Thayer and Lewis Frank.[25] Thayer's is something of a throwback to the tradition of the 1930s, utilizing a rather sensationalist, but eminently readable, anatomy of the worldwide arms trade as a backdrop to an indictment of the Pentagon as its allegedly most egregious perpetrator. Frank's work, while impressive in its display of a bewildering array of data, is somewhat lacking in interpretation of the actual patterns of the trade.

The first real attempt at a comprehensive analysis of the postwar arms trade, replete with a series of typologies to describe its essential segments, is contained in a recent study by Amelia Leiss, Geoffrey Kemp and others of the Center for International Studies at MIT, using data through 1968.[26] Their study is restricted to arms flows in major weapons categories from the major powers to a selected sample of 52 developing nations and is an extension of an earlier work on local conflict which included some analysis of arms transfers.[27] The MIT study forms a pattern for my inquiry, with the subject broken down into such component segments as supplier markets, donor-recipient patterns, transfer modes and the relative modernity of weapons transferred. Additionally, the MIT study includes extensive analysis of long-term trends in the volume of arms transferred on a worldwide basis and of trends in inventories of various weapons systems, by country and by region. Lacking by design a comparative, long-range focus in time, there was no attempt made at "explaining" the patterns evidenced by reference to systems characteristics, nor was there an attempt to correlate these patterns with other measures of internation association, such as alliances.

More recently, during the course of my research for this book, a still more comprehensive survey of the postwar arms trade has been published by the Stockholm International Peace Research Institute (SIPRI).[28] Covering basically much of the same ground as the MIT study, it is distinct methodologically in its effort at quantifying the arms trade on a cost basis rather than by numbers of various weapons systems transferred. Additionally, the SIPRI study is more detailed in its country-by-country coverage of the arms production and arms sales policies of specific major suppliers, and in attention to the growing arms-producing capabilities of a number of nations which heretofore have not been significant factors in the arms markets.

PROBLEMS OF SCOPE, BOUNDARY AND MEASUREMENT

The Arms Trade in the Broader Context of Military Assistance

There are difficult problems in delineating the boundaries which circumscribe the subject of the arms trade or arms transfers. For the actual trade or transfer of completed weaponry is only the core of a larger area of concern which might be defined, more broadly, as the diffusion of military technology, or military assistance. The latter term, as well as that of military aid, is normally used to describe weapons giveaways as distinct from cash sales. Actually, the lines between these concepts are often blurred, both because of the ambiguous nature of some transactions and differing usage.

A broader definition of scope would include such related subjects as the transfer of military skills in the form of advisors, mercenaries and seconded personnel, and the training of recipient-nation personnel in the donor country. Indeed, the MIT study places considerable emphasis on the relationship between these factors and the flow of arms, indicating among other things the importance of the advocate role of military assistance personnel in determining the types and quantities of weapons acquired by some nations.[29] The patterns of the arms trade are affected by these factors as well as by broader systemic ones. And the linkage of military assistance missions to arms trade patterns is itself a function of the overall nature of the diplomatic system, with the nexus having become stronger in a period where arms shipments, to a greater degree, are more purposefully used as instruments of diplomacy.

In some cases, particularly those where recipient nations are engaged in actual conflict, the lines may be blurred between transfers to the recipients and the use of weapons by seconded personnel or "volunteers." Thus, it is difficult to ascertain just how many MIGs sent to the UAR in recent years by the Soviet Union are to be counted as actual internation transfers, as distinct from aircraft being used by Soviet personnel and, therefore, actually remaining within the Soviet Air Force even if flying with Egyptian markings. Similar problems emerge in analyzing American arms transfers to South Vietnam or Laos.

In the 1930s there were similar problems in identifying transfers. The Spanish Civil War affords a good example, where it is somewhat difficult to quantify actual transfers to the belligerents as distinct from the operation of weapons by actual units of outside combatants. On the Loyalist side, there were no instances of actual Russian units operating in the field, although Soviet personnel were interspersed within their operating units. On the Nationalist side, whole units of Italian and German troops were in the field. In the Chaco War between Bolivia and Paraguay both sides employed foreign mercenaries to operate then modern equipment, particularly planes and tanks. This war, like the Spanish Civil War which was to follow some two years later, was used as a testing ground for the weapons of major powers on both sides.[30]

A related problem in the interwar period is demonstrated in the cases of Iraq and Egypt, where nominally independent regimes were in quasi-colonial relationships to Great Britain during most of the 1930s. In both cases, British forces were so intimately intertwined with those of the indigenous regimes as to make analysis of weapons transfers somewhat hazardous. In both Latin America and the Middle East, meanwhile, additional confusion was caused by the fact that the lines between military and civil aviation—and between navies and merchant marines—were often not particularly distinct. In some cases, small civil airlines, operated by personnel from more developed nations, were virtually interchangeable with national air forces, particularly with respect to transport aircraft.

Weapons Components, Ancillary Equipment and Spare Parts

Another boundary problem is that of the extent to which one ought, legitimately, concentrate on the trade in discrete units of weaponry without taking into consideration the scope and significance of the trade in weapons components, ancillary equipment such as radar and other communications apparatus, and spare parts. Needless to say, these are both integral components of a modern military force and an important aspect of the arms trade.

Furthermore, and increasingly, different configurations of ancillary equipment may greatly affect the role and effectiveness of whole weapons systems; a modern jet aircraft's combat performance may hinge critically on whether it is equipped with apparatus for electronic countermeasures against surface-to-air missiles. With jet aircraft, also, associated avionics equipment may represent a substantial portion of the cost of the overall system. Indeed, with the advent of the increasingly electronic nature of warfare, major weapons systems such as aircraft, tanks and various types of warships are becoming mere launching vehicles for very expensive and complex missile systems and corresponding penetration aids and defensive apparatus, as clearly borne out during the 1973 Middle Eastern war.[31]

An analysis of components is particularly important for assessing the extent to which various nations have been able to achieve autarky or some independent production in certain weapons systems. In some cases, a given nation, although capable of producing most of the essential parts of a weapons system, may be critically dependent on an outside power for one or more subsystems. Thus, the French remained dependent on the United States for certain components after having apparently achieved a high degree of independent capability in modern aircraft after 1955. Israel, now striving for independence in aircraft and armored equipment, will remain critically dependent on the United States in the foreseeable future for a number of key bottleneck items, particularly aircraft and tank engines. In recent years France has actually designed, as part of its export drive, certain components, particularly tank guns, to be fitted to older American systems in order to extend their service lives and upgrade them.

In the interwar period a number of middle-range powers were capable of producing airframes for indigenously designed aircraft while still relying on major powers for engines, advanced variable-pitch propellers and certain types of mounted weapons. Thus, it is obvious that in attempting to analyze the arms trade by quantifying transfers of finished weapons systems these partial transfers introduce nagging complications to the analysis. I shall return to this question later in discussing various transfer modes and the degree of weapons-producing capability achieved by nations at various levels of development.

Another problem of scope is presented by spare parts transfers, a critical segment of the arms transfer process to which insufficient attention has been given. Provision for long-term supply of spare parts is usually made in the original contract for a transfer. However, the supplier nation may hold considerable leverage over the recipient by threatening to withhold spare parts necessary to continuing operation of a weapons system. At times this can be used as a unilateral control measure. Recent examples abound, most notably those of the French embargo on Israel and the seemingly successful blockage of spare parts shipments by the United States to El Salvador and Honduras during their brief war which began over an ill-fated soccer match.

The necessity for maintaining existing weapons systems through the flow of spare parts is one factor tending to stabilize donor-recipient relationships, at least from the recipient's standpoint, even in the face of changing diplomatic alignments. Paradoxically, for the recipient it also constitutes an imperative reason for attempting to hold open diversified sources of supply. Some recipients may, however, attempt to develop independent capability in producing critical spare parts after receiving an initial shipment of weapons, among other things in order to reduce the leverage accruing to the supplier over the use of the arms. Israel, for one, has made extensive efforts in this direction in a number of weapons systems. The absence of such capability may force a nation, cut off from spare parts, to cannibalize existing equipment, gradually reducing the number of operable units.

These problems, particularly in their diplomatic aspects, have probably been more important in the postwar period, wherein the supply of weapons and their spare parts has become an instrument of national policy to a greater degree than in the interwar period. However, the lack of detailed information on the flow of spare parts precludes extensive analysis in this study.

Raw Materials and Munitions

Still another problem of scope within a broad construction of the boundaries of the arms trade is that of the supply of strategic raw materials necessary to produce or operate weaponry. As the flow of uranium supplies is important to problems of nuclear proliferation, so may certain raw materials be critical to the conventional arms trade.

In the Middle Ages, most weapons-producing centers were coincident with metals-producing industries. This was the case for cities such as Liége, Solingen, Toledo and Augsburg, all metal industry centers based upon the availability of critical ores such as tin, iron and copper. Until very recently, in fact, the location of many of the major European weapons-producing centers could be traced to these Mediaeval origins. Liége remains, with its vaunted FN works, the primary small arms-producing center of Western Europe.[32]

Nowadays one hears little of the flow of raw materials in relation to arms production. However, a look at the extensive stockpiling efforts made by the United States and other countries, and a glance at the vast detail of the items listed in the United States Battle Act which are prohibited for shipment to Iron Curtain countries, will give some intimation of residual concern in this area.[33] Generally, however, one could hardly cite examples of nations whose arms production has been stifled by raw materials shortages in recent years. This situation may change in the future if some of the ominous predictions about a coming worldwide shortage of many critical raw materials turn out to be accurate. If so, one might speculate that this subject will once again become part and parcel of a discussion on the arms trade.

In the 1930s armaments were referred to, coterminously, as "munitions." In the Nye Committee hearings' reports, extensive emphasis was given to analyzing the international web of chemical companies which dealt, as an important corollary activity, in the trade in explosives and munitions. Due to the close linkage of the chemical and munitions industries, a good part of the crusading literature of the 1930s was devoted to complex anatomical analyses of cartels such as those headed by Nobel, DuPont, I. G. Farben, Loewe, Montecatini, Kuhlmann and Belgian Solvay. These companies were perceived as the epitome of the arms industry and their leading personnel were viewed as archtypical villains in the arms trade.[34] Though some of these companies did manufacture end-use weapons, their importance lay in their manufacture of and trade in those chemicals which were—and still are—utilized in explosives, artillery shells, bombs, ammunition of all sorts and also poison gas. Critical chemical specialties such as TNT, picric acid, cotton cellulose and ethylene (for poison gas) were then warp and woof of the munitions trade.

Presently, one reads little of the role of chemical companies or chemical commodities in the context of the arms trade. Oddly, few of these companies are now commonly identified as part of the military-industrial complex, although some, such as DuPont and Olin-Mathieson, may own subsidiaries which manufacture small arms, while others are giant conglomerates some components of which are military contractors in a variety of areas.[35] As for the chemicals which go into explosives, it may just be that the technology is now too widespread for them to draw notice. They have become mere commodities, far removed from the cutting edge of innovation in military technology. Nevertheless, the trade in such materials remains a relatively important, if unnoticed, substratum of the world arms trade. And, of course, the worldwide flow of petroleum is another aspect of raw materials flows which has important military ramifications. Here, too, greater prominence may be evidenced in the future if the trend toward shortages is further exacerbated.[36]

Some problems are presented here in the comparability of analysis between the interwar and postwar periods. As indicated, interwar analyses of the arms trade focused on munitions as a central component; a major portion of the transfers measured by the League of Nations' *Armaments Yearbook* are in this area. In developing data on major weapons systems for the interwar period—ships, planes and tanks—to afford comparability with the format of the MIT study, much of the arms trade data compiled by the league has had to be ignored.

Small Arms and Artillery Shipments, Revolutionary Movements, Civil Wars and the Clandestine Movement of Arms

A most difficult problem of scope for this study was that of whether to include data on clandestine arms shipments to revolutionary forces or to various factions in civil war situations. This question was linked to that of whether to restrict the study, as done at MIT and SIPRI, to major weapons systems, while omitting the trade in small arms, artillery, jeeps and trucks, and other infantry weapons such as mortars, recoilless rifles, bazookas and so forth.

If small arms were to be beyond the bounds of the study because of lack of information or because of the incredible difficulties inherent in measuring that aspect of the arms trade, then the problem of whether to restrict the study to trade between legitimate or generally recognized regimes became somewhat of a moot point, since in the many revolutionary or civil war situations of the postwar period there were few instances where major weapons systems were involved.

In the interwar period the Spanish Civil War was an exception, as was the earlier multisided Chinese Civil War. Both sides in the Spanish conflict received heavy shipments of major weapons systems. As a result, I have chosen to treat them as separate entities or recipient nations. The Chinese Civil War had, for the most part, abated by the time of the initial Japanese incursions into Manchuria in 1932; only two significant factions remained, the Kuomintang and the Communists. Few major weapons systems were delivered to the Chinese Communists during the 1930s, so that for purposes of analysis the Chiang regime—which curiously received much of its arms from the Soviet Union—will be taken alone as representative of China during this period.[37]

Thus, the analysis will be restricted to major weapons transfers (aircraft, ships and armored equipment) to legitimate or generally recognized regimes. This, in turn, will facilitate those portions of the analysis which focus on the relationship between the arms trade and other types of internation association.

Although data on small arms and artillery will not generally fall within the bounds of this study, some limited information will be introduced in a few sections of the analysis. Overall data on a cost basis, including small arms, will be compared with those for major weapons transfers only, in order to gauge the distortions created in analysis of the supplier markets by restricting the study to major weapons systems. As there are more nations capable of producing, and hence supplying, small arms, one would expect the supplier markets in this area to be less narrowly oligopolistic than for major weapons systems. But although this would be the case for the absolute number of available suppliers, it would not necessarily extend to the breakdown of market shares; that is, unless certain minor nations had developed a specialized capacity in small arms beyond what might have been expected on the basis of size.[38] Slower technological growth rates, smaller requirements for initial investment and lower unit costs do allow some small countries while they are unable to compete in major weapons systems, to be factors in small arms markets.

The information base for small arms transfers is rather sparse. Oddly, the compilations by the League of Nations and their summary by Sloutzki afford a better composite picture of the small arms trade for the interwar period than anything available for the postwar era.[39] For the latter, fragmented information may be gleaned from a volume by W. H. B. Smith which is useful at least for indicating which nations are able to produce their own small arms, whether by their own design or by license.[40] Additional information is contained in the Frank book and in an appendix to the MIT study, the combined resources of which allow at least a rough picture of the patterns of donor-recipient relationships and of the network of licensing agreements in the small arms field.[41]

Actually, inclusion of the small arms trade and shipments to revolutionary forces would require dealing with complexities beyond those of quantifying a bewildering number of discrete arms deals. With major weapons systems, most transfers are relatively straightforward deals from government to government. With many small arms transactions, however, one enters into the murky province of intelligence agencies and private or semiprivate arms brokers such as Interarms (known informally as Interarmco). These relationships are rendered all the more complex by the tendency for many private brokers to operate out of a worldwide web of subsidiaries, that is, as multinational corporations. The fantastic complexity and deviousness of the small arms trade has been described in fascinating detail by Thayer who notes correctly that, despite the tiny percentage of the overall arms trade represented by these activities, they may, nevertheless, be crucial in revolutionary or civil war situations as in Algeria, Biafra and Cuba.[42]

A full analysis of the patterns of small arms transfers would, in any case, be rendered difficult because so many of these transfers are conducted clandestinely. This is the case not only, let us say, for shipments of arms to the IRA from friends in the United States, but also for the operations of the CIA and other intelligence agencies which often disguise the source of their shipments by sending arms originally manufactured by their Cold War opponents. While the CIA may arm its "friendlies" in the Third World with Russian AK-47s—acquired from Israeli stocks captured in the Sinai or from Vietnam—the Soviets may equip their revolutionary cohorts with Western arms acquired from earlier stocks held by Egypt, Iraq, Nigeria or Indonesia.[43] Finally, the incredible longevity of many small arms (as contrasted with tanks or aircraft, many rifles and machine guns remain usable for 50 years) and their frequent involvement in endless, myriad retransfers, makes an anatomy of the small arms trade all but impossible except in a rough qualitative sense—i.e., to the extent of knowing that nation X uses primarily Belgian or Soviet rifles.[44]

Measurement of the Arms Trade

There are cogent reasons for not using overall cost figures to measure the arms trade in lieu of absolute numbers of weapons in various categories such as fighter aircraft, tanks or submarines. These reasons were well stated in the MIT study, which eschewed cost data. I will repeat some of the arguments, which are equally valid for my purposes here, while indicating that there are trade-offs on both sides of the argument.[45]

The primary reason for not using cost data is their extreme lack of comparability, even aside from the problems caused by ambiguities of exchange rates and actual purchasing power. In the postwar period weapons have not always been sold for market prices; in numerous instances they have been given away, sold for bargain basement prices for political reasons or in connection with long-term loans at low interest rates, or exchanged in outright barter. In the interwar period the arms trade was still mostly a private preserve and this problem of comparability was not so acute. However, both Germany and Italy relied heavily on barter agreements toward the end of the 1930s in order to acquire critical raw materials and, additionally, extended long-term loans for arms purchases to buy political influence. Also, during the 1930s the lack of currency convertibility resulted in what effectively became barter agreements in some cases.[46]

Thus, actual cost figures would not seem to be an appropriate measure of the volume of the arms trade. Alternatively, one might have considered assigning a "real" cost to each individual weapons system and then figuring the total cost after ascertaining the number of systems transferred, assuming full payment in all cases. There are hazards here, too, for it is difficult to relate the cost of a weapons system to its real value. Thus, the United States is now selling Phantom jets for about $2.5 million to $3 million each, while the Soviets are selling an only somewhat less effective fighter-bomber, the SU-7, for something like $1 million.[47] These relative figures, even assuming a considerable superiority by the Phantom, may not be indicative of the relative value of the planes transferred. The difference is due to lower labor costs, to less "gold plating" of weapons systems and perhaps to greater willingness by the Soviets, for political reasons, to sell for below actual cost.

The sole remaining alternative would be simply to assume equal costs for reasonably similar equipment, labor costs and other factors aside. This method, however, would seem to offer little advantage over using absolute numbers of weapons transferred. It would represent, simply, a multiple of those figures, while perhaps giving a less vivid illustration of the arms trade, albeit allowing for easier calculations. Such a method has, however, been used by the SIPRI group, at least for portions of their study.

There is, however, one area in which the omission of cost figures may create a serious disadvantage and that is in analysis of inventory trends. The MIT study utilizes a typology which, for each recipient country, characterizes trends in inventories according to such categories as "surge," "accretion," "replacement" or "decretion" over the span of the postwar period.[48] Inferences are then made from these trends to describe the intensity of arms races by dyadic conflict pairs and by regions. However, in this analysis, one plane (or other weapons type) of 1947 vintage becomes equivalent to one of 1967 make even where the firepower of the latter may greatly exceed that of the former.

The problem may be seen in clearer perspective using figures for the interwar period. In the 1930s, a first-line fighter aircraft cost about $20,000 and a bomber in the range of $50,000 to $100,000. Even if one adjusts for inflationary trends, it is apparent that the cost per plane has risen by many orders of magnitude.[49] Moreover, it appears that in most cases the size of air forces, measured in numbers of planes, was much greater in the 1930s than at present. Even middle-range powers such as Romania, Poland and Yugoslavia had air forces in the 1930s ranging up to about one thousand combat aircraft, while Brazil and Argentina had about half that many each. These are considerably greater than present-day figures.

Similar trends are evidenced in weapons systems other than aircraft, as would be immediately apparent in examining, for instance, the size of the larger navies in the late 1930s. The reasons for these trends are fairly obvious—namely, the greater unit cost per system (deflated) in conjunction with much greater firepower or overall capability. These trends have continued within the postwar period since 1945, if only gradually. Thus, it would appear that inventory trends, measured in absolute numbers of weapons systems, would have considerable validity only if controlled both for cost _and_ for performance characteristics.

Truncation of the Interwar Period

For reasons of time economy, the decade 1930—1940 is to be used as representative of the entire interwar period. Some distortion will no doubt result from this truncation, particularly in the analysis of supplier market shares. For one thing, the weakening of the hold on the arms markets by France and Britain, evidenced during the 1930s, would probably have been more apparent if data for the 1920s had been included. In the 1920s, predominance by Britain and France was abetted by the temporary prostration of Germany, American isolation and the fact that rising powers such as Japan, Italy and the USSR were still not competitive in the arms markets to the extent they would be in the following decade.

Despite this caveat, however, it may be said that the real dividing line of the period was in the mid-1930s, following the advent of Hitler, so that the systems characteristics of the early 1930s were generally characteristic of the entire interwar period up to that time. Also, the mid-1930s saw the end of laissez faire in the arms trade in most major supplier nations, making that juncture a watershed in still another important way.

Research Sources

The primary source of data for the interwar arms trade was the files of the Military Intelligence Division of the War Department, located in the Modern Military Division of the National Archives in Washington, D.C. Most of the extensive data were drawn from military attaché reports from the various embassies abroad. Some of the attachés reported on several countries simultaneously (see Appendix B).

The data for aircraft are excellent, the fortunate result of a requirement that an annual aviation summary for each nation be submitted by the attachés. There was no such requirement for armored equipment, although the attaché reports do contain considerable information in this area. However, the data in this category obtained from the military intelligence files had to be supplemented by recourse to a variety of other sources. The libraries of the Army War College at Fort McNair and Carlisle Barracks proved useful. Considerable additional data were ferreted out of military journals from the period such as *Armor, Royal Tank Corps Journal* and *Army Ordnance.* Still more information was gleaned from the incredibly prolific tank buff literature of that period, in which the works of von Senger und Etterlin, Icks and Ogorkiewicz were useful.[50] The data for ships in the interwar period were easily obtainable from *Jane's Fighting Ships* and appear to have been very accurate on the basis of cross-checking with the naval sections of the military intelligence files.

As massive data have been compiled from these sources and then coded according to the MIT format for the postwar period study, it will be impossible to cite the sources for individual transfers in the text. The numbered indexes of the country-by-country files of the Military Intelligence Division are listed in Appendix B. In most cases, that will be the source of a transfer unless otherwise indicated.

For the postwar period most of the data were drawn from the MIT study. The interwar data were coded by the format of that study, except that they were somewhat constricted for my purposes (see Appendix A).

Some additional data on intra-NATO and intra-Warsaw Pact transfers and transfers to nations not included in the MIT study's 52 nation sample have been used. These were culled, variously, from the previously cited works of Frank and Thayer; from the annual of the Institute for Strategic Studies, *The Military Balance* and from a recent series of monographs published by ISS under the series heading of *Defense, Technology and the Western Alliance.* Additionally, the SIPRI work published since the coding of the data has been useful for providing information on recent transfers (since the cut-off date of the MIT study in 1968) and data on some nations not in the MIT sample. SIPRI's annual, *Yearbook of World Armaments and Disarmament*, which includes an annual arms trade register, has also been of use, particularly in allowing for the observation of arms trade patterns since 1968.

Chapter Two

The Differential Impact of Systems Variables on Patterns of the Arms Trade

In outlining a model to describe the relationship between diplomatic systems variables and various dimensions of the arms trade, we have indicated that the following systems variables would appear to have the most direct bearing: (1) the chain of relationships involving polarity, bloc formation, alliance systems and the gradient of power among the major powers; (2) the degrees and types of ideological conflict suffusing relations between the major powers of a period; (3) the degree of "totality" in the conduct of diplomacy and warfare; (4) the dominant modes of international economic intercourse, influenced by the prevailing economic theories of an era; (5) the relative degrees of private and governmental control over decision making on arms transfers; (6) the structure of international business specific to the armaments industry, particularly the degree of internationalization of that industry; and (7) the rate and nature of technological change in weaponry.

The systems variables I have chosen to utilize are not altogether discrete; in some cases, one may act partially as an intervening variable between another and certain dimensions of the arms trade. For instance, the shift away from the dominance of laissez faire economics was one reason for tightened governmental controls on arms sales, which in turn affected donor-recipient patterns. And the ideological nature of postwar international politics has, until recently, tended to freeze the situation of bipolar bloc polarity, which in turn is crucial to the composition of arms supplier markets.

With these caveats in mind, we shall discuss the previously listed systems characteristics in turn, elaborating upon some assumptions that went into our diagrammatic model and paying heed to the complexity, nuance and crosscutting of these relationships. But first, let us look briefly at how some analysts have utilized systems variables at a macrolevel in international situations.

SYSTEMS ANALYSIS IN INTERNATIONAL RELATIONS

Writings on the developmental history of international systems utilize a variety of ways in which to classify successive diplomatic epochs. These characterizations vary by level of abstraction, by differing emphases on "levels of analysis" (types of actors versus structure of the system) and by the lengths of time spans between watersheds demarcating identifiable systems.[1]

Morton Kaplan utilizes a series of ideal types or "states of equilibrium" to describe potential rather than actual past or present systems. His six basic ideal type systems are: balance of power, loose bipolar, tight bipolar, universal, hierarchical and unit veto. Of these, only the first two are considered ever to have had historical counterparts, and then only in approximate form.[2] Kaplan's rules for a loose bipolar system make an approximate fit to the period 1945-1965. The interwar period, with its somewhat fluid alliances and only partially ideological basis of conflict, provides a somewhat lesser approximation to his ideal type for a balance of power system.[3]

Rosecrance, in an avowedly inductive effort at identifying, delineating and classifying actual historical systems, characterizes the structure and practices of nine sequential periods.[4] Except for the modern era, the scope of his scheme is restricted to the European state system. He uses shorter time spans for his systems than do others, identifying basic transformations of the European system within the 1815-1914 period and within the earlier phase of the classical system of European diplomacy between 1648 and the French Revolution.

Aside from sheer classification, Rosecrance, like Kaplan, is primarily concerned with how his systems variables affect the stability, equilibrium, transformation and disintegration of international systems. To answer these questions he adduces a set of systems variables designated by such terms as "resources of the system," the "ethos of elites" and the "regulator." A running commentary is offered on several centuries of European diplomacy, in which these variables are loosely applied. Perhaps the outstanding feature of Rosecrance's analysis, however, is his insistence on the importance of internationally held elite norms with respect to the diplomatic "rules of the game." These subtle factors may be crucial to comparisons of diplomatic periods and also, as we shall see, to an explanation of the patterns of the arms trade.

Coplin, using lengthier time spans than Rosecrance, perceives three distinct periods since the middle of the 17th century which he respectively designates the "classical system" (1648-1815), the "transitional system" (1815-1945) and the "contemporary system" (1945 to the present).[5] The first named of these periods approximates what Kaplan has called a balance of power system, with flexibility of alliances and foreign policy making, dispersion of power centers among six or seven major powers and virtual lack of ideological content to international rivalries, making each nation a potential alliance partner of every other. In the transitional system, newer factors emerge: universalization of the system, pluralization of the foreign policy-making process, the growth of nationalism and the increasing destructive capacity of military weapons. These factors then come to further fruition in the contemporary system, with the additional impact of bipolarity, heightened ideological conflict and nuclear weapons. Importantly, Coplin perceives the interwar period more in terms of its 19th century antecedents than of close parallels with the post-World War II system, a perception which we shall see is quite valid for some practices in the arms trade.[6]

POLARITY, BLOC STRUCTURE, ALLIANCE SYSTEMS AND DISTRIBUTION OF POWER: INTERWAR VERSUS POSTWAR

For our purposes, dealing only with the two most recent identifiable world systems, little use need be made of comparisons of systems boundaries, the nature of political units or of major forms of interaction, as these matters have remained sufficiently stable since 1919. There have, however, been substantial differences in system structure and, to a lesser degree, in the "rules of the game" (totality and ideology).

What, then, have been the basic differences in structure between the two systems, how can they be characterized and of what applicability are they to an analysis of the arms trade?

At first thought, the answer might seem easily forthcoming, with the interwar period one of balance of power (in Kaplan's terms) or multipolarity, and the postwar one of loose bipolarity. But the answer appears surprisingly debatable, for, among the above writers alone, there is significant disagreement over basic characterizations of the interwar and postwar periods, particularly the former. It is hard to say whether these differences are really substantive or merely semantic, with essential agreement on the facts and meaning of interwar diplomacy.

Most commentators describe the postwar period as one in which there has been a recent trend from bipolarity to multipolarity or to bimultipolarity.[7] There have been two major blocs, rigidly held together by the cement of ideology or counterideology, with relatively little shifting of alliances or allegiances. Peripheral Third World neutrals have introduced some flexibility to the system, allowing for a description, in Kaplan's terms, of "loose" bipolarity. On the other hand, additions or subtractions from the two blocs have not usually resulted in significant alterations in the power equation between them.[8] Accruals of power by the hegemonic leaders of the blocs have not normally been secured by alliance policies. Finally, the system has been characterized by a fairly extreme tendency towards totality of warfare and diplomacy, perhaps a 20th century climax of the strands of philosophy represented variously by Marx, Darwin, Clausewitz and Mao.

More recently, of course, there has been a trend toward multi-polarity and loosened alliances with the seeming development of additional major independent centers of power in China, Japan and in the embryonic Western European union. Recent events seem to indicate a trend toward more flexible diplomacy on the part of all major powers, perhaps auguring movement toward a traditional balance of power system in which each of the major powers will be at least potential alliance partners of every other.

In assuming a trend toward multipolarity in the present system, however, there are some intrusions on easy generalizations about shifts away from a world of merely two superpowers. As long as there are only two major nuclear powers, both of which have something approximating first strike capability against the new aspirants to the status of major power, bimultipolarity will remain a perhaps more apt description of the state of the system than multipolarity. The same kinds of analytical problems beset characterizations of the so-called multipolar systems of the 18th and 19th centuries, where there were also serious disparities in power among the various major actors. Throughout much of this period Germany (Prussia) and Britain (or earlier France and Britain) were clearly militarily stronger than Russia or Austria-Hungary. These asymmetries, moreover, were clearly illustrated in arms trade patterns and dependencies. The lesser of the major powers of these periods were considerably dependent on the stronger ones for arms.

The essential consensus among most writers on a description of the basic nature of the postwar system is not, however, matched for the interwar period. Rosecrance, surprisingly, perceives a bipolar alignment, facing off a "status quo, liberal-democratic" bloc against an "expansionist, radical-nationalist" bloc.[9] Russett, on the other hand, defines the same diplomatic constellation as a "balance of power precarious," a designation perhaps intended as closer in meaning to what Kaplan and others perceive for the systems of the 18th and 19th centuries.[10] Rosecrance's characterization of bipolarity would not, at any rate, appear to be accurate for the whole interwar period. It is clearly more applicable to the late 1930s than to the 1920s. But even here the status of the Soviet Union remains obscure. On the one hand, not assigning the Soviets to either bloc is realistic, as they did play somewhat the role of "balancer" in this period, a role held periodically in the "classical system" by Great Britain.[11] However, the role of the Soviet Union in interwar diplomacy cannot be ignored.

Presumably both Japan and Italy are considered by Rosecrance as part of the "expansionist, radical-nationalist" bloc. In terms of their apparent intentions and of the character of their regimes this would be an apt description. Yet in terms of bloc adhesion it should not be forgotten that both of these powers were considering alternative diplomatic alignments in the middle and late 1930s. The cement of ideology with Nazi Germany was not all that strong, not even after the formalizing of the Axis Pact. Italy was on friendly terms with the USSR in the early 1930s, ideology notwithstanding (and, indeed, sold it vast quantities of arms), was at odds with Germany over Austria from 1934 to 1938 and toyed with various anti-German coalitions right up to the outbreak of the war.[12]

Japan's diplomatic maneuvering between Russia and Germany, meanwhile, introduces additional ambiguity to the simple classification of bipolarity during this period, its aims having been based far less on ideological considerations than on achieving a free hand for conquest in China. Finally, the United States, as potentially the most powerful nation of the time, was formally unaligned throughout this period, making its assignment to an identifiable Western bloc questionable before 1940, when the Neutrality Act gave way to Lend-Lease.[13]

A characterization of the interwar system as bipolar, therefore, suffers from a degree of retrospective myopia in which the rise of peripheral powers around the older European state system is ignored. With the perspective afforded by the passage of time, the then latent—if not then perceived—power roles of the United States, the USSR and Japan are much clearer.[14]

What emerges from this is that there is considerable ambiguity concerning the terms bipolar and multipolar. These ambiguities are apparent in examining the way two writers, Rosecrance and Russett, define these terms. Rosecrance, as well as Kaplan and others, defines polarity essentially in terms of confrontations of alliance blocs. Presumably, such a definition would allow either for two hegemonic blocs, each headed by superpowers, as in the postwar period; for two blocs, each composed of several big powers of roughly equivalent strength, as in the immediate pre-World War I years; or for some mixture of these types of alignments.

Russett, on the other hand, presents another definition of bipolarity which is also amenable to rather simple measurement. It has not so much to do with opposing blocs as with the gap in power, measured by GNP, between the two leading powers of a period and those of the next rank.

Russett cites the following statistics to demonstrate the comparison between the two periods with respect to polarity.[15]

Indices of Relative GNP in Standard Prices for Six Major Powers

	1963	*1950*	*1938*
United States	100	100	100
Soviet Union	49	34	47
Germany	19	13	34
Great Britain	16	19	30
France	18	15	24
China	20	18	24

Using these measurements as an approximate valuation of relative power, a characterization of the late 1930s becomes difficult indeed. Even as in the postwar period, one might be tempted to refer to the international system, in Kaplan's terms, as unipolar or hegemonic. DeGaulle, Servan-Schreiber and others have, more or less, so described it, in terms of economic power if not in sheer military terms.[16]

Of course, neither in the 1930s nor later were these measures actually indicative of the true comparative value of United States military power vis-à-vis other major powers. Internal distribution of resources, the tightness of political controls and the power-over-distance gradient are germane to an understanding of this shortfall. For the 1930s, the facts of America's profound neutralism and pacifism require no elaboration.

By Russett's definition of bipolarity, the figures would indicate that there was somewhat less bipolarity in the 1930s than in the postwar period, the recent rise of omitted Japan notwithstanding. Of course, the partition of Germany in the postwar period has had much to do with this. For the interwar period, retrospective judgments on the real comparative military strengths of the major powers would perhaps indicate a degree of quadripolarity, or even quintipolarity, if Japan is conceded great power status and if the Soviet Union's vastly underestimated military power is now retrospectively conceded.[17] Perhaps a preferred designation would be "modified multipolar," with the United States, the USSR, Japan, Britain-France and Germany-Italy constituting the essential polar entities of a system which acquired actual structure only in the latter part of the 1930s.

The differential impact of these structures on the various dimensions of the arms trade have been bruited in the outlining of our model, and will be analyzed in detail in subsequent analysis.

IDEOLOGICAL LOCUS OF CONFLICT AND TOTALITY IN WAR AND DIPLOMACY

Another set of factors affecting the nature of the arms trade is that discussed by Rosecrance under the heading of "ethos of elites." Involved here are subtle and subjective questions of diplomatic usage and conduct—"rules of the game"—and prevailing modes of conducting warfare along a continuum describing degrees of totality and all-out maximization. There is a commonly held assumption about the lack of restraint in war and diplomacy in the 20th century, often contrasted with the 18th and 19th centuries when warfare was generally considered to have retained some degree of civility or even chivalry.

Questions of totality and ideology are closely linked to those of polarity and alliance systems. Historically, warfare and diplomacy appear to have been conducted on a more maximizing basis to the degree conflicting world views have been involved. And those periods where ideological conflict and totality have been in evidence have also tended to be those where the international structure has evolved into rigid bipolar confrontations, with little fluidity in alliances.

There are, actually, serious analytical problems concerning definitions of "ideology" or what constitutes an ideological conflict between pairs or blocs of nations. In the context of the "levels of analysis" problem, Morgenthau and his critics have argued the pros and cons of the relative importance of ideology and national interest as the primary bases for foreign policy behavior.[18] Concerning what constitutes an ideology, there is perhaps a parallel with the "end of ideology" debate in comparative politics, that is, over whether there has been a decline of ideology per se, or rather the dissipation of the force of one particular identifiable ideology. Liberalism, imperialism and nationalism, as well as Marxism or Fascism, can be described as inherently ideological, with corresponding international implications.[19]

But despite difficulties in gauging the ebbs and flows of ideological conflict and degrees of totalism through the centuries, there is still a consensus of sorts on long-range trends going back to the Middle Ages.[20]

The mediaeval period in Europe is normally considered to have had a relative absence of ideological content in diplomacy, due to the hegemony of the Catholic Church. Less totality in warfare and diplomacy was a concomitant, explicable in terms of the zeitgeist of chivalry and the concept of the "just war."[21] On a broader scale, however, there was a bipolar conflict, with an ideological dimension, between Christianity and Islam. This was, indeed, reflected in the practices of the arms trade. The then promiscuous arms salesmen of Liége were somewhat countenanced in their sales of arms to the European enemies of their sovereign, but proscribed from selling to the "infidel" Turk.

At the time of the religious wars in Europe during the Reformation there was a clear bipolar ideological conflict between Catholics and Protestants. The concomitants in terms of diplomatic structure and practice were predictable: rigid alliances, totality of conflict involving massive civilian casualties and also the imposition of licensing restrictions on arms flows, with trade across religious boundaries rigidly prohibited.[22]

Following the period of religious wars ending with the Treaty of Westphalia in 1648 Europe entered into that lengthy and sometimes romanticized phase of its diplomatic history usually characterized as the "classical period of diplomacy," coinciding with the development of the modern nation-state. The structure and practices of that diplomatic period are sufficiently familiar. There were fluid alliances, an essential absence of ideological conflict, dispersion of power among a number of roughly equivalent states and frequent though limited wars devoid of intent to eliminate essential actors. This was the period of set-piece battles, extensive use of mercenaries and widespread transnational mobility of diplomats and military officers.[23] As often noted, in the period preceding that of the burgeoning of modern nationalism the elites of the various nations of Europe had more in common than did the individual national elites and their peoples.[24] Here, too, there was a predictable result in a more laissez faire attitude toward the selling of arms, although this was apparently mitigated by the impact of mercantilism and the correspondingly widespread institutionalization of government arsenals.

Some writers, among them J. F. C. Fuller, date the onset of modern total and ideological warfare with the American and French Revolutions at the end of the 18th century.[25] The development of totalism during this period is said to have been engendered not only by ideological fanaticism, but also by growing industrialization, weapons developments and the advent of modern administrative structures. Hence the rise of the "levee en masse" and "nation in arms." However, in retrospect, some writers perceive this to have been a mere interregnum in terms of total war, followed by an essential resumption of the practices of the classical system up to 1914.

There was, of course, a degree of ideological cleavage in the European state system in the 19th century between relatively liberal-democratic Britain and France on the one hand, and the monarchies of the Holy Alliance on the other. Generally, however, the 19th century is usually characterized as one of relative absence of totality and ideological conflict, despite the intellectual contributions of Clausewitz, Marx and the followers of Darwin, which were to have clearer import in the 20th century. It follows that the arms trade of the 19th century was characterized by a striking degree of laissez faire, private discretion over arms sales and bizarre, almost random transfers not easily related to formal diplomatic alignments.

World War I is cited by Aron and others as the point of origin of a "century of total war," although it was not primarily an ideological war unless fervent rival nationalisms might allow one to so characterize it.[26] Reported practices in the arms trade during this war bear out this paradox. In the literature of the 1930s there is extensive documentation of a lively "anti-national" trade in arms across the lines of World War I, not only in the period immediately preceding the war, but during the war itself. This trade was conducted by arms firms through neutral nations.[27] It was these revelations which subsequently were to give rise to the appellations "arms international" and "merchants of death" in the 1930s.

The subsequent interwar period is perhaps difficult to characterize in terms of totality of diplomatic and ideological conflict, just as it is difficult to define in terms of polarity and alliances.

In the 1920s, the primary locus of ideological conflict was between the new Bolshevik regime and the West, notwithstanding Germany's temporary softening of Soviet isolation in the period subsequent to the Rapallo agreement. From the time of Stresemann's move to the West at Locarno in 1925 up to the advent of Hitler some eight years later, the basic lines of ideological conflict remained those of liberal-democratic versus Bolshevik, both in the international sphere and in the internal politics of many nations in the former category. However, the growth of Fascism in Italy presaged a new force which was to result in the tripolarization of international ideological conflict, a situation increasingly evidenced as the 1930s proceeded.

The growing polarization of ideological conflict was paralleled in the growing totalization of diplomacy in the 1930s. Stimson and others of his generation became increasingly anachronistic in their concerns about "gentlemen opening each other's mail." By the mid-1930s the nature of the arms trade had become a part of this pattern, with the growth of licensing controls, some movement towards the use of arms sales as a purposive instrument of diplomacy and the use of more extensive espionage to ferret out the weapons production and development secrets of rivals. By the late 1930s the odd continuation of some American arms sales to Japan and Germany had perhaps become merely reflective of the pathetic attempts of American liberalism to deal with the world in terms which no longer were consonant with a newer reality.

These factors appear to have affected, critically, the very nature of the arms trade during the interwar period. For its most noticeable characteristic up to the 1930s, with the absence of controls and predictable patterns, was its very casual nature. This had reached a zenith in the 19th century when, as previously noted, arms were often sold to prospective enemies or to members of opposing blocs. And as we shall see, the arms firms of opposing nations were themselves then normally intertwined by interlocking directorates and stock ownership.

These practices continued on through the First World War and well into the interwar period. They were still in evidence in the mid to late 1930s, and not only in the case of the United States selling arms to Germany and Japan. Even the German firms, presumably more closely controlled by an authoritarian regime, were selling arms to imminent victims such as Holland, Romania, Greece and Yugoslavia right up to the eve of the war.

Related to the actual trade in weaponry, in terms of the casual quality of these transactions, was the apparent relative absence of strong concern about retention of technical weapons secrets. Germany, Japan and Russia had surprising access to the latest American and British weapons in the early 1930s, while other donor nations, including the Germans, appear to have traded their most modern weapons quite freely.[28] Again, there was a loose or careless quality to these practices which retrospectively appears surprising in an era where secrecy is of paramount—almost paranoiac—concern.

In summary, one may say that the looseness with which the governments of the interwar period allowed their arms traders to operate somewhat outside the mainstream of diplomacy up to the middle or late 1930s must be viewed as somewhat of an atavism, a remnant of a past era of less than total war.[29] While Aron may be correct in dating the beginnings of the century of total war with the First World War, or Fuller with an earlier date, it is clear that there was a time lag in applicability to the arms trade. We shall now discuss some of the reasons for this apparent anomaly, in the context of dominant modes of economic intercourse and in the structure and practices of international business.

THE RELATIONSHIP OF DOMINANT MODES OF ECONOMIC INTERCOURSE TO GOVERNMENTAL AND PRIVATE CONTROLS OVER ARMS SHIPMENTS

There is another long-range set of problems, not easily visible in a casual review of those systems variables which have affected the nature of the arms trade, which appears to have been crucial: the dominant forms of international economic relations prevailing in given periods and their intellectual underpinnings in prevailing macroeconomic theories. Trends in these variables would appear to have influenced the ebbs and flows of the application of governmental controls on arms sales, as well as relative tendencies toward public and private manufacture of arms.

What then have been the basic phases of economic thought and international economic practice?[30] Most writers seem in agreement that around the year 1600 the precapitalist economic forms of the Middle Ages were superseded by mercantilism, an essentially nationalistic perspective which stressed the importance of accruing gold. Huntington, indeed, claims that the acquisition of gold became the primary goal of international politics during this period, surpassing that of territorial acquisition.[31] The rise of mercantilism appears to have coincided, roughly, with the development of the modern nation-state, and its heyday was also somewhat coincidental with the previously discussed classical period of diplomacy. And during the rise of mercantilism, the previous dominance of private arms traders and armorers was replaced by that of government arsenals, a trend inaugurated by Colbert in France.[32]

The end of the period of mercantilism is usually dated at about the time of Adam Smith's publication of *The Wealth of Nations*. From the turn of the century at around 1800 up to the early part of the 20th century laissez faire appears to have been the dominant theory of international economics. In reality, of course, the situation was far more complex. Laissez faire economics, as applied to the international sphere, was more popular in powerful imperial Great Britain than in nations such as Germany, whose theorists were more inclined toward nationalist economics and a perceived necessity for autarky.[33]

During the course of this century, the older tenets of laissez faire have given way to Keynesian economics and to the practical development of state capitalism and state socialism. These trends have had counterparts in the theory and practice of international economics.

Somewhat congruent with the above trends, the issue of private versus public manufacture and sale of arms has had a rather tortuous and somewhat cyclical history, with a bewildering series of reversals. Today, in a period where governments almost completely control the external flow of arms, it has become something of a dead issue.

During the Middle Ages arms manufacture was primarily the bailiwick of private armorers, although some countries had government arsenals or mixed private and public manufacture. Controls were generally lax. Later, there were instances of licensing, particularly during the wars of the Reformation, while still later, in the 18th century, Colbert inaugurated the organized system of government arsenals in France which became a model for other European nations during the age of mercantilism.

In the 19th century, after a period in which arms manufacture had been conducted primarily by government arsenals in most nations, a reverse trend was set in motion. The roots of this change are explained by Lewinsohn:

> Even so late as Napoleonic times, State manufacture predominated on the Continent. . . . It was only in the course of the nineteenth century that the private manufacture of armaments acquired real importance. Economic liberalism emanating from England paved the way for the private trader in arms as in all else. The principle of industrial liberty and the belief that the private manufacturer stimulated by the desire for gain was capable of greater output, gradually pushed State manufacture into the background. But it was a slow process, nor was it accomplished without bitter opposition. In any case, the years of peace which followed the Napoleonic Wars were hardly favorable to the arms industry. . . . At the time of the accession of Napoleon III in the middle of the last century, a new phase set in. Great names came to the fore, names which have since come to symbolize the arms industry.[34]

Thus, the new trend to privatization of the arms industry appears to have coincided with the advent of the liberal or laissez faire stage of capitalism, a condition which, of course, varied among nations. By the late 19th century, in most countries, both the manufacture and the trade in arms were essentially under private control, with very little interference from governments.

The full extent of these trends is evidenced in the histories of concerns such as Krupp, Vickers and Remington.[35] Salesmen and freewheeling entrepreneurs associated with these and other companies roamed the world, selling to all comers.[36] Often they were able to play off their own home governments against prospective foreign customers. Krupp, for instance, used the threat of sales to France and Austria as a bludgeon in his dealings with the Prussian government.[37] It was these activities which gave rise to the term antinational trade in arms, later popularized after the venting of some of the scandals of the World War I period.

Because of the relative freedom accorded private traders in this period, and because of the relatively low level of arms races at that time, some weapons-making firms actually sold new weapons types abroad even before they were acquired by the home government. The very first submarine was produced in Britain and sold to Greece.[38]

Although the governments of the time applied few restrictions to the arms trade, there were occasional remonstrances in cases of flagrant violation of the national interest. The Prussian defense minister, von Roon, did conjure up some mild annoyance at the Krupps for selling field artillery to Austria before the war of 1866, which guns were used at Koniggratz against Prussian soldiers who were using the same weapons.[39] A similar situation arose at the time of the war of 1870 with France. Such cases were exceptions.

Only in France during part of this period were restrictions on private trade maintained. Then, in 1885, the French government passed a new law giving free rein to private traders, under prodding from arms makers chafing to compete abroad against the British and Germans.[40] After that, free trade was to remain a relatively consistent practice among all major nations up to World War I, and for most of them in most circumstances, up to the mid-1930s.

The upsurge of pacifist, antiwar and anticapitalist sentiment in the period following the trough of the Great Depression had multiple causes.[41] Partly, it resulted from the delayed reaction of fearful publics, with the memory of the slaughter of the trenches still fresh in mind at a time when anxieties about a new holocaust had begun to arise. Additionally, it was the result of highly publicized scandals surrounding the activities of arms merchants in China and South America. The efforts of lobbyists of the arms firms in sabotaging the disarmament conferences of this period added grist to the mills of leftist publicists.[42] Finally, it was probably not altogether accidental that heightened criticism of the laissez faire activities of arms makers occurred in the immediate wake of the Great Depression, when widespread doubts had emerged about the general viability of the capitalist system. There was, therefore, a thrust in the direction of regulatory activities in this area as in others.

The issue of nationalization erupted in all of the major Western nations at this time. It was one of the main points of controversy in the Nye Committee hearings. However, among the major capitalist countries, only France witnessed a significant and wholesale nationalization of its arms industries during the 1930s.[43] This was enmeshed in an internal ideological tug of war which also resulted in extensive state control of the banking system.

In Britain and France, as elsewhere, the result of the furor during the period 1933-1936 was the stringent application of export controls. This had heretofore existed on paper in Great Britain, but controls had apparently been circumvented almost at will, partly via transshipments through foreign subsidiaries. Besides, in the early 1930s the British government seems to have passed almost automatically on virtually all arms export license requests.[44]

In the United States, where laissez faire was a deep-rooted tradition interrupted only periodically by embargoes (and these usually applied only to revolutionary groups in Latin America which threatened American interests), the neutrality laws set up the Munitions Control Board which was required, in liaison with the Treasury and State Departments, to pass upon all shipments of weaponry. Despite these controls, and similar to the British case, arms sales to Germany and Japan were permitted up to the late 1930s, at which time the government entered into a policy of "moral embargoes," enforced implicitly by threats related to the letting of weapons-production contracts.[45]

By the late 1930s the governments of most or all major nations were monitoring and licensing arms exports. But in most cases, this did not extend to the deliberate and purposive use of arms exports as an instrument of policy. Controls were mostly of a negative nature, restricting sales in cases of actual ongoing conflict or in extreme cases where the national interest was thought to be at stake. The initiation of arms deals seems, for the most part, to have been left to salesmen of the arms firms, although military attachés and training groups might be involved in referring prospective customers.

In contrast to the later postwar period, there were but few cases where arms sales to specific countries became hot public issues. This was apparently a reflection of the weight of accepted tradition of private discretion in this matter. The Spanish Civil War was an exception, however, where the question of shipments to the Loyalists was hotly debated by ideological protagonists in the United States, Britain and France.[46]

In short, the practices of the 1930s in the arms trade, at least up to the latter part of that decade, appear to have been an anachronism, a throwback to an earlier age of economic laissez faire. It is interesting that the earlier advent of laissez faire practices in the arms trade followed some decades after the intellectual watershed of Adam Smith. Perhaps in both cases, the explanation lies in the notion of time lags. Just why there should be such time lags in this area is somewhat mysterious.

In the postwar period the issue of private versus public initiative and control of policy has essentially disappeared. All donor nations, whether their arms are manufactured in government arsenals or by private firms on contract, apply strict licensing controls. Further, arms sales have become an important instrument of diplomacy, and government policies are often the subject of public controversy, as witness the controversy in the United States over arms sales to Israel and that in the United Kingdom over sales to South Africa.

Only occasionally nowadays is there an apparent example of circumvention of governmental licensing procedures. Even here, one normally suspects that governmental denial of complicity is a cover to mask the unearthing of connivance. The seemingly bizarre "private" shipments of Swedish and Swiss weapons to Nigeria in 1967, followed by sharp protestations of innocence by the two neutral governments, would seem to fall into that category, along with the stealing of gunboats from Cherbourg harbor by the Israelis.[47]

How, then, have the differences between the two periods on this issue of controls affected the patterns and volume of the arms trade? On the face of it, one might be inclined to hypothesize as follows. The effect upon volume would be indeterminate. At first thought, freedom from governmental licensing might seem to allow for a more freewheeling, unrestricted arms trade, particularly in cases of local arms races in which no agreements could be reached between major powers to restrict the flow of weapons. On the other hand, more recent use of arms transfers as an instrument of diplomacy, in conjunction with government financing and outright giveaways, might well lead to an increase in volume, as the limits imposed upon recipients by cost would be eroded. As a result, the tendency for weapons to be acquired for reasons of sheer prestige might thereby be enhanced. We shall return to these questions later in our discussion of controls in both periods.

Concerning donor-recipient relationships, one might speculate that in a period in which relatively free rein was given to private firms the patterns might be unusual or unexpected in that arms would flow across alliances—that is, they would be incongruent with overall diplomatic constellations. Also, in a freewheeling situation one might expect that purchases would be made mostly on the basis of price or quality of product, rather than following natural client relationships based on diplomatic ties. This, in turn, should lead to more multiple supplier relationships, although this effect would have to be disentangled from those wrought by fluid alliances and less hegemonic blocs.

In short, the impact of the freewheeling nature of the arms trade in the 1930s should have reinforced the tendencies resulting from bloc, alliance and polarity factors. In the bipolar phase of the postwar period the imposition of controls should have reinforced the reverse tendencies. In the present period of seeming movement toward multipolarity and away from hegemonic blocs the maintenance of controls should mitigate trends toward a return to the more random arms trade patterns of the 1930s.

THE INTERNATIONALIZATION OF THE CORPORATE ARMS BUSINESS

Another subject of importance, related to questions of laissez faire and controls, is the very structure of the international arms industry and, specifically, its degree of multinationalization.

The tightly knit transnational nature of the arms industry was a staple object of concern for most of the crusader-writers of the 1930s. Their exposés were adorned by a meticulous—almost prurient—unraveling of the webs of interlocking directorships and stockholdings which allegedly characterized the major arms firms. In some cases, the corresponding accusations bordered upon conspiracy theories of international dimension.

The arms industry was not then, of course, nor is it now the only industry which is transnational in scope and ownership. As Mira Wilkins has recently pointed out, the roots of the multinational corporation go well back into the 19th century.[48] Some writers, however, insisted on seeing something insidious in the multinational nature of the arms industry. Turning Marx upside down, they referred to an "arms international." In alleging that the armaments industry was without a country, they ironically gave it a status and image which American multinationals are now strenuously trying to achieve to stave off the forces of economic nationalism.

The following quotation from Lehmann-Russbuldt gives some idea of the nature of these accusations, as perceived by one interwar critic of the arms firms, in analyzing the pre-World War I period:

> The United Harvey Steel Company was an organization that came into existence in 1901 and ended its career in 1903; but in that brief period the largest armor plate factories and cannon kings in the world were associated with it. Almost all the big French, British, German and Italian firms were represented in it: for example, the powerful British Vicker Ltd., W. G. Armstrong Ltd., Bethlehem Steel, Schneider-Creusot, Krupp, the Dillinger Smelters and the Societa degli Alt Forni Fondiere Acciano di Terni. The last-named, moreover, had unusually close relations with Vickers, which was also intimately connected with another Italian armament firm. Krupp was also a partner in the Austrian Skoda Works and the Russian Putilov Factories. This Russian company, in which Schneider-Creusot was financially interested, ultimately linked up Krupp with the largest French armor plate factory. It is also interesting to learn that Armstrong and Vickers owned one-half of the capital of the Meutoran Armor Plate Factories in Japan. They were also shareholders together with the British firm of John Brown in the Spanish Drydock Naval Construction Works at Ferrol. Six large, well-known British firms founded the Portuguese Shipbuilding Syndicate, for the purpose of helping the Portuguese government build up a powerful fleet. The reconstruction of the battered Russian fleet after the Russo-Japanese War was accomplished by means of the collective action of British, French, German and American firms.[49]

Engelbrecht and Hanighen cite some parallel and reinforcing information emphasizing the role of interlocking directorates:

> The most significant development in directorates, however, was the internationalization of many boards of control. The recently published volume by Launay and Senac, *Les Relationes Internationales des Industries de Guerre*, deals largely with this subject. Alfred Nobel, for instance, the inventor of dynamite, located his companies in almost all parts of the world, from Sweden to South

Africa, from Japan to South America. Most of these scattered interests were gathered into two huge trusts, the Nobel Dynamite Trust Company and the Société Centrale de Dynamite, which united the French, Swedish, Italian, Spanish and South American companies. The boards of these two trusts were made up chiefly of Frenchmen, Englishmen and Germans, but each country represented had one of its nationals among the directors.

The Harvey United Steel Company was governed by a board made up of Germans, Englishmen, Americans, Frenchmen and Italians. The Lonza Company was German owned, but had French, Austrian, Italian and German directors. The Whitehead Torpedo Company had a French, British and Hungarian directorate.

These international trusts insured the arms merchants against all possible developments. In peacetime, they could solicit business everywhere, because their local directors would make the proper contacts. Since most of the larger companies also maintained branch factories abroad, the plea of "home industries" could frequently be made. In wartime, a separation of some kind might become necessary, but this could readily be patched up again when peace returned. Thus, the Great International which political idealists and labor strategists have sought for so long, was actually taking shape in the armament business.[50]

Later, in the interwar period, a number of similar well-known cases were often cited as important examples of transnational investment accompanied by interlocking directorates. Apparently, the chaos of the First World War had not basically changed the structure of the arms international. Schneider-Creusot, the largest arms manufacturer in France, was widely regarded to have owned, in connection with French banks, a large share of Skoda, the important Czech arms-maker. Schneider was also believed to have had substantial interests in various arms firms domiciled in Poland, Rumania and Yugoslavia. Skoda also had important interests in the latter countries. These lines of influence were, for the most part, within the French alliance structure hinged upon the Little Entente.[51]

Krupp of Germany was alleged virtually to have controlled Bofors, the great Swedish arms maker, at least until the 1930s when its shares were bought out by the Swedish government. This was crucial to Germany's being able to carry out important research and development work in Sweden in contravention of the articles of the Treaty of Versailles prohibiting it from rearming.[52] There were similar arrangements elsewhere. Krupp was alleged to have had substantial interests in shipyards in Spain and Holland in which German engineers worked secretly to develop submarines for the future U-boat fleet.

These situations are just samplings from the web of transnational ownership and control which apparently existed up to the 1930s. The literature on the arms trade in this period, and the Nye Committee reports as well, cite an almost endless and bewildering number of such relationships.

In a subsequent chapter we shall examine some of the multinational corporate interrelationships existing in the postwar period, under the heading of "transfer modes." These relationships are not now altogether lacking, but suffice it to say that, despite some extensive American holdings in European arms firms, the extent of these interrelationships is but a shadow of the past.[53] While there has been a recent overall trend toward multinationalization of corporate enterprise, there has been a retrenchment in the armaments field. Governments have become more sensitive about sovereignty over their own arms industries.

Later, in our discussion of the impact of mixes of transfer modes, we shall inquire whether this internationalization of the arms industry may have had an impact upon the actual patterns of the arms trade. For earlier periods, Lewinsohn claims that cartelization was extensive, consisting of controls on production, splitting of markets or delimitation of market spheres and even standardization of prices.[54] Furthermore, agreements among interlocked subsidiaries allowed for easy circumvention of embargoes such as those on China and during the Chaco War. Weapons were merely transshipped via company subsidiaries in nations not participating in the embargo.[55] Similar manifestations have been limited if not altogether absent in the postwar period, another result of closer governmental controls.

THE IMPACT OF TECHNOLOGICAL CHANGE IN WEAPONRY ON THE ARMS TRADE

A final variable factor having a seeming impact upon the arms markets is the rate or extent of technological change in weaponry. Two related but distinct criteria are involved here. First, there is the rate of turnover of generations of weaponry—that is, the time span between the introduction of identifiably qualitative advances in "state of the art" systems. A second criterion involves changes in actual performance characteristics over a given time span, for example, the increase in the range of aircraft over a period.[56]

Curiously, there appears to have been a faster rate of generational turnover in most major weapons systems in the interwar period than in the postwar one. For instance, since the end of the Second World War the United States has gone through only about five or six recognizable generations of fighter aircraft, represented in succession by the F-80, F-84, F-86, F-104, F-4 and F-111, with a newer generation about to emerge with the advanced F-14 and F-15. An approximately similar number of generations have been produced during this period by the other major aircraft producers. The Soviets, for instance, have gone through some seven generations of their MIG interceptor series, numbered in order: 9, 15, 17, 19, 21, 23 and 25. For armored equipment in the postwar period there has been an even fewer number of identifiable generations on both sides of the Iron Curtain. The United States, with its Shermans (World War II vintage), Pershings, Pattons and M-60s, has gone through about four generations, and the Soviets' experience has been somewhat similar. Approximately equivalent patterns could also be demonstrated for Britain and France.

In examining Jane's annuals and some of the compendia of armored equipment in the 1930s, it is fairly apparent that there was then a greater turnover of generations of "state of the art" systems. These trends were also pronounced in the 1920s, so that if one observes trends for the 20 year span of the interwar period it appears that, at least for aircraft and armor, there was then a somewhat higher rate of turnover. The United States and Britain, for instance, seemed to be producing new model aircraft in all categories about every year or two.

On the face of it, this would appear paradoxical or surprising, given the more frantic and better-funded arms races of the postwar period and the more systematic efforts at highly institutionalized research and development. But there are explanations. One is the longer lead times for research and development, and another the far greater unit costs of weapons systems in recent years. For these reasons, the sizes of forces as measured in numbers of planes, tanks or ships was much greater in the 1930s than today. Additionally, these factors may account for the seemingly far larger number of prototypes developed in all of the major countries in the 1930s, although fragmentation of corporate armaments industries in the major Western nations may have had much to do with that.

There is still another possible explanation, contained in Huntington's analysis of alternating or contrasting tendencies between qualitative and quantitative arms races. Huntington was examining this dualism primarily with respect to various dyadic arms races in the past century or more, but one might easily project this distinction onto the plane of worldwide arms races. His basic thesis is that quantitative arms races are more serious, in the sense that they are usually a prelude to war or indicative of high tensions in arms races. On the other hand, he indicates that qualitative arms races are more likely where war is not considered imminent, and where each protagonist can thus concentrate on developing a series of prototypes (with low-level production) in order to keep its weapons technology current.[57]

This analysis would appear to be quite apt as an explanation for weapons developments in the interwar period. In the 1920s and up to the mid-1930s each major nation appears to have produced a large number of prototypes in each weapons category. Later, as arms races heated up and as war began to appear imminent, there appears to have been a drop in the rate of generational turnover and more concentration on actual production. The major fighter aircraft used at the beginning of World War II were those which had been in production for several years.

For the postwar period, perhaps one might claim that the continuous imminency of war, combined with concentration by the major powers on technological development of strategic systems, has resulted in a relatively low turnover for conventional systems, in conjunction with high research costs and long lead times.

There is still one other area of possible explanation for these trends. In the interwar period a number of the then major weapons categories were quite new. Combat aircraft and tanks emerged at the end of World War I. Submarines, and then later aircraft carriers, were also new systems. Perhaps for these reasons, technological growth was rapid, particularly in the early 1930s when previously starved military forces were able to begin to utilize recent technological developments from the civilian sector. In the postwar period, it is perhaps not accidental that the rate of generational turnover has apparently been highest in missile systems, far higher there than with jet aircraft, tanks or various types of ships.

A related measure of technological change is that in combat characteristics over time. This is not easy to measure, as any weapons system will have a number of variable characteristics which will undergo technological improvement over time. Aircraft develop in terms of speed, rate of climb to various altitudes, range, payload and armament, while their effectiveness will depend on the destructiveness and accuracy of armaments, and on communications systems, all-weather capability and the like. Armored equipment will vary according to armament (penetration and accuracy of projectile), speed, maneuverability, range and defensive armor. Similar criteria apply to a variety of combat naval vessels. Tables 2-1 and 2-2 give some sample key measurements of change in combat characteristics for "state of the art" aircraft and tanks in both periods for the major nations.

As indicated in Table 2-1, the rate of change for combat characteristics in aircraft was at least as great in the interwar period as in the postwar. In the 1930s, there were rapid developments in aircraft. The horsepower of aircraft engines rose rapidly, from around 400 HP in 1930 to over 1,000 HP by 1940. Biplanes gave way to monoplanes, wooden fuselages to all metal ones. Armament and navigation equipment improved apace. In the postwar period there have also been rapid changes. But in the 20 year period since 1950 the speed of aircraft has barely doubled (unless one assumes the Mach-3 performance of the MIG-23 as typical), whereas it approximately doubled in the ten years of the 1930s.

Maximum speed is only one characteristic, however. The combat capability of fighter aircraft has improved immeasureably, to a great degree because of the development of air-to-air missiles and associated guidance apparatus. Also, the trend toward all-purpose fighter aircraft which can serve both as interceptors and tactical strike aircraft has resulted particularly in greatly increased capability in the latter area.

Table 2-1.   Interwar and Postwar Fighter Aircraft

Interwar				
Year	Type	Maximum Speed (mph)	Range (miles)	Weight Loaded (lbs)
1930	Hawker Hart Bristol Bulldog Fairey III F Curtiss Hawk Vought Corsair 02U Fiat CR-20 Dewoitine D-27	170-210	400-600	2,800-4,300
1939	Supermarine Spitfire Hawker Hurricane Dewoitine D-527 Messerschmidt 109, 110 Curtiss P-40 Koolhoven FK-58 Breda-65	300-385	600-1,000	5,000-6,000
Postwar				
1950	United States F-84, F-86 MIG-9 Saab-91 Ouragon De Havilland Vampire De Havilland Venom Gloster Meteor	580-700	500-1,200	13,000-20,000
1960	Hawker Hunter Mystere Mirage III Saab Lanssen F-8 Crusader MIG-19	700-1,200	800-1,600	13,000-20,000
1970	Phantom MIG-21, 23 Su-11 Mirage F-1, Milan	1,200-1,450	1,100-1,800	31,000-55,000

Source: Various issues of *Jane's All the World's Aircraft* (London: Sampson, Low, Marsten and Co., annual).

In Table 2-2, comparative data for the two periods is displayed for tanks. Again, average figures or ranges are used for "state of the art" systems for the major countries.

The development of the combat characteristics of tanks is difficult to gauge as there have been different rates of change for various characteristics. In the 1930s the speed of tanks almost doubled, while 37 and 47 mm guns gave way to 75 mm cannon by the end of the period. In the 20 years from 1950 to

Table 2-2.   Interwar and Postwar Tanks

Interwar					
Year	Type	Armament (mm of main gun)	Speed (mph)	Weight (tons)	Range (miles)
1930	U.S. Medium T2 Vickers 6 Carden Lloyd MK6 Fiat Ansaldo 3000 Renault NC-31 Soviet T-26	37-47	15-28	7-14	80-140
1939	U.S. M-2 Valentine Crusader Matilda Somua S-35 PZKW-IV Soviet T-34 Carro Armato M	37-76	20-40	11-26	130-180
Postwar					
1950	Pershing Charioteer Centurion I Soviet T-10 Soviet JS-2 AMX-13	90-120	30-40	30-50	130-150
1960	U.S. M-60 U.S. M-48 Centurion IV Soviet T-54	90-120	30-45	35-50	200-250
1970	Chieftain Leopard Soviet T-62 AMX-30 STRV-103	105-120	30-45	32-52	230-380

Source: Tank data is primarily drawn from F. M. von Senger und Etterlin, *Die Kampfpanzer von 1916-1966* (Munich: J. F. Lehmanns Verlag, 1966); Richard Ogorkiewicz, *Armor* (New York: Praeger, 1960); and K. Macksey and J. H. Batchelor, *Tank: A History of the Armoured Fighting Vehicle* (London: MacDonald, 1970). See also Laurence Martin, Arms and Strategy (New York: McKay, 1973), p. 65.

1970 the maximum speed of tanks remained fairly constant, as did their weights (which vary greatly among light, medium and heavy tanks), while the caliber of the main guns moved up from 75 mm to 90 mm and now to 120 mm with advanced models such as the British Chieftain and German Leopard. A comparison here between periods is difficult due to the varied dimensions involved, but it appears that the rate of technological change was at least as great in the 1930s as in the period 1950 to 1970.

The cost of weapons systems has, however, increased enormously in the postwar period. This is partly the result of the phenomenal increases in the costs of avionics, armaments and missile guidance equipment. Table 2-3 gives some indication of the enormity of these changes for various American postwar weapons systems. Though in both periods the rise in weapons costs has been rapid, the rate of change appears to have been accelerating in the postwar years.

What, then, might be the implications of these rates of change for the patterns of the arms trade? One can state a few hypotheses. First, one might expect the arms supplier markets to be more concentrated in times of rapid technological change, particularly if associated with rapidly soaring costs per system. Middle-range powers would not be able to keep up with the rapid changes produced by the large research and development efforts of the major powers. This actually appears to have happened in the interwar period, with its rapid weapons generation changes. By the late 1930s previous capability of nations such as France, Holland and Czechoslovakia to produce first-line equipment had begun to fade.

Table 2-3.   The Soaring Cost of Weaponry

	Unit Cost (Millions of $)
Air Force Fighters	
P-47 (World War II)	0.1
F-105 (1954-1963)	2.5
F-15 (In development)	10.0
Strategic Bombers	
B-29 (World War II)	0.7
B-52 (1952-1961)	7.9
B-1 (In development)	30.0
Aircraft Carriers	
Essex Class (World War II)	4.7
Enterprise (1961)	451.3
CVAN-70 (planning stage)	900.0
Attack Submarines	
Conventional power (World War II)	4.7
Nuclear power (1968)	77.0
Nuclear power (1971)	175.0

Source: *Business Week,* February 19, 1972, p. 60.

The rate of technological change might be expected to have some impact on the patterns of donor-recipient relationships, although in indeterminate fashion. In periods of rapid turnover of weapons generations, one result might be a continuous freeing for sale to dependent nations of equipment which was becoming obsolete due to technological advances. That is, the arms of the supplier nations would become obsolete more quickly, and the suppliers would then be less reluctant to sell equipment which would no longer be on a par with what their own forces were using. On the other hand, the numbers of any given system which are produced in qualitative arms races may also be small. Hence, a period of rapid change may also be one in which the volume of arms transferred may be constricted. At present, both NATO and the Warsaw Pact are undergoing generational changes in their aircraft and armored equipment. Those on hand from a previous generation (M-48 and T-54 tanks, F-104s and MIG-19s) were produced in large quantities in essentially quantitative arms races. The result, after a long time lag due to the slowness of generational turnover, is the present freeing of huge weapons inventories for resale to dependent nations.

Again, these questions must be analyzed in terms of the complexity of the simultaneous action of a number of systems variables. As we shall see, there was indeed a tendency for more modern weapons to be sold to dependent countries in the interwar period. This may in part have been due to rapid technological change and the tendency toward qualitative arms races. However, the corresponding freedom of private arms firms to sell almost whatever they pleased to whomever they pleased allowed for sales of modern equipment to a degree not present today.

SUMMARY

We have indicated that a broad range of systemic factors are critical to evaluation of changes in the basic dimensions of the arms trade and that an analysis of the worldwide arms transfer patterns at any given time will depend on a complex, specific and sometimes unique cluster of these factors.

A tight delineation of cause and effect would be difficult to achieve. A really sophisticated attempt at attributing causation would depend on quantification of most or all of these variables, so that multiple regression techniques might be used. Clearly, this is not possible. Some of the systems variables are quantifiable to a degree. The gradient of power among major nations can be approximated using GNP figures, while rates of technological change can also be measured, qualified by the fact that numerous combat characteristics would have to be dealt with simultaneously.

On the other hand, some of the really critical systems characteristics are not easily amenable to quantification. Some, such as degrees of totality of conflict and diplomacy, degrees of governmental controls and the structure of international corporate business, involve highly subjective considerations. One can merely attempt to analyze the direction impelled to certain dimensions of the arms trade by changes in these factors, as when a tightening of governmental controls results in less arms being transferred between nations which are not allied or closely associated.

In our subsequent analyses of the supplier markets, donor-recipient patterns, transfer modes and degrees of weapons-producing independence, we shall display and discuss comparative data across the two periods and then attempt to speculate intelligently about how these have been affected over time by changes in specific clusters of diplomatic systems variables.

Chapter Three

A Comparison of the Structure and Behavior of Arms Supplier Markets in Two Diplomatic Periods

We now proceed to investigate the structure of the arms supplier markets in various weapons categories, and also the behavior of both national and bloc actors in these markets in our two diplomatic periods.

Concerning market structure, a number of key, interrelated questions are of interest. Who were the significant producers and suppliers of various major weapons systems in each period? What were the relative market shares of these suppliers and their implications? What consistency has there been in supplier markets across various weapons systems; in turn, what has been the importance of specialization in certain weapons types by some nations? How have the supplier markets changed, either within the two diplomatic periods or between them, and to what extent have changes been attributable to variations in the complex of our diplomatic systems variables? Finally, can analysis of changes in the structure of the arms markets be useful in evaluating the ebbs and flows of national power and influence on a worldwide scale?

Concerning behavior, what has been the difference in arms supply policies among nations described along a continuum from revisionist to antirevisionist, or from expansionist to conservative powers? Have there been differing propensities toward selling different mixes of weapons systems, or weapons of varying modernity and quality?

In seeking generalizations about arms supplier behavior, we shall also attempt to utilize a typology developed by the SIPRI group in a comparative context. Their analysis indicates a division of supplier market behavior into three general types: "hegemonic," "industrial" (market-oriented) and "restrictive," claimed applicable in recent years to such representative nations as the USSR, France and Sweden, respectively.[1] We shall examine whether this typology is useful in longer range analysis.

The central concern of this chapter, however, is that of how the constellation of factors revolving about polarity, alliances, ideology and distribution of power among major nations has affected the degree of monopoly or oligopoly existing in arms supplier markets. This, in turn, is critical to the problem of controls as well as to broader questions of power and influence among nations.

ARMS PRODUCERS AND ARMS SUPPLIERS:
THE PROBLEM OF CONGRUENCE

Initially, the structure of the supplier markets may be discussed on two separate but related levels. First, there is the question of which nations are—or have been—actual producers of weapons systems and hence at least potential factors in supplier markets. Then, more importantly, there is the question of which nations are—or have been—actual factors in the arms markets, of varying significance.

There is not necessarily a one-to-one congruence between capability to produce a weapons system and actually becoming a factor in its supplier market. A smaller nation, stretched for resources and short on production capacity, may be capable of supplying some or all of its requirements in a given system, but may not have the capacity to become a significant exporter. It will also have the problem of breaking into markets controlled by larger nations, backed by superior capabilities in spare parts, maintenance and military training assistance. However, export markets may sometimes be a virtual prerequisite to any weapons production, as the necessary research and development expenditures and plant investment may only be recoverable by achieving economies of scale via export. This is the normal assumption of the underlying basis for current French aggressiveness in the arms export markets. Czechoslovakia, for one, exhibited similar behavior in the interwar period.[2]

On the other hand, neutral Sweden has managed virtual self-sufficiency in almost all weapons categories, with very limited arms sales abroad. The problem of economies of scale has not, apparently, been prohibitive in this case.[3]

Another situation where capability and actuality as a market factor do not coincide is where stipulations of peace treaties from prior wars constitute bars to weapons production. Germany in the interwar period, and Germany and Japan in the postwar period, have been examples. The result has been reduction of the number of significant suppliers.

Generally, the theory of comparative advantage does not appear particularly applicable to analysis of producers and suppliers of arms. As independent arms production is a symbol or normal concomitant of great power status, and necessary for diplomatic independence, most major nations will assume this role, economics aside. In tight, hegemonic alliances (such as NATO throughout most of the postwar period), where a supply of arms is assured the smaller powers, comparative advantage will, however, become operative to a degree. In short, prestige and economic factors are intertwined in determining which nations will choose to become producers, and hence usually suppliers.[4]

Finally, the phenomenon of retransfer introduces an additional complicating element to analysis of supplier markets. Some medium powers—such as the UAR in recent years—have become fairly significant suppliers of arms in some categories without any real independent production capacity.

THE IMPLICATIONS OF MARKET STRUCTURE:
OLIGOPOLY AND CONTROLS

The size or structure of supplier markets has vital implications for the possibility of controls. It is clear that the larger the number of weapons suppliers, the more difficult it will be to achieve agreements on controls either in general or in specific cases.[5] The same point applies to attempts at international embargoes. These assumptions are, however, complicated by the nature of bloc and alliance systems.

There is a psychological as well as a sheer statistical aspect to this point. For the greater the number of suppliers, the easier it becomes for any nation to fall back on the time-honored rationale embodied in such nostrums as: "If we don't sell them the weapons, someone else will."

The problems presented for controls in situations of widespread, dispersed arms production may become more severe in multipolar than in bipolar international systems. Whereas agreements on controls may be simplified by coherent policies within hegemonic blocs headed by one major power, such coordination of policy becomes more difficult in the case of multiple independent power bases. The obverse of this point is also cogent. For those nations which deem themselves in need of arms and which are either unaligned or have poor leverage with major bloc actors relative to their adversaries, the chances for obtaining the necessary arms will be worse in the case of a more constricted supplier market. This problem may be exacerbated in bipolar, hegemonically oriented bloc alignments. The recent experiences of Pakistan and Israel are cases in point.

We shall proceed on the tentative assumption that, other things being equal, tightly oligopolistic supplier markets are more conducive to the chances for international controls of arms flows than more fragmented ones. A counterassumption may have some validity, if one assumes that the competition for extending influence in ideological, bipolar systems may be fierce, and exacerbating of the arms trade in spite of the small number of suppliers.

THE PRODUCERS AND SUPPLIERS OF ARMS
IN THE TWO PERIODS

Let us briefly outline the structure of the supplier markets by identifying the actual producers and suppliers in both periods. In the process, we can indicate broad trends within and between the two periods. Some countries have dropped out at points as suppliers and producers of certain weapons, while others have entered, in response to a variety of political, economic and technological factors.

We have already indicated some hindrances to analysis in our discussion of the distinction between producers and suppliers. There are others, previously touched upon in defining the scope of the arms trade.

One problem is the continuum of relative degrees of independence in research and development of weapons, as well as of production. Then, there is the practice of copying, as well as the activities of some nations in importing many or most components of a weapons system, to be assembled at home. Thus, whereas Japan and Russia appeared to have been independent producers of aircraft in the interwar period, in fact they were merely making copies of purchased Western models, while also importing critical components. The use of licensing is still another type of partial weapons-producing independence.

In some cases, the available data are such that the lines between these degrees of weapons-producing independence are blurred. It is often not clear just what has been copied, licensed or assembled. The scope of the supplier market for a given weapons system is not always restricted merely to those nations capable of independent research, design and production of complete systems. However, to the extent that end-use restrictions have usually been enforced, at least since 1945, the scope of the supplier markets has normally been circumscribed and is generally explicable in terms of the small number of independent bases of arms development.

Combat Aircraft

The combat aircraft—a category including fighter-interceptors, fighter-bombers (strike or attack aircraft), various types of bombers and reconnaissance aircraft—has been, more or less, the "master" weapon throughout both periods under discussion (omitting here weapons of mass destruction and their launchers). The ability to design and produce such aircraft has been—and remains—a hallmark of a militarily advanced nation.

As the types and mixes of aircraft produced have changed considerably since 1930, strict comparison over time is difficult. Partly, this is the result of the introduction in the postwar period of missiles which have replaced some of the previous functions of combat aircraft, particularly that of long-range bombardment.

There has also been a trend away from narrowly specialized functions for aircraft which had previously resulted in the production of a large variety of aircraft types. During the 1930s most major nations were producing specific models for the functions of pursuit, attack, torpedo-bombing and dive-bombing. Each also produced light, medium and heavy bombers, and a variety of amphibious naval aircraft for patrol and antisubmarine warfare (ASW) functions. Still further subdivisions resulted from the specific use of day and night fighters and bombers.

In the postwar period there has been a trend toward multiple purpose aircraft, although variants of a basic model can be configured for different roles. The United States Phantom, for instance, has been variously configured for attack, pursuit and reconnaissance roles. With the once problematic F-111 the trend toward multiple functions reached a zenith, and now is seemingly being reversed in the United States with the F-14 and F-15 (and further with the A-X and LWF) in realization of the limits of cost-effectiveness. These same trends over the two periods have been evidenced in all of the major air forces. It is this, aside from vast increases in development costs, which accounts for the much larger number of prototypes developed during the interwar period.[6]

In the interwar period, the number of nations involved in independent design and production of combat aircraft appears to have been considerably greater than now, although for advanced fighter aircraft, only the United States, Germany, Italy, France and Britain were virtually independent in design and development as well as production. Holland and Czechoslovakia also attained a significant degree of independence, based respectively on the Fokker and Skoda aircraft companies, although, at least in the case of the former, remaining essentially dependent on Britain and France for aircraft engines. Actually, both France and Britain began to import heavily from the United States on the eve of the war. This was due, at least in the case of Britain, as much to inadequate production capability as to shortcomings in design and development.

Meanwhile, Japan and Russia developed independent design capability only by the late 1930s, after a lengthy period of utilizing copies of Western models. In addition to Holland and Czechoslovakia among the middle-range or smaller powers, Poland, Belgium, Lithuania, Yugoslavia and Sweden each developed its own fighter aircraft during this period, although each remained primarily dependent on foreign sources for the bulk of its air forces as well as for engines in indigenously designed models. Only Poland among these exported aircraft to any significant degree, with sales to some of the Balkan nations and to Turkey.

Thus, the number of nations achieving independence in development of combat aircraft in the interwar period was surprisingly high, although qualified by the constricted nature of the aircraft engine market. In addition to engines, some of the nations which gained some measure of independence in the interwar period were also dependent for items such as propellers, navigational equipment and aircraft armament. On the other hand, two nations—Switzerland and Denmark—which did not produce aircraft indigenously, produced advanced aircraft cannon (Oerlikon and Madsen makes) which were used on the fighter aircraft of major nations such as the United Kingdom and France. This, too, would appear to reflect the then freer market nature of the arms trade which allowed for a greater degree of specialization.

In the postwar period only five nations have achieved significant independent design and production capability for fighter aircraft: the United States, the USSR, France, Britain and Sweden. Italy, in addition, has produced one model of a fighter aircraft, the G-91, which has been sold to Germany and Portugal.

France was not really an independent producer before the mid-1950s, before which time she relied primarily upon the United States and Britain, with extensive licensing from the latter. And until very recently, the French had continued to depend on the United States for various electronic accessories. Presently, France, with its Mirage series of fighters, is more or less independent, although increasingly a participant in codevelopment ventures with European partners.

The United Kingdom meanwhile, while independent throughout most of the postwar period, has also come to rely on the United States of late with purchases of Phantoms following the aborting of a deal for F-111s. The British have continued to produce and sell the Lightning interceptor, and in the near future may regain a degree of independence—and a share of the export markets-with the Harrier VTOL fighter (which has already had sales in the United States and Spain), the Jaguar strike aircraft being coproduced with France and the Panavia MRCA fighter being coproduced with Germany and Italy.

Sweden has produced most of its own fighter aircraft in the postwar period, the most recent models being the highly regarded Draken and Viggen fighter-bombers, some of which have been sold to other Scandinavian nations. She has, however, remained dependent on the United States and Britain for licensed engine production, no doubt for reasons of economy.

There have been some halting attempts at further additions to the combat aircraft market. Canada toyed briefly in the late 1950s with a design for its own strike aircraft, the CF-Arrow, but gave up the project. Similarly, an attempt by India and Egypt to codevelop a strike fighter with the aid of refugee technicians in the UAR was abandoned and both countries became rather secure clients of the Soviet Union.

Currently, there are auguries of serious additions to the ranks of combat aircraft producers which may in turn have profound effects upon export markets in dependent nations. China is reported to have finally designed and produced its own fighter aircraft, although none have been sold abroad.[7] Japan is also making moves in this direction with its new Mitsubishi aircraft.[8] Israel, meanwhile, is now reported to be in production on its own design of a fighter plane, the Barak, probably copied from the French Mirage and to be powered by engines licensed from the United States.[9] Then, too, the several codevelopment efforts now underway among Western European nations indicate the possibility of further changes in the makeup of the market.[10]

Generally, however, in terms of significant impact on the export markets, the number of effective suppliers of fighter aircraft has remained at four or five throughout the postwar period.

Similar comparative patterns have obtained for bombers. As noted previously, a more complex and functionally specific mix of aircraft in this category was produced in the interwar period. Still, only the United States, the United Kingdom, Germany, France and Italy were significant suppliers during that period, although there was also some bomber production in Russia, Japan, Czechoslovakia and Holland. In the postwar period, only the United States, the Soviet Union and Britain have produced heavy bombers, while some French aircraft—the Vautour and new Mirage models—have been capable of ordnance delivery in the medium bomber range.

Transport Aircraft

In transport aircraft, there has been close correspondence with design and production capability for bombers, with fewer supplier factors than for fighter aircraft.

In the interwar period the primary factors in the transport aircraft market were the United States (Boeing, Curtiss, Lockheed, Douglas), Britain (Armstrong-Whitworth, Bristol, Handley-Page, Vickers), France (Bordelaise, Breguet, Potez), Germany (Henschel, Junkers) and Italy (Bergameschi, Caproni). Fokker was also a minor supplier factor while Czechoslovakia (Avia), Switzerland (Comte) and Japan (Nakajima copies of Douglas models) produced transports without becoming involved in export sales. Sweden was also a supplier of transport aircraft in the early 1930s, but this was based on production by a Junkers facility domiciled outside of Germany to evade treaty restrictions.

In the postwar period only the United States, the USSR, the United Kingdom and France have been significant developers of transport aircraft, although, in addition, Italy and the Netherlands have produced light transports, as has Israel with a STOL model. The difference between the two periods is, however, essentially accounted for by the absence of Germany and Japan from the postwar transport markets.

Trainer and Utility Aircraft

In both periods a large number of nations have achieved independent design and production capability in trainer and utility aircraft, although this has not translated significantly into very broad supplier markets. Also, many of the smaller nations which have developed this capability have still remained dependent on the larger nations for the bulk of their own air forces' requirements.

In the interwar period significant development of light aircraft was achieved, in addition to the major nations, by Yugoslavia, Belgium, Argentina, Brazil, Mexico, Austria, Finland, Lithuania, Poland, Rumania, Spain, Sweden and China. However, only a small number of transfers from these sources were recorded.

In the postwar period jet trainers have been developed independently by nations such as Italy, Czechoslovakia, Poland and Yugoslavia, in addition to the major powers, while prop-driven utility aircraft have been developed by most developed nations as well as by Brazil and Argentina. Of considerable import has been the use made by numerous developing countries of the armed jet trainers produced by France and Italy (Magister and Macchi models) for counterinsurgency purposes.

In general, however, the number of nations engaged in independent design and production of smaller aircraft appears to have declined from the 1930s to the present.

Aircraft Engines

As previously indicated, in both periods the number of nations involved in independent design and production of aircraft engines usable for military purposes has been smaller than the number of nations possessing capability in airframe design and production. This is aside from the larger number of nations engaged in license production of engines, which includes otherwise independent Sweden. Table 3-1 indicates the scope of the aircraft engine market for the interwar period. In addition, the Soviets and Japanese were large-scale interwar engine producers, licensing and copying foreign designs.

In the postwar period the number of independent sources of jet aircraft engines has been reduced to four: the United States (General Electric and Pratt and Whitney), the United Kingdom (Rolls-Royce), France (SNECMA and Turbomeca) and the Soviet Union. It is perhaps this factor above all which makes for a highly constricted aircraft supplier market and which at least potentially allows for controls applied by a very limited number of nations, if those controls were to be extended to licensing agreements.

Helicopters

In the interwar period, while a number of nations developed rotary-driven aircraft prototypes, there was no significant use of helicopters for military purposes. In the postwar period the market has been roughly similar to that for combat aircraft, despite a somewhat larger number of nations having achieved some independent design and production capability.

For the most part the helicopter supplier markets have been

Table 3-1.   Interwar Combat Aircraft Engine Producers

Country	Producer
Great Britain	Bristol, Rolls-Royce, Armstrong-Siddeley, Napier
United States	Allison, Pratt and Whitney, Wright, Kinner
France	Lorraine, Gnome-Rhone, Hispano-Suiza
Germany	BMW, Junkers, Siemens, Argus, Daimler-Benz, Hirth
Italy	Piaggio, Isotta-Fraschini, Alfa-Romeo, Fiat
Czechoslovakia	Skoda, Walter

Source: *Jane's All the World's Aircraft*. (London: Sampson, Low, Marsten and Co., annual).

dominated by the United States (Sikorsky, Bell, Lycoming, among others), the United Kingdom (Westland), France (Alouette and Frelon series) and the Soviet Union (Mi-series). Some other nations have become significant factors through sales of licensed craft; Italy, with its Bell Agusta helicopters, is one good example. Although Brazil, Canada, Czechoslovakia, West Germany, Hungary, Italy, Japan, Netherlands, Poland, South Africa and Spain have designed their own rotorcraft, none has achieved significant production, much less noticeable impact as suppliers. This market too is narrowly oligopolistic.

Tanks and Armored Cars

As with combat aircraft, the number of independent centers of design and production of armored equipment was somewhat greater in the interwar period, but with recent additions to the ranks seemingly auguring a return to the basic structure of the earlier period.

In the interwar period tanks were independently designed by the United States, the United Kingdom, France, Germany, Italy, Sweden and Czechoslovakia, with Japan and Russia again constituting additional market factors through copying and licensing. Poland and Spain also developed indigenous prototypes in abortive projects.[11]

In the earlier postwar period tank development was centered in the United States, the USSR, Britain and France. Sweden also has been a producer of innovative, indigenously designed tank equipment, but has not been a supplier factor, nor has Switzerland with its specially designed mountain armor equipment. India and Israel have both produced independently designed modifications of foreign tanks. More recently, however, China, Japan and West Germany have embarked on indigenous tank development programs with the German Leopard tank now widely used in Western Europe. It may be anticipated that they will subsequently become factors in the tank export markets.[12]

Until very recently, then, the interperiod difference in tank development has been explained by the dropping out of the Czechs and Italians, and the addition of the Swiss.

Armored cars were a much more significant class of military equipment in the 1930s than they are now, although this type of vehicle can still be useful in many developing nations for counterinsurgency purposes and for reconnaissance and light combat in certain types of terrain.

In the interwar period armored cars were produced and exported by the United States (Marmon-Harrington, Ford), Britain (Morris, Guy, Crossley, Lanchester), France (Renault, Panhard), Italy (Fiat), Czechoslovakia (Skoda), Sweden (Landskrona) and Austria (Steyr). As we shall see, Austria was among the leading suppliers of these vehicles, based on extensive sales of its small Steyr armored car in Eastern Europe.

In the postwar period the number of supplier factors has declined in line with the reduced importance of this weapons system. The Soviet Union has not sold any, and the United States only a few. The bulk of the market has been controlled by the British (Ferret, Humber, Staghound, Saladin models) and the French (Panhard). Recent heavy sales of the French Panhard vehicle to South Africa do indicate the retention of some significant export markets for urban counterinsurgency purposes.

Naval Vessels

A detailed analysis of the scope of the markets in the various categories of naval vessels would require too lengthy a discussion at this point. Some generalizations may be made, however. As with other types of weapons systems, the supplier markets are more concentrated in the most sophisticated and expensive categories of vessels. There are far more developers, producers and suppliers of patrol craft and gunboats in both periods than of battleships or aircraft carriers.

Another clear generalization is that the number of nations able to achieve independent development capability was somewhat greater in the interwar period than at present. These trends are clearer, however, for the less expensive items. Again, this is primarily accounted for by the dropping out of a number of middle-range powers—mostly in Europe—from the supplier markets, a concomitant of the bipolar, hegemonic alliance system of the postwar period.

In the 1930s a surprising number of nations were independently producing their own warships. Besides the major powers, all of which were substantially able to satisfy their internal markets, these included Holland, Denmark, Sweden, Norway, China, Spain, Finland and Portugal. However, similar to the broader base of aircraft production in that period, these nations tended to be dependent on the major nations for supply of—or licensing of—key components such as naval engines and fire control equipment. There was also considerable shipbuilding activity by subsidiaries of major nations' firms in a number of the middle-range powers, including Spain, Portugal and Finland.

Concerning the actual export market for naval ships, it is rather clear that in both periods there has been a far higher incidence of retransfers than has been the case for other weapons systems. This has enabled a number of smaller powers to become significant secondary suppliers. The greater longevity of naval vessels as contrasted with aircraft and armored equipment accounts for this. Even today there is a lively trade among developing nations for World War II vintage naval vessels, often with prestige implications transcending those of actual combat requirements. The scope of the interwar naval supply markets is indicated in Table 3-2.

For the postwar period the markets have been severely narrowed, although with extensive license-production and offshore procurement conducted by European clients of the two superpowers. United States and Soviet models are dominant, with Britain, France, Sweden and Japan maintaining some

Table 3-2.   Interwar Naval Craft Developers

Type of Craft	Developers
Warships	United States, Britain, France, Germany, Russia, Japan, Brazil, Romania, Poland, Finland, Sweden, Norway, Spain, Portugal, Netherlands, Denmark, Canada
Submarines	United States, Britain, France, Germany, Russia, Japan, Romania, Turkey, Sweden, Spain, Netherlands, Denmark
Patrol Boats, Gunboats, Motor Torpedo Boats	United States, Britain, France, Germany, Russia, Japan, Brazil, Cuba, Poland, Norway, Netherlands, Denmark, Australia, Belgium
Transports, Oilers, Support Vessels	United States, Britain, France, Germany, Russia, Japan, Argentina, Turkey, Sweden, Spain, Portugal, Netherlands, Denmark

independent design and development. American-licensed patrol boats and missile-destroyers are built in Spain, Portugal, Japan and Germany. Otherwise, the broadest markets are in the areas of patrol craft and torpedo boats, where independent development has been achieved in the shipyards of a number of essentially weapons-dependent nations: Argentina, Ceylon, India, Indonesia, Mexico, Thailand, Turkey, Brazil, North Korea, South Korea and Israel. In addition, in the small warship category, India, Chile, Argentina and Indonesia have produced some frigates and submarine chasers, without becoming real factors in the supplier markets.

Missiles

As the development of missiles of various types (air-to-surface, air-to-air, surface-to-surface, surface-to-air, ship-to-ship, etc.) was still embryonic in the interwar period, there is no basis here for comparisons between periods. However, with the growing importance of missiles of all sorts, some brief commentary is in order on the development of missile markets in the postwar period.[13]

Despite the considerable concentration of missile production among the major powers, a lack of market concentration relative to categories such as combat aircraft and tanks is observable. Presumably, as with small arms, trainer aircraft and patrol boats, the explanation is in smaller unit costs, even in the face of high technological requirements.

Each of the major powers has produced a full range of modern missiles, although only the superpowers, and now China, have developed and produced advanced ICBMs. In the conventional missiles category, significant independent development has been achieved by Israel (surface-to-surface), Italy (surface-to-surface, air-to-surface, antitank, surface-to-air), Japan (antitank), Norway (antisubmarine and antiship), West Germany (various), Switzerland (antitank and surface-to-air), Australia (surface-to-surface), Sweden (antitank and surface-to-air) and Brazil (surface-to-surface, surface-to-air and antitank). Some of these nations have developed export markets, an example being Israel's sales of the proven Gabriel missile to Iran and Singapore. France, with an excellent conventional missile industry, has even succeeded in breaking into American military procurement markets in this field.[14] In the future, with the expected increased combat effectiveness of antitank and surface-to-air systems, this segment of the international trade in arms will no doubt assume more crucial importance.

It should be stressed, however, with the lessons of the 1973 Middle East War in mind, that the qualitative aspects of missile performance will be critical in determining the future shape of supplier markets. And it should be noted, for instance, that at the level of sophisticated surface-to-air missiles, only the several major powers are now competing for exports.

THE STRUCTURE OF THE SUPPLIER MARKETS

In this section we shall examine the market shares achieved by various suppliers for each of the major weapons categories in both periods. Then, we shall try to summarize by evaluating the overall role of major suppliers in both periods across all major systems.

Using the data on market shares, we shall measure the degrees of market concentration for each weapons system in each period. This is done at various levels, by indicating the shares of the markets held by the first, first two, first three, first four, and first five largest suppliers. As earlier indicated, the degree of market oligopoly or concentration should have important implications for controls.

Additionally, we have aggregated the data on market shares by identifiable blocs in both periods. For the postwar period the shares of the NATO and Soviet blocs are compared and then further broken down into categories which might more closely represent the present apparent trend towards multipolarity. Thus, a further breakdown is made of the United States, the Warsaw Pact, China and Western Europe (within NATO).

For the interwar period two types of bloc arrangements for the data are used. First, assuming a crude tripolar arrangement, we have combined market shares according to a West-Axis-Soviet alignment, with the United States assumed to have been part of an incipient Western bloc. Then, a quintipolar breakdown is used: the United States, France-Britain, Germany-Italy, Japan and the USSR.

Data on market shares by bloc can be illustrative in analyzing trends in market shares within periods. This allows us to examine whether there have been parallel trends in the expansion or contraction of the arms markets of identifiable expansionist or status quo blocs. A central thesis here is that expansionist powers or blocs have tended, within periods, to expand their arms clientele at the expense of status quo or conservative powers or blocs.

Combat Aircraft

In Table 3-3 we have the basic breakdown of the supplier market for combat aircraft in both periods. As indicated, the United States has been the

Table 3-3.   Comparison of Market Shares in Combat Aircraft

Interwar (from 1930)				*Postwar (to 1968)*			
Rank	*Country*	*Number*	*Percent*	*Rank*	*Country*	*Number*	*Percent*
1	United States	3,218	22.8	1	United States	2,512	29.7
2	United Kingdom	2,435	17.3	2	USSR	2,390	28.2
3	France	2,204	15.6	3	United Kingdom	1,234	14.6
4	Italy	1,786	12.7	4	France	651	7.7
5	Germany	1,336	9.5	5	China	481	5.7
6	USSR	784	5.6	6	UAR	352	4.2
7	Netherlands	429	3.0	7	Sweden	203	2.4
8	Poland	306	2.2	8	West Germany	201	2.4
9	Other	1,614	11.3	9	Other	438	5.1
		14,112	100.0			8,462	100.0

Other Suppliers: Belgium, Canada, Czechoslovakia, Sweden, Switzerland, Japan, Denmark, Yugoslavia, Mexico

Other Suppliers: Poland, Jordan, Czechoslovakia, Italy, Israel, Iraq, Argentina, Mexico

Bloc Market Shares (percent)

West:	56.4	United States	22.8	NATO:	54.6	United States	29.7
Axis:	22.7	Britain-France	32.9	Sino-Soviet:	34.4	Western Europe	24.9
Soviet:	5.6	Soviet	5.6			Warsaw	28.7
		Japan	0.5			China	5.7
		Germany-Italy	22.2				

Levels of Concentration (percent)

	Interwar	*Postwar*
Single largest supplier	22.8	29.7
Two largest suppliers	40.1	57.9
Three largest suppliers	55.7	72.5
Four largest suppliers	68.4	80.2
Five largest suppliers	77.9	85.9

Rank Order Correlation of Interperiod Suppliers

r_s	*Significance*
.60	.015

major supplier in both periods, although with a somewhat higher percentage of the market in the postwar era up to 1968. We shall see that the United States, with the highest GNP throughout the time span since 1930, has been a disproportionately stronger factor in the aircraft markets than in any other category. It is still noteworthy, however, that the United States was the world's premier supplier of combat aircraft even in the period of its semi-isolation before World War II.

After the United States, the USSR has been the second largest supplier since 1945, its role having gradually increased over the span of this period. In fact, massive Soviet aircraft transfers to the Middle East since 1968 would probably now put it in first place. The United Kingdom and France have been the third and fourth largest. Actually, the 1968 terminal date of the MIT research has probably resulted in this author's understating the French postwar supplier role as it might now appear from the perspective of the early 1970s, since in the period 1969-1972 the French secured a number of markets, particularly for Mirage fighters, which previously were dominated by other powers. Sales of these jets have been made to such varied recipients as Argentina, Colombia, Peru, Libya, Lebanon, Saudi Arabia, Kuwait, Malaysia, Pakistan, Greece, Portugal, Australia, India, South Africa, Switzerland and Belgium.[15]

At first glance, it might appear surprising that the UAR, a nonproducer of indigenously developed combat aircraft, would be a stronger market factor than some of the major nations. The reason, of course, has been significant numbers of retransfers of Soviet and other aircraft to nations such as Nigeria, Guinea, Ghana and the Sudan, perhaps often in cases where the Soviets have wished to achieve a low profile for these transactions.

The breakdown of market shares by bloc in the postwar period indicates an almost tripolar pattern of influence. While overall NATO sales of combat aircraft have far exceeded those of what was once known as the Sino-Soviet bloc, it is noteworthy that the combined shares of the Western European members of NATO have not lagged far behind those of the United States alone. Here, extensive retransfers of American equipment to Third World nations have been important.

In the interwar period, the United States as the leading supplier was followed by the United Kingdom, France, Italy and Germany. As we shall see later, the patterns of transfers from the United States were somewhat different in that period. American sales were then concentrated in Latin America and in China. As indicated in the table, the Western bloc was collectively dominant over the Axis grouping, although the rise of the latter as a combined market force toward the latter part of the period is masked by using data for the whole ten year interval.

The Soviet Union, then with the second highest GNP in the world, was not a very significant aircraft supplier in the 1930s. During this period the Soviets were just beginning to develop an independent aircraft industry, based on foreign copies. Most production was absorbed by the Soviet Air Force, although there were some concentrated sales to Loyalist Spain, the Kuomintang in China, Turkey and Czechoslovakia.

Somewhat in contrast with the postwar period, none of the significant interwar suppliers achieved that status by retransfers of secondhand equipment. This was probably due to the more rapid turnover of weapons generations as well as to less restrictive controls on the transfer of modern equipment and the absence of large numbers of developing countries to provide an end-market for weapons sold through two or more stages.

Just because a given supplier held only a tiny fraction of the market—even around one percent—does not necessarily mean that it could not have been an important supplier in specific situations. In absolute terms, the number of aircraft supplied by Japan to Thailand in the late 1930s, or by Czechoslovakia to a few of the Balkan countries, was still quite large.

It is clear that there has been a higher level of market concentration in the postwar period at all levels. In either period, it is clear that controls could not easily have resulted from agreements among two or three suppliers, although the production-base limitations of the smaller suppliers might have afforded this to some degree.

Transport Aircraft

The figures for supplier shares in transport aircraft shown in Table 3-4 indicate somewhat different patterns than for combat aircraft. The most striking feature has been the clear dominance—although well short of mono-poly—of the United States in both periods, with around half of the market. One might speculate that this has been, in both periods, a by-product of dominance in commercial aircraft, many of which are developed from the same prototypes. In the 1930s, for instance, military versions of the Douglas DC-3—then tops in its field—were widely sold.

The rather small second place share of the postwar market by the Soviet Union is no doubt explicable in light of the retarded state of that country's commercial air fleet, at least until very recently.

As indicated in the table, the scope of the interwar market was quite small. There were only eight identifiable sources of traded transports. Also, in absolute numbers, the size of the market appears to have been quite limited. Extensive long-range transport both of military personnel and cargo was then in its infancy.

In the postwar period there have been a large number of smaller supplier factors. This is explained by the fairly lively market in retransferred transports. As with a number of categories of naval craft, transport aircraft appear to have considerable longevity, which accounts for this significant retransfer market.

In contrast with combat aircraft, the degree of market concentration

Table 3-4   Comparison of Market Shares in Transport Aircraft

Interwar (from 1930)				*Postwar (to 1968)*			
Rank	*Country*	*Number*	*Percent*	*Rank*	*Country*	*Number*	*Percent*
1	United States	158	53.6	1	United States	1,011	46.6
2	Italy	38	12.9	2	USSR	308	14.2
3	United Kingdom	30	10.2	3	United Kingdom	224	10.3
4	Germany	29	9.8	4	France	165	7.6
5	France	21	7.1	5	UAR	32	1.5
6	Sweden	12	4.1	6	Canada	31	1.4
7	Netherlands	6	2.0	7	Czechoslovakia	28	1.3
8	Switzerland	1	0.3	8	Other	370	17.1
		295	100.0			2,169	100.0

Other Suppliers: None

Other Suppliers: Belgium, Italy, India, Netherlands, Switzerland, China, Poland, West. Germany, South Africa, Iran, Iraq, Argentina, New Zealand, Jordan, Zambia

Bloc Market Shares (percent)

West:	70.9	United States	53.6	NATO:	72.0	United States	46.6
Axis:	22.7	Britain-France	17.3	Sino-Soviet:	20.3	Western Europe	19.9
Soviet:	0.0	Soviet	0.0			Warsaw	20.1
		Germany-Italy	22.7			China	0.2
		Japan	0.0				

Levels of Concentration (percent)

	Interwar	*Postwar*
Single largest supplier	53.6	46.6
Two largest suppliers	66.5	60.8
Three largest suppliers	76.7	71.1
Four largest suppliers	86.5	78.7
Five largest suppliers	93.6	80.2

Rank Order Correlation of Interperiod Suppliers

r_s	*Significance*
.13	.328

appears to have been greater for transports in the interwar period. This is accounted for primarily by the degree of American dominance in the earlier period. In terms of various identifiable bloc shares, it is clear that the West, paced by the United States, has been dominant throughout, although Junkers and Caproni transports from Germany and Italy were beginning to make inroads into Western markets in the late 1930s. Meanwhile, recent developments in

Soviet and Western European commercial aviation may later lead to erosion of present American markets in transports, a trend already well underway.

Trainer Aircraft

In Table 3-5 it is demonstrated that the United States has also been the major supplier of trainer aircraft in both periods. While in the interwar period the United States was just narrowly ahead of the United Kingdom, Germany and France in an essentially quadropolistic market, it has since assumed an altogether dominant position.

As indicated in the table, there have been a far higher number of suppliers in the postwar period, even with the somewhat smaller absolute number of trainer aircraft traded. Again, a large portion of the market is accounted for by retransfers by nonproducing nations.

One point which stands out, in contrast to some other categories, is the small number of transfers originating from the Soviet Union. As we have noted, the USSR has also been a rather weak market factor in transport aircraft. Clearly, the Soviets appear to have concentrated their aircraft sales in the combat category, that is, have emphasized ordnance delivery systems over those not expressly designed for use in combat roles. The reasons for this appear to be mixed. On the one hand, it reflects the order of battle of the Soviet Air Force, particularly in the transport field. On the other, the Soviets have appeared—perhaps more so than the United States—unwilling to pressure clients to accept less sophisticated systems in lieu of advanced fighters. Where Western suppliers have transferred "combat" trainer aircraft to many developing African nations, the Soviets have donated MIGs to the air forces of Uganda, the Sudan, Somalia and Guinea. In these cases, prestige reasons probably outweigh those of rational choices of acquisition in terms of foreseeable combat contingencies.

It is emphasized that trainer aircraft can often be significant for combat purposes in "local war" situations. They are often a very rational purchase for a small nation on a cost-effectiveness basis.[16] The Israelis made good use of their French Fouga Magister trainers for tank-busting purposes in June of 1967. South Africa, perhaps anticipating an extensive counterinsurgency operation, has license-built hundreds of Italian Macchi trainers for possible combat use. Similar purchases were made in the interwar period. Britain, with its DeHavilland Moth series, the United States with its Stearmans and Harvards, and Germany with its Bucker and Arado trainers made numerous sales to smaller countries unable to afford advanced combat aircraft.

Observing the data on market concentration, it is apparent that a third type of pattern emerges here, where in neither period has there been consistently more concentration at all levels. Higher concentration at the level of the first and second largest suppliers in the postwar period gives way to higher concentration for the interwar period at the levels of the third through fifth largest. Here, an attribution of higher concentration in one case or the other

Table 3-5.   Comparison of Market Shares in Trainer Aircraft

Interwar (from 1930)				*Postwar (to 1968)*			
Rank	*Country*	*Number*	*Percent*	*Rank*	*Country*	*Number*	*Percent*
1	United States	1,311	25.6	1	United States	1,892	42.5
2	United Kingdom	1,231	24.0	2	United Kingdom	531	11.9
3	Germany	954	18.6	3	France	339	7.6
4	France	834	16.3	4	USSR	282	6.3
5	Czechoslovakia	152	3.0	5	Netherlands	169	3.8
6	Italy	146	2.8	6	Canada	130	2.9
7	Other	496	9.7	7	Czechoslovakia	119	2.7
				8	Spain	100	2.2
				9	Italy	86	1.9
				10.	Other	799	18.2
		5,124	100.0			4,447	100.0

Other Suppliers: Netherlands, Sweden, Switzerland, Finland, Mexico, Brazil

Other Suppliers: Belgium, India, Israel, Sweden, Switzerland, UAR, Poland, West Germany, Japan, Norway, Indonesia, Iraq, Argentina, Laos

Bloc Market Shares (percent)

West:	68.2	United States	25.6	NATO:	72.6	United States	42.5
Axis	21.4	Britain-France	42.6	Sino-Soviet:	9.1	Western Europe	26.8
Soviet:	0.0	Soviet	0.0			Warsaw	9.1
		Germany-Italy	21.4			China	0.0
		Japan	0.0				

Levels of Concentration (percent)

	Interwar	*Postwar*
Single largest supplier	25.6	42.5
Two largest suppliers	49.6	54.4
Three largest suppliers	68.2	62.0
Four largest suppliers	84.5	68.3
Five largest suppliers	87.5	72.1

Rank Order Correlation of Interperiod Suppliers

r_s	*Significance*
.50	.042

becomes somewhat ambiguous. It would appear, however, that the larger number of suppliers in the postwar period, due to extensive retransfers, makes controls more difficult.

Utility Aircraft

The category of utility aircraft is something of a catchall for aircraft not placed in other categories. Mostly, it consists of small army scout or observation planes which can be distinguished from trainers or from longer range observation planes. Many of the functions of these planes have now been assumed by helicopters.

The MIT study included data and analysis in this category. As the number of these transfers identified for the interwar period was quite small (175 total), comparative analysis would not be warranted. Suffice it to say that the United States has been the largest supplier in both periods, as in other types of aircraft. In the interwar period, Holland was surprisingly the second largest supplier, based on specialization in this area by the Fokker firm. For the postwar era, a virtual American monopoly has been softened somewhat by the significant market positions of Canada, Britain and West Germany.

Helicopters

The market patterns for helicopters in the postwar period have been somewhat similar to those for other aircraft categories. The United States has been by far the largest supplier, followed by the Soviet Union and France. Only Italy, Britain and West Germany, in addition, have been significant factors.

One might speculate that an extension of the time-frame for the data beyond 1968 might have divulged a stronger role for the French, who in recent

Table 3-6. Comparison of Market Shares in Helicopters

Postwar (to 1968)			
Rank	Country	Number	Percent
1	United States	620	42.8
2	USSR	406	28.0
3	France	253	17.4
4	United Kingdom	50	3.4
5	Italy	41	2.8
6	West Germany	30	2.1
7	Others	50	3.5
		1,450	100.0

Other Suppliers: Belgium, UAR, Japan, South Africa, Austria, Brazil

Bloc Market Shares (percent)

NATO:	68.6	United States	42.8
Sino-Soviet:	28.6	Western Europe	25.8
		Warsaw	28.6
		China	0.0

Levels of Concentration (percent)

Single largest supplier	42.8
Two largest suppliers	70.8
Three largest suppliers	88.2
Four largest suppliers	91.6
Five largest suppliers	94.4

years have been as successful with sales of Super Frelon and Alouette helicopters as with Mirage jets. They have found markets in numerous nations, including particularly heavy sales to South Africa.

The supplier market for helicopters has been highly concentrated, more so at the level of the five largest suppliers than has been the case for any of the other aircraft categories in the postwar period.

Tanks

One striking fact emerging from the comparative patterns of tank supply, in contrast to those for aircraft, is the lack of dominance in both periods by the United States.

For the interwar period, America's relatively small role should come as no surprise. The backwardness of American tank development during that period was often commented on by military observers, who recognized the lead taken by Britain, France and Germany under the impetus of the doctrines then being propounded respectively by Liddell-Hart, DeGaulle and Guderian. Private tank producers in the United States sometimes had more success selling their models abroad than at home. The famous Christie tank, later copied as the Soviet T-34 and rated the best of its kind in the Second World War, was sold not only to Russia but to Britain as well before interest was finally evidenced by the United States War Department.

Britain and France were dominant in tank sales during the 1930s. The British were the acknowledged quality leaders in this field and achieved numerous export contracts with the Vickers and Carden-Lloyd models. France's first place in overall sales was primarily the result of one major concentrated licensing deal with Russia, following the Franco-Soviet Pact of 1935, in which some 500 Renault R-35 tanks were transferred. Italy was also a significant market factor, with sales in Latin America and elsewhere of its then highly rated Fiat-Ansaldo light tank. Germany's armor developments, peaking in the late 1930s, came too late for it to be a major exporter throughout the interwar period. Actually, its earlier doctrine of building light and mobile tanks was proved a failure in combat in Spain, and the poor performance of its armor there no doubt affected its exports.

In the postwar period (up to 1968) the Soviets have led in tank sales and recent massive shipments to the Middle East have no doubt increased this lead. This might have been expected from the structure of the Soviet military establishment, which emphasizes massive armored forces. Correspondingly, the emphasis placed on air and naval forces by the United States, partly a function of geographical location, has resulted in a smaller number of tanks being available for export, a point made very clear in the October War, when United States tank inventories were seriously depleted by replacement shipments to Israel. Several of the Arab countries, and Israel as well, have been significant exporters of secondhand armor.

Table 3-7. Comparison of Market Shares in Tanks

Interwar (from 1930)				*Postwar (to 1968)*			
Rank	*Country*	*Number*	*Percent*	*Rank*	*Country*	*Number*	*Percent*
1	France	1,091	27.9	1	USSR	5,393	37.4
2	United Kingdom	1,017	26.1	2	United States	4,206	29.1
3	United States	574	14.7	3	United Kingdom	1,435	9.9
4	Italy	424	10.9	4	France	1,139	7.9
5	Czechoslovakia	270	6.9	5	UAR	718	5.0
6	USSR	220	5.6	6	Czechoslovakia	250	1.7
7	Germany	160	4.1	7	West Germany	250	1.7
8	Sweden	122	3.1	8	Other	1,043	7.3
9	Poland	26	0.7				
		3,904	100.0			14,434	100.0

Other Suppliers: None

Other Suppliers: Italy, Israel, Iraq, Sweden, China, Poland, Syria, Indonesia, Cuba, Jordan

Bloc Market Shares (percent)

West:	68.7	United States	14.7	NATO:	49.4	United States	29.1
Axis:	15.0	Britain-France	54.0	Sino-Soviet:	39.2	Western Europe	20.3
		Soviet	5.6			Warsaw	39.8
		Germany-Italy	15.0			China	0.7
		Japan	0.0				

Levels of Concentration (percent)

	Interwar	*Postwar*
Single largest supplier	27.9	37.4
Two largest suppliers	54.0	66.5
Three largest suppliers	68.7	76.4
Four largest suppliers	79.6	84.3
Five largest suppliers	86.5	89.3

Rank Order Correlation of Interperiod Suppliers

r_s	*Significance*
.55	.035

Here, too, if data had been included since 1968 France's share might well have been much larger. In comprehensive arms deals also involving planes and ships, France has had success in selling its new AMX-30 tank to a number of countries in Asia, Africa and the Middle East, as well as in selling the older AMX-13 to Ecuador, Guatemala and El Salvador. Meanwhile, the reputed excellence of its armored equipment has afforded Britain a continuing significant role in this market. The Centurion proved superior to both American and Soviet models in both the India-Pakistan and Arab-Israeli conflicts, and, more recently, Britain has developed the new Chieftain tank, perhaps the best in the world and already sold in large volume to Libya and Iran.

In the postwar period huge Soviet sales of tanks have resulted in a more even distribution of bloc market influence than with aircraft. Regarding concentration, it appears that the postwar period has exhibited more oligo-polistic tendencies than the interwar, but with the gap closing to relative insignificance by the fifth level. At this level, the degree of market concentration is similar to that in many of the aircraft categories.

Armored Cars

As in the market for tanks, we get a clear divergence from the dominance of the United States in armored cars, a category which clearly had more important military implications in the 1930s than today.[17]

For the interwar period the market was quite dispersed, with seven significant suppliers. Austria's leading share was based on its heavy sales of the small Steyr reconnaissance vehicle in Eastern Europe. Otherwise, the United States, with its Marmon-Harrington vehicle, and Germany, France, Czecho-slovakia, Britain and Russia were all active in this market. Soviet sales were mostly of the Bronieford model, copied and mass-produced from an American Ford armored car, large shipments of which were made to the Spanish Loyalists.

The postwar period has seen Britain as the largest supplier, with its well-known Saracen and Saladin types. The United States has been second and France third. More recently, France has concluded a large deal with South Africa for its Panhard armored car, which has also been sold to Iraq and Saudi Arabia. Britain's strong supplier role would appear a result of its experiences in desert warfare in World War II and the subsequent retention of markets in the Middle East at least until the mid-1960s.

The Soviets have been altogether absent from the armored car markets of the postwar period. This has resulted from the requirements of the Soviet military itself, which has eschewed these vehicles in favor of tanks and armored personnel carriers.

There has been greater market concentration in armored cars in the postwar period at all levels. This appears merely to represent the growing obsolescence of this armor type in the postwar period, with some specialization being maintained by a few countries. In the interwar period armored cars had been a key weapons system, replacing the previous role of cavalry for reconnaissance while constituting an inexpensive alternative to tanks.

Submarines

In the next several sections we shall examine the breakdown of supplier market shares for various categories of naval vessels—submarines, warships and patrol boats. We shall see that the relative standings of major

Table 3-8.   Comparison of Market Shares in Armored Cars

	Interwar (from 1930)				*Postwar (to 1968)*		
Rank	*Country*	*Number*	*Percent*	*Rank*	*Country*	*Number*	*Percent*
1	Austria	400	25.0	1	United Kingdom	1,430	43.7
2	United States	288	18.0	2	United States	1,051	32.1
3	France	189	11.8	3	France	572	17.5
4	Germany	183	11.4	4	West Germany	60	1.8
5	Czechoslovakia	165	10.3	5	Belgium	55	1.7
6	USSR	160	10.0	6	Others	105	3.2
7	United Kingdom	130	8.1				
8	Others	85	5.4				
		1,600	100.0			3,273	100.0

Other Suppliers: Italy, scattered   Other Suppliers: Sweden, scattered

Bloc Market Shares (percent)

West:	37.9	United States	18.0	NATO:	96.8	United States	32.1
Axis:	12.3	Britain-France	19.9	Sino-Soviet:	0.0	Western Europe	64.7
Soviet:	10.3	Soviet	10.0			Warsaw	0.0
		Germany-Italy	12.3			China	0.0
		Japan	0.0				

Levels of Concentration (percent)

	Interwar	*Postwar*
Single largest supplier	25.0	43.7
Two largest suppliers	43.0	75.8
Three largest suppliers	54.8	93.3
Four largest suppliers	66.2	95.7
Five largest suppliers	76.5	97.5

Rank Order Correlation of Interperiod Suppliers

r_s	*Significance*
.131	.348

suppliers in both periods have been somewhat at variance from those in the aircraft and armor fields, often based on the differing military structures of the supplier nations themselves. And, similar to the armor categories but differing from those in aircraft, the role of the United States has been comparatively modest.

In the interwar period Britain and Italy were the largest suppliers in each of the naval vessel categories. Britain's role, of course, comes as no surprise. From the perspective of the 1970s, however, a perusal of the sections on the British Navy in any edition of Jane's annual in the 1930s is still an eye opener; the size of the British fleet at that time was simply awesome. One corollary was the capacity to dispose of numerous surplus craft, many of which dated back to the buildup during World War I.

Italy was the second largest supplier of submarines during this period although, as indicated in Table 3-9, the absolute number transferred during this period was quite small. The Italians found markets for their submarines in the 1930s in Argentina, Brazil, Thailand, Turkey, Romania and Nationalist Spain. France, the United States, Germany and Japan were also market factors.

In the postwar period the Soviet Union has been the leading supplier of submarines, followed by the United States and Britain. Most of the other market factors have been nonproducers engaging in limited numbers of retransfers.[18] Soviet transactions have been concentrated in several key client states, most notably the UAR and Indonesia. The leading position of the Soviets in the postwar submarine market is easily accounted for by its own navy's concentration in underseas warfare, a pattern paralleled in patrol vessels.

Due to the absence of retransfers in the interwar period, market concentration in submarines was higher then than in the postwar period. In both periods, the Western bloc nations have held a lesser aggregate share of the market than in most of the aircraft and armor systems. This has probably been an indirect result of both Axis and Soviet attempts at countering the preponderance of the Anglo-Saxon surface fleets with submarines.

Warships

The warship category includes all ships not under the other naval categories of submarines, patrol vessels, transports, and support and auxiliary ships; namely battleships, aircraft carriers, cruisers, destroyers, minesweepers, minelayers, frigates, sloops and coastal defense ships.

As indicated in Table 3-10, Britain was altogether dominant in warship sales during the 1930s. Its transfers were scattered among a wide range of recipients around the globe. Italy, a distant second, found outlets in Argentina, Iran, Romania, Greece and Nationalist Spain. Smaller shares were taken by France, Spain, Japan (mostly to Siam) and the United States. Clearly, the United States was a very minor factor, despite its fairly sizeable navy. The explanation is not clear.

In the postwar period the virtual absence of the Soviet Union as a supplier has been striking. Again, this has reflected the Soviets' neglect, until recently, of their own surface fleet, with concentration on building of submarines and patrol vessels. As a result, the United States, Britain and Canada have, up to now, been the world's largest suppliers of warships (much of it World War II surplus), with a plethora of middle-range and smaller powers having participated through retransfers. The apparently high incidence of retransfers of warships has been based on their longevity. Cruisers and destroyers of World War II vintage, or even earlier, are still traded among developing nations, often for mere prestige purposes.

Table 3-9.   **Comparison of Market Shares in Submarines**

	Interwar (from 1930)				*Postwar (to 1968)*		
Rank	*Country*	*Number*	*Percent*	*Rank*	*Country*	*Number*	*Percent*
1	United Kingdom	18	36.0	1	USSR	26	28.6
2	Italy	12	24.0	2	United States	18	19.8
3	France	5	10.0	3	United Kingdom	11	12.1
4	United States	4	8.0	4	Chile	7	7.7
5	Japan	4	8.0	5	Italy	6	6.5
6	Germany	4	8.0	6	Japan	4	4.4
7	Others	3	6.0	7	Peru	4	4.4
				8	Thailand	4	4.4
				9	Others	11	12.1
		50	100.0			91	100.0

Other Suppliers: Holland, Spain   Other Suppliers: Israel, UAR, Poland,
                                                                 Argentina, Brazil

Bloc Market Shares (percent)

West:	54.0	United States	8.0	NATO:	38.4	United States	19.8
Axis:	40.0	Britain-France	46.0	Sino-Soviet:	30.8	Western Europe	18.6
Soviet:	0.0	Soviet	0.0			Warsaw	30.8
		Germany-Italy	32.0			China	0.0
		Japan	8.0				

Levels of Concentration (percent)

	Interwar	*Postwar*
Single largest supplier	36.0	28.6
Two largest suppliers	60.0	48.4
Three largest suppliers	70.0	60.5
Four largest suppliers	78.0	68.2
Five largest suppliers	86.0	74.7

Rank Order Correlation of Interperiod Suppliers

r_s	*Significance*
.13	.295

This, in turn, accounts for the relatively higher level of market concentration in the interwar period for warships. And in contrast to the bloc breakdown for submarines, the Western nations have been more significant suppliers in both periods relative to their Axis and Soviet competitors.

Patrol Vessels

The patrol vessel (including here gunboats and motor torpedo boats) has been an important naval system in both periods. Both before and after World

Table 3-10.   Comparison of Market Shares in Warships

Interwar (from 1930)				Postwar (to 1968)			
Rank	Country	Number	Percent	Rank	Country	Number	Percent
1	United Kingdom	76	58.9	1	United States	116	27.8
2	Italy	23	17.8	2	United Kingdom	87	20.9
3	France	13	10.1	3	Canada	27	6.5
4	Spain	5	3.9	4	Argentina	18	4.3
5	Japan	5	3.9	5	Netherlands	16	3.8
6	United States	3	2.3	6	Brazil	15	3.6
7	Others	4	3.1	7	USSR	15	3.6
				8	Italy	15	3.6
				9	Others	108	25.9
		129	100.0			409	100.0

Other Suppliers: Portugal, Estonia

Other Suppliers: France, India, Spain, Sweden, Switzerland, UAR, Japan, Indonesia, Poland, Portugal, Peru, Germany, Estonia, Mexico, Chile, Thailand, Pakistan, Colombia

Bloc Market Shares (percent)

West:	71.3	United States	2.3	NATO:	65.0	United States	27.8
Axis:	17.8	Britain-France	69.0	Sino-Soviet:	4.6	Western Europe	30.7
Soviet:	0.0	Soviet	0.0			Warsaw	4.6
		Germany-Italy	17.8			China	0.0
		Japan	0.0				

Levels of Concentration (percent)

	Interwar	Postwar
Single largest supplier	58.9	27.8
Two largest suppliers	76.7	48.7
Three largest suppliers	86.8	55.2
Four largest suppliers	90.7	59.5
Five largest suppliers	94.6	63.3

Rank Order Correlation of Interperiod Suppliers

r_s	Significance
−.01	.499

War II, many navies have considered them a potentially potent, low-cost destroyer of larger ships. As far back as the 19th century there were debates in international naval circles over whether to concentrate resources on heavy warships or on smaller torpedo boats which could close with and destroy them.[19] A few years ago, the sinking of an Israeli destroyer by Egyptian-manned patrol boats firing ship-to-ship Soviet Styx missiles engendered a similar debate which has been reinforced by the lessons of the 1973 war, in which Israeli missile-firing patrol boats apparently prevailed over Soviet-supplied Arab counterparts.[20]

In the 1930s the Italians were the leading sellers of patrol vessels and motor torpedo boats, based on the then strong reputation of their Ansaldo-type craft. They achieved markets for patrol boats in numerous small nations, as well as in the USSR during the brief Stalin-Mussolini rapprochement in the early 1930s. The British and Germans were also very significant market factors, with Thorneycroft and Lurssen makes. As in other categories of naval equipment, the United States was then a rather negligible market factor.

In the postwar period the Soviet Union has achieved first rank as a supplier of patrol boats, many of the missile-firing variety. Its Osa and Komar class patrol vessels, armed with Styx missiles, have been sold in great numbers to the UAR, Syria, Algeria, Indonesia, Cuba and India. The United States and the United Kingdom have also been strong factors, as has China, which has built copies and licensed versions of the Soviet systems.

As indicated earlier, a fairly large number of smaller powers have achieved an indigenous development and production base in patrol vessels. Although the combat viability of such systems is now highly dependent upon associated missile systems and electronic gear, significant numbers of them have been sold by such nations as North Vietnam, Brazil, Mexico, Yugoslavia and others. This in turn has resulted in considerably less market concentration than existed in the 1930s.

As with submarines, the position of the Western bloc in both periods has been rivaled by the Axis and Soviets to a degree abnormal in comparison with some other systems. One might speculate again that, in either period, the Axis and Soviet-bloc nations have concentrated on selling smaller craft due to the overwhelming maritime predominance of the Americans and British, although the makeup of the Axis and Soviet navies has also been explanatory.

Summary of Market Factors by Weapons Systems in Interwar and Postwar Periods

The rank orderings of the first five suppliers in each weapons category for both periods are displayed in Table 3-12, to allow for a summary comparative view.

In the postwar period, the United States-USSR duopoly is evident in all categories except trainer aircraft, armored cars and warships, where the United States and the United Kingdom have been leading suppliers. The United States has been dominant in all aircraft categories in both periods. Meanwhile, in the 1930s the United Kingdom and Italy are seen to have led as suppliers of naval vessels.

Perhaps the most profound change from the interwar to the postwar period has been the rise of the Soviet Union from a position of virtual insignificance even at a time when it had the second highest GNP in the world to

Table 3-11.   Comparison of Market Shares in Patrol Vessels

Interwar (from 1930)				Postwar (to 1968)			
Rank	Country	Number	Percent	Rank	Country	Number	Percent
1	Italy	143	47.2	1	USSR	400	27.3
2	United Kingdom	62	20.5	2	United States	318	21.7
3	Germany	40	13.2	3	United Kingdom	166	11.3
4	United States	11	3.6	4	China	98	6.7
5	Spain	10	3.3	5	France	46	3.1
6	Japan	8	2.6	6	Netherlands	40	2.7
7	Others	29	9.6	7	Italy	36	2.5
				8	West Germany	33	2.3
				9	North Vietnam	32	2.2
				10	Brazil	27	1.8
				11	Mexico	23	1.6
				12	Yugoslavia	22	1.5
				13	Others	222	15.3
		303	100.0			1,463	100.0

Other suppliers: Canada, France, USSR, Norway, Finland, Hungary, plus some transfers of unknown origin

Other Suppliers: Canada, India, Israel, Spain, UAR, Japan, South Africa, Iran, Indonesia, Australia, Peru, Cuba, Argentina, Thailand, Colombia, Pakistan, Philippines, South Korea, Venezuela, Chile, Dominican Republic, South Vietnam, Nigeria, Malaysia

Bloc Market Shares (percent)

West:	24.3	United States	3.6	NATO:	43.7	United States	21.7
Axis:	63.0	Britain-France	20.6	Sino-Soviet:	38.0	Western Europe	21.9
Soviet:	0.2	Soviet	0.2			Warsaw	27.3
		Germany-Italy	60.4			China	6.7
		Japan	2.6				

Levels of Concentration (percent)

	Postwar	Interwar
Single largest supplier	47.2	27.3
Two largest suppliers	67.7	49.0
Three largest suppliers	80.9	60.3
Four largest suppliers	84.5	67.0
Five largest suppliers	87.8	70.1

Rank Order Correlation of Interperiod Suppliers

r_s	Significance
.21	.230

Table 3-12. Summary of Arms Market Shares Across Weapons Systems

Interwar

Rank	Combat Aircraft	Transport Aircraft	Trainer Aircraft	Tanks	Armored Cars	Submarines	Warships	Patrol Vessels
1	United States	United States	United States	France	Austria	United Kingdom	United Kingdom	Italy
2	United Kingdom	Italy	United Kingdom	United Kingdom	United States	Italy	Italy	United Kingdom
3	France	United Kingdom	Germany	United States	France	France	France	Germany
4	Italy	Germany	France	Italy	Germany	United States	Spain	United States
5	Germany	France	Czechoslovakia	Czechoslovakia	Czechoslovakia	Japan	Japan	Spain

Postwar

Rank	Combat Aircraft	Transport Aircraft	Trainer Aircraft	Tanks	Armored Cars	Submarines	Warships	Patrol Vessels
1	United States	United States	United States	USSR	United Kingdom	USSR	United States	USSR
2	USSR	USSR	United Kingdom	United States	United States	United States	United Kingdom	United States
3	United Kingdom	United Kingdom	France	United Kingdom	France	United Kingdom	Canada	United Kingdom
4	France	France	USSR	France	West Germany	Chile	Argentina	China
5	China	UAR	Netherlands	UAR	Belgium	Italy	Netherlands	France

its current position as one of the two leading suppliers. The end of the colonial era allowed the Soviets to emerge from isolation and to expand their influence beyond the captive Eastern European markets, becoming a leading supplier to developing nations beginning in the mid-1950s.

At the bottom of the several tables on interperiod market structure, a Spearman's rank order correlation (rho) has been computed to measure congruence or continuity between the two periods. As indicated, there have been vast changes in the makeup of these markets across periods. World War II was indeed a watershed dividing distinct phases of the arms supplier markets.

The highest level of continuity between periods has been evidenced in combat aircraft, trainer aircraft and tanks. This is partly explicable by the role of the Soviet Union, which was a more significant factor in the combat aircraft and tank markets of the 1930s than in other systems, while in the postwar period the Soviets' virtual absence from trainer aircraft markets has also provided continuity. The higher correlation in these categories appears to be explained, to a lesser degree, by continuity in the market shares of Germany, Italy and Czechoslovakia. Meanwhile, the much more prominent role of Britain and Italy in the naval markets of the 1930s contributes greatly to the low levels of correlation between periods for these categories.

COMPARISON OF SUPPLIER MARKETS

Earlier, we explained the reasons for comparing data between the two diplomatic periods by weapons types, rather than by aggregate cost figures. As there have, however, been attempts at aggregating information on the overall arms trade by cost for both periods, we may now briefly display these data and compare them with our own. This in turn may raise questions about contrasting interpretations of market structure.

Data on Individual Weapons Systems and Weapons Transfers as Reported by the League of Nations and SIPRI

Table 3-13 contains a summary of the League of Nations' arms trade data, as compiled by Sloutzki. Several problems arise in attempting to draw a comparison with our own data. First, the league data omitted naval and aircraft transfer costs, while encompassing small arms, ammunition and heavier army equipment. It was therefore essentially a measure of the small arms and munitions trade. A more serious problem was that of accuracy, which is readily admitted by Sloutzki. As he notes, some of the major suppliers in the 1930s, notably the "closed societies" of Germany, Italy and the USSR, were known seriously to have underreported the costs of their arms transfers to the league, which apparently did not utilize alternative data sources for correction. Just how serious the resulting inaccuracies were is difficult to say.

Table 3-13.   Export of Arms and Ammunition of Principal Exporters, 1929-1938 (in millions of former gold $)

	1929	1930	1931	1932	1933	1934	1935	1936	1937	1938	Average	Grand Total (percent)
United Kingdom	21.8	17.0	13.4	10.1	10.1	8.5	9.6	9.7	11.9	17.1	12.9	25.0
Czechoslovakia	3.2	5.3	3.9	1.4	3.2	8.7	10.5	7.7	7.2	14.3	6.5	12.6
Germany	7.5	6.5	5.2	3.8	4.1	3.3	2.5	5.3	9.0	8.4	5.6	10.9
France	9.4	7.0	2.7	9.3	8.5	8.0	6.6	10.6	6.7	6.8	5.5	10.7
United States	10.7	6.5	3.9	2.9	3.2	3.7	3.3	4.3	5.6	6.9	5.1	9.9
Sweden	3.0	4.3	3.7	3.7	3.4	3.7	3.3	2.9	5.7	7.8	4.2	8.1
Belgium	3.0	2.5	1.5	1.5	1.4	2.1	2.5	2.4	3.2	6.1	2.6	5.0
Italy	3.7	3.8	2.2	0.6	1.5	1.6	0.7	0.7	1.6	2.2	1.9	3.7
Switzerland	0.5	1.0	1.1	0.7	1.1	0.8	0.4	2.4	5.0	5.8	1.9	3.7
	62.8	53.9	37.6	34.0	36.5	40.4	39.4	46.0	55.9	75.4	46.2	89.6
Others	9.6	8.3	2.8	4.6	5.6	4.6	3.7	3.9	4.5	6.5	5.4	10.4
Grand Total	72.4	62.2	40.4	38.6	42.1	45.0	43.1	49.9	60.4	81.9	51.6	100.0

Source: Nokhim M. Sloutzki, *The World Armaments Race, 1919-1939* (Geneva: Geneva Research Center, 1941), p. 71.

In comparing these data with those summarized in Table 3-12 a discrepant picture emerges. It is difficult to tell the degree to which this represents variance between the supplier markets for small arms and those for major weapons systems, or rather the inadequacy of the league data for the 1930s.

If the league data are to be believed, Great Britain was far and away the largest supplier of arms in the 1930s, while the shares of the United States and Italy were well below those found for major weapons categories. In the case of the United States, this was not likely to have been a matter of underreporting, but rather a reflection of American specialization in aircraft sales, then disproportionate relative to sales of armored and naval equipment.

Czechoslovakia is here indicated to have been the second largest arms supplier in the 1930s. This no doubt reflects a major role for Skoda in small arms and artillery exports which was not duplicated for aircraft and armor. Likewise, the relatively large shares of Sweden, Belgium and Switzerland as small arms suppliers indicates the residual roles of the traditional arms makers of Bofors, FN and Oerlikon, respectively, in countries with light capacity for major weapons systems.

Some other interesting points and trends are indicated in the league data. First, it is apparent that the overall reported volume of arms flows dipped sharply in parallel with trends in overall trade during the depression years. Only by 1937 did the volume again reach the levels of 1929. Next, the small percentage of the arms trade, according to the league figures, which was represented by small countries under the heading of "other countries," coincides with the data for major weapons systems. This seems again to indicate a low level of arms retransfers during this period. Finally, it is clear that both British and French arms manufacturers declined as suppliers as the 1930s progressed, corresponding to the erosion of their nations' joint influence and power throughout the world, a trend clearly manifested in any number of ways.

In Table 3-14 we have summarized data from the SIPRI study showing trends in major weapons exports to Third World nations by the various major suppliers. The sample of the countries represented on the recipient side is similar to, but broader than, that of the MIT study from which our data were derived.

The SIPRI data are organized both on an annual basis and by five year moving averages. The latter make for easier observation of long-range trends by smoothing out the effects of severe ups and downs from year to year. Large up and down movements in arms sales figures are the rule, with nowhere near the relative constancy or gradual trending to be observed in overall trade figures. The reason is the normalcy of large one-shot arms deals at given junctures. As the table indicates, some examples are the abnormally large figures for the United States in 1965 at the time of the Vietnam buildup, and the equally abnormal figures for the Soviets in 1967 when they were replacing the vast stores of

Table 3-14. Major Weapon Exports by Main Suppliers, 1950-1969

Supplier		50	51	52	53	54	55	56	57	58	59	60	61	62	63	64	65	66	67	68	69
United States	A	50	130	130	210	290	250	270	240	630	300	470	230	200	280	250	420	290	270	300	580
	B		130	160	200	230	260	340	340	380	370	370	300	280	290	300	300	370	300		
USSR	A	20	30	40	40	—	50	80	160	120	80	370	280	510	210	180	200	400	710	380	320
	B		20	120	120		50	80	110	150	80	110	280	510	210	180	200	400	710	380	
United Kingdom	A	70	30	80	90	110	130	140	190	260	140	170	180	50	80	80	140	110	60	170	200
	B			80	90	120	130	170	170	190	190	160	120	110	110	90	90	110	140		
France	A	—	—	—	30	50	40	120	50	100	40	40	30	70	110	90	50	70	40	120	90
	B			20	30	50	50	60	70	50	50	30	60	70	80	70	70	40	70		
Canada	A	20	5	—	20	50	60	80	30	70	50	50	50	60	70	80	40	5	5	30	10
	B		30	10	20	30	30	70	50	50	50	10	50	100	70	40	20	10	20	30	
Italy	A	5	30	10	—	—	10	20	10	20	20	10	10	30	10	10	5	10	10	30	40
	B			10	10	5	5			10	10	10	5	10	10	5	5	10	20		
China	A	40	40	20	10	—	—	—	40	80	60	10	—	5	—	—	5	30	10	5	—
	B			20	10	5			20	30	30	30	20	10	10	5	5	10	10		
West Germany	A	—	—	—	—	—	5	—	—	10	20	10	10	20	10	30	40	110	30	10	—
	B					5	5	5	5	10	10	20	10	20	30	30	40				
Czecho-slovakia	A	—	—	—	—	—	30	40	5	20	40	30	5	5	10	30	40	5	5	5	—
	B									30	20	20	5	5	5	5	5	5	5		
Sweden	A	—	—	10	5	5	5	5	5	30	5	—	20	10	5	—	5	—	—	—	—
	B			5	5	5	5	10	10	10	5	5									
Japan	A	—	—	—	—	20	—	5	10	10	—	—	10	20	20	10	10	10	30	10	—
	B							5	5	5	5	5	10	10	20	20	10	10	10		
All other	A	20	10	5	20	—	70	10	5	30	30	5	20	30	10	10	40	20	30	5	40
	B			10	20	20	20	20	30	10	30	20	10	20	20	20	20	30			
Total	A	220	270	210	520	510	610	770	760	1310	770	860	760	890	840	690	930	1050	1190	1070	1280
	B	350	350	420	520	630	790	840	890	890	920	820	810	820	880	940	990	1100	1100		

A = yearly figures, B = five year moving averages

Source: SIPRI, *The Arms Trade with the Third World* (New York: Humanities Press, 1971), pp. 882-883.

materiel lost by the Arabs, since altogether superseded by still more massive transfers in 1973-1974.

In general, the picture presented by the SIPRI data is not greatly at variance with our own. This is expected, as their data were derived from first identifying transfers by types and then multiplying by an arbitrary assumed cost for that system.

Some trends are clear from the table. First, the United States and the USSR are depicted as having had a fair degree of duopolistic dominance of the arms markets over recent decades, with Britain and France the next two most important factors. The Soviets are indicated as having gradually and inexorably moved from a position of insignificance to one of near-supremacy, as reflected in the last five year moving averages computed with 1967 as a base year, a trend no doubt significantly heightened by 1974. With the use of constant 1968 dollar prices, the United States is indicated as having leveled off as an arms supplier in absolute figures, after a climb up to 1958. There was a period of considerable decline in 1962-1963.

British arms sales are indicated as having gone into a considerable decline after 1959, the result of the loss of numerous previously captive arms markets in the wake of decolonialization. Many of those markets were taken over by the Soviets. British sales began to pick up again after 1967, as did those of France which have increased rapidly since 1969. Finally, Italy is shown to have become a rapidly more significant arms trader in the late 1960s, not a surprise in view of its heavy arms sales to South Africa and to some of the sub-Saharan African nations.

Having anticipated some of the within-period trends in both eras, we now proceed to examine them in detail.

Trends in Market Shares within Periods

Up to now, we have ignored market trends within the two periods. We have indicated, however, that there are usually large variations in market shares from year to year. Beyond that, there is the question of longer range trends.

A number of important interrelated issues are raised here. One involves the relationship between ebbs and flows of arms supplier shares and the basic thrust of national foreign policies. We had speculated, on the basis of a cursory examination of market trends, that those nations identifiable in either period as "revisionist" powers appear to have acquired a greater and greater share of the arms markets as the periods progressed, at the expense of the "status quo" powers.

These generalizations raise questions about definitions of revisionist and status quo as applied to specific countries.[21] There is little argument about the validity of these terms in the interwar years, when Germany, Italy and Japan were rather explicit about revisionist aims, and when Britain and France could, with little debate, have been characterized as status quo-oriented. For the postwar period, however, one might well argue their validity as applied to the American-Soviet confrontation. Depending upon ideological perspective, one might find characterizations of the foreign policies of both as imperialistic.[22] For the most part, however, this writer's view is that a revisionist-status quo dichotomy is essentially valid as a definition of the reality of the postwar bipolar confrontation. In addition, recent French diplomacy might well be characterized as revisionist in a broad political sense, perhaps not irrelevant to its change in arms sales policy.

In Tables 3-15 and 3-16 we have disaggregated the supplier market shares for the major powers in both periods. For the interwar the data are merely broken down into two five year subperiods, halving the decade of the 1930s. Besides giving an even division of time, this breaking point coincides quite nicely with the real upsurge in the expansionist policies of the Axis powers. For the postwar period we have chosen a more complicated measure of within-period trends. The data for market shares were first broken down into five year periods between 1945 and 1968, except for the final period which covers only a three year span. Those for 1945-1949 and 1950-1954 were then averaged to obtain representative figures for the early postwar period. The data for 1960-1964 and 1965-1968, albeit with those for 1965-1968 somewhat disproportionately weighted, were averaged to obtain figures for the late postwar period, which emphasizes the most recent trends. One reason the ten year periods were used is because it was thought that merely using the data for 1945-1949 would exaggerate the American, and understate the Soviet, roles in the immediate postwar period when the latter had not really begun to compete in the arms markets.

The data for within-period trends do indeed indicate gradual but significant takeovers of arms markets in both periods by revisionist powers. In the interwar period the increase in United States market shares for most weapons systems runs counter to this generalization, primarily in aircraft categories. The roles of the British and French, though, are seen clearly to have declined during the 1930s. If data for the 1920s had been included this decline would certainly have been even more marked. Meanwhile, the Germans, Italians, Japanese and Soviets all achieved overall increases in their arms market shares as World War II approached.

The German and Italian figures, however, indicate some degree of mutual dependence. Where the one became stronger, the other became weaker. They were competing in many of the same markets in Latin America, Eastern Europe, China and the Middle East. And there were some countertrends, particularly in warships, where the British role actually increased in the late 1930s.

For the postwar period, long-range trends have been rather stark. The United States has had a severe long-range decline in arms market

Table 3-15.   Interwar Trends in Market Shares for Major Suppliers (percent)

	Combat Aircraft	Transport Aircraft	Trainer Aircraft	Tanks	Armored Cars	Submarines	Warships	Patrol Vessels
United States								
1930-1934	17.3	40.9	15.3	21.7	44.0	9.8	0.0	1.3
1935-1940	25.0	55.8	33.7	10.6	1.2	0.0	3.4	2.6
Change	+ 7.7	+14.9	+18.4	-11.1	-47.8	- 9.8	+ 3.4	+ 1.3
United Kingdom								
1930-1934	24.6	0.0	32.9	34.0	14.7	26.8	42.7	16.7
1935-1940	14.2	12.0	17.1	21.4	3.9	13.7	46.6	12.9
Change	-10.4	+12.0	-15.8	-12.6	-10.6	-13.1	+ 3.9	- 3.6
France								
1930-1934	26.1	4.5	34.7	38.8	28.5	12.2	2.4	—
1935-1940	11.3	7.6	1.9	21.6	1.0	0.0	12.5	—
Change	-14.8	+ 3.1	-32.8	-17.2	-27.5	-12.2	+10.1	—
Germany								
1930-1934	4.5	27.3	2.1	0.0	0.0	0.0	—	10.3
1935-1940	11.5	6.8	31.5	6.5	18.8	7.8	—	8.4
Change	+ 7.0	-20.5	+29.4	+ 6.5	+18.8	+ 7.8	—	- 1.9

Table 3-15.—Continued

	Combat Aircraft	Transport Aircraft	Trainer Aircraft	Tanks	Armored Cars	Submarines	Warships	Patrol Vessels
Italy								
1930-1934	14.7	11.4	0.1	2.2	2.4	14.6	19.5	20.5
1935-1940	11.8	13.1	5.0	15.9	0.0	11.8	8.0	33.4
Change	− 2.9	+ 1.7	+ 4.9	+13.7	− 2.4	− 2.8	−11.5	+12.9
Japan								
1930-1934	0.0	—	—	—	—	0.0	1.2	0.0
1935-1940	0.7	—	—	—	—	7.8	4.5	2.1
Change	+ 0.7	—	—	—	—	+ 7.8	+ 3.3	+ 2.1
USSR								
1930-1934	0.0	—	—	1.2	0.0	—	—	2.6
1935-1940	7.8	—	—	8.2	16.4	—	—	0.0
Change	+ 7.8	—	—	+ 7.0	+16.4	—	—	− 2.6

Table 3-16. Postwar Trends in Market Shares for Major Suppliers (percent)

	Combat Aircraft	Transport Aircraft	Trainer Aircraft	Tanks	Armored Cars	Submarines	Warships	Patrol Vessels
United States								
1945-1949	65.2	53.8	100.0	66.7	0.0	100.0	33.3	62.7
1950-1954	37.1	73.0	41.6	38.1	59.2	100.0	46.0	37.0
1960-1964	23.6	40.6	48.1	35.8	2.2	57.1	49.2	19.0
1965-1968	26.5	23.9	29.8	23.7	29.6	0.0	73.0	15.0
Average: 1945-1954	51.2	63.4	70.8	52.4	29.6	100.0	39.7	49.9
Average: 1960-1968	25.1	32.3	39.0	29.8	15.9	28.6	61.1	17.0
Change	-26.1	-31.1	-31.8	-22.6	-13.7	-71.4	+21.4	-32.9
USSR								
1945-1949	0.0	0.0	0.0	0.0	0.0	0.0	0.0	0.0
1950-1954	0.0	0.0	0.3	0.0	0.0	0.0	6.0	0.0
1960-1964	44.5	22.1	6.9	44.1	0.0	28.6	27.1	51.3
1965-1968	32.9	18.6	4.9	53.2	0.0	100.0	0.0	24.0
Average: 1945-1954	0.0	0.0	0.0	0.0	0.0	0.0	0.0	0.0
Average: 1960-1968	38.7	70.4	5.9	48.7	0.0	64.3	13.6	37.7
Change	+38.7	+70.4	+ 5.9	+48.7	0.0	+64.3	+10.6	+37.7

Table 3-16.—Continued

	Combat Aircraft	Transport Aircraft	Trainer Aircraft	Tanks	Armored Cars	Submarines	Warships	Patrol Vessels
United Kingdom								
1945-1949	21.7	46.2	0.0	33.3	0.0	0.0	22.7	23.9
1950-1954	43.1	26.3	52.6	18.3	35.6	0.0	44.0	9.0
1960-1964	11.0	9.7	8.7	7.7	70.1	14.3	22.0	5.5
1965-1968	7.3	5.9	12.9	0.0	5.9	0.0	16.0	28.0
Average: 1945-1954	32.4	36.3	26.3	25.8	17.8	0.0	33.4	16.5
Average: 1960-1968	9.2	7.8	10.8	3.9	38.0	7.2	19.0	16.8
Change	-23.2	-28.5	-15.5	-21.9	+20.2	+7.2	-14.4	+0.3
France								
1945-1949	0.0	0.0	0.0	0.0	*	*	*	*
1950-1954	0.0	0.0	0.0	37.5	*	*	*	*
1960-1964	4.9	13.3	9.2	3.3	*	*	*	*
1965-1968	8.2	0.0	18.6	5.0	*	*	*	*
Average: 1945-1954	0.0	0.0	0.0	18.8	*	*	*	*
Average: 1960-1968	6.6	6.7	13.9	4.2	*	*	*	*
Change	+6.6	+6.7	+13.9	-14.6	*	*	*	*

*Data not available by subperiods from MIT study.

participation in all categories except that of warships. The Soviets, meanwhile, have achieved huge corresponding increases in market shares all across the board. Britain has suffered decreases in most categories, although more recent data for the early 1970s might well indicate a reversal of these trends.[23] Finally, the gradual increase of French shares is indicated in our data, although the cut-off point of 1968 does not allow for observation of what certainly has been a far greater climb in recent years, perhaps strongly related to the impasse in Franco-American relations and a global revisionist thrust to French foreign policy.[24]

Thus, the suggestion that there may be a tendency for revisionist powers to expand arms markets at the expense of status quo powers does appear valid, based on information from these two periods. A more rigorous evaluation of this proposition would require inferences from a larger number of situations. Also, it must be remembered that the German role in the early 1930s was severely curtailed because of treaty restrictions. Further, some of these trends, such as the increased roles of Japan and the USSR in the 1930s or that of the Soviets since 1945, may have been due to enhanced relative technological capability as well as to revisionist foreign policy behavior.

The apparent reciprocal relationship between the market share trends of revisionist and status quo powers does have important implications for controlling the arms trade. What is implied is that unaggressive arms trading activity on the part of conservative powers may merely create vacuums into which expansionist powers, bent on upsetting the world order, may move with alacrity. Examples from the recent past abound, as witness the loss of arms markets—and hence general diplomatic influence—by the West in India and in the Arab world in the face of Soviet incursions.[25]

Henry Kissinger has been quoted as saying that "whenever peace—conceived as the avoidance of war—has been the primary objective of a group of powers, the international system has been at the mercy of the most ruthless of the international community."[26] The problem of controlling the arms trade, as indicated in the within-period trends in supplier market shares, may constitute a corollary. We shall return to this theme later in a more comprehensive discussion of the history of attempts at controls.

Analogy to Concentration of Corporate Industrial Market Shares

In a recent volume on the application of economic theories to the study of international relations, Michael Gort suggested a number of hypotheses on industrial concentration which may be applicable by analogy to analysis of the arms trade.[27] Without attempting rigorous testing of this analogy, we may nevertheless briefly indicate some possible parallels as an heuristic pointer to further research. Gort's generalizations are as follows, as summarized by Russett.

First, stability is, indeed, related to the degree of concentration, as is predicted by most theories of oligopoly and which would tend to support analogous propositions favoring the concentration of international power in a few large nations. Second, stability is positively related to the degree that products are differentiated—ideological competition, which fosters clear preference for the "product" of one large nation over that of a competitor, would here be seen as a factor for "brand loyalty," and stability of shares or spheres of influence. Finally, stability is negatively related to the overall growth rate of the industry—periods of rapid technological development and social change produce many opportunities for a unit to grow at the expense of others through vigorous competition.[28]

As indicated in our data for the two diplomatic periods, there has been considerable instability in the arms supplier markets in both periods. Comparison of the relative degrees of instability is difficult, because one period under study is considerably longer than the other and because short-run instability in the arms markets is more normal than in many industrial categories where the year-to-year demand is more stable. Further, degrees of market concentration in various weapons systems in either period have not been too dissimilar but have varied between weapons systems. In both periods, there has been only moderate market concentration combined with quite considerable market stability.

According to Gort, ideological competition should be conducive to stability, due to the hold of "brand loyalty" or spheres of influence. We shall examine this question more closely in our subsequent analysis of donor-recipient patterns. Suffice it to say now that this hypothesis does appear valid as applied to arms trade patterns. We shall demonstrate that the breakdown of ideologically oriented clientele patterns in the past few years has created considerable instability in arms transfer patterns. This need not, however, be reflected in supplier market shares, as each of the major suppliers may both gain and lose markets in periods of instability. In fact, however, we shall see that the Soviets, more than the United States, have been able to take advantage of market instability created by the loosening of "brand preferences," perhaps because of the greater willingness of a revisionist power to use arms supplies as a means of extending influence in the face of efforts at controls by rival status quo powers.

The relationship between technological change and market stability is complex. There is an assumption that periods of rapid technological growth will bring new factors into the market, while others exit. In the arms markets, it has been rare that a nation of less than leading rank has been a technological innovator, although both the French and the Israelis have come up with surprises in recent years, at least in missiles.[29] On the other hand, one can point to examples where rapid technological growth has resulted in the dropping out of marginal suppliers from some markets, also an aspect of instability. We have cited some examples, among them the French decline in the aircraft markets of the 1930s. Likewise, the earlier postwar desuetude of the Western European arms industries could be attributed to the pressures of rapid technological change now being surmounted by cooperative codevelopment ventures among consortia of European nations.

Congruence of the Distribution of Market Shares with the Distribution of National Power as Measured by GNP

The relative measurement of national power has long been a preoccupation of international relations scholars. Some, like Klaus Knorr, have relied on a combination of quantitative indices and relatively subjective criteria for analysis.[30] Others, such as Marshall, have simply concluded that any real attempt at measuring power is inherently inadequate to the complexities of the subject.[31] Otherwise, GNP has normally been used as a rough measure under the assumption that it provides a viable balancing of population and per capita income or level of economic development.

Using GNP as a rough approximate measure of national power, we may examine the relationship of the distribution of power among major nations with their shares in the markets for various weapons systems. Our hypothesis was that congruence would be greater in the postwar period. Conversely, it was assumed that in the interwar period, with its freer flow of uncontrolled weapons sales, the production and sale of arms was still—to some degree—the accidental result of the location of the older arms industries in Europe. Also, it was assumed that there was then a greater degree of weapons-production specialization among the major powers, whereas in the postwar period all major powers have striven for autarkic capability in all fields of weaponry.

The GNP rankings of the 12 countries which were the most significant suppliers across all categories in each period are indicated in Table 3-17. For the interwar period, the national income figures for 1938 were used. For the postwar, the figures for 1957 were chosen as representative, as it falls roughly midway in the period between 1945 and 1968. Of course, relative GNP standings do change—sometimes markedly—within periods, so that the 1957 figures do not adequately reflect the startling postwar economic developments in West Germany and Japan.

Using the GNP figures in Table 3-17 in conjunction with market shares for various weapons systems, we may correlate the two to probe for congruence. As indicated in Table 3-18, congruence between market shares and GNP appears far higher in the postwar period than in the interwar, as expected. For the interwar period the degree of congruence in some categories is low, as indicated in the figures for levels of significance.

Several points emerge here. In both periods, the congruence of

Table 3-17.   Breakdown of GNP

Interwar–1938		Postwar–1957	
Country	National Income (millions $)	Country	GNP (millions $)
United States	$67,375	United States	$443,270
Germany	23,000	USSR	121,920
United Kingdom	22,100	United Kingdom	61,379
USSR	17,850	West Germany	49,906
France	10,800	China	46,256
Japan	6,070	France	41,563
Italy	5,830	Canada	32,291
Canada	3,986	Japan	27,844
Spain	2,875	Italy	25,003
Sweden	2,830	Sweden	10,166
Netherlands	2,730	Netherlands	9,216
Czechoslovakia	2,000	UAR	3,423

Sources: For interwar period, W. S. and E. S. Woytinsky, *World Population and Production* (New York: Twentieth Century Fund, 1953). For postwar, Bruce Russett et al., *World Handbook of Political and Social Indicators* (New Haven: Yale University Press, 1964).

market shares with GNP is generally higher in the various categories of aircraft than for armor or naval equipment. This appears to reflect the dominant role of the United States in both periods as a supplier of aircraft, corresponding to its lead in GNP. Then, the virtual absence of the Soviets—a leading 1930s power in terms of GNP—from the interwar arms markets lends a degree of incongruence to the comparative figures. The weak role of the United States as a supplier of naval vessels in that period had the same effect. Likewise, the seemingly outsized

Table 3-18.   Pearson's *R* Correlation of Market Shares for Various Weapons Categories with GNP

	Interwar		Postwar	
	R	Significance	R	Significance
Combat Aircraft	.76	.002	.80	.001
Transport Aircraft	.93	.001	.98	.001
Trainers	.77	.002	.96	.001
Tanks	.38	.112	.71	.005
Armored Cars	.77	.002	.54	.035
Submarines	.19	.276	.64	.013
Warships	.10	.374	.78	.001
Patrol Boats	.00	.496	.76	.002
Average .49			Average .77	

role of Italy as a naval supplier in the 1930s, along with Britain's dominance, caused further incongruence with the breakdown of GNP. It seems clear that GNP has become a better predictor of overall distribution of arms market shares in the postwar period than it was in the interwar—that is, arms market shares seem to have become more reflective of national power. This is to be expected, given that major nations have gone at the business of selling arms in a more purposive and politically motivated way in the recent period. To a lesser degree, the production and supplying of arms has become a matter of idiosyncratic choice or chance. No longer is it likely that an Austria or an Italy would be a leading supplier in any category.

An Approximate Measure of the Qualitative Content of Transfers

Raw data on the number of weapons systems transferred obscure the important question of the quality of the weapons themselves. This in turn raises the question of whether certain suppliers, or certain types of suppliers, have been more apt to sell arms of greater modernity or quality than others. In tense and sustained arms races between dependent nations this can be quite crucial, as witness the furor in the Arab world over earlier transfers of the vaunted Phantom to Israel by the United States, subsequent anxiety in Israel over the apparent transfer of swift new MIG-23s to the UAR and Syria, and mutual concerns over transfer to either side of sophisticated missile systems and electronic warfare technology.

There are a number of ways in which assessments may be made of the quality of weapons transferred. For a truly sophisticated measurement one would utilize a mixture of combat performance characteristics—speed, armament, range, ordnance load, etc.

In the MIT study, a simpler method was used for approximate evaluation of qualitative characteristics by merely measuring the modernity of the system. Arms transfers were categorized by the length of time elapsed since initial production of the system in the original supplier nation. A three-way typology was devised: systems transferred within less than five years from the initial date of production, those transferred five to ten years from this initial date and those transferred over ten years after that time. A built-in assumption here is that at any given point in time the advanced weapons systems of the major nations will be of roughly equal quality. The Phantom, MIG-21 and Mirage III had fairly close initial dates of production.

We may first look at the aggregate of transfers in both periods, looking for noticeable differences between them. The average degree of modernity for weapons in each category for all supplier nations in either period is indicated in Table 3-19.

The difference in the figures for the two periods is rather startling and seemingly significant beyond any chance of error in method. On the average,

Table 3-19.   Modernity Indices—Aggregate Comparison of
Interwar and Postwar Systems (percent)

	Interwar			Postwar		
	Years			Years		
	Under 5	5-10	Over 10	Under 5	5-10	Under 10
Combat Aircraft	85.8	11.0	3.2	16.9	50.4	32.7
Transport Aircraft	65.5	8.8	25.4	17.1	30.5	52.4
Trainers	74.5	21.2	4.4	17.0	32.6	50.4
Tanks	74.8	14.9	10.3	13.0	27.8	59.2
Armored Cars	67.1	4.4	28.5	33.3	27.2	39.5
Submarines	98.9	1.0	0.0	27.5	20.9	51.6
Warships	93.5	2.4	4.1	38.8	18.5	42.7
Patrol Vessels	95.6	0.9	3.5	59.4	16.3	24.3

arms traded in the 1930s were of much greater modernity than those in the postwar period, and this is the case for all types of weapons.

Some of the possible reasons for this difference were adumbrated in the context of differing rates of technological change between the two periods. We then averred that the apparent faster turnover of weapons generations in the 1930s ought to have led to transfers of more modern arms, as they would become obsolete more quickly in the inventories of the major powers. Also, there is the factor of longer lead times for contemporary systems. And finally, the fantastic rise in the unit costs of weapons of all types has made purchase of new ones by dependent nations an expensive proposition.

There are also political reasons, namely, the tighter controls now exercised by governments over arms sales. The United States, for instance, has been reluctant until recently to sell Phantoms to any but the closest of allies. The introduction of such aircraft to regional cockpits such as the Middle East could upset the balance of power and lead to matching moves by other suppliers.

These kinds of political restrictions on the modernity of transfers seem, relatively, to have been absent in the 1930s for reasons which remain somewhat obscure, except as explained by the greater freedom of arms suppliers to make such decisions. This is immediately apparent in perusing a list of aircraft transfers in Europe in the 1930s. Both Britain and Germany were then selling, in volume, their latest aircraft—Spitfires, Hawker Hurricanes, Messerschmidt 109s and Junkers bombers—to recipient nations such as Yugoslavia, Romania and Turkey.

As indicated in Tables 3-20 and 3-21, however, there is scant evidence that revisionist powers have sold weapons of greater modernity than status quo powers. In both periods, there has been great similarity between the major supplier nations on this count. Perhaps the fact that so many dependent

Table 3-20.   Interwar—Modernity of Transfers by Weapons System (percent)

Years	Combat Aircraft	Transport Aircraft	Trainer Aircraft	Tanks	Armored Cars	Submarines	Warships	Patrol Vessels
United States								
Less than 5	96.7	84.8	91.2	56.4	11.1	100.0	100.0	100.0
5-10	0.5	4.4	7.8	0.0	0.0	0.0	0.0	0.0
Over 10	2.7	10.8	1.1	43.6	88.9	0.0	0.0	0.0
United Kingdom								
Less than 5	72.2	0.0	64.1	74.9	60.0	100.0	94.7	88.7
5-10	19.5	0.0	25.4	22.9	24.6	0.0	5.3	0.0
Over 10	3.2	100.0	10.5	2.2	15.4	0.0	0.0	11.3
France								
Less than 5	70.1	66.7	35.7	82.7	78.8	100.0	100.0	100.0
5-10	27.9	33.3	56.8	11.0	5.3	0.0	0.0	0.0
Over 10	2.0	0.0	7.4	6.3	15.9	0.0	0.0	0.0
Germany								
Less than 5	91.3	34.5	89.3	100.0	45.4	100.0	—	87.5
5-10	7.0	0.0	9.1	0.0	0.0	0.0	—	0.0
Over 10	1.6	65.5	1.6	0.0	54.6	0.0	—	12.5

Table 3-20.—Continued

Years	Combat Aircraft	Transport Aircraft	Trainer Aircraft	Tanks	Armored Cars	Submarines	Warships	Patrol Vessels
Italy								
Less than 5	82.6	89.5	89.7	90.6	26.7	91.7	78.3	95.8
5-10	15.1	0.0	8.2	9.4	40.0	8.3	0.0	2.8
Over 10	2.2	10.5	2.1	0.0	33.3	0.0	21.7	1.4
USSR								
Less than 5	99.7	—	—	11.4	100.0	—	—	100.0
5-10	0.0	—	—	81.8	0.0	—	—	0.0
Over 10	0.3	—	—	6.8	0.0	—	—	0.0
Japan								
Less than 5	83.3	—	—	—	—	100.0	100.0	87.5
5-10	0.0	—	—	—	—	0.0	0.0	0.0
Over 10	16.7	—	—	—	—	0.0	0.0	12.5

Table 3-21.   Postwar—Modernity of Transfers by Weapons System (percent)

Years	Combat Aircraft	Transport Aircraft	Trainer Aircraft	Tanks	Armored Cars	Submarines	Warships	Patrol Vessels
United States								
Less than 5	14.8	2.9	5.0	16.9	19.1	22.2	30.2	48.4
5-10	54.8	27.5	28.3	27.8	30.9	0.0	22.4	14.2
Over 10	30.4	69.6	66.7	55.3	50.0	77.8	47.4	37.4
USSR								
Less than 5	14.3	17.2	1.1	13.9	—	15.4	0.0	31.4
5-10	66.9	38.6	17.1	15.0	—	65.4	26.7	51.0
Over 10	18.8	44.2	81.9	71.1	—	19.2	73.3	17.6
United Kingdom								
Less than 5	15.6	33.0	3.6	5.2	57.7	63.6	52.9	46.4
5-10	61.8	47.3	74.8	61.7	25.1	0.0	25.3	22.3
Over 10	22.6	19.6	21.7	33.1	17.2	36.4	21.8	31.3
France								
Less than 5	68.7	21.8	1.2	21.5	11.4	—	0.0	54.3
5-10	26.7	6.7	16.5	42.6	27.1	—	0.0	0.0
Over 10	4.6	71.5	82.3	35.9	61.5	—	100.0	45.7

nations have been engaged in actual arms races, to one degree or another, has tended to even out the quality of transfers among the suppliers. In dyadic arms races, such as those between Israel and the Arabs or India and Pakistan, there is no doubt a tendency toward matching of weapons supplies to both sides in terms of quality.[32]

For the postwar period the relatively high modernity of arms transferred by the French in the combat aircraft, tank and patrol boat categories has stood out. France has gone all-out in recent years to pry arms markets from both of the superpowers. No doubt, it has been impelled toward offering more modern arms as a substitute for the diplomatic backing normally associated with a superpower-client relationship. One can cite some examples. When the United States refused to sell Phantoms to Peru and Brazil, and insisted they purchase the less sophisticated F-5 Freedom Fighter, the French moved in with modern Mirages. And the French have recently begun to make similar moves in the Arab world, where the Soviets have, to a degree, moderated the quality of arms transferred in balancing United States arms transfers to Israel.

The SIPRI Typology of Arms Supplier Behavior

The SIPRI group has developed a three-way typology to describe different patterns of behavior or policy by major suppliers. They define and discuss three types of supplier patterns—hegemonic, commercial and restrictive—realizing that often the policies of individual suppliers will combine aspects of two or three of these patterns.[33]

A hegemonic pattern of supply is one in which a major power uses arms sales in a comprehensive attempt to spread influence and achieve or maintain spheres of influence. In a stronger sense of the term, arms sales are said to be used to achieve dominance over dependent nations. The arms supply policies of the United States and the USSR in the postwar period are claimed usually to have followed this pattern, that is, to have been primarily for political purposes.

An industrial pattern of supply is defined by the SIPRI group as one where it is important to maintain an advanced domestic defense industry and where this is possible only through the extensive export of weapons. In this pattern, in purest form, commercial rationales are the only or primary function of arms trading and arms are supplied indiscriminately to any recipient which can afford to pay for them. France is said to represent this pattern most closely in the modern period, although not without hegemonic overtones, while Britain—which once fell in the hegemonic category—is said to have substantially assumed this stance of late. Also, the shift in American policy in the early 1960s under the aegis of Kennedy and Kuss is said to have represented a partial shift in this direction, away from a primarily hegemonic pattern.

Finally, there is a restrictive pattern of supply. Its characteristic feature is that arms are not supplied to countries where they may, directly or indirectly, involve the supplier in a local or internation conflict. This is a policy of considerable restraint, exemplified, at least until recently, by Sweden and Switzerland whose policies ostensibly have been to sell arms only in cases where they are almost sure not to be used.[34] As a curious commentary on some of the more ludicrous aspects of the arms trade, this amounts virtually to a policy of selling arms only where they will be used solely for prestige or show purposes.[35]

This typology would not appear to have been as applicable to differential supplier behavior in the interwar period. Generally, and certainly up to the late 1930s, one could probably say that all governments then had essentially industrial patterns of supply. Some qualification derives from the efforts of military attachés in pushing arms sales in foreign markets, but the thrust of this activity was usually more commercial than hegemonic, in the sense used by SIPRI. By the late 1930s, however, some of the arms-selling activities of the Axis powers in Latin America and in the Middle East had begun to savor of the hegemonic pattern. As was later to be the case, this policy was afforded by the use of barter agreements, long-term government loans and some outright aid. This hegemonic pattern was particularly evident in German and Italian arms sales to Argentina and Chile right before the outbreak of World War II.

It is difficult to cite any arms supplier behavior in the 1930s which would have fit the restrictive category. The intent of the United States neutrality laws allows a description of American policy in the late 1930s along these lines, but these restrictions were applicable only to actual ongoing conflict, not to potential use, as with present Swedish policy. And during the interwar period neither Swedish nor Swiss neutrality was reinforced by the kind of restrictive policy now in force; both then sold arms to nations on the brink of conflict.

In our final chapter we shall discuss some current American policy problems with respect to arms sales. At this point, we may merely point out that some of the proposals made in recent years by Senator Fulbright and others have appeared to be prescriptions for a move towards a restrictive policy, that is, one without either strong political or commercial purposes.

Summary

We have indicated that some of the major comparative generalizations for the supplier side of the market are as follows:

1.   The number of producers of major weapons systems, and hence the number of potential suppliers, tends to be held down in systems characterized by hegemonic bipolar blocs.
2.   In both the interwar and postwar periods there has been a moderate degree of market concentration in most weapons systems, varying from the least to the most sophisticated. Among the major nations, the degree of concentration has been highest in the bipolar postwar period. However, the higher incidence of retransfers has resulted in more dispersed supplier

markets for some systems in the postwar period, at least for secondhand weapons.

3.   There have been strong apparent trends indicating that revisionist powers have gradually taken over markets from status quo powers as both periods progressed.

4.   The overall level of modernity of weapons sold was far higher in the interwar period, due apparently both to technological factors and to the freer nature of a still somewhat privately controlled arms trade.

5.   In the postwar period there has been much greater congruence of arms market shares with national power as represented by GNP. That is, the arms supplier markets have become a pretty good measure of the influence and power of the major nations, which have tried to maximize the extension of influence by these means.

In the following chapter we shall pursue questions on the patterns of donor-recipient relations, paraphrasing in effect the Lasswellian definition of politics: Who sells arms to whom, when and how many?

Chapter Four

A Comparison of Donor-Recipient Arms Transfer Patterns in Two Diplomatic Periods

In both the interwar and postwar periods, the networks of international arms transfers have been of bewildering, almost staggering, complexity. We shall attempt here to unravel these complex relationships, searching for patterns, generalizations and tentative explanations. Let us first, however, illustrate what is involved with some examples taken from narrow slices of time and geography within our two periods.[1]

Take, for instance, the arms acquisition patterns of India and Pakistan between their wars of 1965 and 1971. Since 1965, after the brief embargo imposed by the United States and Britain, India has widened its arms sources. From the USSR it has received a massive infusion of MIG-21 and Sukhoi-7 fighters, Tupolev bombers, PT-76 and T-54 tanks, helicopters, frigates, patrol boats and submarines. Simultaneously, however, the Indians have acquired Hawker Hunter and Gnat fighters and Seacat shipboard missiles from Britain, as well as some ex-British Seahawk navy fighters from West German stocks. A version of the British Vickers-37 tank has been mass-produced by license. From the eager French have come Breguet patrol aircraft, Alouette helicopters and Daphne submarines, as well as Nord air-to-air missiles to complement Atoll missiles acquired from the Soviets. The United States, relatively inactive in Indian arms markets during this period, has chipped in with some small arms and considerable economic aid which has indirectly financed arms purchases from other suppliers.

Pakistan's rival patterns of arms acquisition have been equally intriguing. Since 1965 it has received numerous MIG-19 fighters, IL-28 bombers and MI-6 helicopters from China, systems earlier licensed by the latter from Russia. From the United States have come Martin B-57 bombers, Lockheed Hercules transports, Sidewinder missiles, Patton tanks and M-113 armored personnel carriers, as well as F-86 Sabre jets transshipped from West Germany via Iran. The French have contributed Mirage fighters, the same Alouette helicopters which have been supplied to India and three Daphne submarines to match the same number sent to New Delhi. Having become India's primary supplier, the Soviets, nevertheless, have donated some 100 T-54 and T-55 tanks to Pakistan. The United States, having virtually embargoed Pakistan since the 1971 war, had by 1974 begun to resume arms shipments, in line with the new, less inhibited arms-selling policy of the Nixon administration.

During the same approximate period, the patterns of arms transfers to both sides of the Arab-Israeli conflict have been equally interesting. Egypt, of course, has benefited from massive shipments of all types of Soviet equipment before, during and after the 1973 conflict, including jet fighters and bombers, missiles of all types (including modern SAMs), tanks, armored personnel carriers, self-propelled artillery, submarines and missile-firing patrol boats. Nevertheless, the UAR is now negotiating with both Britain and France for alternative sources of supply and is apparently on the verge of a large helicopter deal with the former. It was suspected, anyway, that recent shipments of French Mirages and British Chieftain tanks to Libya actually had the UAR as their intended destination, if for no other reason than that they could not be absorbed by the tiny Libyan armed forces.[2] Indeed, the Mirages were used by Egypt during the 1973 war. Syria, like the UAR, has been primarily a Soviet client but has recently also received patrol boats from France and some equipment from Britain. Iraq, also primarily dependent on the USSR, has recently turned to France for Alouette helicopters and Nord Noratlas transports (originally licensed to France by the United States) and to Britain for Hawker Hunter fighters and Provost jet trainers. Jordan has long relied on the United States and Britain for its weapons but has recently bought some artillery and antiaircraft equipment from the Soviet Union. Its sister monarchy, Saudi Arabia, after extensive purchases of Patton tanks and Hawk missiles from the United States and Lightning and Hunter fighters and Thunderbird missiles from Britain, is now acquiring Alouette helicopters and Panhard armored cars from France and Agusta Bell helicopters from Italy. Recently, it has made newer deals with all three major Western nations, including purchases of F-5 fighters from the United States, helicopters and an integrated air defense system from the United Kingdom and probably Mirage jets from France. On the periphery in the Mahgreb, both Algeria and Morocco have balanced acquisitions from both Soviet and Western sources. Still within the Arab League, Lebanon has relied on a combination of Western sources, Kuwait on the British and the two Yemeni regimes on the Soviets. Lebanon has also bought Mirage fighters and Crotale surface-to-air missiles from France.

Israel's acquisitions are more familiar. Long reliant on the French for most weapons, the Israelis have now become essentially dependent on the United States, buying Phantoms, Skyhawks, Hawks, helicopters, tanks, artillery and a variety of missiles. Nevertheless, there were continuing shipments of Centurion tanks from Britain (at least up to 1973), following earlier sales of retransferred Patton tanks from West Germany and helicopters from Italy.

Captured Soviet tanks have also been integrated into Israel's force structure to supplement aging American and British tanks which have been re-fitted with bigger French 105 mm. guns.

In some of the less publicized corners of the world transfer patterns have been equally bewildering. Uganda acquired Soviet MIGs while its army was being equipped and trained by Israel. The Cambodian army, after the fall of Sihanouk, was hurriedly re-equipped with American arms to complement what had been a primarily Chinese-supplied arsenal. Ceylon recently received simultaneous emergency shipments of arms from Britain and Russia to combat its Maoist guerrillas. Yugoslavia has alternated between Soviet and Western arms deals, while Finland and Austria have acquired arms from both, simultaneously, over a long period of time, as well as from neutral Sweden.

In the interwar period, some of the patterns of arms transfers were, if anything, even more complex due to their relative lack of political content in an era of lingering laissez faire. China in the late 1930s was acquiring major weapons systems from the United States, Britain, Italy, France, Germany and the Soviet Union. In the early 1930s it had even received some naval equipment from Japan, on the eve of the Manchurian invasion. Meanwhile the Japanese, while at war with China in the late 1930s, were licensing, copying and purchasing military equipment from all of the sources which were simultaneously supplying China, with the exception of the Soviet Union. Turkey, Romania, Yugoslavia, Bulgaria, Greece and Finland—as well as Iraq, Iran and Afghanistan—were purchasing modern equipment from both sides of the escalating West-Axis confrontation. In the late 1930s Holland, Denmark and Norway were buying German and Italian aircraft, as was every single one of the South American republics, although still not abandoning earlier established pipelines to American, British and French arsenals. Japan, meanwhile, was still purchasing aircraft from the United States up to 1938.

Of course, not all arms trade relationships have been either complex or surprising. One expects that Cuba has received most of its arms from the Soviet Union since 1960, and that Taiwan and South Korea have acquired most of theirs from the United States. These relationships are on one end of a continuum, exemplifying sole supplier ties based on obvious ideological affinity.

Amidst this welter of detail—with its combined elements of realpolitik, pathos, venality and comedy—it is our task to formulate some generalizations about styles of acquisition, and about the political import of such transactions. Several interrelated problems will be discussed.

We shall examine the varying propensities of recipient nations to acquire their arms either from sole suppliers, from a dominant supplier or from a multiplicity of suppliers. In cases of multiple sources of supply, we shall further analyze these patterns as either within or across definable alliance blocs.

These various styles of acquisition go to the very heart of the arms acquisition process, to the power relationships, bargaining and diplomacy within which it is imbedded. Relative tendencies toward selectivity or eclecticism in arms acquisitions have important implications for controls as well. They are also critical indicators of trends in diplomatic systems variables, such as the extent of polarity. What would appear to be a tautology here is merely a reflection of reciprocity in cause and effect.

Parallel to our analysis of the supplier markets, we shall also here look at trends both within and between the two periods. We shall briefly examine the stability of arms trade relationships across the divide of World War II.

Another area of inquiry is the congruence of arms trade patterns with those of other cross-national indices of association. In a crude sense, this involves seeking explanations of arms trade patterns in relation to other types of ties. Space limitations will preclude more than a cursory coverage of this subsidiary theme, but we will discuss briefly the juxtaposition of arms trade patterns upon those of formal alliances. We will also note that such an analysis could be conducted on a broader scale, utilizing patterns of overall trade, membership in intergovernmental organizations or foreign economic aid.

The extent of these congruences should, we speculate, depend upon the mix of systemic variables characteristic of an era. We would expect that in the postwar period, with arms transfers having become so manifestly an instrument of diplomacy, that the patterns of the arms trade would hew more closely to what might be expected on the basis of other ties, particularly those of alliances. With overall trade, one would naturally expect a weaker associational link than for arms transfers.

THREE BASIC STYLES OF RECIPIENT ACQUISITION PATTERNS

Following the typology used by the MIT group for the postwar period, we may identify three general patterns or styles of recipient acquisition: sole supplier, principal or dominant supplier and multiple supplier. Actually, we are dealing with a continuum along which we have chosen arbitrary dividing lines to allow for a workable typology. Later, we shall have to subdivide the latter two categories according to within- and across-bloc patterns. Also, the concept of multiple supplier style will be disaggregated according to the simultaneity of weapons acquisitions from different suppliers.

These categories can be used either to analyze arms transactions by individual weapons systems (as done in the MIT study) or by the aggregate of transfers to given nations. We will use aggregated data. The categories are defined as follows:

1. Sole supplier relationship—where a single donor has supplied all of the weapons received by a given recipient.

2. Principal or dominant supplier relationship—where a single donor has supplied 60 percent or more, on the average, of all weapons systems or is the primary supplier in most or all of them.
3. Multiple supplier relationship—where no one supplier has transferred over 59 percent of the weapons acquired by a given recipient nation.[3]

Advantages or Disadvantages of Acquisition Styles to Suppliers and Recipients

Moving from one end of the continuum to the other—from sole supplier relationship to extreme eclecticism—advantages or disadvantages may accrue either to suppliers or recipients. These factors in turn may determine the degree to which these patterns lend themselves to controls of various sorts.

Of course, the recipient nation does not always have a choice of acquisition style. For some dependent nations, sole supplier relationships are imposed by diplomatic position and they may count themselves lucky to have even that. The present relationship between Israel and the United States is an example. These are complex matters about which we may make some tentative generalizations, while illustrating with examples.

For the recipient in a sole supplier relationship, certain clear advantages are apparent. Acquiring all or most weapons (or at least all of those in one weapons category) from one supplier allows easier integration of one's defense forces and the coordination of arms, ammunition and ancillary equipment (radar, electronics gear, repair facilities) which is particularly important within functional combat areas such as air defense, counterinsurgency or antisubmarine warfare. Furthermore, this allows for coordination and efficiency in the broader aspects of military assistance, particularly in training. A tight sole client relationship will usually entail a strong role for foreign military training groups in the arms acquisition process itself. Relationships between the military forces of the donor and recipient are apt to be close, with an intimate web of friendships between their respective officers'corps.[4]

The language factor may be important, as it affects the use of training manuals, maintenance instructions and directions for use of arms. A nation receiving arms from a multiplicity of sources will be forced to acquire proficiency in translating and using a correspondingly mixed batch of training manuals and other materials. In short, there are real efficiencies and economies to be gained by making one's armed forces and equipment a virtual carbon copy of the donor's. And the costs of switching suppliers are beyond what is involved in merely buying new equipment.

The seriousness of these problems may, however, depend on the technical and intellectual resources of the recipient. Some nations—Japan in the interwar period and Israel in the postwar one are examples—have managed to integrate the equipment of numerous suppliers by resourceful cannibalization and extensive modifications based on indigenous technology. For most nations, particularly the less developed ones, such indigenous input is beyond their capacity.

There have been some cases where multiple supplier relationships have really been combinations of sole supplier relationships to respective armed services in dependent nations. The best known case was pre—World War I Turkey, whose army was equipped and trained by the Germans while its navy was tied to the British.[5] Somewhat similar circumstances have existed in Indonesia in recent years. In these cases the problems normally associated with multiple dependence relationships are reduced, although the result may be severe interservice rivalry.

Another possible advantage of a single supplier relationship involves the prestige of the supplier, in terms of the efficacy of the arms themselves as well as of the broader diplomatic relationship surrounding their supply. These factors can be difficult to separate. It appears that the Soviet military was humiliated by the use to which its weapons were put in 1967, all the more so as the weapons systems as well as the users were called into question. Soviet aircraft were outperformed by French Mirages and Soviet tanks by British Centurions. This may in turn have given impetus to the shipping of still more modern and improved arms to the Arabs after that war and up through the 1973 conflict, during which Soviet arms were not found wanting in quality.

In both the past and present, and most recently in the 1973 conflict, conflicts between dependent nations have been used as testing grounds for the arms of major powers. The Spanish Civil War was the classic case, where, incidentally, Soviet tanks and planes were considered superior to those of Germany and Italy, the outcome of the war notwithstanding. One result of this was extensive redesigning of German military equipment preparatory to World War II.[6] The Chaco War between Paraguay and Bolivia was also openly used as a proving ground, but seems less to have engaged the prestige of suppliers.[7]

On balance, it does seem that a sole supplier relationship may more readily involve the prestige of the supplier's arms and hence make intervention on behalf of the recipient more likely. This is, however, somewhat tautological, as sole or dominant supplier relationships are themselves usually reflective of close diplomatic ties and corresponding obligations.

On the other hand, there are certain disadvantages to the recipient nation which is tied to a sole or dominant supplier. Most important is the dangerous degree of dependence upon sometimes precarious sources of arms and spare parts. Sudden cutoffs or restraints may result from shifts of policy or alignment, pressures from rival nations or international organizations, or from domestic opinion in the donor nation. The seemingly traditional use of embargoes applied to all belligerents in conflict situations may imperil the narrowly based client at a critical juncture, either at the outbreak of, or during, a war. The Israelis were to learn this lesson in the wake of the 1967 war, when they were cut off by the French embargo after having built an air force primarily from that source. Pakistan was also to learn this lesson, first in 1965 and then again more recently, when its largely American-supplied forces were subject to interruptions in the flow of previously ordered arms. In both of these cases the problem for the recipient was mitigated by alternative sources of supply, albeit also precarious ones.

At any rate, a recipient nation which has been tied to a sole or dominant supplier relationship, and which has been cut off by an embargo or change of policy, may be in the unhappy position of having to build its forces from scratch with new relationships. This is a particularly acute problem if spare parts have been cut off, forcing the dependent nation to scavenge and cannibalize to stretch the use of existing inventories. A good example was Indonesia after the overthrow of Sukarno. Its predominantly Soviet-supplied forces were cut off from their accustomed source and forced into comprehensive revamping on the basis of newer ones.

Sometimes the competition of either the supplier's own forces or other recipients for scarce supplies may cause problems for the recipient in a sole supplier relationship. Soviet cutbacks to the Spanish Loyalists in 1937 appear partly to have been based on the exigencies of arming expanding Soviet forces, and those of China against Japan as well.[8] The Israelis appear to have had some problems acquiring Phantoms in desired numbers because of the competing requirements of the Vietnam War and the competing requests of other nations allied to the United States. There were similar problems regarding American armor shipments to Israel during and after the 1973 conflict.

Another disadvantage to the recipient in a sole supplier relationship, particularly if no alternative exists, is that it may be forced to acquire weapons which are inappropriate—in terms of combat-effectiveness—for the mission of its forces or to the level of its technical ability. For better or worse, the recipient's forces must become virtual carbon copies of the supplier's. The South Vietnamese Army's effectiveness sometimes appeared to have suffered for these reasons, it having become a copy of an American army which itself often appeared not to function well in the jungle terrain of Southeast Asia. American rifles have proven too heavy for the Vietnamese soldier, while other highly sophisticated items of equipment have sometimes appeared to be merely expensive hindrances.

In another example, the Egyptians have sometimes seemed to regret their dependence on Soviet arms. Until recently, the Soviet Air Force concentrated disproportionately on fighter-interceptors, which were markedly inferior to French and American craft in ground support and tactical bombing roles. Also, Soviet tanks had earlier proved unreliable for desert warfare, perhaps because of the lack of sand filters which in 1967 caused frequent breakdowns in combat. And even despite the improved performance of Soviet arms during the 1973 conflict, all of the Arab states were seeking alternative sources of supply in the aftermath of that war.[9]

In the interwar period there were fewer examples of sole or

dominant supplier relationships but then, too, their disadvantages were illustrated in some cases. The several Eastern European nations tied to France by sole or dominant supplier relationships came to realize the inferiority of French arms to those of Germany and Britain. They woke up very late. On the eve of the Second World War they made frantic and inevitably futile efforts at re-equipping their forces from Britain and America, but by then this could not be done on a sufficient scale due to the competing needs of the latter's forces.

There are also both advantages and disadvantages to the recipient in a more eclectic acquisition pattern. Again, the crucial elements are integration of training and equipment, economics, built-in diplomatic support and assurance of continuing supply. And there is another matter which bears discussion at length, the leverage in arms markets afforded by multiple supplier sources.

Leverage in the Arms Markets by Dependent Nations

Multiple available sources of supply reduce the dangers of sudden cutoffs or embargoes. And even for recipient nations in sole or dominant supplier patterns the mere existence of relatively assured alternative sources will enable them to bargain between suppliers and to deter embargoes or controls.

There are several good recent examples of the kind of leverage afforded by alternative sources of supply. Both Jordan and Iran have used the threat of acquiring Soviet arms to squeeze additional or more sophisticated hardware from reluctant America and Britain. The threat has been made credible by the actual acquisition of small amounts of Russian military equipment. Syria has taken advantage of the competition between the USSR and China for leadership of the Third World to pry additional arms from the former under the threat of turning to the latter.[10] Egypt and Libya have played the same game in bargaining with the Soviets, using the threat of turning to France or Britain as a lever, with the former now making overtures to the United States as well, concurrent with the apparent Egypto-American detente.[11] Several nations in Latin America have learned that the best way to get the most modern equipment from the United States is to turn to Western European sources. And in situations where the recipient has had less leverage, South Africa has apparently begun to erode the British embargo with its massive purchases from France, while Pakistan has been able to get at least a trickle of arms from the United States in recent years only because of the threat of turning to China.[12]

The leverage held by the dependent nation in these situations has combined psychological and economic components. The original supplier nations know that the net effect of a cut-off may be negligible because of optional sources. As a result, they may choose, pragmatically, to continue in their roles. In doing so they may be able to maintain some diplomatic influence over the recipient, and of course make a contribution to their balance of payments positions in the process. These rationales have been used by the United States, for example, in continuing arms sales to Greece, Pakistan and Portugal, despite opposition at home and abroad.[13]

Relative leverage, then, is critical to an understanding of the processes of the arms trade. Of course, the leverage held by a nation in its quest for weapons is useful in other areas as well, say for obtaining economic aid or for getting one's way on a vote in the United Nations. The criteria for favorable leverage are fairly clear: size, economic strength, strategic geographic position, possession of scarce raw materials, and influence and connections with other nations.

There are certain nations—India is a good example—whose size, position and influence afford them great leverage in enabling them to play off the larger powers and to force continuing massive arms shipments as a price for the influence which goes with a supplier-recipient relationship. And the very magnitude of a nation's arms market will be a factor determining leverage. India buys a lot more planes and tanks than do smaller nations. The initial fears of French arms manufacturers about the loss of the Israeli market were soon quieted by the realization of far greater profits to be made playing the other side of the street.

In some cases, high leverage on one side of a conflict pairing will translate almost automatically into low leverage on the other. The Arabs, in a good leverage situation due to their combined populations, resources and strategic territory—and close ties to a broad spectrum of Afro-Asian nations— have not only been able to bargain for vast arms shipments from a number of suppliers, but have also had some success in forcing those suppliers not to ship arms to Israel. France, Germany and Britain have by now effectively acceded to this pressure, although the counterleverage afforded by the Jewish vote in the United States has up to now forestalled its application to Israel's last available supplier. India has had less success in cutting off arms supplies to Pakistan despite a favorable leverage situation, although its pressures appear to have become increasingly successful of late, at least with the United States. Still, both the French and Soviets have supplied Pakistan with some arms, while simultaneously arming India. This would appear to indicate that India's leverage over its suppliers, while high, is not equivalent to what the Arabs have achieved with their oil resources and the threat of expropriation as a trump card.[14]

France, in a number of cases, has played an anomalous role, almost beyond explanation by ordinary criteria. It has assumed the role of scavenger in numerous situations where previous suppliers had bowed out due to embargoes, international pressures or the low leverage of the recipient. It has replaced the Anglo-Saxon nations as a prime supplier to Greece, Portugal, Spain, South Africa and Rhodesia, while still maintaining client relationships with leftist regimes in Libya, Iraq and Algeria, and with a raft of sub-Saharan African states. The explanation seems to lie in the French having somewhat successfully consolidated a reputation for an apolitical approach to arms sales—an industrial or commercial policy of supply—which has come to be grudgingly accepted by nations which would not readily accept the same stance by the United States or Britain.[15] The case of the French embargo on Israel seems to be an exception.

Otherwise, they have circumvented the problem of leverage by making their sell-to-all-comers doctrine credible in maintaining an image of almost militant and defiant cynicism. Britain, by contrast, was roundly condemned by black African states when it merely hinted at the resumption of arms sales to South Africa.[16]

Looking at these questions somewhat differently, it would appear that there are situations where a supplier nation wants to be a supplier—i.e., is an eager supplier—but others where the supplier assumes its role only with reluctance. In the latter case, the recipient nation is usually either short on leverage or is a "pariah state" which many other nations do not want to see acquire weapons. Sometimes, even a pariah can obtain weapons because of putative moral concerns of one supplier, or because the economic rewards of supplying it may be tempting enough to at least one of the potential suppliers even under threats from nations with high leverage. France's role as "jackal state of the arms trade" has been pursued in some circumstances where these calculations seem to have been made and where benefits appeared on balance to outweigh costs.

In a later section we shall see that pariahs or nations with low leverage will often move toward independent arms production to forestall the threat of cutoffs, and in doing so may sometimes increase their chances of getting arms from reluctant suppliers who will then rationalize that they are going to be armed anyway.

In the interwar period, when governmental controls over the destination of arms were minimal, low leverage and pariahs in the arms trade do not seem significantly to have existed. It is difficult to cite an example where these factors were operable, perhaps with the exception of the difficulties of the Spanish Loyalists in obtaining arms from Britain and the United States. At a time when private suppliers acted somewhat independently from prevailing diplomatic forces there were few cases where one could contrast "reluctant" and "willing" suppliers.

For the recipients in the 1930s, there appears to have been scant expectation that their suppliers might have been unwilling to sell to antagonists. There was minimal furor during the Chaco and Sino-Japanese conflicts, in which the same arms manufacturers were purveyors to both sides. Logically, the conditions for applying pressure existed but simply appear not to have been used, perhaps merely because of the weight of established tradition. It was accepted that all supplier nations (or their arms firms) had essentially commercial arms sales policies. Also, the threat of retaliation by cutoff of raw materials or expropriation of assets may then have been generally less usable or credible.

Where alternative sources of supply are not readily available, a sole supplier relationship will give the supplier a large degree of control. In the postwar period this has allowed in some cases for arms sales policy to be used as a coercive diplomatic instrument. The donor nation may make further arms shipments—or continuation of spare parts shipments—contingent upon the satisfaction of certain conditions by the recipient. Before the 1973 Mideast war the United States appeared to be using this type of pressure on Israel both with respect to troop withdrawals (the Rogers Plan) and to signature of the Non-Proliferation Treaty and then again after the war, to pressure Israeli withdrawals from its expanded frontiers. Similar pressures exerted on Pakistan, despite Nixon's "tilt" in its favor in 1971, were only marginally effective because of existent alternative sources of supply, namely, China and France.

There has been at least one case in which the sole supplier of two nations in conflict was able virtually to force cessation of hostilities by shutting off further shipments of arms and spare parts. This was done rather effectively by the United States in bringing a halt to the 1969 "soccer war" between Honduras and El Salvador. At least during the duration of the conflict, alternative sources of supply—particularly from cross-bloc sources—were inconceivable for the two belligerents.[17]

Still, this type of control by a supplier will often backfire in the aftermath of a conflict, as nations once embargoed may subsequently attempt to broaden their bases of supply. This happened after the Indo-Pakistan War of 1965, in which the United States and Britain were able effectively to embargo both sides. Afterwards, India turned to Russia and Pakistan to China, although both retained remnants of previous client relationships. Of course, the contrast between this situation and that in Central America is explained to a great degree by geography and by recognized big power spheres of influence.

Again, in the interwar period there was little to compare with this kind of coercive arms diplomacy. Embargoes were formally applied in the Chinese Civil War, the Chaco and in Spain, in response to moralistically inspired public opinion pressures. But in each case the multiplicity of available suppliers with commercial policies, sufficient leverage on both sides and the weakness of controls over arms transactions rendered attempts at controls almost laughable. The arms trade of those days was normally—almost always—a buyer's market.

A COMPARISON OF DONOR-RECIPIENT PATTERNS

As indicated, the MIT study analyzed donor-recipient patterns according to the previously indicated acquisition styles—sole, predominant and multiple supplier—and by individual weapons systems, while we have aggregated the data across all weapons systems, using the same basic typology of acquisition patterns, This results, of course, in there being fewer identified sole supplier relationships, since the probabilities for multiple patterns rise if data for all categories are combined.

A few initial comments are appropriate to the organization of the data in Tables 4-1 through 4-6 regarding the size and composition of the respective samples of recipient nations. For the interwar period the sample is virtually global, excepting a few small nations for which no record of transfers of major weapons could be found.[18] For the postwar period our data base is the MIT sample of 52 developing countries, which accounts for only a portion of the some 130 independent entities now in existence.

We have supplemented the MIT data with additional information from the SIPRI study for developing nations not in the MIT sample. Also, the NATO and Warsaw Pact countries, and some other developed countries, have been included. Despite this, a number of developing countries are still omitted. Many, however, have not yet acquired any arms in the major weapons categories. Bahrein, Lesotho, Burundi, Mauritius, Fiji and the Maldives Islands, among others, are still mercifully bereft of fighter aircraft and tanks.

It was felt that the omission of these nations would not result in altering the validity of the analysis significantly. In fact, the inclusion of all nations in the postwar world would probably have resulted in heightening one of the major conclusions to emerge, namely, that there has been a greater tendency towards sole supplier relationships and a lesser tendency towards multiple supplier, cross-bloc relationships. Many of the omitted nations are either small African states still extensively tied to excolonial powers, or equally small Caribbean and Pacific nations most of which are primarily clients of the United States or the United Kingdom and only for small arms.

A more serious methodological problem arises with the time periods used and the simultaneity of transfers in the multiple supplier pattern. The MIT data, for the most part, were aggregated over a 13 year time span, from 1955 to 1968, while our corresponding data for the interwar period were aggregated over a 10 year period. As we shall explain, the concept of multiple supplier relationship might then subsume any of a number of distinct patterns, with significantly different implications. We shall discuss and define them in turn, and later analyze the data within this framework.

A multiple supplier relationship might first refer to a situation in which a recipient nation had, throughout most of a period, simultaneously received its arms from a number of suppliers, either across or within blocs. One example is postwar Morocco, which has simultaneously received a fairly steady stream of both Soviet and American arms over a period of many years. India has been another such example of late.

At the other end of the continuum the concept of multiple supplier relationship might actually be something of a misnomer. With the data aggregated over a lengthy time span, what appears to be a multiple supplier relationship might really consist of successive phases of sole or dominant supplier relationships. And, in terms of cross- or within-bloc patterns, the long-term compilation of transfer data might obscure some changes of acquisition patterns of great political import. Take Cuba, for example. Up to

1960 it received all of its arms from the United States and Britain; since then all its arms have come from the USSR. Yet if one were to look at the whole of the postwar period, Cuba would be in the multiple supplier category. As we shall see, there are numerous such examples in the postwar period, although few in the 1930s.

Within the multiple supplier category, these two types of cases are merely pure ideal types at the poles of a continuum. There are actually many cases which defy easy categorization. Iraq, for instance, was entirely a Western client up to the late 1950s, then switched to purchasing most of its arms from the Soviet Union while still retaining low-level client ties with France and Britain. This then is a modified segmented pattern under the rubric of multiple supplier pattern. Indonesia, meanwhile, has gone through at least three identifiable phases. In the first, it received all of its arms from various Western powers. Then it turned to the Soviets, but continued to purchase some Western arms. In a third phase, after Sukarno's demise, the Soviet source was abandoned and Western ones again expanded. Here, then, we have a combination of sole supplier and multiple supplier segments, which sum as a multiple acquisition pattern for the entire period. In still other cases, dominant within-bloc supplier patterns are broken by minor acquisitions from the other bloc, perhaps to establish the credibility of threats to change bloc suppliers. Jordan and Iran have previously been cited as examples. Finally, there are some cases in both periods within the multiple supplier category which defy easy categorization even within these more specific subcategories. There are cases of long-term simultaneity of cross-bloc supply which, nevertheless, contain phases where one or more suppliers or blocs have been dominant.

With these concepts in mind, the acquisition patterns for the two periods are broken down according to sole, predominant and multiple supplier relationships in Tables 4-1 and 4-2. The predominant supplier relationships are further subdivided according to whether the chief suppliers were from the Western bloc in either period or from the Axis or Soviet blocs. In turn, the predominant supplier relationships are further broken down according to whether the remainder of a given nation's acquisitions were all from within the alliance bloc of the dominant supplier or also included transfers from the rival bloc. This indicates whether bloc rivalries for arms influence have occurred at all. Finally, multiple supplier acquisition patterns are similarly divided. Some multiple acquisition patterns have involved only transfers from within blocs, while others have evidenced cross-bloc rivalries. The latter pattern is most highly indicative of bloc rivalries and cross-pressures on dependent nations. It is these countries which, more than others, have been the arenas for major power and bloc rivalries, keeping in mind the apparently less purposeful national pursuit of such rivalries at least up to the mid-1930s.

In Tables 4-3 and 4-4 the acquisition patterns for both periods have been rearranged to demonstrate more visibly the role of major suppliers in sole

**Table 4-1.   Postwar Donor-Recipient Patterns (to 1968),
by Acquisition Style**

Sole Supplier		*Predominant Supplier*		*Multiple Supplier*
West Bloc		*West Bloc*		*West Bloc*
Bolivia	US	Colombia	US	Venezuela
Nicaragua	US	Argentina	US	Israel
South Korea	US	Brazil	US	Jordan
Liberia	US	Chile	US	Lebanon
Malawi	UK	Dominican Republic	US	Saudi Arabia
Gambia	UK	Peru	US	Tunisia
Togo	Fr	Mexico	US	Zaire
Upper Volta	Fr	Rhodesia	UK	South Africa
Senegal	Fr	Zambia	UK	Ivory Coast
Gabon	Fr	Kenya	UK	Singapore
Chad	Fr	Dahomey	Fr	Sweden
Central African Republic	Fr	Cameroon	Fr	Switzerland
Abu Dhabi	UK	Niger	Fr	
Bahrein	UK	Malagasy	Fr	*Soviet Bloc*
Muscat and Oman	UK	Rwanda	US	none
		Thailand	US	
Soviet Bloc		Philippines	US	*Cross-Bloc*
Afghan	USSR	South Vietnam	US	Burma
Guinea	USSR	Kuwait	US	India
Yemen	USSR	Also: all NATO,		Pakistan
China	USSR	New Zealand,		Indonesia
		Spain, Japan,		Laos
		Australia		Cambodia
		Soviet Bloc		Morocco
		North Korea	USSR	South Yemen
		North Vietnam	USSR	Libya
		Mali	USSR	Mauritania
		Also: all Warsaw		Congo
		Pact	USSR	Uganda
		West Bloc with		Ghana
		Cross-Bloc ties		Tanzania
		Iran	US	Nigeria
		Ceylon	UK	Sudan
		Ethiopia	US	Finland
		Soviet Bloc with		Austria
		Cross-Bloc ties		Yugoslavia
		Cuba	USSR	
		Iraq	USSR	
		Syria	USSR	
		UAR	USSR	
		Algeria	USSR	
		Cyprus	USSR	
		Somalia	USSR	

Note: Identity of Sole or Predominant Supplier indicated in columns to the right of
country, where appropriate.

**Table 4-2. Interwar Donor-Recipient Patterns,
By Acquisition Style**

Sole Supplier		Predominant Supplier		Multiple Supplier
West Bloc		*West Bloc*		*West Bloc*
Cuba	US	Australia	UK	Guatemala
Egypt	UK	Canada	UK	Loyalist Spain
Haiti	US	Costa Rica	Fr	South Africa
Honduras	US	Dominican Republic	US	Belgium
Saudi Arabia	UK	Eire	UK	Czechoslovakia
New Zealand	UK	Estonia	UK	
		Mexico	US	*Axis Bloc*
Axis Bloc		Poland	Fr	None
Albania	It			
		West Bloc with		*Cross-Bloc*
		Cross-Bloc ties		Argentina
		Colombia	US	Austria
		Greece	UK	Bolivia
		Iraq	UK	Brazil
		Latvia	UK	Chile
		Nicaragua	US	China
		Portugal	UK	Denmark
				Ethiopia
		Axis Bloc with		Finland
		Cross-Bloc ties		Iran
		Afghan	It	Lithuania
		Bulgaria	Ger	Norway
		Ecuador	It	Peru
		Hungary	It	Rumania
		Paraguay	It	El Salvador
				Sweden
		Axis Bloc		Switzerland
		Nationalist Spain	It	Thailand
				Turkey
				Uruguay
				Venezuela
				Yugoslavia
				Netherlands

Note: Identity of Sole or Predominant Supplier indicated in columns to right of country, where appropriate.

and dominant supplier relationships. As indicated, four suppliers in the postwar period and five in the interwar achieved this status in at least one dependent nation.

In Tables 4-5 and 4-6 we have further disaggregated the acquisition patterns in the predominant and multiple supplier categories in order to correct for the problem of simultaneity and the segmentation of phases of supplier influence. We shall subsequently define these subcategories, illustrating with examples. This greater specificity with regard to cross-bloc patterns will enable

Table 4-3.   Postwar Donor-Recipient Patterns (to 1968), by Suppliers

Supplier	United States	United Kingdom	France	USSR
Sole	Bolivia Nicaragua South Korea Liberia	Malawi Gambia Abu Dhabi Bahrein Muscat and Oman	Togo Upper Volta Senegal Gabon Chad Central African Republic	Afghan Guinea Yemen China
Predominant (within-bloc pattern)	Colombia Argentina Brazil Chile Peru Dominican Republic Mexico Rwanda Thailand Philippines South Vietnam All NATO Japan New Zealand Australia Spain	Rhodesia Zambia Kenya Kuwait	Dahomey Cameroon Niger Malagasy	North Korea North Vietnam Mali All Warsaw Pact
Predominant (cross-bloc pattern)	Iran Ethiopia	Ceylon	None	Cuba Iraq Syria UAR Algeria Cyprus Somalia

Multiple Supplier (within West bloc)

Venezuela
Israel
Jordan
Lebanon
Saudi Arabia
Tunisia
Zaire
South Africa
Ivory Coast
Singapore
Sweden
Switzerland

Multiple Supplier (within Soviet bloc)

Multiple Supplier (cross-bloc)

France	USSR
Pakistan Indonesia Cambodia Morocco Mauritania Tanzania Yugoslavia Nigeria Austria Ghana	Burma India Laos South Yemen Libya Congo Uganda Sudan Finland

Table 4-4. Interwar Donor-Recipient Patterns, by Suppliers

Supplier	United States	United Kingdom	France	Italy	Germany
Sole	Cuba Haiti Honduras	Egypt Saudi Arabia New Zealand	none	Albania	none
Predominant (within-bloc pattern)	Dominican Republic Mexico	Australia Canada Eire Estonia	Poland	Nationalist Spain	none
Predominant (cross-bloc pattern)	Colombia Nicaragua	Greece Iraq Latvia Portugal	none	Afghan Ecuador Hungary Paraguay	Bulgaria
Multiple Supplier (within West bloc)	*Multiple Supplier (within Axis bloc)*				*Multiple Supplier (cross-bloc)*
Guatemala Loyalist Spain South Africa Belgium Czechoslovakia	none				Argentina Bolivia Brazil Chile Salvador Peru Uruguay Venezuela Austria Denmark Finland Lithuania Norway Rumania Sweden Switzerland Yugoslavia Netherlands China Ethiopia Iran Thailand Turkey

**Table 4-5.   Postwar Multiple and Predominant Supplier
Relationships (to 1968), Within-Period Segmentation Patterns**

Multiple Supplier Pattern—Whole Period			
Austria Finland Yugoslavia			
Multiple Supplier Pattern—Shift of Influence from West to Soviet Bloc with Approximate Date of Shift of Influence			
Morocco	1961	India	1965
Ghana	1961	Pakistan	1965
Mali	1961	Uganda	1966
Indonesia	1962	Nigeria	1967
Somalia	1963	Mauritania	1969
Congo	1964	Sudan	1969
Cambodia	1964		
Multiple Supplier Pattern—Shift of Influence from Soviet to West Bloc			
Indonesia	1965		
Cambodia	1970		
Predominant West Pattern—Shift Towards Cross-Bloc Pattern			
Ceylon	1971		
Predominant Soviet Pattern—Shift Towards Cross-Bloc Pattern			
None			
Predominant Soviet Pattern—Shift from West to Soviet Bloc			
Syria	1955		
UAR	1955		
Iraq	1958		
Cuba	1960		
Algeria	1962		
Somalia	1963		
Cyprus	1964		
Predominant Western Pattern—Shift from Soviet to West Bloc			
None			

Table 4-6.   Interwar Multiple and Predominant Supplier Relationships, Within-Period Segmentation Patterns

Multiple Supplier Pattern – Whole Period			

Ethiopia (to 1935)			
China			
Turkey			
Switzerland			
Sweden			

Multiple Supplier Pattern – Shift of Influence from West to Axis Bloc with Approximate Date of Shift of Influence

Peru	1934	Argentina	1937
Rumania	1934	Bolivia	1937
Austria	1934	Venezuela	1937
Uruguay	1934	Norway	1937
Lithuania	1935	Finland	1938
Chile	1936	Brazil	1938
Iran	1936	Thailand	1938
Yugoslavia	1936	El Salvador	1938
Denmark	1936		

Multiple Supplier Pattern – Shift of Influence from Axis to West Bloc

None

Predominant West Pattern – Shift Towards Cross-Bloc Pattern

Colombia	1933	Latvia	1937
Greece	1935	Iraq	1938
Portugal	1936	Nicaragua	1938

Predominant Axis Pattern – Shift Towards Cross-Bloc Pattern

None

Predominant Axis Pattern – Shift from West to Soviet Bloc

Hungary	1934
Afghan	1937
Ecuador	1937
Paraguay	1937

Predominant Western Pattern – Shift from Axis to West Bloc

None

us to trace overall shifts of influence in individual countries and in regions by supplier nations and major power blocs.

Sole Supplier Relationships

Sole supplier relationships in either period have usually been reflective of very close ties between supplier and recipient, often bordering on the status of protectorate for the latter. Another rather consistent characteristic has been the small size of all of the recipient nations in this relationship. There are two apparent reasons for this. First, a smaller nation will normally have relatively low volume requirements for arms, making it more likely that its demand can be satisfied by one nation. Second, it is less likely to have the kind of market leverage we have previously discussed. It is thus less able to bargain among the major suppliers for the honor of being one of their recipients.

In the interwar period only seven of some 60 then existing independent states were consistently in a sole supplier relationship. None of these relationships was particularly surprising. Cuba, Haiti and Honduras were then virtual American satrapies. Egypt was practically a British protectorate, while Saudi Arabia was also under considerable British influence. Albania was under Mussolini's thumb during this period and perhaps did not dare to seek arms elsewhere in defiance of him.

In the postwar period the larger number of nations in the sample include, correspondingly, a larger number of nations in a sole supplier relationship. As indicated in the tables, the majority have been African nations still somewhat tied to their former British and French overseers, along with three Persian Gulf sheikdoms until recently under the umbrella of the British navy. Otherwise, Bolivia and Nicaragua have been alone among Latin American nations in not seeking some of their arms outside the American orbit, at least until very recently, when Nicaragua has apparently bought some from Israel. South Korea is an obvious case of overwhelming American influence, and Liberia an anomaly among the African states.

Four nations have been involved in sole supplier relationships with the Soviets. Ideology is explanatory in the cases of Guinea, Yemen and China, although since the early 1960s the latter has had to build its own armaments base while continuing to rely on Soviet licenses transferred before then. Afghanistan, which has received some American economic aid, appears tied to the Soviet arms orbit on the basis of sheer territorial propinquity.

Predominant Supplier, Within-Bloc Relationships

Nations in this category are normally in a situation similar to those in sole supplier relationships. In some cases, inroads on the dominance of one major supplier may be explained by weapons specialization on the part of supplier nations. Britain has supplied surplus naval craft, for instance, to South American nations otherwise wholly dependent on the United States and armored cars in other cases, on the basis of sheer specialization.

In the interwar period the United States and Britain accounted for most of the acquisition patterns in this category. In Australia and Canada predominant British influence was diluted by some American arms sales, anticipating later shifts of influence after 1945. Eire bought some weapons from Sweden. Estonia was a rare case for interwar Eastern Europe, escaping the competing pressures of Axis and Soviet influence in the late 1930s despite its geographic distance from Britain. American shares in Mexico and the Dominican Republic were somewhat undercut by Britain and France, with the former having considerable success with combat aircraft sales to Mexico in the early 1930s. The case of Costa Rica was somewhat unusual, with French firms having preempted one arms market in Central America from the Americans, although not as unusual as El Salvador, where Italian influence actually became dominant in the late 1930s.

Poland alone among the middle-range powers of interwar Europe relied primarily on France for its arms, a pattern set early in the 1920s when surplus French arms were acquired for use against the invading Bolsheviks. Poland's almost total reliance on French arms was to result in that country's being very poorly equipped in its brief attempt at stopping the German juggernaut in 1939.

Nationalist Spain was the only political entity in the interwar period to have been in either a sole or dominant supplier relationship to an Axis power. It received massive amounts of the most modern German and Italian planes, tanks and submarines between 1936 and 1940, both during and after the Civil War.

The fact that only Nationalist Spain was in a predominant relationship with the Axis powers during this period is, of course, not altogether indicative of the relative balance of influence between Western and Axis arms firms. As we shall see, numerous nations which were arms clients of the Western powers in the early 1930s later shifted to predominant Axis or multiple supplier relationships. Neither Germany nor Italy were significant factors in the arms markets up to 1935, with a few exceptions: Italy's arms sales to the Soviet Union in the early 1930s and some aircraft sales by a German Junkers subsidiary operating out of Sweden.

Since 1945 the United States has had predominant influence in almost all of the Latin American republics. Recently, however, France, Britain, West Germany, Italy and Canada have begun to make strong inroads, particularly in Brazil, Argentina, Peru, Venezuela, Ecuador and Chile.[19] The remainder of the cases of American predominance are quite predictable with the exception of the tiny African nation of Rwanda. Except for Rwanda, Ethiopia, Liberia and Zaire, American postwar arms influence on the African continent has been minimal.

The remaining cases of predominant, within-bloc relationships with France and Britain as suppliers are easily explicable in light of prior colonial relationships and Kuwait's traditional close ties to Britain.

The cases listed under predominant supplier, within-bloc pattern for the Soviet bloc are those where Soviet and Chinese arms sales have coincided (North Korea and North Vietnam) or where transfers have occurred among the Eastern European countries, all of which license-build Soviet weapons.

Predominant Supplier, Cross-Bloc Relationships

In this category, the competing influences of rival blocs have been at play, albeit with one major power from one of the rival blocs still having accounted for the bulk of transfers over a period. However, as indicated, the designation for this category may obscure some very distinct patterns with differing implications.

In the interwar period there were several nations—Colombia, Greece, Portugal, Iraq and Latvia—which received the bulk of their arms throughout the whole decade of the 1930s from either the United States or Britain but which were engaged in concurrent purchases from the Axis powers by the late 1930s. Colombia and Nicaragua were following the same pattern as most of the remainder of the Latin American nations. Greece, like the remainder of the Balkan nations, acquired large amounts of weapons from the Germans late in the decade. Portugal, under Salazar, followed Franco Spain's close ties to the Axis. Iraq, meanwhile, became a hotbed of Axis activity just prior to the Second World War, despite the British bases at Basra and Habbaniya.

There were no cases of nations with predominant arms ties to an Axis client during the whole period of the 1930s, in which there were shifts in reverse of those just described. There were, however, a number of cases where the data for the whole period aggregate to a predominantly Axis client pattern, but where this relationship was formed only after an initial phase of total Western influence. These cases are listed in Table 4-6. Italian arms shipments to Afghanistan, Ecuador and Paraguay were sufficiently heavy from 1937 to 1940 to constitute over 60 percent of the total transfers for the entire decade. Italy's ties to Hungary and Germany's to Bulgaria were formed earlier, reflecting the closeness of relationships between the Axis powers and the fascist regimes which later were to join them, formally, in declaring war.

Thus, the within-period trends for nations having predominant suppliers, either Western or Axis, were all in the direction of increasing Axis influence as the period progressed. We shall see that these trends were repeated in the numerous cases of multiple supplier, cross-bloc relationships.

In the postwar period, among those nations which have received the bulk of their arms from one Western supplier, Ceylon is the one case of considerable recent movement towards Soviet influence. The Bandaranaike government has purchased MIGs and other equipment to combat its Maoist insurgents. In Ethiopia and Iran overall American predominance has been broken by small, almost token, shipments of Soviet arms, which would not yet appear to reflect significant shifts of diplomatic influence, although Iran's economic ties with the Soviets have grown much closer in recent years.

There are a number of cases where the Soviets have predominated over the whole postwar period, but where the pattern has been one of a shift from an earlier Western client relationship to almost complete Soviet influence. Syria, Iraq and the UAR came into the Soviet orbit in the middle to late 1950s. Each has, however, received small amounts of Western arms since, and each is now being entreated by the French to diversify its purchases. Algeria's case has been very similar, while that of Cuba has been one of very distinct phases. Perhaps more surprising is the case of Cyprus, which had become part of the Soviet sphere of arms influence prior to the recent war and subsequent to the waning of a previously strong British presence.[20]

As in the interwar period, all of the within-period shifts in predominant supplier, cross-bloc patterns have been away from Western bloc influence. Again, it is clear that revisionist powers (or their arms firms) have consistently gained markets at the expense of status quo powers. This point is perhaps also backed up by France's takeover of numerous previously American areas of arms influence since the late 1960s.

Multiple Supplier Within-Bloc Patterns

This category is similar to that of predominant, within-bloc suppliers, except that no supplier nation, or its firms, achieved up to 60 percent of a dependent nation's arms purchases. Here, too, aggregated data for whole periods may subsume identifiable phases in which there have been marked shifts of influence from one supplier to another. An example is Israel, which received most of its arms from France between 1955 and 1967 and from the United States between 1967 and the present.

In the interwar period, for instance, Loyalist Spain received most of its arms from France and Britain, although with significant additional supplies from Russia and Holland, among others. But during most of the Spanish Civil War, Russia was actually the leading supplier, with heavy shipments of tanks and planes.

South Africa split its sales between Britain and the United States, and Belgium between Britain and France although, like many other European nations on the eve of the war, it bought aircraft from the United States in the late 1930s. Guatemala, like Costa Rica, had fairly close arms ties with France during the 1930s to balance purchases from the United States.

Czechoslovakia's patterns of arms purchases in the 1930s were quite diverse. Actually, the Czechs had a fairly well-developed arms industry of their own, which also allowed them to license-produce a broad spectrum of French and British equipment, some of which subsequently was transshipped to the other members of the Little Entente. On the eve of Munich, the Czechs purchased from the Soviet Union some 60 bombers which had originally been built on license from one of the American aircraft firms.

The nations in the postwar period displaying multiple supplier, within-bloc patterns are a diverse group. They represent various combinations of

American, British and French influence, either simultaneously or in phases. Israel's case has been noted. Venezuela was the first of the Latin American nations to break away from the prevailing pattern of American influence after 1945, spreading its purchases among a number of European countries. Jordan and Saudi Arabia have split theirs mostly between the United States and Britain, although the Saudis are now turning to France. Tunisia and Lebanon have purchased arms from each of the three major Western powers, with Tunisia also among the small number of developing countries to have bought aircraft from Sweden. Singapore, wealthy despite its small size, has been a rather diversified collector of Western arms in the past few years. It was one of the first nations to receive American M-16 rifles and has also purchased used French tanks from Israel.[21]

Postwar arms purchase patterns by Sweden and Switzerland contrast with those of the 1930s. Then, their neutrality was backed by what appeared to have been careful balancing of acquisitions from both the Axis and Western powers. This overtly neutralist pattern has been followed in the postwar period only by Finland and Austria. Sweden has built a formidable arms industry of its own, although still relying on the United States and Britain for aircraft engines and helicopters, while Switzerland has heavily license-produced a range of Western equipment.

Multiple Supplier Cross-Bloc Patterns

The bulk of the nations in this category in either period are those in which the rival efforts of major blocs or their firms for arms-selling influence have been played out. Again, a number of distinct subpatterns have been evidenced, ranging from cases where arms have been acquired simultaneously from rival blocs over most or all of a period to those where there have been distinct phases demarcated by definite shifts of influence. It is in examining trends in this category that we can see the extent to which recent postwar trends have become quite reminiscent of the earlier period.

Actually, in both periods there have been relatively few cases in which nations of rival blocs have simultaneously sold arms to recipients over a lengthy period. In the postwar period only the European buffer states have fit this pattern. And here there has been a difference between the acquisition styles of Finland and Austria on the one hand and Yugoslavia on the other. The former have had avowed policies of balancing arms purchases from both sides of the Iron Curtain to emphasize their status as neutrals although also purchasing from other neutrals. Yugoslavia, meanwhile, with an odd mix of American, French and Soviet equipment, has appeared to shift back and forth in response to the mysterious movements of Tito's diplomacy between East and West.[22]

In the interwar period there were a few important recipient nations which exhibited multiple, simultaneous acquisition patterns over the span of the period or for most of it. Ethiopia's purchases were balanced between Italy,

France, Britain and Holland before its downfall in the short war of 1935. On a much larger scale, however, both China and Turkey exhibited rather extreme cross-bloc, eclectic acquisition patterns throughout the 1930s. The transactions are itemized in Tables 4-7 and 4-8 to illustrate the contrast with the postwar experience and perhaps to anticipate future patterns.

China, as indicated, received significant amounts of major weapons systems from all of the major powers of that period, including the Soviet Union. There were even small shipments from Japan in 1931. Even here, however, one can perceive segmented phases in China's acquisitions, obviously linked to phases in the diplomacy of that era. The United States and Britain accounted for the bulk of China's purchases up to about 1934. From then up to 1937 the two Axis powers began to challenge, at a time when their arms trading activities were expanding almost everywhere. Then in 1938, with Japan having joined the Axis and being also involved in an undeclared war with the Soviets on the Siberian border, Russian arms began to flow to the embattled Chiang. Simultaneously there were large shipments of American armor.

Turkey in the 1930s was an equivalently fickle and eclectic arms recipient. Its purchases were, like China's, from each of the major powers, including the Soviets, and additionally from Czechoslovakia, Spain and Sweden. In this case, also, phases in which one or another supplier was dominant can be discerned. The significance which must have been attached by the British at that time to maintaining influence in Turkey can be gauged by the number of the most modern aircraft sold there. This was at a time of near panic in Britain over the comparative production rates of German and British aircraft factories.

The remaining large number of nations in the 1930s exhibiting multiple acquisition patterns were cases either where there were sharp demarcations between periods of Western and then Axis influence or where earlier Western influence gave way to a mixed pattern. The dates of these shifts are indicated in Table 4-6. It is clear that Axis market shares gradually increased in a large number of previously Western bailiwicks as the period progressed, reaching a crescendo by 1937 and 1938. These shifts, in combination with others we have noted in the predominant supplier category, were spread over all regions. Every one of the South American republics was affected; by the late 1930s there was furious competition between the arms salesmen of all of the rival major powers excepting the USSR.

In Europe, most of the Balkan and other Eastern European nations were acquiring arms from both Western and Axis nations by the late 1930s. Here, even more than in Latin America, the arms races were intense. Even nations the size of Romania and Yugoslavia acquired hundreds of modern combat aircraft and tanks. Meanwhile, the Middle East also became an arena for arms competition between the rival blocs, with Iran, Iraq and Afghanistan diversifying their acquisitions by about 1937 away from earlier reliance on Britain. Norway and Denmark, along with Finland and Sweden, surprisingly also

Table 4-7.   China's Arms Acquisition Pattern in 1930s

Year	Number	Model and Type, System	Supplier Nation
1930	10	Vickers Vespa trainers	Britain
	7	Arrow trainers	Britain
	6	Armstrong Whitworth Atlas bombers	Britain
	24	Carden Lloyd gun carriers	Britain
	3	North American Waco J-5 trainers	United States
	3	Stearman transports	United States
	2	Ford ISD transports	United States
	10	Vought Corsair fighters	United States
	15	Renault M-26 tanks	France
1931	5	Aichi observation planes	Japan
	1	Cruiser	Japan
	35	Douglas 0-38 fighter bombers	United States
1932	25	Avro 634 trainers	Britain
	13	Armstrong Whitworth bombers	Britain
	15	Douglas observation planes	United States
	15	Vickers 6 Ton tanks	Britain
	6	Hotchkiss tanks	Britain
	5	Vickers light tanks	Britain
	3	Armored cars, unspecified	Britain
	1	Junkers Ju-52 bomber	Sweden
1933	25	DeHavilland Tiger Moth trainers	Britain
	12	Vickers Carden Lloyd tanks	Britain
	10	Whippet tanks	Britain
	100	Fleet trainers	United States
	50	Curtiss Hawk fighters	United States
	16	Caproni bombers	Italy
1934	16	Avro Avian trainers	Britain
	4	Cutty Sark ASW craft	Britain
	20	Vought Corsair fighters	United States
	20	Curtiss Shrike fighters	United States
	1	Curtiss Condor bomber	United States
	38	Vought V-90 fighter bombers	United States
	10	Breguet fighter bombers	France
1935	40	Fleet PT-11C trainers	United States
	12	Douglas C2NCL observation planes	United States
	46	Northrop 2E bombers	United States
	2	Boeing 247 D bombers	United States
	10	Boeing IPOL fighters	United States
	20	Breda 27 fighters	Italy
	12	Fiat Cr-32 fighters	Italy
	20	Breda BT-25 trainers	Italy
	24	Savoia-Marchetti S-72 bombers	Italy
1936	2	Douglas DC-2 transports	United States
	2	M.A.S. torpedo boats	Italy
	5	Thorneycroft torpedo boats	Britain

Table 4-7.—*Continued*

Year	Number	Model and Type, System	Supplier Nation
1937	2	Douglas DC-2 transports	United States
	2	Ryan reconnaissance planes	United States
	2	Patrol boats	Britain
	20	Fiat Br-3 bombers	Italy
	13	Junkers K-47 bombers	Germany
	10	Junkers transports	Germany
	20	Focke-Wulf Stieglitz trainers	Germany
	6	Heinkel He-111 bombers	Germany
1938	120	I-15 fighters	USSR
	120	I-16 fighters	USSR
	120	SB-2 and SB-3 bombers	USSR
1940	10	SDKfz 222 armored cars	Germany
	200	Tanks, various	United States

purchased significant amounts of arms from the Axis in the late 1930s, also generally representing diversification away from British sources. In fact, Poland, Estonia and Belgium were the only nations in Europe which were not buying arms from either Germany or Italy or both by the late 1930s.

In summary, the great majority of nations in all regions of the world were, by the late 1930s, purchasing arms from both of the rival blocs in patterns ranging along a continuum of relative influence between them. Partly, this appears to have been a result of the freedom of private traders and the lack of political controls or even strong diplomatic content to these transactions. Perhaps also, a moderate degree of outright ideological conflict—in comparison with the postwar period—made purchases from either bloc by most dependent nations at least a possibility. There seem to have been few of the "unthinkable" arms client relationships there would be in later years. Alternatively, however, the wave of fascist movements which swept over a good part of the globe in the late 1930s, especially in most of Eastern Europe and Latin America, may have opened possibilities for Axis suppliers on an at least partially ideological basis.

There is one other facet to these problems which did not fall within the purview of our research. It is possible that there may have been a link between the comparative production outputs of the Axis and Western powers and shifts of market influence. The vast expansion of the arms production capacities of Germany and Italy in the mid-1930s, not immediately matched by the United States, Britain and France, may have allowed for volume sales to nations whose preferences, on the basis of ideology, were not too strong.

In the postwar period a rather similar trend has been evidenced in shifts toward multiple supplier relationships. A large number of nations once mostly within the Western arms supply orbit have developed multiple supplier

Table 4-8.   Turkey's Arms Acquisition Pattern in 1930s

Year	Number	Model and Type, System	Supplier Nation
1930	25	Junkers A-20 bombers	Sweden
	4	Destroyers	Italy
	12	Gordou Leseurre fighters	France
	10	Citroen armored cars	France
1931	16	Savoia S-55 ASW aircraft	Italy
	30	Smolik 28 trainers	Czechoslovakia
	1	Collier ship	United States
1932	6	Curtiss Fledgling trainers	United States
	3	S.V.A.N. motor torpedo boats	Italy
	2	Submarines	Italy
	2	Destroyers	Italy
1933	45	Breguet-19 fighter bombers	France
	4	Supermarine Southampton ASW	Britain
	2	Bombers, unspecified	USSR
1934	12	Consolidated fleet trainers	United States
	35	Curtiss Hawk interceptors	United States
	36	Dewoitine 21 interceptors	France
	6	Vickers flying boats	Britain
	10	Vickers A light tanks	Britain
1935	60	PZL fighters	Poland
	1	Submarine	Spain
	10	T-28 tanks	USSR
	100	Bronieford armored cars	USSR
	62	T-26 tanks	USSR
	5	T-27 tanks	USSR
1936	20	Martin bombers	United States
	40	Vultee B-12 bombers	United States
	6	DeHavilland Rapide and Dragon trainers	Britain
	10	Focke-Wulf 58 Weihe fighter bombers	Germany
	1	Submarine tender	Germany
1937	12	Bristol Blenheim bombers	Britain
	5	Lurssen torpedo boats	Germany
1938	40	Grumman FF-1 fighter bombers	United States
	60	Gotha trainers	Germany
	24	Heinkel He-111 bombers	Germany
	75	Skoda armored cars	Czechoslovakia
	20	Praga tanks	Czechoslovakia
1939	50	Curtiss Model 22 trainers	United States
	14	Curtiss Hawk model I trainers	United States
	25	Hanriot trainers	France
	30	Morane-Saulnier interceptors	France
	4	Submarines	Germany
	15	Hawker Hurricane fighters	Britain
	30	Supermarine Spitfire fighters	Britain
	30	Blackburn Skua dive bombers	Britain
	26	Fairey Battle fighters	Britain
	25	Avro Anson bombers	Britain
	25	Miles Magister trainers	Britain
	4	Submarines	Britain
	3	Minelayers	Britain
	4	Destroyers	Britain
	5	Vickers tanks	Britain

relationships which include the Soviets. The progress of these trends is depicted in Table 4-5, along with parallel trends in those nations which have been predominant clients of the USSR despite some earlier ties with Western nations.

Since the early 1960s the Soviets have edged into a number of erstwhile Western markets: Morocco, Ghana, Mali, Somalia, Congo-Brazzaville, Indonesia, India, Uganda, Nigeria, Pakistan, Mauritania and the Sudan. Some of these Third World nations, such as Ghana and Mali, formed ties with the Soviets in the wake of the decolonialization process and on the basis of moderately strong ideological ties. Others, such as India and Pakistan, originally turned to them out of pique at the reluctance of Western arms suppliers to back them in crises. Nigeria, too, found the USSR a willing supplier of arms in its conflict with Biafra, while some of the Western nations held back from more than desultory deliveries for allegedly moral reasons. Morocco, a monarchy, constitutes at least one case where a distinct ideological shift was not involved in the reduction of Western influence. Its move toward splitting arms purchases between the two blocs followed its disagreement with the United States over Strategic Air Command bases built there and later dismantled.

In the interwar period we have seen that there were no cases where Axis influence, once having achieved a foothold, was later reversed, although in both China and Turkey Axis arms sales appear to have trailed off by the end of the 1930s. In the postwar period, however, there have been two cases in the multiple supplier pattern category in which Soviet bloc influence has been totally reversed. One was Indonesia. A client of the West up to 1962, it shifted markedly into the Soviet orbit, ranking with the UAR, India and Cuba among the Russians' largest arms customers. Then in 1965 came the bloody counterrevolution and the deposing of Sukarno, resulting in an end to arms acquisitions from the Soviets and a return to American and French sources, among others. Cambodia, meanwhile, was primarily a Western client up to 1964. Then, Sihanouk began to purchase most of his arms from China. In 1970, with the Lon Nol regime beginning to fight alongside ARVN against the North Vietnamese, the Cambodians began hurriedly to supplement their predominantly Chinese arsenal with American equipment. So far, these cases remain unique. However, recent halting trends away from the Soviet arms orbit in the UAR, Algeria, Iraq and the Sudan may auger further such developments.

Summary

Some of the primary conclusions to emerge from comparison of the arms acquisition patterns of the two periods are as follows:

1. The number of sole supplier relationships has been rather small in both periods, although more frequent in the postwar period because of the lingering hold of old colonial ties. For the most part, however, these client relationships have been characteristic of small nations tied ideologically to

great powers or existing as virtual protectorates of the latter because of territorial propinquity. Most of the sole supplier relationships in either period have involved Western suppliers, partly because of the weakness of the revisionist powers at the outset of each period.

2. There has been a definite trend of late toward cross-bloc, multiple supplier relationships, in parallel with the breakdown of the loose bipolar arrangement of the early postwar period. This appears to be reminiscent of what happened in the late 1930s, although still muted because of the more ideological nature of present day diplomacy. Also, the relative absence of governmental controls in the 1930s allowed these patterns to be even more pronounced.

3. There have been pronounced shifts in both periods toward more and more arms markets either being taken over by revisionist bloc powers or shared by them with previously dominant status quo suppliers. This reinforces the conclusions of our analysis of the shifts in supplier market shares over time between revisionist and status quo powers.

4. In both periods the major peripheral powers—India and Indonesia in the postwar; China, Turkey and Japan in the interwar—have had the most eclectic multiple supplier acquisition patterns. This seems to have been reflective of size and associated leverage. In the postwar period positive leverage has sometimes—as in the Middle East—been associated with denying arms to rivals from one's own suppliers. This type of leverage was not possible or was not used in the interwar period, thereby contributing towards multiple supplier relationships in many countries.

In the future it is possible that present trends toward an increase in the number of competitive multiple supplier relationships will be amplified. One might predict this on the basis of the seeming trends towards multipolarity and the decline of ideological totality. Also, the predicted increase in the number of competitive supplier factors in major weapons systems would militate in this direction. There could be an ironic and somewhat unexpected outcome from a reduction of big-power ideological conflict. The increase in the number of countries acquiring arms from both major blocs may exacerbate local arms races, giving leverage to a larger number of countries. Such a trend in Latin America, for instance, could greatly increase the flow of arms into that region, and has already been presaged by the onset of major Soviet arms deliveries to Peru in 1973-1974.[23] And in contrast to the interwar period, the willingness of some major suppliers to give arms away would make such arms races even more uncontrollable.

In the interwar period practically the whole world had become an arena for the arms sales of all major suppliers, private or national. Heretofore, most of Latin America and a large number of nations in Africa and Asia have been spared this situation by the unthinkability of certain client relationships on the basis of ideological incompatibility. This could change. In the past decade there have been strong trends toward a return to the situation of the 1930s. If these trends are further developed, the chances for controlling the arms trade will become much slimmer, other things remaining equal.

THE CONTINUITY OF DONOR-RECIPIENT PATTERNS FROM THE INTERWAR TO THE POSTWAR PERIOD

We have already discussed the continuity of arms trade patterns between the two periods in terms of recipient acquisition styles. A second aspect involves the actual continuity of specific donor-recipient relationships across the two periods, and regional patterns of influence on the part of suppliers and blocs. Clearly, this is but an aspect of the larger question of the regional continuity of diplomatic influence by major powers across the divide of World War II.

Even a cursory examination of the donor-recipient patterns of the two periods would reveal that there has been a profound absence of interperiod continuity in arms supplier relationships.

The greatest continuity is evidenced in those countries of Latin America where American influence has been uninterruptedly strong since the interwar period (although now waning) and in some ex-British and ex-French colonial possessions—now independent nations— where ties have not yet fully been sundered by the forces of nationalism and Marxism.

In some areas, particularly in Eastern Europe and the Middle East, the Soviets in effect filled vacuums left by the defeat and subsequent loss of influence by Germany and Italy. In others—particularly in southern South America—Western influence took up some of the slack left by the withdrawal of the Axis. Mostly, however, it is apparent that many areas in which there was mixed West-Axis influence in the interwar period later fell solely into either the Western or Soviet spheres, although some of these areas are now returning to a cross-bloc pattern.

In Europe, the pattern of extensive cross-bloc competition for arms markets in the 1930s has changed to rigid within-bloc client relationships since 1945, parallel with the diplomatic arrangements within and across the Iron Curtain. In the Middle East, the USSR has simply replaced the Axis powers as a significant supplier of arms in a number of nations while the United States has become a much more significant supplier where its influence had been altogether absent with the exception of Turkey. But, corresponding to overall diplomatic developments, the most significant interperiod change has been the sharp decline of British arms sales in this region at least until very recently, when massive British arms deals with Iran, Egypt and some of the Persian Gulf sheikdoms have begun to reverse this pattern.

In Africa some continuity has been afforded by the lingering hold of client relationships based on previous colonial ties. Britain still dominates the arms markets of Malawi, Gambia, Zambia and Kenya, while competing with the Soviets in Nigeria, Ghana, the Sudan and a few others. France, meanwhile, has clung to more excolonial markets than has Britain, no doubt a reflection of the closer political and economic ties maintained within the French Union. Soviet influence, meanwhile, has either replaced or coexists with that of the excolonial powers in a number of African countries: Mali, Somalia, Guinea, Ghana, Nigeria, Mauritania and the Sudan. Thus, while there is more long-range continuity in this region than elsewhere, the old bonds appear gradually to be dissolving.

Likewise, in Asia present arms client relationships bear little resemblance to the past. India, Pakistan, the nations of Indochina, Thailand, China, Japan, Burma and Ceylon are all involved in supplier relationships which are greatly at variance with those of the 1930s. This is true both of nations then independent and those still in various stages of colonialism.

In short, the arms acquisition patterns of the interwar period have pretty much been obliterated by time and by vast changes in overall diplomatic relationships. It is difficult to cite any case where arms-trading ties have long survived changes in the basic diplomatic context, which is not surprising as they are perhaps the best of all indicators of relations between any pair of countries.

PATTERNS OF ARMS ACQUISITIONS AND
FORMAL ALLIANCES

We have examined donor-recipient patterns somewhat as if they were isolated phenomena, though presumably—at least for the postwar period—the reader will have been able to place these relationships somewhat automatically in a broader context. Nevertheless, one is left with questions about the extent to which these patterns could, in either period, be explained by reference to other traditionally used measures of association. Or, less ambitiously, and without attempting to explain anything, one may still wish to examine the congruity of arms trade patterns with other kinds of ties.

Among the commonly used indicators of the strength of internation ties are formal alliances, overall trade patterns, and memberships and voting patterns in intergovernmental organizations.

Needless to say, an attempt to correlate data in all of these areas with our data on arms flows would be a huge task, and phases in all of these relationships would have to be juxtaposed to the previously indicated shifts of arms acquisition patterns. As we have noted, arms trade patterns tend to fluctuate much more on a year-to-year basis than do overall trade patterns, which tend toward considerable short-run stability.

We did, cursorily, examine some overall trade data for both periods, in League of Nations and United Nations sources.[24] One distinction between the interwar and postwar periods was striking. In the 1930s the United States,

Britain and Germany ranked as the leading exporters—in one order or another—to the vast majority of the world's nations. As with the arms trade, there seems to have been little channeling of overall trade along the lines of ideological relationships, as would be the case after 1945. This brief examination of overall trade data for the 1930s also indicated rather steady patterns from year to year, even in the face of considerable fluctuation in arms client relationships. This has not always been the case in the postwar period. When nations such as Cuba, the UAR, Syria and others have become Soviet arms clients their overall trade has tended to change accordingly and drastically.

Closer analysis of the relationship between arms trade and overall trade patterns might, however, have proved interesting in one respect. There is an old maxim about "trade following the flag." In a pure sense, movement of the flag has referred to conquest, colonization or some level of imperial control. One might, however, think of arms sales as one other important way of showing the flag, and it might be interesting to know whether arms sales have tended to precede—and in a sense cause—overall trading relationships, or the reverse. One suspects that this relationship is not a clear one and that examples could be found indicating precedence in either direction. In the recent past, Soviet arms deals with some of the aforementioned countries appear to have been opening wedges for larger trading relationships. Likewise, the French now seem to be using arms deals in the Middle East as a door-opener for broader economic influence, particularly with respect to oil concessions.[25] Of course, to the extent that arms deals often involve barter or some expectation of reciprocity, the import of weapons by a nation will often automatically steer its exports towards the arms supplier. This has been true of many recent Soviet clients. In the interwar period, German imports of raw materials were often linked to arms deals in a period of blocked currencies.

For a brief foray into the connection between arms transactions and other measures of internation association, we may, however, examine congruence with formal alliances. One obvious hypothesis emerges here from a comparison of the two periods by our systems variables. The arms trade patterns of the postwar period should, clearly, have been more congruent with formal alliances in a period of seemingly greater politicization of the arms trade. That is, the cluster of factors operating in the 1930s should have lent themselves to a more random pattern of arms flows which could not be related too closely to the network of formal alliances because of the relative absence of governmental constraints on arms sales.

There are some problems in defining what constitutes an alliance, or the real meaning of a given alliance. Their mere existence is sometimes obscure or arguable. Also, there are different types of alliances, with differing implications for arms transfers.

Singer and Small, in their compilation of alliances for the interwar and still earlier periods, divided them into three categories running along a continuum from defense pacts, to neutrality and nonaggression pacts, to mere ententes or consultative agreements. That is, alliances were divided into categories indicating degrees of military commitment, and implicitly, closeness of ties which ought to be relatively important in terms of arms-trading ties.[26]

Another problem in dealing with the juxtaposition of alliance patterns to those of arms transfers is posed by identifying terminations of the former. Many alliances are not formally terminated either at the time their original intent or spirit fades or when new relationships are formed. A case in point is the recent relationship of Pakistan to SEATO. The CENTO organization, formed in the heyday of Dulles' "pactomania," is still another example of a formal treaty never having been abrogated despite its having become effectively defunct.

In the interwar period, particularly in the couple of years preceding the outbreak of war, nonaggression pacts and consultative agreements appear to have been signed almost indiscriminately. This appears to have reflected the propaganda warfare and diplomatic shifts of that twilight period in which many nations were maneuvering to avoid being odd man out in case of war. Some of these agreements—such as the Franco-German alliance of 1938—appear in retrospect to have been little more than eyewash, or temporary promises by would-be aggressors not to attack other signees until other victims had been devoured. At any rate, one would not expect these alliances to be reflected in arms client relationships, and generally they were not. The Soviet Union, in particular, seems to have specialized in rather meaningless nonaggression pacts during this period.

We shall discuss the juxtaposition of alliances and arms transfers for the two periods by regions. Most of the alliances in both periods have been regional in any case. Two pertinent problems bear examination here. One has to do with the relationship between suppliers and recipients—i.e., the congruence of formal alliances with different acquisition styles, namely, those of sole, dominant and multiple supplier. A second question bears on the extent to which arms-dependent members of regional alliances tend to acquire their arms either from the same or different sources, within or across major power alliance blocs.

Interwar Alliances and the Arms Trade: Analysis by Regions[27]

Latin America.   In the 1930s, as later, the network of formal alliances in Latin America was a comparatively simple one. It evolved in two stages. First, in 1933, a nonaggression pact was signed by a number of countries: Argentina, Brazil, Chile, Mexico, Paraguay and Uruguay. Colombia and Panama joined this pact in 1934 and 1936, respectively. Then, in 1936, a consultative pact was formed by the entire body of Western Hemisphere nations, headed by the United States, a precursor to those signed after World War II.

In juxtaposition to arms acquisitions in Latin America in the 1930s, what stands out is the absence of any formal alliance ties in Latin America with the Axis nations. Oddly, the broad alliance of 1936 was signed just when Germany and Italy were beginning to make serious inroads into the Latin American arms markets, a trend which accelerated up to about 1939. It was also a period of considerable Axis economic penetration into this region.

On the face of it, one might assume that the alliance formed in 1936, of consultative nature only, was not of great import given the spheres of influence achieved by those nations against whom the alliance was presumably directed. But there is some tendency for the nations which formed the earlier—1933—nonaggression pact to have constituted a subgrouping within Latin America. As a group, with the exception of Mexico, they were later to go relatively further toward becoming Axis arms clients. On the other hand, a number of nations in this region who were not parties to the 1933 pact—Ecuador, Venezuela, Bolivia, Nicaragua and El Salvador—were also later to exhibit strong cross-bloc acquisition patterns.

The Middle East.   Among the small number of truly independent Middle Eastern states in the 1930s there was a rather complex set of interlocking alliances. The northern tier states of Afghanistan, Iraq, Iran and Turkey were tied in pairs by bilateral pacts which were combined into a multilateral nonaggression pact in force from 1937 to 1939. In addition, Afghanistan and Persia were involved in nonaggression pacts with the Soviet Union dating back to 1926 and 1927, respectively. Meanwhile, Iraq and Egypt were tied to Britain by defense pacts in 1932 and 1936, respectively, in the wake of the granting of nominal independence in exchange for basing rights. Finally, Turkey, tied to the other regional states by various agreements, was also involved in a web of extraregional pacts. It had a nonaggression pact with the Soviets from 1925 to 1939, a defense pact with Greece, Romania and Yugoslavia, and nonaggression pacts with Italy, Hungary, Bulgaria and France.

In the northern tier group, each of the four nations exhibited some cross-bloc arms acquisitions. In Turkey's case this accorded with its complex alliance arrangements and with similar cross-bloc acquisition patterns of its alliance partners in the Balkans. Many nations in the Near East appear to have been hedging their bets during this period. Iraq's arms purchases from Italy, despite its defense pact with Britain, are more difficult to explain, as are Iran's purchases in the face of its close (although not formalized in an alliance) ties to Britain.

Asia and the Far East.   In Asia there was little alliance formation during this period. The only ones were Japan's adherence to the Axis Pact in 1936, China's nonaggression pact with the USSR in 1937 and the latter's alliance with Mongolia in the same year.

As Japan was, for the most part, independent in arms production by the late 1930s, its pact with the Axis was not too significant in terms of arms transfers, although there was some shifting from Western sources to Germany for aircraft engine acquisitions. China's alliance with the Soviets, however, a nonaggression pact, was accompanied by extensive arms transactions. After 1937 Russia replaced the Axis powers in the Chinese arms market, although China continued to rely simultaneously on the United States, with whom there was no alliance.

Sub-Saharan Africa.   In Sub-Saharan Africa during this period colonial ties prevailed. There were no apparent alliances tying the two then independent nations—Ethiopia and Liberia—to outside powers. And Ethiopia, in the period up to its demise in 1935, was the only independent nation in this region to receive major weapons systems from outside powers.

Europe.   There were major contradictions between the arms trade patterns of Europe in the 1930s and corresponding networks of formal alliances.

The ostensible hinge of the anti-German status quo coalition was France's ties with Poland and the Little Entente (Czechoslovakia, Romania, Yugoslavia), with the latter arrangement having also been directed at potential Hungarian or Austrian revisionism. French ties with these Eastern European states would appear to have been strategically sound and, in fact, were backed up by considerable arms transfers and licensing agreements. Toward the end of the period, however, this ring around Germany began to break down because of Czecho-Polish antagonism, the vitiation of the thrust of these arrangements after Locarno and the installation of fascist-type regimes all over Eastern Europe except in Czechoslovakia.

Consequently, the other members of what was ostensibly a French alliance system in Eastern Europe became arms clients of the Axis powers as well as of the West, with France a diminishing factor due also to the faltering of its arms industries. The diplomatic shift by Yugoslavia was actually registered by a nonaggression pact with Italy in 1937. Poland alone remained an arms client of France during the whole of the 1930s, even in the face of a pact with Nazi Germany in 1934.

The Soviet Union signed a host of nonaggression pacts in Europe during this period. Among the cosignees were Turkey, Germany (first up to 1936), Lithuania, Finland, Latvia, Estonia, Poland, Italy and Czechoslovakia. Of these, only Turkey was a significant customer for Russian weapons, although the Czechs did seek last minute succor just prior to the Munich debacle, while Poland, Latvia, Lithuania and Finland all purchased small lots of Soviet arms. Germany and Russia were, of course, involved in some exchanges of military equipment in the post-Rapallo period, perhaps extending through about 1930.[28] And Russia's pact with Italy in the early 1930s was reflected in extensive shipments of arms from the latter to the former.

One alliance which related closely to arms flows was that signed by Austria, Hungary and Italy in 1934 and terminated in 1938. It was accompanied by considerable arms supplies flowing from Italy to the other two, both of which continued throughout the period simultaneously to purchase arms from Western and neutral sources.

In the Baltic there was a consultative pact between Estonia, Latvia and Lithuania. Their arms acquisitions were not, however, similar or coordinated. The first two used Britain as a primary source, while Lithuania spread its bets between the Axis and the Soviet Union.

In summarizing the interwar alliance and arms trade nexus it appears that alliances did not, generally, parallel arms client relationships. In many cases—in Latin America, the Middle East and Europe—arms supplier relationships appear to have existed almost in defiance of crazy-quilt and fast-changing alliance ties. To a great extent the then lack of substance to what were to become the wartime Western and Axis alliances seems explanatory. These alliances were primarily incipient up to the outbreak of war, and there were no strong ties to either side on the part of most peripheral states.

Postwar Alliances and the Arms Trade: Analysis by Regions[29]

Latin America. The postwar alliance system in Latin America has been similar to that of the interwar period, excepting the anomalous situation of Cuba since 1960. In the immediate aftermath of World War II the entire hemisphere was drawn together under the American umbrella in the collective security arrangements embodied in the Chapultepec Agreement and the Rio Treaty.

Despite recent trends toward multiple within-bloc acquisition patterns, signalling the demise of the United States as an overwhelmingly dominant force in Latin American arms markets, the situation has been markedly different from that in the 1930s. Guatemala's brief period of acquiring arms from the Soviets in 1954, before the CIA-inspired counterrevolution, had been the only case of cross-bloc arms acquisition other than Cuba before 1973. Recently, large shipments of Soviet tanks and other equipment to Peru appeared to signal the introduction of cross-bloc rivalry to the region.

The Middle East. In this region, the interrelationship of arms acquisition patterns and alliance arrangements has been—and remains—quite complex.

Formally, the CENTO pact remains in force, although its scope has recently been further reduced by the formal withdrawal of Pakistan after the disastrous Bangladesh war. Turkey, Iran and Pakistan have also had bilateral defense treaties with the United States to underscore the intent of CENTO. As previously indicated Pakistan and Iran have, nevertheless, acquired some arms from the Soviet bloc, albeit on a small scale in the case of the latter. Originally, the British role in CENTO was supposed to have been enabled by its presence in Cyprus, which has become a Soviet arms client, further vitiating the earlier intended role of the alliance.

Despite its preeminent role as supplier of arms to the left-leaning Arab states faced off against Israel, the Soviets, until very recently, have not had formal military alliances in this area, although there have been "treaties of friendship" with Iraq and the UAR.

Britain, meanwhile, does have extant treaties with Malta, Cyprus, Bahrein, Quatar, the Trucial States and Libya. It remains the primary arms supplier to the Persian Gulf States and is an increasingly significant supplier to Egypt and Saudi Arabia. Its alliances with Libya and Cyprus would appear effectively to have withered, as evidenced by their very contrary arms acquisition patterns.

All of the Arab states are tied together by the defense arrangements built into the Arab League. Indeed, all of these nations did formally declare war on Israel in 1967, and again in 1973, although for many of them nothing more than a gesture was involved. Within the Arab League, however, different adherents have had varying arms acquisition patterns. As in the interwar period, within-region alliances have been combined with both cross-bloc and within-bloc arms acquisition patterns of all sorts. Syria, Iraq, the UAR, the Sudan, the Yemens and Libya have taken arms from the Soviets, with several of these nations having also purchased arms from Western sources, particularly France. Jordan, Lebanon, Saudi Arabia and Kuwait have been Western clients, while Morocco and Mauritania have had simultaneous cross-bloc supplier relationships. There have been some similarities between the present external orientation of this region and the balance which existed in the 1930s between British and Axis influence.

Sub-Saharan Africa.   All of the states in this region are members of the OAU, begun in 1963, and which has a Defense Commission that has been of seemingly negligible import up to now. At this level, the connection between alliances and arms acquisition patterns has been very weak.

Otherwise, there has been considerable congruence between arms client patterns and alliances, perhaps more than in other regions. In particular, there has been a close fit between arms acquisitions and the system of pacts tying individual French-speaking nations to the excolonial power. France has remained the primary armorer of Cameroon, Chad, Dahomey, Ivory Coast, Niger, Malagasy, Senegal, Togo, Upper Volta and the Central African Republic, to all of whom she is formally allied. There have been a few breaks in the monotony of this pattern. Within the "Union Africaine and Malagache," Congo-Brazzaville and Mauritania have acquired some arms from the Soviet bloc, and Rwanda from the United States. Congo-Brazzaville and Mauritania also have bilateral ties with France, despite their partial arms dependence on the Soviets.

Britain has had pacts only with Uganda and Kenya among its former colonies. Clearly, it has not held onto its former ties with the same tenacity as France. The pact with Kenya has been backed up with a predominant arms supplier relationship, while that with Uganda has been broken by Soviet inroads. Britain does not have formal alliances with other excolonies to whom she still remains the primary arms supplier—i.e., Gambia, Malawi and Zambia.

The Soviet Union has not had formal alliance ties with any of its African clients—Guinea, Mali, Somalia, Ghana, Tanzania, Mauritania and Uganda. However, some of the major Soviet clients were tied together by the Casablanca Pact grouping in 1961. The UAR and Morocco were also signees, which probably relates to the shift of Morocco at that time from dependence on American arms to mixed dependence on both superpowers.

Otherwise, south of the Sahara, bilateral alliances formed in the early 1960s by Ethiopia and Kenya and by Gambia and Senegal appear to have run across the lines of British and French arms supplier ties, reflecting mere propinquity.

Asia and the Far East.   On the noncommunist side, the primary alliance in this region has been the moribund SEATO arrangement, originally including the United States, Australia, New Zealand, Britain, France, Pakistan, Thailand and the Philippines, with stipulations providing for consultation in the case of aggression against the three states of Indochina. Since its signing, Britain and France have more or less disengaged, while Pakistan has dropped out. With respect to arms shipments, the primary linkage is with American arms supply predominance in the Philippines and Thailand as well as in Australia and New Zealand. Pakistan, again, has turned elsewhere.

Within the Anglo-Malaysian Defense Agreement, and a coordinate arrangement called ANZAM in which Britain, Australia and New Zealand coordinate defense policy in the Malaysian area, Britain has been a significant but not altogether dominant arms supplier to Malaysia and Singapore, rivalled now by the French. Otherwise, strong congruence between arms transfers and alliances has been exhibited in American relationships with the Philippines, South Korea and Taiwan, and Soviet relationships with North Korea and Mongolia.

Neither Burma nor Indonesia, both very eclectic cross-bloc acquirers of weapons, have been tied by alliance. This has also been the case for India throughout most of the postwar period, during its phase of avowed neutralism. More recently, a pact with the Soviets would appear to indicate a swing to one side, highlighted by the increasing dependence of India on Soviet weapons, some of which—including the MIG-21 fighter—are now being license-produced, and also by India's giving the Soviet Navy valuable basing rights on the Indian Ocean.

Europe.   The facts of the postwar European alliance networks are too well known to warrant further exploration here. Both NATO and the Warsaw Pact have been closely tied together by coordinated weapons development and production arrangements. There has been no evidence of conflict between arms supplier relationships and alliances in this region, in contrast to the very complicated crosscutting patterns of the 1930s. Cross-bloc acquisition patterns have been evidenced only by the buffer states of Austria, Yugoslavia and Finland. Spain's extra-NATO defense arrangements with the United States have been backed up by massive arms supplies, although with increasing recent competition from France.

Summary

We may attempt to summarize these relationships by looking at the alliance behavior of nations in both periods which have been respectively in sole, predominant and multiple supplier patterns. Analysis along these lines is made difficult by the segmented or phased nature of many of the arms client relationships, and because the tenure of alliances has often covered only a portion of the diplomatic periods.

First, let us look at the sole and predominant supplier relationships, where we would expect—if anywhere—close alliance ties. In the interwar period, 14 of the 21 dependent nations in these categories were tied to the supplier nation by formal alliance. Each of the nations tied closely by arms transactions to the United States, France and Italy was also formally allied to its supplier. Britain, however, was in alliance with only five of the eleven countries for which it was a dominant arms supplier, with Portugal, Latvia, Greece, Estonia, Eire and Saudi Arabia the exceptions. Likewise, Germany had no alliance with Bulgaria, where its arms were dominant.

In the postwar period up to 1968, of those 51 nations outside of NATO and the Warsaw Pact which have had sole or predominant supplier relationships with one or the other major power, 32 have had alliances with them. The exceptions were Rwanda and Ethiopia for the United States; Malawi, Gambia, Rhodesia, Zambia and Ceylon for the United Kingdom; and Afghanistan, Guinea, Yemen, North Vietnam, Mali, Cuba, Syria, Algeria, Cyprus, the UAR, Iraq and Somalia for the USSR. As in the interwar period, Britain seems to have had a high percentage of close arms client relationships which have not corresponded to formal alliances, for reasons not at all clear. Meanwhile, the Soviets, who in the interwar period were signing alliances with everyone in sight, including some which were patently absurd, seem to have been cautious in openly formalizing what have clearly been close relationships as measured by arms transactions. Perhaps what this adds up to is that various nations, at different times, for reasons which may not be obvious, will have differing proclivities toward formal alliance formation, although not toward close association as measured by other criteria.

The percentage of dependent nations in either period in sole or predominant supplier relationships which have corresponded to alliances has been quite similar: 63 and 67 percent. Differences emerge, however, in comparisons of within-bloc and cross-bloc multiple supplier relationships. In the interwar period some 60 percent of those nations in these acquisition patterns were allied with one or more of the major supplier nations at some point. In multiple supplier, cross-bloc relationships, the figures were high partly because of the large number of Latin American nations—formally allied to the United States—whose arms acquisitions fit this pattern, although there were also a number of European nations in this situation.

In the postwar period the percentage of nations in multiple supplier relationships, within- and cross-bloc, which have been in alliance with one or more of the major powers has been much smaller, around 33 and 21 percent, respectively. The reason is that the postwar sample of nations includes so many Third World countries, many of which have insisted upon—or have been forced into by geography—a formally neutralist posture which was apparently less frequent in the 1930s, partly because most independent nations were in close proximity to major powers.

Chapter Five

A Comparison of the Use of Transfer Modes in Two Diplomatic Periods

Up to now we have been treating all arms transfers as if they were an undifferentiated mass of transactions. Actually, the notion of weapons transfer subsumes a multiplicity of mechanisms or vehicles by which weapons technology is diffused. Hence the virtually self-explanatory term transfer mode which has come into recent vogue among arms trade analysts.[1]

In turn, the varying use of different transfer modes may have important diplomatic implications, often being indicative of the closeness of ties between donors and recipients and of degrees of technological dependence by the latter on the former. And, as we shall see, our analysis here leads into that on weapons-producing independence, since some nonexport transfer mechanisms have been used as halfway houses on the road to self-sufficiency. We shall proceed to examine how the use of these various mechanisms has varied between our two diplomatic periods and how some important long-run changes can be explained by our systems variables.

Transfer modes can be viewed along two separate, crosscutting dimensions. One describes the source or destination of arms transfers as either governmental or private and has been touched upon before in our discussion of controls over their destination. There are government-to-government transactions, private-governmental transactions in either direction and others which involve only private entities at both ends. In reality, of course, many transactions are difficult to so characterize, as they involve mixed participation by both private and government bodies. Nowadays, most transactions are effectively government-to-government, regardless of the source of the arms or of their financing. A shipment of arms from an armaments manufacturer to a foreign government or group is normally within the decision-making purview of the supplier government, although some initiative for the sale may have originated with the manufacturer.

Along another dimension, there is a continuum of transfer mechanisms which involve varying technological input by donors and recipients. This continuum runs from straight export through licensing, off-shore assembly and the activities of arms corporations' subsidiaries in foreign countries, and through coproduction, codevelopment, stealing, copying, loaning, retransfer and the transnational movement of arms technicians. We shall first define and describe each of these, illustrating with examples, and then proceed to compare their use in the interwar and postwar periods. However, it should be made clear that the identification of any given arms transfer within one of these categories is often not easy. Many transactions involve mixed, simultaneous use of two or more transfer modes, as for example when a weapons system first licensed from one country to another is subsequently retransferred to or copied by a third.

Straight export sale is the most common form of transfer, as when the United States sells Phantom jets to Great Britain for cash. Of course, not all export transfers are for full cash value. There is a continuum here from trade to aid, with intermediate situations entailing loans, barter or trade-offs for base rights or other items of exchange. All of these transfer mechanisms are, however, on one end of a continuum describing degrees of technological input by the recipient. Research, development and production of the weapons are all conducted solely by the supplier nation.

Next, there are the sometimes overlapping categories of licensing and overseas assembly. Licensing entails the sale of the technology itself—i.e., patents, blueprints and production methods. The research and development having been conducted in the donor country, rights are then purchased by the recipient, which carries out the production work. Some present examples are the licensing of M-60 tanks by the United States to Italy and of Mirage jets from France to Switzerland.

An intermediate category between straight export and licensing involves final assembly of finished parts by the recipient nation. Actually, there are numerous cases of mixed use of licensing and assembly, with the recipient nation manufacturing some parts on license and importing others for final assembly. Often a recipient will build an airframe on license, but import the engine, which is the most difficult aircraft component for which to develop indigenous manufacturing capability. A present example is the production of MIG-21 fighters by India, which apparently is able to produce some but not all of its parts.

In some cases, two or more countries will agree jointly to produce and/or develop a weapons system. Where the research and development work originates in one country, and where the production is then conducted in others as well, it is usually referred to as coproduction. This concept is sometimes used almost coterminously with licensing, usually distinguished only by the original simultaneity of joint production, although it also refers to arrangements in which two or more nations divide production of components for a system. A current example is provided by the new Mirage fighter being produced jointly by France and Belgium. The growing use of such arrangements in the armaments field is merely a subset of broader trends emerging with the growth of multinational corporations.

In still other cases, in what is a rapidly burgeoning contemporary phenomenon, the research and development as well as the production of a system becomes the object of joint effort, so that the system ceases to have a clear original national identity. The present joint effort by Britain and France on the Jaguar strike fighter is an example. Here, one can hardly speak of an actual weapons transfer between the participating nations, although, as we shall see, there may be novel implications for subsequent transfers to third parties.

There are other more seldomly used mechanisms, some of which have been of great importance in specific situations. In the interwar period it was a common practice for some nations to buy up single units of given weapons systems and then to copy and produce them in large quantities. This apparently allowed for avoidance of licensing fees, albeit with the handicap of working without actual blueprints. Both Russia and Japan built whole air forces in the 1930s by this method. And, of course, weapons systems can often be copied without first purchasing a unit, either from captured weapons or by espionage. In still other cases usable quantities of weapons will be stolen or captured. The Israelis have stolen gunboats previously ordered from—and then embargoed by—the French from Cherbourg harbor, and have also incorporated a sizeable force of Soviet tanks captured in the 1967 and 1973 wars into their order of battle.

Still another way in which arms technology has been diffused is by the emigration of arms technicians. In the Renaissance, Spain, weak in indigenous arms technology, imported large numbers of armorers from the Low Countries in an attempt to compete with Britain and Sweden.[2] As we shall see, this form of transfer is not often evidenced nowadays, although there have been a few interesting contemporary cases.

Finally, there are retransfers and loans. Retransfer has been a very frequent and important mechanism in both the interwar and postwar periods. And, of course, one can point to numerous cases where weapons have been retransferred more than once. Referring to our continuum describing relative technological input by donor and recipient, the retransfer mechanism is unique in there being no such input on either end of the transaction, except where the supplier is itself a licensee. The donor is usually merely a conduit for arms developed and produced by an original supplier. The loaning out of weapons systems, meanwhile, is a seemingly newly developed transfer mode with only a few cases identifiable to date. It may become still more significant in the future.

Again, we stress that many arms transactions involve complex combinations of two or more transfer mechanisms. Let us cite some examples. The United States has licensed Agusta Bell helicopters to Italy, some of which later were retransferred to Israel. Israel has assembled French Magister trainers, some of which later were retransferred to sub-Saharan African nations. In the 1930s the Soviets copied several American combat aircraft models, some of which were later sold to Czechoslovakia, then captured by the Germans and subsequently sold or given to Bulgaria. There were transfers of aircraft from Germany to Chile in the late 1930s which involved essentially German-designed craft mounting Wright Cyclone engines originally licensed from the United States. In some cases, captured arms have been copied and then mass-produced, as with recent Israeli production of Soviet Katyusha rockets.

The possible combinations of the use of mixed transfer modes are legion. We shall, nevertheless, discuss each important identifiably discrete transfer mechanism in turn in an attempt to draw some generalizations about how their use has varied between our two periods.

THE VARYING USE OF ARMS AID AND TRADE BETWEEN PERIODS

It would be impossible, within space limitations, to analyze the policies of all of the major suppliers in both periods on the distribution of their transfers between cash sales, outright aid or various intermediary hybrid situations of long-term loans at low interest rates (many of which are never repaid), barter for raw materials or exchanges for basing rights. Indeed, as we have indicated, the virtual impossibility of identifying individual transfers in these categories was one good reason for our not using monetary value to measure the volume of arms transactions. Much of this information remains in the realm of more or less secret diplomacy, as Thayer has pointed out in his analysis of the Pentagon-Eximbank complex prior to 1967.[3]

There is, however, one marked difference between our two periods which is clear beyond any qualification stemming from inadequacy of data. In the interwar period there was practically no such thing as military grants and aid.[4] Indeed, our research was able to uncover no more than a few clear-cut cases where arms apparently were being transferred free of cost. One was in the early 1920s, when the French lavished quantities of World War I surplus equipment on the Poles, who under Weygand's direction were then attempting to stem the westward tide of bolshevism. Later, during the Spanish Civil War, it was apparent that many of the German, Italian and Soviet arms shipments were gratis to the recipients, although the financial details were not clear from our sources. Then, in the late 1930s, the Germans apparently offered outright military aid to Argentina and perhaps to other South American countries. With Argentina, these overtures were rebuffed because of the political strings attached. The Axis powers were, however, able to make considerable use of loan and barter deals in Latin America during that period. There may well have been a small handful of other cases of military aid, although we were unable to identify them.

The reasons for the absence of significant military aid during the interwar period are not readily apparent. One might speculate that governments then were reluctant to enter into an area where the prerogatives of arms-dealing corporations had long been established by tradition. Or, one can merely point to the virtual absence of the hegemonic arms supplier policies attributed to the major powers in the postwar period by the SIPRI study. Even the Soviets, as far as one can tell, were not nearly as charitable with gifts of arms during the 1930s as they later would be after 1955, although in the earlier period their activities were obviously limited by production capacity.[5]

In the postwar period outright arms aid has become an important instrument for the spreading and maintaining of diplomatic influence. Vast stores have been given away free of charge or at very low cost. Most of the arms aid has been donated by the United States and USSR, with the other major supplier nations having more usually pursued an industrial policy. As we shall discuss in our concluding chapter, these trends have presented new barriers to the chances for instituting controls on arms flows for now even the economic constraints which had previously kept the lid on their overall volume have evaporated.

Actually, the postwar policies of the USSR and the United States have trended in curiously opposite directions. Earlier in the postwar period it had been the United States (and also Britain) which had most readily contributed arms aid, spurred by mountains of World War II surplus. Later, with the advent of the Kennedy era and the installation of Henry Kuss as America's supersalesman of arms, a virtual volte face was executed which resulted in a greater emphasis on sales. The alleviation of balance of payments deficits came to match in importance the arming of allies around the Sino-Soviet periphery.[6]

The Soviets, on the other hand, appear to have moved somewhat in the opposite direction. Once insistent upon economic payment of some kind—such as the absurdity of the long-term mortgaging of cotton crops in Egypt and the Sudan for earlier arms deals—the Soviets now appear to have moved toward arms giveaways at least where payment is not realistic or where returns are otherwise high.[7] Soviet arms deliveries to some Arab nations after 1967 quite clearly were not being paid for fully except by the exchange value of the basing rights so crucial to Soviet naval expansion policy along the Mediterranean-Red Sea-Indian Ocean littoral, although there were indications that replacement shipments during and after the 1973 conflict were being paid for by oil revenues. In another relative reversal by the two superpowers, the Soviets have recently emphasized arms aid over economic aid, while the United States has seemed to move the other way. The lesson of India's gravitation toward its arms supplier—and away from its agricultural provider—after 1965 has doubtless not been lost on the Kremlin.[8]

Outright arms aid in the postwar period has pretty much been a two nation game, despite some gifts by Britain and France. Britain gave some military aid to Greece, Turkey, Jordan and Lebanon in the early postwar years as did France to some of the smaller African states. Mostly, though, the middle-range powers have been constrained to pursue an industrial policy to finance the maintenance of indigenous arms industries.[9] Curiously, the pursuit of such a policy without political strings can be quite successful, as it has been in Latin America where some nations have apparently grown weary of American nagging over their arms acquisitions.[10]

A COMPARISON OF THE INTERWAR AND POSTWAR NETWORKS FOR THE VARIOUS TRANSFER MODES

Licensing

An analysis of licensing ought, we suppose, to begin with an examination of why either the respective donors or recipients choose this mechanism over straight export. Normally there are mutual advantages, although in some cases one side may successfully insist on licensing, and in others the transaction may be linked to trade-offs in other areas of a relationship. Basically, however, we may separate the criteria for the choice of a licensing arrangement into economic and political aspects.

On the economic side, there is an unfortunate paucity of available information on the comparative costs for donors and recipients. It is not even clear just how the amount of payment for a license is normally arrived at. Apparently this can vary between a lump payment for the transfer of technology and an agreed sum per item of a system produced by the recipient.[11] In the interwar period at least, the latter method was apparently most common, according to some discussion in the military intelligence files.

For the recipient, the unit costs of licensing a system may or may not be less than in importing. This will depend on the number of systems eventually produced. For the donor, overall profits are presumably usually lower in licensing deals. However, licensing permits entry into a foreign market at minimal investment cost, and there may sometimes be economic benefits to the donor in that it may not want continuously to adjust its production facilities to accommodate foreign demand. For the recipient, the desire to maintain employment in its arms industries is an additional economic factor. And it may wish, despite becoming dependent on foreign weapons technology, to keep its hand in the arms business and to maintain, thereby, a viable establishment of weapons engineers and technicians. In Japan and Germany, licensing has allowed retention of arms industry bases which could be expanded if necessary, forming nuclei for research and development work which could then lead to production of indigenous systems.

For France in the immediate postwar period licensing was conducted on the base of a declining arms industry which later was revived. For developing nations licensing may be the first step toward independent capability in design and development. India and Israel have moved along these lines, first licensing systems from major powers and then beginning to develop their own.[12] The same basic pattern was followed by Japan and Russia in the interwar years.

Actually, the web of interlocking licensing agreements among the NATO nations since the 1950s must be viewed in the context of requirements for logistical coordination as well as on a sheer economic basis. Licensing agreements have been one aspect of a thrust toward integrated force structures and interchangeable weapons systems. Mostly, the transfer of technology has been unidirectional, from the United States to Europe, although this has begun to change in recent years.[13]

There is also a prestige factor in a recipient's decision to license. Some nations may eschew heavy reliance on licensing because of a feeling that a blow to their prestige will result from having their forces armed with another nation's products. France has sometimes appeared to be affected by such considerations in recent years. However, on a more objective basis, and given the fact that end-use restrictions are usually tied to licensing agreements, it is clear that a nation such as France which wishes to pursue an independent foreign policy will be better served by a fully independent arms development base.[14]

There is still another political aspect to the choice of licensing—that of the subjective degree of the visibility of transfers. A supplier may feel, particularly where it is a reluctant supplier and where a recipient has low leverage, that extending licensing agreements may be less unsettling to rivals of the recipient than outright exports. In recent years both the United States and France have licensed weapons systems to Israel—in the latter case despite an announced embargo—seemingly under the assumption that this would be less aggravating to the Arabs than the export shipment of the same systems.[15] It makes it appear that the Israelis are producing their own arms. We have previously noted a similar technique for achieving low visibility with the use of third nations as retransfer conduits, even where—as with Soviet shipments to Egypt in 1955—the real origin of the arms is readily apparent to all concerned.

What then are some of the assumptions with which one might approach the comparative use of licensing between our two periods? How might the networks of licensing agreements have been expected to vary with our systems variables?

At first, one might expect there to have been more licensing with rigid bipolarity and relative stability of alliance systems. In particular, one might expect there to have been more licensing by essentially middle-range powers which are capable of license-production and which will see no need for costly development programs of their own so long as they are tied to a hegemonic alliance leader.

Few nations would be imagined to wish to license arms, particularly new technology, to allies or friends whose allegiance is not entirely secure, as the diffusion of technology, once accomplished, cannot be recalled. The Soviets must, in recent years, have rued their earlier generosity in licensing most of their advanced systems to China. A number of interwar Western nations must have been similarly chagrined by 1941 over licensing to Japan. Supplier nations will not want to issue licenses unless fairly well assured that end-use restrictions will be honored. There is an element of trust to this and that trust may be breached if donor-recipient relations cool off. China has not only made continuing use of Russian licenses, but has also sold these licensed systems to Pakistan, the rival of an important Soviet client.[16]

Generally, then, licensing arrangements should be reflective of close and expectedly stable relationships. If multipolarity or a more fluid alliance system would be expected to restrict the extent of licensing, however, the kind of private discretion exercised in the 1930s would be expected to have militated in the opposite direction. Logic then would predict that the relative extent of licensing—similar to the relative extent of multiple sources of acquisition—would have been the result of counterbalancing tendencies.

There is also a technological aspect to these questions to be examined later in greater detail. With the passage of time, the gradually increasing technological capability of smaller nations, reflected in their ability to conduct licensed production, will be balanced by more stringent technological requirements.

Because of the composition of our two samples of recipient nations, it would not make sense to compare the two periods by the overall percentages of arms transfers accounted for by licensing agreements. Our interwar sample is global, including all of the European nations, while our postwar recipients consist mostly of developing nations. Clearly, comparative analysis would only be afforded if we had data on the numbers of systems transferred within NATO and the Warsaw Pact by licensing. In the absence of such information, it will still be worthwhile to examine these questions for the interwar period alone, to gain some picture of the importance of the licensing mechanism, assuming that it has not varied drastically between our two periods.[17]

In Table 5-1 we have determined, for eight of our major weapons systems, the relative number of transfers accounted for by licensing by major interwar supplier nations. In the categories of transport and supply ships, and for utility aircraft, licensing was not sufficiently significant to warrant inclusion.

Several points emerge from these data on interwar licensing. One is that licensing accounted for a fairly significant proportion of the total transfers during that period, averaging near 20 percent for categories other than warships and submarines. Second, licensing was most frequently used in the aircraft categories, next most frequently in armor and least in the naval categories, excepting patrol boats. One reason there was less licensing of ships was that a number of middle-range powers—Sweden, Denmark, Norway, Holland—which license-built most of their aircraft, were simultaneously able independently to design and construct their own naval craft.

Table 5-1. Transfers Accounted for by Licensing, Interwar Suppliers (percent)

Supplier Nation	Combat Aircraft	Transport Aircraft	Trainer Aircraft	Tanks	Armored Cars	Submarines	Warships	Patrol Vessels
Czechoslovakia	31.4	0.0	67.1	14.8	0.0	0.0	0.0	0.0
France	26.3	0.0	13.8	10.5	0.0	0.0	61.5	0.0
Italy	2.1	0.0	41.1	0.0	0.0	0.0	0.0	69.9
Netherlands	31.7	0.0	0.0	0.0	0.0	0.0	0.0	0.0
Sweden	40.4	0.0	0.0	24.6	0.0	0.0	0.0	0.0
United Kingdom	34.5	100.0	25.4	16.9	0.8	27.8	15.8	11.3
United States	8.5	15.2	12.0	52.3	69.4	0.0	0.0	0.0
Poland	68.6	0.0	0.0	0.0	0.0	0.0	0.0	0.0
Germany	23.8	27.6	49.5	0.0	0.0	50.0	0.0	0.0
All Suppliers	17.5	21.0	23.8	17.0	15.7	7.6	11.8	23.4

As one might expect, licensing was most frequent in those weapons requiring the least technological sophistication, namely, trainer aircraft and patrol boats. This held true consistently within the categories of aircraft, armor and ships.

Only some of the active interwar arms suppliers were involved in licensing: Czechoslovakia, France, Italy, Netherlands, Sweden, the United States, Poland and Germany. Others—the USSR, Belgium, Canada, Switzerland and Japan—were not at all active. Of these, however, only the USSR and Japan were really significant independent designers of their own equipment, and they were themselves primarily on the receiving end of licensing agreements up to the late 1930s while striving for self-sufficiency. With the USSR, however, traditional extreme cautiousness in exporting technology may have been an important factor and has still been the case in the postwar period. Since 1945 the Soviets have engaged in only a few licensing agreements—in Yugoslovia and India—outside the zone of their tight political control.

In Table 5-2 we have listed the major licensing agreements for the interwar period by suppliers.[18] In conjunction with the data in Table 5-1, it can be seen that the licensing propensities of major suppliers varied somewhat, and in turn varied greatly between major weapons categories.

In aircraft, Britain, Germany and Czechoslovakia licensed a relatively high proportion of their transfers, while the United States was a reluctant licensor, as was Italy except in trainer aircraft. For the United States the explanation is fairly clear. The bulk of its interwar aircraft transfers were to non-European clients, with sales concentrated in Latin America, China, Thailand and Turkey. These nations simply had less capacity for license-production than did those European nations essentially dependent on other major European suppliers. Britain, particularly its Hawker Aircraft Company, licensed a fairly high proportion of its aircraft transfers, most significantly to Belgium, Sweden, Denmark, Norway, Czechoslovakia, Yugoslavia and Finland, as well as to its Commonwealth partners.

Germany was also a significant licensor of aircraft in the late 1930s, belying any speculation based on the Soviet experience that totalitarian or revisionist powers might inherently be less prone to transfer technology in this manner. Its varied customers were located in Europe, Latin America, Russia and Turkey. Italy, meanwhile, specialized in licensing trainer aircraft, primarily in Eastern Europe. France's aircraft licensing agreements, too, were mostly with its allies in Eastern Europe. Most of these transactions took place in the early 1930s, with Germany and Britain later taking over these markets.

In the two categories of armored equipment, tanks and armored cars, only a few nations were active licensors: Czechoslovakia, France, Sweden, the United Kingdom and the United States. In contrast with aircraft, the United States had the highest proclivity toward licensing armor, primarily the result of two rather large transactions with the USSR and South Africa. On the basis of a

Table 5-2.   Interwar Licensing Agreements

Licensor	Licensee	Systems Licensed
United Kingdom	Australia	Hawker Demon, Vickers tanks, patrol sloops, escort destroyers
	Canada	Vickers Vedette, DeHavilland Puss Moth, Delta and Bolingbroke bombers, Super Stanraer ASW, Westland Lysander, Norseman transport, Blackburn Shark, DeHavilland Tiger Moth
	South Africa	Westland Wapiti, Hawker Hart, Avro Tutor
	Czechoslovakia	Avro 626, Carden-Lloyd and Vickers tanks
	France	Short Calcutta ASW, Carden-Lloyd tanks
	Hungary	Straussler tanks and armored cars
	Japan	Gypsy Moth, Gloster Gamecock, Short Flying Boat, DeHavilland Puss Moth, Hawker Nimrod, Vickers and Carden-Lloyd tanks, Rolls Royce AC
	Poland	Vickers and Carden-Lloyd tanks
	Russia	Vickers and Carden-Lloyd tanks
	Yugoslavia	Hawker Fury, Hurricane, Blenheim, Yarrow destroyers
	Finland	DeHavilland Puss Moth, Blackburn Ripon, submarines, MTBs, coastal defense ships
	Portugal	Destroyers, Vickers Valparaiso
	Netherlands	Destroyers, MTBs
	China	Avro 634
	Greece	Atlas Reconnaissance, Avro 626, Avro Tutor, Blackburn Velos
	Norway	DeHavilland Puss Moth, DeHavilland Tiger Moth, Gloster Gladiator
	Denmark	Bristol Bulldog, Avro Tutor, Hawker Nimrod
	Sweden	Hawker Hart, DeHavilland Puss Moth, Tiger Moth, Hawker Osprey
	Belgium	Fairey Firefly and Fox, Avro 504, Gloster Gladiator

Table 5-2.—_Continued_

Licensor	_Licensee_	_Systems Licensed_
	Spain	Vickers Vildebeest, Blackburn torpedo, Hawker Super Fury, Avro Cadet
United States	USSR	Bellanca transport, Martin bomber, Ford armored car
	Japan	Vought Corsair, Fairchild utility, Curtiss Hawk
	Australia	North American 33 trainer
	Canada	Fairchild 71 and 51 trainers
	Sweden	North American BT-9A trainer, Douglas-Northrop 8A-1 bomber
	Romania	Fleet trainers
	Brazil	Destroyers
	Turkey	Martin bombers, Curtiss Hawk
	China	Douglas U-38 fighter bomber
	Thailand	Curtiss Hawk, Vought Corsair
	Mexico	Fairchild KR-34 trainer, Vought Corsair
	Chile	Curtiss Falcon
	South Africa	Marmon-Harrington tanks
France	Belgium	Breguet observation planes, Morane trainers, Berliet armored cars
	Japan	Renault tanks and armored cars
	Poland	Potez fighters, Breguet observation planes, Renault tanks
	Romania	Potez bombers, Renault tanks
	Yugoslavia	Hanriot trainers, Dewoitine fighters, Breguet bombers, Potez observation planes, Renault tanks
	Russia	Destroyers
	Czechoslovakia	Dewoitine interceptors
	Switzerland	Dewoitine observation planes, Morane fighters
	Portugal	Morane trainers, Potez observation planes
	Spain	Breguet fighters and bombers
Germany	Turkey	Submarines, Gotha trainers
	Argentina	Focke-Wulf Stieglitz trainers

Table 5-2.—*Continued*

Licensor	Licensee	Systems Licensed
	Yugoslavia	Dornier-17 bombers
	Hungary	Heinkel utility aircraft
	Austria	Focke-Wulf Stieglitz trainers
	Switzerland	Bucker Jungmann, Jungmeister trainers
	Sweden	Heinkel observation craft, Junkers-86, F-W Stieglitz, He-115 bomber
	Netherlands	Dornier Wal ASW, Dornier-24 bomber
	Spain	Dornier Wal ASW, submarines
	Russia	Heinkel observation craft, Junkers bomber and observation craft
Italy	Russia	MAS MTBs
	Bulgaria	Caproni 113 trainers
	Romania	Nardi trainers
	Norway	Breda trainers, Caproni-310 bombers
Netherlands	France	Koolhoven FK-58 fighter
	Hungary	Fokker bombers
	Belgium	Fokker fighters
	Poland	Fokker bombers
	Norway	Fokker fighters and bombers
	Denmark	Fokker fighters and bombers
	Switzerland	Fokker fighters
Czechoslovakia	Poland	Skoda armored cars
	Romania	Skoda armored cars
	Switzerland	Kolben-Danek tanks
	Yugoslavia	Avia fighters
	Finland	Smolik trainers
	Belgium	Avia reconnaissance planes
	Russia	Avia interceptors
Austria	Hungary	Daimler armored cars
Poland	Turkey	PZL interceptor
	Romania	PZL interceptor
Sweden	Hungary	Landverk Toldi tanks

Ford license, the Soviets copied and then mass-produced large numbers of armored cars some of which were used by the Loyalists in the Spanish Civil War.

Britain, the undoubted leader in armor technology during this period, licensed its highly rated Vickers and Carden-Lloyd tanks and gun carriers to a considerable number of nations, including some which otherwise were essentially independent producers—Russia, Czechoslovakia, France and Japan. Both France and Czechoslovakia, meanwhile, had some success of their own in licensing armored systems, particularly armored cars where Renault and Skoda were competitive.

There were not very many licensing agreements involving naval systems during this period. Only the United Kingdom, France, Germany and Italy were at all identifiable as licensors. Mostly, these transactions consisted of the licensing of the competing Thorneycroft, Lurssen and MAS patrol boats produced by Britain, Germany and Italy, respectively.

On the recipient side, there were varying propensities toward producing arms by license. In general—and this has been true in both periods—the more advanced nations have license-produced higher proportions of their arms requirements.

The Netherlands, Russia, Japan and Czechoslovakia received a high proportion of their external transfers in this form, but as these were primarily autarkic nations this pertains only to that fraction of their arms which came from abroad.

Of the predominately dependent nations, the most significant licensees were Argentina, Australia, Canada, Denmark, Finland, Hungary, Mexico, Norway, Poland, Portugal, Nationalist Spain, Switzerland, Turkey, South Africa, Yugoslavia and Belgium. Each of these license-produced, across the range of the various weapons, something over 20 percent of their requirements. Of these, only a few—Canada, Australia, South Africa, Switzerland and Belgium—were later to maintain an equivalent postwar licensing capacity.

In Table 5-3 we have listed the major identifiable postwar licensing agreements, again arranged by licensor. As clearly indicated, most of these transactions have been within the NATO and Warsaw alliances. Indeed, only a small number of developing countries have been on the recipient end of licensing agreements. The major exception has been India, which has worked its way toward a modern armaments industry by licensing aircraft and frigates from Britain, fighter aircraft and missiles from the Soviet Union and helicopters from France. Israel, Argentina and Brazil are the remaining significant exceptions, each having license-produced some trainer and utility aircraft and with the latter having initiated some production of STOL aircraft licensed from Japan. Argentina has also license-produced French tanks.[19]

The United States has been a prolific postwar licensor of all kinds of military equipment to allies and close associates. Systems such as the F-84, F-86 and F-104 fighters, Sikorsky and Bell helicopters, Hawk missiles and several

Table 5-3. Postwar Licensing Agreements (up to 1968) (partial list)

Licensor	Licensee	Systems Licensed
United States	France	Hawk missiles, Sikorsky S-58 helicopters
	Belgium	Lockheed F-104, North American F-86, minesweepers, Hawk missiles
	Italy	F-84, F-86, F-104, Bell Iroquois helicopters, M-113 Armored Personnel Carrier, M-47, M-48 tanks, Hawk missiles
	Netherlands	F-104, F-5
	Japan	F-86, F-104, F-4, AT-33, 34 trainers, Bell Iroquois helicopters, Neptune ASW
	Canada	F-104, F-86, F-5, AT-33 trainer, Neptune ASW
	West Germany	F-104, Bell Iroquois helicopters, Charles Adams destroyers, Hawk missiles
	Britain	Sikorsky S-51 helicopters
	Spain	Frigates, F-5 fighter
	Portugal	Frigates
	Australia	F-86, A-4
	Sweden	Aircraft engines
	Mexico	LASA 60 aircraft
	Argentina	U3A and T-34 aircraft
	Taiwan	Bell helicopters
United Kingdom	France	Vampire, Sea Venom fighters
	Belgium	Hawker Hunter, Gloster Meteor fighters
	Italy	Vampire fighters
	Australia	Vampire fighters, Canberra bombers
	Switzerland	Vampire, Venom fighters
	Sweden	Aircraft engines
	Netherlands	Sea Fury, Hunter, and Meteor fighters, submarines, Leander class frigates
	India	Vampire and Gnat fighters, Andover aircraft, Leander class frigates
	Denmark	Vosper patrol boats
	United States	Canberra bombers
	Canada	CC-106 Yukon and CL-28 Argus aircraft

Table 5-3.—Continued

Licensor	Licensee	Systems Licensed
France	Switzerland	Mirage fighters, Magister trainers
	Australia	Mirage fighters
	West Germany	Magister trainers
	Israel	Magister trainers
	Denmark	U-4 coastal submarines
	South Africa	Panhard armored cars, Magister trainers, AMX tanks
	Belgium	Mirage V fighter (co-production)
	Spain	Daphne submarines
	Brazil	MS-760 Paris aircraft
	Sweden	Alouette helicopters
	United States	Breguet patrol craft, Alouette helicopters
	Argentina	MS-760 Paris aircraft, AMX tanks
	Dominican Republic	AMX-13 tanks
	India	Alouette helicopters
USSR	China	MIG-15, 17, 19, 21 fighters; T-34, T-54, PT-76 tanks; BTR Armored Personnel Carriers, Riga type frigates, W-type submarines
	Poland	Submarines, T-34 tanks, minesweepers, destroyer escorts
	Czechoslovakia	MIG-15, 17, 19, 21 fighters, BTR
	India	MIG-21 fighters, Atoll missiles
	Yugoslavia	T-34 tanks
West Germany	Spain	Lurssen Patrol boats, He-111 aircraft
	France	Lurssen Patrol boats
	Denmark	Coastal submarines
	Pakistan	Cobra missiles
	Brazil	Do-27, Do-28 transports
Italy	West Germany	Fiat G-91 fighters
	South Africa	Macchi MB-326 trainers
	Australia	Macchi MB-326 trainers
	Argentina	MB-308 aircraft
	Brazil	MB-226 aircraft
Netherlands	Italy	Fokker S-11 aircraft
	Brazil	Fokker S-11 and S-12 aircraft
Japan	Brazil	STOL transports
Canada	Argentina	Otter aircraft

types of naval craft have each been licensed to a number of other nations. This has resulted in considerable interchangeability of the forces of the United States-led alliance structure, while also allowing for the maintenance of armaments industries in a number of nations which have not been significantly engaged in indigenous research and development.

The United States has not, however, by any means accounted for all of the license transfers within the Western bloc. Britain, before the recent apparent decline of its aircraft industry, had considerable success in licensing its Vampire, Meteor and Hunter fighters to other European nations, including Switzerland, and to Australia. More recently, France has replaced Britain as the second most significant licensor, following the United States. The Magister jet trainer, used to great advantage by the Israelis in the 1967 War for tank-busting purposes, has been licensed to a number of nations, including West Germany. The vaunted Mirage fighter, which established the reputation of the French aircraft industry in 1967, has been licensed to Australia and Switzerland in competition with American models.

The web of licensing agreements among Western nations has not always consisted of transfers of technology from the stronger to the weaker powers. More recently, there has been evidenced a more reciprocal pattern of cross-licensing, coincident with the trend toward codevelopment schemes. Germany has built quantities of Italy's Fiat F-91 fighter, while Italy has produced Dutch Fokker aircraft. Even the United States, long only an exporter of arms technology, has recently been on the receiving end of some transactions, licensing helicopters, ASW aircraft and missiles from France, and a V-STOL strike aircraft from VFW-Fokker of Germany. Further, by 1974 consideration was being given to coproduction of a still newer British V-STOL fighter, as well as to licensing of the British Rapier missile.[20]

The United States has also been pushed out of a number of erstwhile secured markets in Western Europe. Belgium is now rebuilding its air force with Mirages to replace the F-104. Other nations are replacing the once standard Patton tanks with German Leopards. Denmark is purchasing Swedish aircraft. We shall return to discussion of this trend later in looking at recent West European codevelopment ventures.

Japan has perhaps been the most prodigious licensee of all, having had until recently no indigenous arms development. But it has maintained a small, high-quality fighting force in all areas, armed almost exclusively with American-licensed equipment, including large quantities of F-86, F-104 and F-4 fighters, Lockheed and Beech armed trainers, Bell helicopters and Lockheed Neptune ASW aircraft. It has maintained the manufacturing capacity which allows for rapid movement toward indigenous arms development any time it should choose independence. The first steps have already been taken with the development of an indigenously designed tank and a prototype Mitsubishi fighter aircraft.[21]

The Soviet Union has allowed considerable license-production among its dependents in Eastern Europe, ranging across a variety of weapons systems. Only Czechoslovakia and China, however, in addition to India, have been given access to the technology for the MIG series of fighter aircraft, while only Poland, Yugoslavia and China have license-produced Soviet tanks. With the exception of some indigenous small aircraft in Poland and Czechoslovakia, there has been no independent development of modern weapons systems within the Soviet bloc outside the Soviet Union.

A few summary points may be made in comparing the licensing networks of the two periods. Most importantly, there seems to have been some decrease in the capability of smaller and less developed countries to produce weapons on license. This trend has been most evident for combat aircraft. In the 1930s, for instance, Turkey was license-producing American Martin bombers and Curtiss Hawk fighters; Thailand, Curtiss Hawks and Vought Corsairs; and Mexico, the Corsairs. China, then very underdeveloped, was licensing Douglas bombers. Perhaps the most indicative case was that of Yugoslavia, which in the period of its frantic cross-bloc acquisitions in the late 1930s was simultaneously license-producing Britain's advanced Hurricane fighters and Blenheim bombers and Germany's advanced Dornier bombers.

The decline of license-production by small or middle-range powers is noticeable for the smaller, developed European powers, as well as for developing nations. In the 1930s Norway, Denmark, Spain, Portugal, Greece, Yugoslavia and others produced a high proportion of their weapons inventories on license. Nowadays they rely almost solely on imports. Presumably, this is the result of increased technological requirements for aircraft production, which have caused the once embryonic aircraft industries of many smaller nations to become defunct. Relatively assured supply from nations heading hegemonic alliances has no doubt also played a role; if necessary, Norway and Denmark could no doubt match Israel in the development of a modern aircraft industry.

Otherwise, there has been a great increase in licensing by nations just below the rank of major power. A number of nations once independent in arms development have become primarily licensees. Germany, Italy, Czechoslovakia, Japan and, to a lesser degree, Britain and France fall into this category. Thus, one might characterize the major change from the interwar to the postwar period as one in which the locus of license-production activity has moved a few notches up the scale of economic development or national power. These facts jibe, of course, with those describing the constriction of supplier markets in some categories.

Earlier, we had stated that licensing arrangements ought to be closely reflective of strong internation ties. As a result, we would expect there to be few examples of cross-bloc multiple supplier licensing relationships. This certainly has been the case for the postwar period. Most licensing has been within the frameworks of the two major alliance systems, except for some Western nations' licensing to the European neutrals. India, meanwhile, contributes the sole example of cross-bloc acquisition of weapons technology by this method, having license-produced weapons both from the Soviet Union and from Britain.

In the interwar period, however, there were many more such cross-bloc arrangements, following from the overall pattern of donor-recipient relationships. Of the twenty-two nations in that period which received arms from both of the major bloc groupings, seven were not a party to any licensing agreements. These were all small nations—Bolivia, Ethiopia, Iran, Lithuania, El Salvador, Uruguay and Venezuela. Of the remaining fifteen, eight licensed arms from only one of the major blocs: Brazil, Argentina, Chile, Thailand, China, Austria, Denmark, Finland and Hungary. Of these only Argentina and Austria were licensees of the Axis nations. There were eight nations—Hungary, Turkey, the Netherlands, Switzerland, Sweden, Yugoslavia, Romania and Norway—which were licensees from both major blocs. In the case of the neutrals, this is a further indication of the maintenance of an evenhanded policy, manifested in a variety of ways. For the others, one could probably claim that they were, more than other nations, the focal point for cross-bloc competition for arms influence, having close ties with the arms industries of both blocs. Turkey and Yugoslavia stand out in volume of license production based on transfers from firms of both blocs.

Unlike the postwar period, there was then very little licensing by Germany, France, Italy and the United Kingdom, reflecting their virtual arms independence. Also, there was a minimum of cross-licensing among the major powers within identifiable blocs. This pattern would become prevalent only after 1945. One exception was France's licensing, just before the war, of the Dutch Koolhoven fighter, in a last ditch effort at overcoming the weakness of the French aircraft industry.

In comparing the licensing networks of the two periods, then, we may make the following points. First, that the extent of licensing in the interwar period appears to have been, if anything, even greater than in the postwar, despite the fluidity of alliances. In the interwar period, licensing agreements occurred even where there were fairly low levels of internation association, in conjunction with cross-bloc acquisition patterns, and frequently involving relatively underdeveloped nations.

In the postwar period, meanwhile, increasing technological requirements and tighter alliance blocs appear to have restricted most licensing to within the major alliances, or to nations closely associated with the alliance leaders. Only very advanced dependent nations have been able to license-produce the most modern weapons systems.

Coproduction and Codevelopment
The linked phenomena of coproduction and codevelopment are quite modern developments, primarily the result of the contemporary economics of major weapons production and of increased needs for cost-effectiveness in research and development in the North Atlantic area.

As previously indicated, the distinction between these two transfer modes is sometimes blurred, there being an intermediary grey area between them. Lewis Frank has stated the distinction as follows:

> Coproduction or joint production is being increasingly resorted to in Western Europe. It allows the participants to take advantage of the latest in technology and share defense costs as well as to ensure an adequate market for the systems. It provides some political assurance as well, and allows both sides to exercise their comparative advantage in production while taking advantage of commonality in sales efforts and maintenance. ... Codevelopment, which may eventuate into coproduction, depends upon the satisfactory identification of bilateral or multilateral hardware and politico-military requirements early in the research and development production cycle. The shared cost and technological spillover benefits can thus be exploited to a greater advantage earlier in the program.[22]

Thus, at one end of the range the term coproduction becomes more or less coterminous with licensing, although with more distinct overtones of prior commitment and planning. Development is by one nation; production by two or more. Or more comprehensive agreements may be formulated, with cross-licensing programs involving shared production of a number of weapons systems.

Robert James, writing for the Institute for Strategic Studies, offers a somewhat altered terminology, distinguishing between ab initio NATO standardization in major weapons projects—as in the G-91 and Atlantique programs—and standardization achieved by common production of existing equipment by NATO members. He indicates that the point at which planning of combat requirements for a system takes place is critical, as is the type and direction of financing for collaborative ventures. His description of the complexities of the Hawk missile coproduction scheme is illustrative.

> The Hawk, together with the Sidewinder air-to-air missile and the Bullpup air-to-surface missile, was one of the missiles offered to NATO countries by the United States in 1958 after the shock of the first Russian Sputnik. It was selected by France, Germany, Italy, the Netherlands, and Belgium. The British, who considered that their needs were more than adequately met by the Thunderbird missile, kept firmly out of the program from its inception. In order to initiate the program, the United States bore the major financial liability until full arrangements could be agreed between the participating countries. In the event, it was not until October, 1963, after over two years of difficult and delicate negotiations, that the respective obligations and functions of industry and the participating governments were finally agreed. At that stage, it was estimated that the total cost of the program would be $620 million, of which the

United States' contribution was $30 million for grant assistance and $80 million for reimbursement assistance. The production contract alone was worth $286 million. The final cost was $667 million, of which $32 million came from U.S. grant aid in the form of technical assistance, documentation, and training, etc. . . . The Hawk project was adopted as a NATO program in February, 1958, and the NATO Hawk Production Organization set up. The consortium, the Société Européene de Téléguidage (SETEL), was established in 1959, consisting of Compagnie Française Thomson-Houston (France), Philips (Netherlands), Telefunken (Germany), Finmeccanica (Italy), and Atéliers de Constructions Électriques de Charleroi (Belgium). . . . Three assembly centers (HAMCO) were established in Germany, France, and Italy. . . . The project was administered by a Production Agency, which came under criticism for being too large and unwieldy.[23]

In addition to the above facets of this arrangement, over 650 European technicians were trained in Hawk technology in the United States and numerous production drawings were sent to the European manufacturers involved along with critical materials and parts. This is a hybrid arrangement within our transfer mode classification, somewhere between a traditional licensing agreement and a codevelopment venture. It is an arrangement which is fairly typical of many which have evolved within the Atlantic alliance in recent years.

Despite the seeming comprehensiveness of agreements such as that for the Hawk (which did not include the British), earlier hopes for all-NATO standardization have gone awash, giving way to a complex web of interlocking bipartite and multipartite agreements. This has been the case, according to James, despite the development of a rather vast bureaucratic infrastructure for planning and coordination. He asserts that standardization and interoperability have been achieved in some aspects of NATO equipment, but principally at a relatively low level (standardization from the bottom). On major projects the results have, to date, been far from satisfactory. Most difficulties, he says, have been caused by the failure of the alliance to create a really effective NATO procurement agency.[24]

Up to the early 1960s the bulk of Atlantic alliance cooperative production efforts were based essentially on American technology. Then, spurred by growing European fears of inexorable American technological dominance so well popularized by Servan-Schreiber, a newer trend emerged featuring codevelopment among European nations, variously on bipartite, tripartite or still more broadly based arrangements.[25] However, the United States still remained a party to many such ventures. A recent ISS annual listed the ongoing codevelopment ventures as of 1970, which are reproduced in Table 5-4.

Table 5-4.   Current International Defence Production Projects

Project	Years	Participating Countries	Main Contractors	Joint Project Type	Remarks
AIRCRAFT					
Panavia 200 variable geometry Multirole Combat Aircraft (MRCA)	1969-	Britain, Germany, Italy	Panavia consortium: (British Aircraft Corporation; Messerschmitt-Bolkow-Blohm; Fiat)	Project definition, development and production	Reported total requirement –900
SEPECAT Jaguar strike/trainer	1965-	Britain, France	Société Européenne de Production de l'Avion École de Combat et Appui Tactique (SEPECAT): (British Aircraft Corporation; Breguet)	Design, development and production	Initial production–400
Transall C-160 transport	1959-	France, Germany	Transporter Allianz (Transall): (Nord Aviation; Messerschmitt-Bolkow-Blohm; VFW-Fokker)	Development and production	Initial production–169, some of which have been built
'Helicopter Package'—Sud SA-330 Puma tactical helicopter; Sud SA-341 Gazelle light observation helicopter; Westland WG-13 utility helicopter	1967-	Britain, France	Westland Aircraft; Sud Aviation	Development and production	Planned and/or actual production: SA-330, 275; SA-341, 450; WG-13, 335-375
Breguet Atlantic maritime patrol aircraft	1959-	Belgium, France, Germany, Holland, United States (financing only)	Fairey, SABCA, Fabrique Nationale, Breguet, Sud Aviation, Dornier, VFW-Fokker	Development and production	

Table 5-4.—*Continued*

Project	Years	Participating Countries	Main Contractors	Joint Project Type	Remarks
AERO-ENGINES					
M-45 advanced turbofan series for civil and military use	1964-	Britain, France	Rolls Royce (Bristol Engine Division); Société National d'Étude et de Construction de Moteurs d'Aviation (SNECMA)	Design, development and production	
TF-41 turbofan to power the LTV A-7D fighter-bomber (also designated RB.168-62/66 and 912-B3/14)	1966-	Britain, United States	Rolls Royce; Allison Division, General Motors Corporation	Development and production	
XJ99-RA-1 advanced V-STOL lift engine	1965-	Britain, United States	Rolls Royce; Allison	Development	
RB. 153 and RB. 193 lift-cruise turbofan engines	1963, 1965 respectively	Britain, Germany	Rolls Royce; MAN-Turbo	Design, development and production	
RB-172-T-260 (Adour) turbofan for Jaguar SSI. ST	1965-	Britain, France	Rolls Royce; Turbomeca	Development and production	
RB-199 turbofan for MRCA	1969-	Britain, Germany, Italy	Rotar Union (Rolls Royce, Motoren und Turbinen Union, Fiat)	Development and production	
T-112 shift turbine for auxiliary power unit role in VFW prototype VAK 191B V-STOL fighter	1966-	Britain, Germany	Rolls Royce (Small Engines Dvision); Klockner-Humboldt-Deutz	Development and production	

Table 5-4.—Continued

Project	Years	Participating Countries	Main Contractors	Joint Project Type	Remarks
MISSILES					
Martel teleguided-antiradar air-to-surface missile	1964	Britain, France	Engins Matra; Hawker Siddeley Dynamics; Marconi; Electronique Marcel Dassault	Development and production	
Milan wire-guided antitank missile	1965	France, Germany	Nord; Messerschmitt-Bolkow-Blohm	Development and production	
HOT wire-guided antitank missile	1965	France, Germany	Nord; Messerschmitt-Bolkow-Blohm	Development	
Roland surface-to-air missile	1966	France, Germany	Nord; Messerschmitt-Bolkow-Blohm	Development and production	
GUNS					
155mm towed	1967	Britain, Germany	Vickers, Rheinmetall, Faunwerke	Development and production	
Self-propelled version	1970	Britain, Germany	Vickers, Rheinmetall, Porsche	Development and production	
ELECTRONICS					
NATO Air Defence Ground Environment (NADGE) infra-structure	1967-	Britain, France, Germany, Italy, the Netherlands, the United States	NADGECO consortium (Marconi, Thomson-CSF, Telefunken, Selenia, Hollandse Signaal-apparaten, Hughes Aircraft)	Development and production	This integrated air defence system is due for completion in 1971

Source: *The Military Balance: 1970-1971* (London: Institute for Strategic Studies), pp. 113-115.

Several points stand out from this compilation of codevelopment ventures. First, a strong trend toward intra-European armaments procurement is apparent, despite—or perhaps because—of France's seeming continuing alienation from American and NATO diplomacy. On the other hand, at least two agreements which involve Franco-American collaboration on a weapons system are indicated: the Breguet Atlantique maritime patrol aircraft and the NATO Air Defense Ground Environment (NADGE) infrastructure. These agreements have coincided with growing Franco-American arms competition in Western Europe as well as elsewhere.[26]

Cooperation between France, Germany and Britain is seen to have become very tight, clearly representing a move away from excessive weapons dependence on the United States, particularly on the part of Germany. The growing independence of Western Europe as a grouping within the NATO alliance is clearly reflected in these developments, perhaps presaging further trends toward an independent diplomatic stance. There has also, however, been a recent move by neutral Sweden to become part of this trend, with coproduction offers to Belgium and Holland for the Saab Viggen fighter.[27]

These codevelopment arrangements will, in the future, account for a substantial portion of what will be a newer generation of NATO weapons in the late 1970s and early 1980s: the Jaguar and MRCA combat aircraft, PUMA helicopters and a wide range of missiles.[28]

Of necessity, these ongoing codevelopment efforts within NATO are obviously based on strong anticipation of the continuing cohesiveness of the alliance, or at least upon an expectation of easily coordinated future diplomacy within the EEC grouping, now to be augmented by a British presence. One point, however, remains somewhat obscure. How will these developments affect future arms sales outside of NATO and Western Europe?

Up to now, there have been, so far as we can discern, only a few instances of transfer of a codeveloped weapons system outside the orbit of NATO. A few Transall transport aircraft, jointly developed by France and West Germany, have been sold to South Africa, while some codeveloped Puma and Gazelle helicopters have been sold by France to Brazil and Kuwait. The former transaction would not have been expected to cause problems in the coordination of arms transfer policy, as neither France nor West Germany has cooperated in the United Nations' embargo on South Africa, while French and British policies do not significantly differ with respect to either Brazil or Kuwait.

But difficulties in policy coordination might easily be envisaged in any number of other instances, particularly where policy toward a given country differs among partners to a codevelopment venture. What would happen in the case of a request for an Anglo-French codeveloped system from Pakistan, India or South Africa? Will the Jaguar swing-wing fighter later be made available to one of the combatants in the Middle East? Will weapons emerging from joint Franco-German projects be made available to leftist Arab regimes such as Iraq, Syria or Algeria, now small-scale clients of the French? More intriguing still, what of sales of products of joint Franco-American systems to any one of a number of nations where policy now diverges in basic principle?

Little evidence now exists to indicate how arms sales will be handled in such cases. Possibly, the parties to codevelopment ventures will be left to make such decisions on their own, selling surplus equipment from their own stocks. This would represent a change from the norm, with many arms deals being based on preproduction agreements on long-range contract. One might speculate, on the other hand, that policy might often be determined on the basis of the lowest common denominator. This might conflict with strong trends toward industrial arms sales policies by most Western European nations, although on the other hand, in the wake of the events of 1973, the arms-selling policies of the Western European countries appeared to be converging. The situation has no apparent precedent.

Outside NATO, the Soviet bloc has also achieved considerable standardization of equipment, indeed surpassing that of NATO. Here, however, there is little evidence of codevelopment in the sense of coordinated, prior procurement planning. Presumably, decisions on procurement, design and development are still made in the USSR. And needless to say, Soviet hegemony within its alliance has precluded discernible conflict over the destination of arms exported outside it. Despite some evidence presented by Thayer indicating a degree of independence by the Czech Omnipol organization, and some recent Czech arms sales to Latin America, it is difficult to imagine any Eastern European nation selling major weapons systems in the face of Soviet opposition, although it should be noted that Rumania is now *buying* some helicopters from the United States.[29]

There are intriguing future possibilities for codevelopment ventures involving other nations, such as China or Japan. And there has been at least one attempt at a codeveloped weapons system outside of the developed nations, that by India and the UAR to jointly decrease their dependence on major powers for jet fighter aircraft. Their aircraft was based on a model earlier developed by emigré German technicians associated with the Hispano Aviation Company, domiciled in Spain, and was originally intended for use by the Spanish Air Force. Later, the project was moved to Egypt and employed scientists and technicians from a number of Western nations. After a series of bizarre developments, the project was abandoned, having merely achieved the output of a small number of aircraft delivered to the Indian Air Force as the HAL Marut. The project's original impetus was dissolved as both of the participants became arms clients of the Soviet Union.[30]

This somewhat aborted project is important for what it indicated about the limits of codevelopment ventures among essentially underdeveloped countries. However, if the major powers later come to agreements on limiting arms sales to certain developing countries, this project could be a harbinger of similar future developments. Here too, however, as with ventures among developed countries, strong and stable diplomatic relations would appear to be prerequisite, particularly given the long lead-times associated with the development of modern weapons systems.

The phenomena of coproduction and codevelopment are apparently new, without historical precedent either in the interwar period or before. The only identifiable approximation to an interwar precedent was the halting move by the French-led Little Entente alliance in the 1930s toward a limited degree of weapons standardization. For the most part, this involved extensive use of French licenses, and some Czech licenses, by Yugoslavia and Romania and was a fairly rudimentary arrangement. It broke down in a welter of disagreement, mostly over charges by Romania that it was being used as a dumping ground for unwanted Czech equipment, and also over Czech charges of French dominance in the agreement. Although earlier disagreements were primarily economic in nature, the arrangement later collapsed altogether with the withering of the Little Entente, the rise of fascist-type regimes in Yugoslavia and Romania and the eventual competition of arms from the Axis nations. Clearly demonstrated was the precondition of a tight and enduring alliance as a prerequisite for joint arms development and production and for standardization on a significant level.

It is to be wondered whether a trend toward multipolarity and more fluid alliances, if further eventuated in the future, especially as it affects intra-European and intra-NATO relationships, will serve to attenuate present trends toward codevelopment. Perhaps more likely is a gradual withdrawal of the United States from participation in Western European arms markets, with tighter ties among the Europeans if still closer political integration should occur.

Copying and Stealing

If codevelopment and coproduction seem to be recently emergent transfer modes, that of copying—at least of a certain type—appears to have become archaic. Copying can take any of several forms.

In the postwar period it has often been alleged that Soviet aircraft have borne suspiciously close resemblances to earlier American-produced planes. This type of copying is conducted by espionage, either by the stealing of plans and documents or by close analysis of photographs. These cases involve copying without the approbation of—and in the face of resistance by—the original source of the technology. A well-publicized recent example involved an apparent attempt by Israeli intelligence to acquire information on a new French Mirage fighter through bribery of a Swiss engineer involved in its license-production.[31]

In the interwar period, however, with its laxness of controls and relative freedom of private firms, the art of copying was institutionalized in a different form. Nations short on indigenous weapons development talent were then able to make a practice of buying up one or a few units of given systems, which they then copied or modified. This was done with the knowledge—and apparent resigned tolerance—of the original developers, who in turn were not usually restrained by their own governments.

The use of widespread copying was most effectively employed during the 1930s by Japan and Russia, both of which thus developed the bulk of the weapons they were to use during World War II. They pursued a parallel policy, almost in lockstep, sometimes simultaneously copying the very same systems from Western arms manufacturers. The method was simple. Each bought up one or a few copies of almost every major American, German, British and French system produced up to the late 1930s, tested them, and then determined whether they were worth copying. Many times, amalgams of different systems were subsequently produced, so that the final version might hardly be recognizable. Alternatively, licensing agreements were sometimes entered into, or else a complex, confusing combination of copying and licensing was often employed for production of a single system.

In both Japan and Russia this policy was pursued at full tilt from the early 1920s to the middle or late 1930s. By the end of the 1930s both nations, having acquired sufficient technological expertise, began to design indigenous equipment, while still continuing to "borrow" technology. However, the Japanese were not able to move ahead very rapidly during the war itself after being cut off from erstwhile Western sources. Their aircraft were superior to American models at Coral Sea and Midway, but vastly inferior by 1945.[32]

The magnitude of the copying by Japan and Russia may be illustrated by some of their purchases during that period, particularly in aircraft. Take the case of Japan. In the period 1937-1938, not long before Pearl Harbor and long after the outline of Japan's aggressive foreign policy had been made abundantly clear in China and with the signing of the Axis Treaty, the following purchases were made from the United States alone: one copy each of the Kinner Envoy, Northrop 2J, Stinson Reliant, North American Waco YPF-7, Chance Vought V-143, North American NA-16 Harvard trainer, Fairchild Amphibious transport, Lockheed 12A transport and Fairchild 24K; five Douglas DC-3 transports, ten Lockheed 14-W63 transports; and eight Seversky 2-PA pursuit aircraft.[33]

The licenses for these purchases, incidentally, were actually issued by the United States Munitions Control Board up to June of 1938, after which it was decided to crack down, not so much on the premise of clear future national interest, but on the stated basis of outrage over Axis bombing of civilians in China and Spain.

Japanese purchases from the United States in the late 1930s were merely a culmination of what had long been an Herculean effort at copying from numerous sources. As early as 1933 the Japanese were producing at least ten different combat aircraft engines copied or licensed from Bristol of Britain, BMW and Junkers of Germany, Salmson of France and Wright and Pratt and

Whitney of the United States. These engines were, in turn, installed in airframes copied from previously purchased Western aircraft.

Some of the resulting aircraft were Rube Goldberg amalgams, composed of combinations of Wright Cyclone engines, Hamilton-Standard propellers, Handley-Page wing slots, Curtiss retractable landing gears and Junkers cantilever wings. However, more readily identifiable copies were made of the Boeing B-26, Douglas DC-2, Short Flying Boat, several Junkers and Dornier bombers, and Gloster pursuit planes. The Japanese air armada which astonished the world in late 1941 was the end-product of an incredibly clever amalgamation of the best of weapons technology produced by the United States, Britain, France and Germany. It was not the first or the last time the Japanese would display a talent for absorbing foreign techniques.

Not to be outdone, the Soviets pursued an almost identical course of eclectic borrowing of foreign technology, leaning on the latest products of Western capitalist firms, ideology and Stalinist demonology aside. This policy of seeking foreign military assistance had been presaged in the 1920s by Russian cooperation with the German military, particularly in the development of tank and gas warfare.

Relative to the Japanese, the Russians relied disproportionately on Britain and the United States in the middle and late 1930s, after a spell during which French and Italian technology was borrowed. They made extensive use of copied Douglas bombers and Seversky fighters, originally purchased in small lot orders and then mass-produced.

The primary thrust of Soviet copying efforts was, however, in armor, obviously critical to a nation contemplating a mobile land war on the plains of Northern Europe. In the early 1930s the Soviets copied and licensed a number of British Vickers, French Renault and Italian Fiat models. In at least one instance, a British tank was purchased for copying before it had been issued to the British army.

From the United States the Soviets purchased and copied the Bronieford armored car, later used in large numbers by the Spanish Loyalists. Much more important, however, was the copying of the famed Christie tank, at first ignored by the United States War Department, which later emerged—with modifications—as the Soviet T-34. It may have been the finest tank of the Second World War.[34] While armored developments languished in the United States, the Soviets were able to mass-produce tens of thousands of T-34s and Vickers tanks, barely in time to face the onslaught of German Panzers by 1941.

Institutionalized copying is no longer anywhere in evidence. Those few recent identifiable instances of copying have been based on espionage, as with the Israeli attempt at gaining the secrets of Mirage production. China has apparently availed itself of extensive copying based on espionage since being cut off from Soviet technology in the early 1960s. Up to that time the Chinese had been given licenses for most advanced Soviet systems, up to and including the then first-line MIG-19 fighter. Since then China has managed to produce the more advanced MIG-21 fighter, apparently copied. This would no doubt have been an easy matter, given close Chinese ties with some Soviet recipients, Syria in particular.[35]

Mostly, copying has been the instrument of catch-up powers, as demonstrated by Russia and Japan in the 1930s and by China in recent years. For those who can obtain licensing agreements, and can afford them, the need for copying does not normally exist.

Stealing or capturing of arms in bulk quantities has also served as a transfer mechanism in some cases. Many of the anticolonial guerrilla movements of the earlier postwar period were armed in this fashion. Chinese Communist forces in their successful civil war used large stocks of abandoned Japanese arms, as did the Viet Minh against the French and Indonesian rebels against the Dutch. Castro's revolutionary forces were armed with American weapons captured from the incumbent Batista regime.

The Israelis' success in incorporating Soviet tanks captured in 1967 has already been mentioned. Actually, these tanks have been modified, now being equipped with American radio equipment and machine guns. This is a good example of the combinative use of mixed transfer modes.

There are obvious drawbacks to the use of captured or stolen equipment if it comes to form a significant part of one's order of battle. The equipment will gradually be rendered useless unless spare parts can be acquired or production facilities set up to manufacture them and the correct caliber ammunition. It helps, therefore, if a nation which captures a good sized arsenal is able to purchase spare parts from another nation which is—or was—a client of the original supplier. Otherwise, the booty will be drawn down by gradual cannibalization. However, this type of arms supply is also the special realm of private arms brokers such as Interarmco, which over the years have acquired stocks of weapons and parts from all of the major suppliers. Secondary deals to fill gaps in a recipient's armory are their stock in trade.[36]

The Multinationalization of the Armaments Industry and the Activities of Offshore Corporate Subsidiaries

Earlier we had explained in our discussion of systems variables that, since the interwar period, the world armaments industry appears to have undergone a degree of deinternationalization. This trend could be measured by the decrease in interlocking stockholding and directorships and by the decreased activities of arms corporations' subsidiaries in weapons-dependent nations. These trends, in a way, appear paradoxical in view of the strong thrust toward multinationalization of corporate business. But they might well have been predicted as arms transfers became more important instruments of national diplomacy.

Hence, the international arms cartel has become an anachronism, aside from the impact wrought by the socialization of economies in the Soviet bloc and elsewhere, effectively removing some areas of the world from the purview of Western corporations. Earlier, pre-1914 Russia had been the quintessential case of a dependent nation, with its arms manufacturing owned and operated by foreign corporations.

One question is the extent to which donor-recipient patterns, or the flow of weapons technology, were affected by these phenomena in prior periods. Two separate problems are involved here. One is the extent of technology transfer when an arms corporation domiciled in one country owns a piece of one in another—i.e., whether this is conducive to extensive cross-licensing. Secondly, there is the impact of basing wholly owned corporate subsidiaries in recipient countries where, in effect, they act as equivalents of licensees, albeit owned and controlled from abroad.

We have indicated previously that cross-national ownership and interlocking direction of arms industries had earlier been quite extensive, but the extent to which these relationships, in combination with those determined by bank loans, directed the flow of licensing agreements or even the destination of exported arms is not clear. Usually, arms manufacturers in recipient nations maintained a national identity, even if essentially controlled from abroad. Sometimes, however, the activities of the subsidiaries of arms corporations were more visible.

We have previously noted that the foreign subsidiaries of German companies were crucial in carrying out offshore research and development work while domestic arms development was prohibited by the Treaty of 1919. A Junkers subsidiary built bombers in Sweden, many of which were subsequently retransferred elsewhere. Dornier had plants in Switzerland and Italy responsible for bombers and ASW aircraft which served as prototypes for subsequent domestic German models.[37] Krupp subsidiaries built submarines in Holland and in Spain.

Wholly owned subsidiaries were not used only by German firms. British shipbuilding companies had full-blown subsidiaries abroad, with a Crichton-Vulcan shipyard in Finland and Yarrow's in Yugoslavia. And America's export-minded Curtiss-Wright Corporation set up plants abroad to make fighter planes in Turkey, Mexico and Chile. In addition there were the numberless subsidiaries of the chemical firms making munitions, with DuPont, ICI, Montecatini, I. G. Farben and Rhone-Poulenc having wholly owned munitions plants all over the globe. This practice of setting up subsidiaries to make whole weapons systems abroad is seemingly entirely absent today.

This does not mean, however, that cross-national ownership of arms corporations is altogether passé. Indeed, a recent monograph of the Institute for Strategic Studies by C. J. E. Harlow included data on a fairly significant web of cross-national ownership, displayed in Table 5-5. The data are for European arms

Table 5-5.   Cross-Nationally Owned Armaments Firms Within NATO Bloc

Country of Domicile of Company	Company	Industry	Largest Shareholders	Licensed Production (if any)
Belgium	Société Anonyme Belge de Constructions Aéronautique (SABCA)	Aircraft	50% Fokker (Netherlands)	Breguet Atlantique, F-104G, Breguet 941
	S. A. Fairey	Aeroengines	100% Fairey Co. Ltd. (UK)	Lockheed F-104G, Breguet Atlantique
	Bell Telephone Manufacturing Company	Electronics	100% ITT (US)	
	COBELDA	Electronics	50% Hughes Aircraft (US), 50% SABCA	Doppler for Breguet Atlantique
United Kingdom	Pye of Cambridge	Electronics	90% Philips Gloeilampen (Netherlands)	
France	SNECMA	Aeroengines and electronics	10% Pratt & Whitney (US), remainder held by government	Hercules piston engine for Noratlas from Hawker-Siddeley; Orpheus for G-91, Pratt and Whitney producers
	Precilec S. A.	Electronics	20% United Aircraft (US)	
	Bull General Electronics	Electronics	50% General Electric	
West Germany	Bolkow	Aircraft and missiles	25% L. Bolkow, 20% Family-Essen, 25% Boeing Co, 25% Nord Aviation	MF1-9 Junior Light aircraft from Malmo Flygindustrie, Klemm KI-107 monoplane, Daystrom products, joint producers of missiles with Nord

Table 5-5.—Continued

Country of Domicile of Company		Industry	Largest Shareholders	Licensed Production (if any)
	AEG-Telefunken Group	Electronics	10% General Electric	Cross-licensed agreements with Marconi, RCA, EMI, CSF, Philips, Siemens, GE, Decca and Bendix radar equipment
	VFW (Vereinigte Flug-technische Werke) formerly Focke-Wulf, Weserflug and Heinkel	Aircraft	20% Friedrich or Fr. Krupp, 6% A. G. Weser, 26% Hanseatische Indus-trie Beleiligungen GmbH., 26% United Aircraft, 12% Heinkel	Joint production of Transall, F-104, G-91, Fouga Magister, Piaggio P-149, Noratlas 2501
	Robert Bosch	Electronics	Association of ITT	
	Honeywell	Electronics	100% Honeywell	
	IBM	Electronics	100% World Trade Corporation (IBM)	
	Teldix	Electronics	Joint subsidiary of Bendix-Telefunken	
Italy	Aeronautica Macchi	Aircraft	20% Lockheed (US)	Fokker S-11 (As M-416), Lockheed AL-60, F-104-G
	Contraves Italiana	Electronics, Missiles	Subsidiary of Contraves, Zurich, Switzerland	
	Selenia	Electronics	45% Raytheon, 10% Fiat, 45% Finmeccanica	Hawk missile, Sparrow missile for F-104S and other Raytheon products
	Soc. Italiane Telecom-municazioni Siemens	Electronics	Subsidiary of Siemens (Germany)	

Table 5-5.—Continued

Country of Domicile of Company	Industry	Largest Shareholders	Licensed Production (if any)
Netherlands			
N. V. Koniklijke Nederlanse Vliegtuigfabriken Fokker	Aircraft, Electronics	20% Northrop	Hawk missile, Lockheed F-104G, Hawker Hunter, Gloster Meteor
Hispano-Suiza (Netherland), N.V.	Ordnance	H-S-CFTH (France)	
Sweden			
Svenska Radio AB	Electronics	71% L. M. Ericsson 29% Marconi (UK)	
Standard Radio and Telefon AB	Electronics	ITT (US)	

Source: In C. J. E. Harlow, *The European Armaments Base: A Survey* (London: Institute for Strategic Studies, 1967).

firms only, and do not include any information—if it would be pertinent—on foreign interests in American military contractors.

It is clear from the data that there is considerable American investment in European arms companies. American companies have substantial, if only partial, interests in some of the leading aircraft and missile manufacturing firms in Europe: SNECMA, Bolkow, VFW, Fokker and Macchi. In some of these cases, the tie-in with past and present licensing arrangements is apparent. Fokker, partly owned by Northrop, is now producing that company's F-5 aircraft, while Macchi of Italy, partly owned by Lockheed, is a licensee of the latter's F-104 Starfighter. Other tie-ins are indicated in Selenia of Italy's production of Hawk missiles, SNECMA of France's production of Pratt and Whitney engines and the German AEG group's production of General Electric components.

Recently, there have been indications that European arms firms may be moving toward some buying out of companies in the United States, paralleling overall trends in multinational corporate ownership. France's Aerospatiale has bought out the Vought Helicopter Company from LTV, now operated as a wholly owned subsidiary.

To some extent, then, cross-national stock ownership of Western armaments companies is explanatory of donor-recipient patterns. These activities have apparently accounted for a considerable flow of weapons technology.

American penetration into French military-related industries is noteworthy. The matter became a sore point with General DeGaulle, who was not only sensitive to the symbolic partial loss of sovereignty, but to actual restrictions which might be applied to French arms exports where American and French policies diverged. General Electric's purchase of a 50 percent interest in Machines Bull, the major French computer firm, became a cause célèbre in France.

In summary, however, there has been a considerable degree of deinternationalization of arms industries since the 1930s. This corresponds with our general impression of increased governmental controls on arms production and sales, increased coordination of armaments firms into the national security bureaucracies of all nations and the constriction of international corporate activity as governments have become decreasingly tolerant of encroachment on decision making and control by outside entities. The newer trend toward codevelopment ventures is a novel form of reinternationalization.

The Mobility of Arms Technicians and Makers

Earlier, we commented on the significance of transnational movements of arms technicians in earlier times. During the Renaissance, and even as recently as the late 19th century, emigration of arms experts was frequent and seemingly tolerated by victims of brain drains. No doubt this was merely an aspect of the more significant population migrations characteristic of earlier periods.[38] Cipolla has demonstrated, for example, that the movement of arms technicians was not only critical to the arming of Spain and Portugal in Renaissance Europe, but also to the build-up of arms industries in India, China and Japan.[39]

In the late 19th century men like Hotchkiss and Maxim, the original developers of automatic weapons, moved about in quest of the highest bids for their talents. Hotchkiss was an American and yet one of France's largest arms manufacturers, Thomson-Hotchkiss-Brandt, still bears his name. Maxim, too, was an American who took up citizenship in Great Britain, where his machine guns were developed.

Movements of arms experts have not been a very significant factor in the diffusion of weapons technology in either the interwar or postwar periods. However, there have been a few interesting exceptions. In the interwar period, while the restrictions of the Versailles Treaty were still nominally respected, German arms technicians carried on in outposts in Russia, Switzerland, Holland, Italy and Spain. Tank developers such as Christie and Straussler also moved about, as had the machine gun inventors of the previous era, selling their ideas to the most interested bidders.

Since 1945 there has been some limited movement of weapons experts. There was, of course, the postwar emigration of German rocket experts to both the United States and the Soviet Union. Then there were the peripatetic remnants of the old Messerschmitt aircraft engineering group, finding a haven for work on new jets first in Spain and then in Egypt.[41] Israel has also availed itself of foreign aircraft engineers, some instrumental in setting up the embryonic Israeli aircraft industry. South Africa, meanwhile, is alleged to have taken advantage of recent recessions in the aircraft industries of the United States and Britain to lure away skilled engineers.

The fact that the UAR, Israel and South Africa have been the most noticeable beneficiaries of this transfer mechanism indicates its residual importance for middle-range powers aspiring to the beginnings of an independent arms base.

In the past, with more primitive technology, it was easier to transfer the technology itself merely by moving small numbers of personnel. Now, when all armaments industries require enormous capital investment as well as personnel, the movement of skilled technicians as a transfer mechanism is limited. Also, most governments are now far more chary of allowing personnel with knowledge of classified information to move elsewhere. There has been a big change on this point over the past several decades, another aspect of the end to casualness in arms trade diplomacy.

Retransfer

The term retransfer is virtually self-explanatory, referring to secondary, tertiary or additional transfers beyond that from original suppliers. Actually, a considerable range of activities is here subsumed, as weapons can be retransferred by any of a number of the transfer mechanisms we have discussed—i.e., straight export, licensing, copying, and so forth.

Critical to analysis of the use of retransfer is the extent to which end-use restrictions are applied and enforced by the original supplier. This is not a simple matter. It is clear that, in contrast with the interwar period, end-use restrictions have been more frequently and stringently enforced since 1945. But, as pointed out in the SIPRI study, there is still some variation in the extent to which different suppliers monitor secondary transactions. Some nations—the United States, France, West Germany and Switzerland—insist on formal agreements as part of all transactions, forbidding resale without permission. Others—the United Kingdom, Italy and Canada—require such agreements only for some deals. According to SIPRI, France and Germany go furthest in assuring that end-use agreements are respected, by threatening to sequester monetary deposits required for this purpose.[42]

Contrary to what might have been expected, the use of retransfer appears to have been far greater in the postwar period than in the interwar. This is perhaps surprising only because in the earlier period of relatively freewheeling and privatized arms sales one might have expected that end-use agreements, if they existed at all, would have been casually enforced.

These factors were operative, but counterbalanced by others. Most importantly, there were far fewer small developing countries than at present. These now constitute the bulk of the market for retransferred arms. Also, there is now the fact that a number of major suppliers—Germany, Italy, and the Netherlands for example—have themselves been equipped largely by American licenses so that their arms sales have perforce been mostly retransfers. In the postwar period, then, these two factors—the large number of developing nations and the arms-dependency of relatively major suppliers—have resulted in what is commonly identifiable as a two-step process by which many nations are armed.

There is another possible explanation for the small number of retransfers in the interwar period. The less stringent governmental export controls of that period may have made it easier for smaller nations to acquire first-line equipment from original suppliers. And there was a higher average level of modernity of transfers in the 1930s, to some extent based on the more rapid turnover of weapons generations. As secondhand weapons were more quickly spun off by the major powers' forces, this may have lessened the need for acquiring arms through secondary markets. Finally, there is the cost factor. As unit costs for major weapons systems have soared, first-line military equipment has been priced out of the range of many smaller nations, who are thus more likely to acquire secondhand arms by retransfer, if not from the older surplus stocks of original suppliers.

According to the MIT data there has been an increase in retransfers since 1945. Their data indicate that while between 1950 and 1954 only 48 identifiable aircraft retransfers occurred, between 1965 and 1968 this figure had climbed to 576. The latter figure represents about one-seventh of the 3500 or so aircraft transferred during this period, a measure of the growing importance of this transfer mechanism.[43] Again, the reason quite clearly is the growth, since the 1950s, of a large number of small independent nations, building their armed forces from scratch.

As further indicated in the MIT study, the frequency of retransfers varies by weapons system and is normally most frequent in those with the greatest longevity. In both the interwar and postwar periods ship retransfers have been more frequent than those for combat aircraft or armor. In small arms, numerous retransfers are commonplace, since, in a field of technology which has not seen profound change in the past 40 years, these weapons may have useful lives spanning decades. Old warships are also frequently retransferred, as they are as often acquired for prestige as for expected combat purposes.

Of the 1500-odd arms deals of the 1930s, only about 50 were identifiable as retransfers. Contrary to the postwar experience, European nations such as France, Germany and the Netherlands were not normally the sources for such transactions. The most frequent retransfer conduits during that period were the offshore German subsidiaries in Sweden and Italy, particularly the German Junkers' subsidiary in Sweden. In addition, the USSR was a fairly frequent source of retransferred equipment, selling weapons produced on Western licenses to Turkey, Loyalist Spain and Czechoslovakia. There is no indication that the issue of end-use restrictions arose in these cases.

In the postwar period retransfers have often been used either to thinly disguise the sources of transfers or to mitigate their diplomatic impact. Thus, West Germany was induced by the United States to sell Patton tanks to Israel in 1965, a move which severely strained Arab-German relations and led to retaliation through recognition of East Germany in the face of the Hallstein Doctrine.[44] The Soviets, in turn, have used Algeria and the UAR as retransfer conduits to sub-Saharan African nations presumed sensitive about the sources of their acquisitions.

There have been other cases in which there has been ambiguity over whether end-use restrictions have actually been violated, or whether complaints from the original suppliers were merely used as covers once the essential nature of the transactions had become known. After the United States embargo on Pakistan in 1965, a retransfer of United States-licensed equipment from West Germany, supposedly originally intended for Iran, was the subject of much public hand-wringing by American officials sensitive to Indian remonstrances.[45] It is hard to believe, however, that the Germans and Iranians acted independently, given the potential for future sanctions available to the original supplier.

In the 1930s there was perhaps only one identifiable case where a retransfer became the subject of recriminations by the original supplier. During the Spanish Civil War, with the United States having announced an embargo on all belligerents, a number of American aircraft were rapidly retransferred to the Loyalists via Mexico. It is not likely that this was done with the connivance of the United States government, given the climate of that period. Rather, it appears that private groups in the United States sympathetic to the Loyalists attempted to circumvent the embargo.

In the near future there is likely to be a flood of retransferred weapons moving to developing countries from Western Europe. As NATO introduces a new generation of combat aircraft and tanks, large quantities of systems originally licensed from the United States, particularly F-104 and F-5 fighters and M-48 tanks, will become surplus. Presumably, the United States will exercise supervision over the disposition of these systems. In fact, an Italian firm has already been given the task of collecting and renovating M-47 and M-48 tanks from all over Western Europe, for sale to third countries.[46]

The potential for retransfers may later present severe problems for controls of arms to smaller countries. Some of the better armed developing countries—India, the UAR, Israel, Syria and Algeria among others—now have on hand huge stocks of military equipment, much of which will soon become obsolete for their purposes. Some of these nations may be tempted to sell off much of this equipment, if only to help finance new acquisitions from the original suppliers. For nations such as India and the UAR, which have high leverage with the major suppliers, end-use restrictions are not likely to be strongly enforced.

Loaning of Arms

The loaning out of military equipment is a transfer mechanism which appears to be a rather recent phenomenon, without apparent historical precedent.

In the interwar period we found just one case which involved a loan, that of the transfer of some ships from Britain to New Zealand. In recent years, but dating back to the 1950s, the United States has begun to use this method of arming some of its allies, among them Spain, Pakistan, Taiwan and Greece, on a limited basis and mostly with naval craft.[47]

The use of loans of military equipment by the United States seems to have originated in response to congressional criticism of military aid policy, so that these transfers have been made to appear merely temporary or conditional. The loans have renewal clauses, and continuing renewals are usually pro forma.

Whether there will be expanded use of loans by the United States and by other suppliers remains to be seen. There has been advocacy for their use as an intermediary form of arms control in which dependent nations would be granted military equipment only where there is immediate military threat. This recommendation neglects, however, the question of how a nation would be able to make use of loaned equipment without continuous prior training. Thus, it is difficult to imagine that the dependent nations as a group would be willing to be armed on this basis or that an agreement to do so could be reached among the major supplier nations.

Summary

We have found a number of significant differences between our two periods in the frequency of the use of various transfer modes. There has been a significant increase in the use of military aid in the postwar period. While the use of licensing has not varied greatly between the two periods, the identity of the most frequent licensees has changed, with powers just below the top rank having become dependent on this means of arming in the postwar period, while in the interwar period licensing was more frequent among less developed countries. There have been very significant increases in the use of retransfer, coproduction and codevelopment in the postwar period, each explicable by changes in systems variables. The increasing use of retransfer appears to be primarily the result of the vast increase in the number of smaller dependent nations, while the increased use of coproduction and codevelopment schemes seems a function of tight and stable alliances, along with the vastly increased costs of independent weapons programs which have channeled efforts into collaborative ventures. Finally, the use of copying from purchased models, important in the 1930s, has become virtually nonexistent, as has the diffusion of arms technology by movement of weapons technicians.

Chapter Six

Dependence and Autarky in Weapons Acquisition

Are there long-term trends pointing toward increasing weapons dependence by a larger number of nations? Or, are there just shifts in the levels of dependence exhibited by different classes of nations? The answer may depend on just what weapons one is talking about, over a range of sophistication and cost.

In discussing relative weapons dependence, we shall draw together some disparate strands from the preceding chapters on supplier markets, donor-recipient patterns and transfer modes.

Clearly, the number of nations able to achieve independence in weapons development and production will directly affect the basic structure of the supplier markets. In turn, the extent to which intermediate sized nations are compelled to seek an autarkic arms-production base will depend on those aspects of donor-recipient patterns related to the assurance of outside supply: polarity, leverage and alliance patterns. Also, the ability of some nations to achieve weapons-producing autarky will depend on whether they are able to utilize transfer modes such as licensing and copying, which may, in turn, lead to substantial independence as the recipient builds on a base of borrowed expertise. Finally, the outside limits of weapons-producing capability for powers of middle rank are linked to some obvious requisites for controls. Controls applied by major suppliers will only be effective insofar as there are hard constraints on the capability of recipients to produce their own arms, once cut off wholly or partially from outside supply.

We shall examine several interrelated problems here. First, we shall compare our two diplomatic periods according to the dependence exhibited by nations at various levels of economic development. Then, we shall assess the limits on weapons-producing independence imposed by levels of economic capacity and development, that is, by different mixes of GNP and per capita GNP. We shall want to examine whether either low GNP or low per capita GNP has been more of a handicap to an independent arms-producing base. We shall then look at the economic or resource constraints operating on those nations—mostly middle-range powers—which in either period have attempted strenuously to overcome the disabilities of small size in response to insecurity about continued arms supplies. Anticipating our summary chapter on controls, we shall examine the impact of embargoes and imposed controls in impelling additional nations toward autarky, and hence toward becoming additional factors in the supplier markets.

We shall briefly extend our analysis to problems of nuclear proliferation. Our examination of dependence in conventional arms ought to shed some additional light on a closely related subject.

THE DEPENDENCE-AUTARKY CONTINUUM

Surveying weapons production capacity and orders of battle for the range of nations one can perceive a graduated and complex continuum running from total independence to total dependence. There is considerable and expected variation by weapons systems, with many more nations dependent for jet aircraft than for infantry rifles.

We have broken the continuum up into six categories describing various states of dependence, with arbitrary breaks because there are no really discrete compartments. With the aid of examples drawn from both periods, the essentials should be made clear, along with some important political implications.[1]

Level 1: Total Independence

This category needs little elaboration, referring to complete independence in research and development as well as production for given weapons systems. The essential independence of a given nation in a weapons category will not be considered compromised by a small number of foreign acquisitions where qualitative preference for another supplier's arms, or marginal cost factors, have dictated a very limited degree of outside dependence. Thus, the United States may be considered fully independent in aircraft development and production at present, despite the Marine Corps' recent purchase of some British Harrier V-STOL aircraft. The United States has benefited from comparative advantage in a few isolated cases where choices may have been dictated by political as well as economic and technological factors.

Level 2: Near-Total Independence

At this level, a nation which is close to independence in development and production of a weapons type, and which would have no trouble achieving such independence if it so chose, nevertheless has allowed itself to remain dependent for some key bottleneck components. The reason will usually be cost-effectiveness, along with assurances of continuing outside supply, while indigenous production could be attained fairly rapidly if necessary.

One example is Sweden's aircraft industry, which produces indigenously developed models but which relies entirely on licensing of American and British engines. Presumably, the Swedes could design and develop their own engines, particularly as they could easily copy the engines now produced on license.

A further assumption at Level 2 is that independent research and development could easily be sustained beyond the point where copied equipment has become obsolete, in contrast to a case such as China after it was cut off from Soviet technology in the early 1960s.

Level 3: Mixed Independence-Dependence

This category incorporates several types of dependence, each differing from the preceding level only by degree. First there are situations where most or all systems are produced by licensing or copying. There is clear independence in production, but essentially total dependence for research and development. Dependence for the latter is assumed not to be essentially a matter of choice but the result of inability to match the efforts of more advanced nations.

Thus, where Switzerland and the Netherlands now license-produce most of their aircraft, it would appear unlikely, although not impossible, that they could match the major powers in research and development for indigenous products. At the very least, this could not be done without a substantial internal shift of resources, which would have important economic implications even if export markets could be developed to defray some of the costs.

Another typical situation of this category is where a nation makes significant efforts at indigenous development and production in some particular area within a major weapons category. In the 1930s, for instance, the Czechs manufactured a considerable range of indigenous aircraft, but remained critically dependent on France and others for the most advanced types. It was difficult for the Czechs to keep pace, either quantitatively or qualitatively, once the European arms race accelerated in the late 1930s.

Level 4: Mixed Dependence-Independence

At this level, a nation exhibits some fairly significant license-production capacity, or very limited independent R and D capability in a weapons type, but remains essentially dependent on imports or licensing, usually weighted towards the former.

Conceivably, a nation in this category, by considerable stretching of resources, could attain Level 3 capability. It is, however, considered altogether out of the running for Level 1 or Level 2 capacity, even with an Herculean effort. Some current examples in the aircraft category are India and Spain, both involved in significant license production, and in the case of the former, with a limited indigenous development program. Both remain, however, essentially dependent for combat aircraft.

Level 5: Near-Total Dependence

Nations in this category may have demonstrated very limited capability for license-production, or even for development of some unsophisticated systems of their own, such as patrol boats or utility aircraft. At best, however, they may have limited arms-production bases which might, with extensive effort, allow for moving up to Level 4. Current examples are Mexico's or Turkey's aircraft industries, producing small numbers of unsophisticated aircraft with numerous components supplied from abroad.

Limited efforts toward reducing dependence at this level may be explicable only by prestige factors. There are numerous smaller nations whose efforts at building an armaments base would appear to be otherwise futile. Sometimes, limited production facilities are mere adjuncts to minor capability for repair and overhaul of systems supplied by major powers.

Level 6: Total Dependence

At this level a nation has no production facilities, much less research and development capability. Usually, no such capability has ever existed. This has, of course, been the normal situation for the majority of nations throughout history.

Before analyzing our two periods by this typology, a few qualifications ought to be cited. The most serious one involves the collapsing, for reasons of economy, of the diverse categories of weapons into aircraft, armor, naval and small arms. Obviously, dependence may not be uniform within these categories. As we have had to simplify somewhere, we have attempted to make an average assessment for each nation, for each major weapons category. More weight has been given to the important "master" weapons for each category: fighter aircraft, tanks and warships. In reality the dilemma exists only for a small number of nations.

A second problem has been touched upon before in our analysis of supplier markets—that of capability in contrast to the actual facts of development and production. In some cases, dependence will be opted for where capability exists. Again, cost-effectiveness and assuredness of supply will usually be the central reasons.

In still other cases, the absence of production capability will merely reflect the lack of national requirements for certain weapons types. Switzerland and Czechoslovakia, for instance, do not produce naval craft, although their industrial capacity would allow for it if it were necessary. In Tables 6-1 through 6-5, these cases have been entered at Level 6. The reader will be able to interpret this information accordingly in a small number of cases.

A final problem is that of changes in dependence levels undergone by some nations within the two periods, although usually these changes have been marginal. Particularly in the direction of lessened dependence, such changes are not easily come by. China in the past decade has been an outstanding exception. Israel, India and Iran are now bidding to become others. As previously noted, in the late 1930s a number of European nations which had exhibited some independence were forced into dependence relationships toward the end of the period. They could not keep pace in a period of rapid technological change.

COMPARATIVE ANALYSIS OF DEPENDENCE
LEVELS BY WEAPONS SYSTEMS

In Tables 6-1 through 6-5 we have organized our data on dependence levels for both periods in a number of ways. In Tables 6-1 and 6-2 dependence levels for nations in both periods are indicated for the four weapons categories of aircraft, naval, armor and small arms. Nations are ranked by GNP for the postwar period and by national income for the interwar. Data and ranks for per capita GNP and per capita national income are also included, allowing for comparison of these ranks with those for GNP.

Only 36 of the 65-odd independent nations of the interwar period are included. For the remainder, below the indicated level of national income, across-the-board Level 6 dependence for arms was nearly uniform. The few exceptions are noted at the bottom of Table 6-1.

Likewise, for the postwar period only 60 of 140-odd independent entities have been included. For nations at levels of economic capacity below that of Burma or North Vietnam total arms dependence has been almost uniformly the case, again with the few exceptions noted at the bottom of Table 6-2. The omission of a large number of nations in both periods from the tables for space economy should not obscure the important fact of the large number of them which have no arms industries whatsoever, and which are therefore altogether dependent.

In Tables 6-3 and 6-4 we have rearranged the data by weapons systems, indicating which nations have been at which levels of dependence in each of the weapons categories.

In Table 6-5 we have juxtaposed the dependence levels for the two periods by nation. Only nations which were politically independent in both periods have been included, excepting India, an important case of an excolonial possession which has come considerable distance toward an independent arms industry.

In many cases, a clear majority, there has been no change between periods in dependence levels in any weapons category. Where there has been a change, it is so indicated. Plus changes denote movement towards independence and minuses the reverse. At the bottom of Table 6-5 the aggregate changes for each weapons category have been summed to afford a very rough indication of the overall change in worldwide dependence.

Table 6-1.   Interwar Arms Dependence Levels, by National Income and Per Capita National Income

Country	Rank	National 1938 Income (millions of current $)	Rank	Per Capital Income ($)	Dependency Levels			
					Aircraft	Naval	Armor	Small Arms
United States	1	$67,375	3	$519	1	1	1	1
Germany	2	23,000	9	335	1	1	1	1
United Kingdom	3	22,100	4	465	1	1	1	1
USSR	4	17,850	26	105	3	3	3	1
France	5	10,800	13	260	2	1	1	1
China	6	7,700	36	17	5	6	6	5
Japan	7	6,070	29	86	3	2	2	2
Italy	8	5,830	23	133	1	1	1	1
Canada	9	3,986	7	357	4	6	6	4
Australia	10	3,825	2	556	5	4	6	3
Poland	11	3,350	27	96	2	6	4	3
Spain	12	2,875	18	173	4	3	6	4
Sweden	13	2,830	5	447	3	1	3	1
Netherlands	14	2,730	10	314	2	1	5	3
Argentina	15	2,657	15	186	5	4	6	4
Yugoslavia	16	2,640	19	171	4	4	5	3
Belgium	17	2,200	12	262	4	6	5	1
Czechoslovakia	18	2,000	16	185	3	6	1	1
Brazil	19	1,990	35	50	5	5	6	6
South Africa	20	1,860	14	186	4	6	3	5
Switzerland	21	1,850	6	440	4	6	4	1
Hungary	22	1,500	21	167	5	6	6	5
Denmark	23	1,170	11	308	4	1	6	1
Mexico	24	1,100	34	58	5	6	6	5
Turkey	25	1,060	33	60	5	5	6	5
Austria	26	1,056	22	154	5	6	4	4
Egypt	27	1,030	32	63	6	6	6	6

Table 6-1.—Continued

Country	Rank	National 1938 Income (millions of current $)	Rank	Per Capita Income ($)	Dependency Levels			
					Aircraft	Naval	Armor	Small Arms
Norway	28	1,000	8	345	4	1	6	5
New Zealand	29	907	1	567	6	6	6	5
Chile	30	840	17	183	5	6	6	6
Ireland	31	724	14	250	6	6	6	6
Bulgaria	32	682	25	110	5	6	6	5
Finland	33	625	20	169	5	5	6	4
Colombia	34	625	31	72	6	6	6	6
Greece	35	550	30	77	4	6	6	6
Venezuela	36	440	24	125	6	6	6	6
Cuba	37	400	28	95	6	6	6	6

Note 1 Most remaining nations in this period with low national incomes had Level 6 dependence in all systems. The exceptions were: Iran (Level 4 in small arms), and Lithuania (Level 5 in aircraft).

Note 2 National Income figures not available for Portugal (Level 5 in aircraft and naval, Level 4 in small arms); Romania (Level 4 in aircraft and small arms, Level 5 in armor); and Thailand (Level 4 in aircraft).

Source: National Income and per capita income figures for 1938 are from Woytinsky and Woytinsky, *World Population and Production* (New York: Twentieth Century Fund, 1953), pp. 389-390.

Table 6-2.   Postwar Arms Dependence Levels (as of 1968), by GNP and Per Capita GNP

Country	Rank	GNP-1965 (billions $)	Rank	Per Capita GNP ($)	Dependency Level			
					Aircraft	Naval	Armor	Small Arms
United States	1	$696	1	$3,575	1	1	1	1
USSR	2	313	17	1,357	1	1	1	1
West Germany	3	112	9	1,900	3	2	1	1
United Kingdom	4	99	11	1,818	2	1	1	1
France	5	94	8	1,924	1	1	1	1
Japan	6	84	25	861	3	3	3	3
China	7	76	53	109	3	4	4	3
Italy	8	57	20	1,104	3	3	3	2
India	9	49	56	101	4	4	4	3
Canada	10	48	3	2,473	4	4	5	4
Poland	11	31	23	978	5	3	4	3
Australia	12	23	6	2,002	3	3	4	3
Czechoslovakia	13	22	14	1,561	3	6	4	1
Brazil	14	22	42	267	4	4	4	4
East Germany	15	22	19	1,260	6	4	6	3
Sweden	16	20	2	2,549	2	2	2	3
Mexico	17	19	33	455	5	5	6	3
Netherlands	18	19	15	1,554	3	3	6	4
Spain	19	18	32	561	4	4	6	3
Argentina	20	17	28	770	4	4	4	3
Belgium	21	17	12	1,804	3	5	5	1
Romania	22	15	27	778	6	6	6	5
Switzerland	23	14	4	2,333	3	6	3	1
Pakistan	24	11	54	109	6	6	6	5
Hungary	25	11	21	1,094	6	5	6	3
South Africa	26	11	30	611	4	5	3	3
Indonesia	27	10	58	99	5	5	6	3
Denmark	28	10	5	2,120	6	3	6	3
Austria	29	9	18	1,287	5	6	6	3
Yugoslavia	30	9	34	451	5	3	3	3
Turkey	31	9	41	282	5	5	6	5
Finland	32	8	13	1,749	6	3	6	3
Venezuela	33	8	24	882	6	6	6	6

Table 6-2.—Continued

Country	Rank	GNP 1965 (billions $)	Rank	Per Capita GNP ($)	Dependency Levels			
					Aircraft	Naval	Armor	Small Arms
Norway	34	7	10	1,890	6	3	6	3
Bulgaria	35	7	26	829	6	5	6	3
Iran	36	6	43	251	6	6	6	5
Greece	37	6	29	687	6	6	6	5
New Zealand	38	5	7	1,980	6	6	6	3
Philippines	39	5	49	160	6	6	6	6
Colombia	40	5	40	282	6	5	6	6
Nigeria	41	5	59	84	6	6	6	6
Chile	42	5	31	565	5	5	6	5
UAR	43	5	50	159	5	6	6	5
Peru	44	4	37	367	6	6	6	5
Thailand	45	4	52	129	6	5	6	5
Portugal	46	4	35	406	6	3	6	4
Israel	47	4	16	1,422	5	6	4	2
Cuba	48	3	36	393	6	6	6	5
South Korea	49	3	55	105	6	5	6	5
Malaysia	50	3	38	306	6	6	6	6
Taiwan	51	3	45	227	5	6	6	5
Ireland	52	3	22	980	6	6	6	6
Algeria	53	3	46	222	6	6	6	6
Morocco	54	3	48	196	6	6	6	6
North Korea	55	3	47	207	6	5	6	3
South Vietnam	56	2	51	150	6	5	6	6
Ghana	57	2	39	285	6	6	6	6
Iraq	58	2	44	231	6	6	6	6
North Vietnam	59	2	57	100	6	6	6	6
Burma	60	2	60	71	6	5	6	5

Note 1 Most remaining nations in this period with low GNPs have Level 6 dependency in all systems. The exceptions are: Ceylon (Level 5 in naval), Dominican Republic (Level 5 in armor and small arms), El Salvador (Level 5 in small arms), Paraguay (Level 5 in small arms), and Rhodesia (Level 5 in small arms).

Source: Postwar GNP and per capita GNP data are from Yale World Data Analysis Program.

Table 6-3.   Summary of Interwar Dependence Levels by
Weapons System

Weapons System	Level	Countries
Aircraft	1	Germany, United Kingdom, United States
	2	France, Poland, Netherlands
	3	USSR, Japan, Sweden, Czechoslovakia
	4	Canada, Spain, Yugoslavia, Belgium, South Africa, Switzerland, Denmark, Norway, Greece, Romania, Thailand
	5	China, Australia, Argentina, Brazil, Hungary, Mexico, Turkey Austria, Chile, Bulgaria, Finland, Lithuania, Portugal
	6	All remaining nations
Naval	1	United States, Germany, United Kingdom, France, Italy, Sweden, Netherlands, Denmark, Norway
	2	Japan
	3	USSR, Spain
	4	Australia, Argentina, Yugoslavia
	5	Brazil, Turkey, Finland, Portugal
	6	All remaining nations
Armor	1	United States, Germany, United Kingdom, France, Italy, Czechoslovakia
	2	Japan
	3	USSR, Sweden, South Africa
	4	Poland, Switzerland, Hungary, Austria
	5	Netherlands, Yugoslavia, Belgium, Romania
	6	All remaining nations
Small Arms	1	United States, Germany, United Kingdom, USSR, France, Italy, Sweden, Belgium, Czechoslovakia, Switzerland, Denmark
	2	Japan
	3	Australia, Poland, Netherlands, Yugoslavia
	4	Canada, Spain, Argentina, Austria, Finland, Portugal, Romania, Iran
	5	China, South Africa, Hungary, Mexico, Turkey, Norway, New Zealand, Bulgaria
	6	All remaining nations

Aircraft

The number of independent nations in either period has been very small, with that number narrowing from trainer or utility aircraft to modern fighters. At present, only the United States and the Soviet Union, and now perhaps France, are fully autarkic in all areas. And France, along with Britain and Germany, is now diluting its arms independence by participation in numerous codevelopment ventures which may later result in making these nations independent as a bloc. Sweden is somewhat of an anomaly, backing up its neutralist diplomatic stance with a near-independent aircraft industry but relying on foreign sources for engine licenses and helicopters.

In the interwar period the number of nations at total or near

Table 6-4.   Summary of Postwar Dependence Levels by
Weapons System

Weapons System	*Level*	*Countries*
Aircraft	1	United States, USSR, France
	2	United Kingdom, Sweden
	3	West Germany, Japan, China, Italy, Australia, Czechoslovakia, Netherlands, Switzerland, Belgium
	4	India, Canada, Brazil, Spain, Argentina, South Africa
	5	Poland, Mexico, Indonesia, Austria, Yugoslavia, Turkey, Chile, UAR, Israel, Taiwan
	6	All remaining nations
Naval	1	United States, USSR, United Kingdom, France, Japan
	2	West Germany
	3	Italy, Poland, Australia, Netherlands, Denmark, Yugoslavia, Finland, Norway, Portugal
	4	China, India, Canada, Brazil, East Germany, Spain, Argentina
	5	Mexico, Belgium, Hungary, South Africa, Indonesia, Turkey, Bulgaria, Colombia, Chile, Thailand, South Korea, North Korea, South Vietnam, Burma, Ceylon
	6	All remaining nations
Armor	1	United States, USSR, West Germany, United Kingdom, France
	2	Sweden
	3	Japan, Italy, Switzerland, South Africa, Yugoslavia
	4	China, India, Poland, Australia, Czechoslovakia, Brazil, Argentina, Israel
	5	Canada, Belgium, Dominican Republic
	6	All remaining nations
Small Arms	1	United States, USSR, West Germany, United Kingdom, France, Czechoslovakia, Belgium, Switzerland
	2	Italy, Israel
	3	Japan, China, India, Poland, Australia, East Germany, Sweden, Netherlands, Spain, Argentina, Hungary, South Africa, Indonesia, Denmark, Austria, Yugoslavia, Finland, Norway, Bulgaria, Iran, New Zealand
	4	Canada, Brazil, Mexico, Portugal
	5	Romania, Pakistan, Turkey, Greece, Nigeria, Chile, UAR, Peru, Thailand, Cuba, South Korea, Taiwan, Burma, Dominican Republic, El Salvador, Paraguay, Rhodesia
	6	All remaining nations

independence was somewhat greater and the composition of the group was somewhat different. Germany, Italy, Britain and the United States were fully autarkic, while France, the Netherlands and Poland were close, although suffering qualitative inferiority.

The dependence of the USSR and Japan during this period has been commented upon, in the context of their efforts at overcoming reliance on

Table 6-5. Changes in Dependence Levels Between Periods

Country	Aircraft Interwar	Postwar	Change	Naval Interwar	Postwar	Change	Armor Interwar	Postwar	Change	Small Arms Interwar	Postwar	Change
Afghan	6	6	—	6	6	—	6	6	—	6	6	—
Albania	6	6	—	6	6	—	6	6	—	6	6	+1
Argentina	5	4	+1	4	4	—	6	4	+2	4	3	+1
Australia	5	3	+2	4	3	+1	6	4	+2	3	3	—
Austria	5	5	—	6	6	—	4	6	-2	4	3	+1
Bolivia	6	6	—	6	6	—	6	6	—	6	6	—
Brazil	5	4	+1	5	4	+1	6	4	+2	6	4	+2
Bulgaria	5	6	-1	6	5	+1	6	6	—	5	3	+2
Canada	4	4	—	6	4	+2	6	5	+1	4	4	—
Chile	5	5	—	6	5	+1	6	6	—	6	5	+1
China	5	3	+2	6	4	+2	6	4	+2	5	3	+2
Colombia	6	6	—	6	5	+1	6	6	—	6	6	—
Costa Rica	6	6	—	6	6	—	6	6	—	6	6	—
Cuba	6	6	—	6	6	—	6	6	—	6	5	+1
Czechoslovakia	3	3	—	6	6	—	1	4	-3	1	1	—
Denmark	4	6	-2	1	3	-2	6	6	—	1	3	-2
Dominican Republic	6	6	—	6	6	—	6	5	+1	6	5	+1
Ecuador	6	6	—	6	6	—	6	6	—	6	6	—
Eire	6	6	—	6	6	—	6	6	—	6	6	—
Egypt	6	5	+1	6	6	—	6	6	—	6	5	+1
Ethiopia	6	6	—	6	6	—	6	6	—	6	6	—
Finland	5	6	-1	5	3	+2	6	6	—	4	3	+1
France	2	1	+1	1	1	—	1	1	—	1	1	—

Table 6-5.—Continued

Country	Aircraft			Naval			Armor			Small Arms		
	Interwar	Postwar	Change	Interwar	Postwar	Change	Interwar	Postwar	Change	Interwar	Postwar	Change
Germany	1	3	−2	1	2	−1	1	1	—	1	1	—
Greece	4	6	−2	6	6	—	6	6	—	6	5	+1
Great Britain	1	2	−1	1	1	—	1	1	—	1	1	—
Guatemala	6	6	—	6	6	—	6	6	—	6	6	—
Haiti	6	6	—	6	6	—	6	6	—	6	6	—
Honduras	6	6	—	6	6	—	6	6	—	6	6	—
Hungary	5	6	−1	4	5	−1	4	6	−2	5	3	+2
India	6	4	+2	6	4	+2	6	4	+2	6	3	+3
Iran	6	6	—	6	6	—	6	6	—	4	3	+1
Iraq	6	6	—	6	6	—	6	6	—	6	6	—
Italy	1	3	−2	1	3	−2	1	3	−2	1	2	−1
Japan	3	3	—	2	1	+1	2	3	−1	3	4	−1
Mexico	5	5	—	6	5	+1	6	6	—	5	4	+1
Nicaragua	6	6	—	6	6	—	6	6	—	6	6	—
Norway	4	6	−2	6	3	+3	6	6	—	5	3	+2
Panama	6	6	—	6	6	—	6	6	—	6	6	—
Paraguay	6	6	—	6	6	—	6	6	—	6	5	+1
Peru	6	6	—	4	1	+3	4	4	—	6	6	—
Poland	2	5	−3	4	2	+2	4	4	—	3	3	—
Portugal	5	6	−1	6	6	—	6	6	—	4	4	—
Romania	4	6	−2	6	6	—	6	6	—	4	5	−1

Table 6-5.—Continued

Country	Aircraft			Naval			Armor			Small Arms		
	Interwar	Postwar	Change	Interwar	Postwar	Change	Interwar	Postwar	Change	Interwar	Postwar	Change
Salvador	6	6	—	6	6	—	6	6	—	6	5	+1
Saudi Arabia	6	6	—	6	6	—	6	6	—	6	6	—
Spain	4	4	—	3	4	−1	6	6	—	4	3	+1
Sweden	3	2	+1	1	2	−1	3	2	+1	1	3	−2
Switzerland	4	3	+1	6	6	—	4	3	+1	1	1	—
Thailand	4	6	−2	6	5	+1	6	6	—	6	5	+1
Turkey	5	5	—	5	5	—	6	6	—	5	5	—
United States	1	1	—	1	1	—	1	1	—	1	1	—
USSR	3	1	+2	3	1	+2	3	1	+2	1	1	—
South Africa	4	4	—	3	5	+1	3	3	—	5	3	+2
Uruguay	6	6	—	6	6	—	6	6	—	6	6	—
Venezuela	6	6	—	6	6	—	6	6	—	6	6	—
Yugoslavia	4	5	−1	4	3	+1	5	3	+2	3	3	+2
New Zealand	6	6	—	6	6	—	6	6	—	5	3	—
Netherlands	2	3	−1	1	3	−2	3	6	−1	3	3	+2
Belgium	4	3	+1	6	5	+1	5	5	—	1	1	—
	Aircraft			Naval			Armor			Small Arms		
Aggregate Changes	+15			+27			+17			+31		
	−23			−11			−11			−8		

foreign sources by copying and licensing which later led to development of indigenous models. Otherwise, there was Czechoslovakia's effort at an independent aircraft industry base, which proved futile and led to hasty purchases from Britain and Russia preceding the Munich debacle.

Most surprising in the interwar period was the number of nations capable of partially fulfilling their needs either by indigenous development or by licensing. Fighter aircraft were developed by Romania, Yougoslavia and even Lithuania, while Greece, Norway, Thailand and Denmark each had sufficiently developed production facilities to build significant proportions of their aircraft by licensing. Later, after 1945, these nations' aircraft industries were to decline substantially. Further up the ladder, once independent or near-independent nations such as Germany and Italy were to become primarily licensees of American aircraft. There were economic benefits and an assured source of supply.

There have been some important developments on the upward mobile side since the 1930s. Perhaps the most significant moves toward decreased dependence, in addition to the Soviet Union, have been made by China, India and Australia. More recently, China has produced a new jet aircraft, designated the F-9 and reported to be a copy of the Soviet MIG-21. There have not been corresponding reports of indigenous Chinese development of transports or helicopters, although these can be expected later. China clearly is moving toward weapons-producing autarky, although it remains to be seen if it can match its rivals in quality. If not, its situation will be reminiscent of France in the 1930s, with prestige of indigenous development unmatched by combat capability.

India is also moving toward independence in this field. It has long engaged in license production of modern aircraft: Vampire and Gnat jets from Britain, the MIG-21 from the USSR and Alouette helicopters from France. The indigenous development of its own HAL-Marut, in collaboration with the UAR, may signal a move toward real independence, particularly if now relatively secure outside sources of supply should become less assured. Meanwhile, India has now gone into production with a number of indigenously designed and produced trainer and utility aircraft, as well as with aircraft engines built to power them. Its recent nuclear test, along with reports of associated missile developments, may augur future enhanced weapons independence.

Australia had only a rudimentary aircraft industry in the 1930s. It still has not entered the lists as an indigenous designer, but significant license production of advanced American and French combat aircraft has given it, along with nations such as Germany, Italy and Japan, the capability to move in that direction if desired.

There have been some signs of indigenous aircraft development by a number of other developing countries: Argentina, Brazil, Israel, Chile, Indonesia,

Turkey, the UAR and also South Africa. Each of the three Latin American nations has developed its own trainer and utility aircraft, although in all cases they are powered by engines from abroad. None has yet been able to license-produce a modern jet fighter, although both Brazil and Argentina have moved toward this option by license-building the Italian MB-26 armed trainer and Brazil is now considering license-production of either the United States F-5, the French Mirage III or the Italian G-91.[2]

South Africa, likewise, license-produces the MB-26, and may also be moving toward independent development capability because of its fears of a more comprehensive arms cutoff if the now extant United Nations embargo should later be adhered to by France and Italy. Israel is in a similar and perhaps more precarious position. It has taken the first steps towards independence with its indigenous Arava STOL transport and license-production of the French Fouga Magister trainer. More recently, Israel has become the first of the smaller developing nations to move toward actual independence in combat fighter aircraft.[3] It has produced a modified version of the French Mirage—the Barak—to be powered by American-supplied jet engines. The development of such a craft has not resulted in any significant degree of independence, however, as the necessity for offshore engine purchases will remain for the foreseeable future, as will the need for importing sophisticated strike aircraft with modern avionics equipment and stand-off missiles.

In summary, the overwhelming bulk of nations in either period have been totally dependent for their aircraft. Despite some moves toward reducing this dependence by some small and middle-range powers there are not likely to be significant changes in the near or even distant future.

As indicated at the bottom of Table 6-5, there has appeared to be a trend toward greater aggregate dependence on a worldwide level for aircraft, as measured in this rather simplified and crude way. This is primarily the result of the decline of the indigenous development capabilities of the middle-range powers of Europe—Germany, Italy, Belgium and the Netherlands—and also of Denmark, Yugoslavia and Poland. Further, there has been a decline in the license-producing capacity of some developing nations such as Mexico, Thailand, Turkey and Chile, although still other small nations have acquired the capacity to produce trainer or utility aircraft on license.

For the future, one might easily project a reversal of these trends. Japan, China and perhaps some of the Western European nations, as well as Israel and India, appear to be moving toward increased independence. When or if that is achieved, particularly with China and Japan, the implications for controls will be profound. And if nations such as India and Israel can achieve independence, which to be meaningful would require the development of aircraft which could match those produced by the major powers, the diplomacy surrounding the arms trade in the South Asian and Middle Eastern regions would be changed accordingly. Control of events in these areas by major powers would be reduced.

Naval Craft

Here some rather odd changes of dependence have occurred, some but not all of which parallel developments in aircraft. In the 1930s four small European nations—Sweden, Norway, Denmark and Holland—each with a strong maritime tradition, had maintained indigenous shipbuilding capacity which was comprehensive and included capital ships. Otherwise, excepting the major powers, there were very few nations with significant development or production capability. Several—Yugoslavia, Finland, Portugal, Turkey and Spain—did produce some naval ships with the aid of licensing, copying or the domiciling of subsidiaries of foreign shipbuilders.

Across the watershed of World War II there have been some changes. While the major powers, including in this case Japan, have maintained independent shipbuilding capacity, the medium size powers of Europe have come to rely on imports or licensing. Of course, the number of warships in their inventories is now much smaller, so it is not surprising that they have not chosen to keep their dockyards in operation.

The Soviet Union, which in the interwar period had been very weak in shipbuilding, is now fully independent and perhaps on the verge of becoming the world's leading maritime power.

Perhaps more striking is the number of smaller nations which have developed some capability for building naval craft other than warships and submarines. These strivings for a degree of independence have, no doubt, been encouraged by the decline in the importance of warships in favor of patrol craft and torpedo boats, a trend perhaps to be accelerated by newer developments in ship-to-ship missilry.

For some time Argentina, Chile, Ceylon, India, Indonesia, Mexico, South Africa, Thailand and Turkey among the smaller powers have had indigenous shipbuilding capacity. Argentina, Chile and India have built frigates, and the latter seaward defense boats as well. Indonesia has built its own submarine chasers. The remainder have all constructed patrol boats.

There are very recent developments pointing to lessened dependence. Argentina and Brazil are now building submarines under license, and South Africa is thought to be considering their construction. North Korea and South Korea have entered into construction of submarine chasers and patrol boats, respectively. Both Israel and Iran are also moving toward capability for building small combat vessels.[4]

Overall, as indicated in Table 6-5, there seems to have been decreased aggregate dependence by the world's nations since the 1930s. The reason, in contrast to aircraft, would appear to be a slower rate of technological change, and perhaps also a less steep curve in the rise of costs. But it remains to be seen whether newer developments in naval warfare will significantly lower levels of dependence for smaller nations.

Armor

Here, as with naval craft, and in some contrast to aircraft, there appears to have been a trend toward lessened overall dependence. This may, however, merely reflect the newness of tank technology in the 1930s, when such vehicles were being built by only a few nations and when others were even still relying on traditional horse cavalry.[5]

At the levels of independence and near-independence, Italy and Czechoslovakia have dropped out to become mere licensees, while the USSR, Sweden and Switzerland have reduced their dependence. Basically, the strong barriers to becoming independent in this category have not changed.

Near the middle of the continuum, once significant indigenous producers of armored equipment such as Holland, Poland and, to a lesser degree, Austria and Hungary have become totally dependent and have even abandoned license-production.

Among the smaller nations there have been some few attempts at moving toward an independent base. China, paralleling its efforts in aircraft, has moved from continued copying of old Soviet tanks to indigenous development. India, before receiving a vast number of Soviet armored vehicles, experimented briefly with its modification of a British model known as the Vijayanta. Argentina has licensed French AMX-13 tanks and assembled Swiss Mowag armored cars, and South Africa, French Panhard armored cars. Israel earlier built a modified version of the old American Sherman tank known as the Isherman, refitted with larger caliber French and British cannon, and is now producing the Ben Gurion, fitted with French guns. The only attempt in the developing world, however, at a fully indigenous armored system is Brazil's Cutia fully tracked armored reconnaissance vehicle which has not yet entered full production.[6]

Basically, the overall level of worldwide dependence for armored vehicles has not changed much since the 1930s. There have been considerable technological advances and increased costs which have fully kept pace with the efforts of smaller powers to reduce their foreign dependence. There seem to be few auguries of change here, although in some cases, as in Brazil and Argentina where automotive industries are now expanding, there may later be more indigenously developed armored systems.

Small Arms

In small arms, where technological and economic requirements are relatively minimal, one might have expected a large number of nations to have developed independent bases of supply. If it were the case, it would be potentially significant, as in many situations this would allow for fighting at least a low-level conflict on an independent basis.

However, the number of nations capable of producing their own small arms, even by license, has remained surprisingly small. And this is despite a rather promiscuous policy by FN of Belgium, which has allowed licensing of some of its NATO-standardized weapons to just about anyone.[7]

There has, however, been a gradual increase in the number of smaller nations with their own small arms arsenals. In the 1930s only Argentina, Iran, Mexico, Turkey and China were at all active. Now Nigeria, Paraguay, Peru, Thailand, Indonesia, Salvador, Ceylon and the Dominican Republic, among others, have their own armories, usually working with licenses. Most of these nations, however, still rely on foreign imports for at least part of their needs, and while some are virtually independent for rifles and machine guns, few have reached that stage for artillery, grenades or mortars. According to the SIPRI study only Argentina, Brazil, India, Israel and South Africa among the smaller or medium powers have achieved that.[8]

A few smaller nations have produced indigenously designed small arms. Turkey and Argentina have strong traditional small arms industries. India and the Dominican Republic have now designed their own rifles. Israel has developed its UZI submachine gun, which has subsequently been exported and licensed abroad to Germany and Belgium, among others. It is now also reported to be in production on a new rifle (Galili) and machine gun, hoped to be equal or even superior to the presently standard NATO small arms.[9]

Actually, efforts toward independence by developing nations in small arms may not be all that critical for controls. Almost nobody is sanguine about controlling the arms trade at this level. The ease of clandestine shipment and the vast stores of small arms held by private brokers all over the world render controls on the small arms trade almost impossible.

The development of jet aircraft by a number of new nations would be—and may in fact turn out to be—devastating to the chances for controls. Similar developments in small arms would be almost superfluous. In the past decade, the world has virtually been flooded with Belgian FN rifles and with China's copy of the popular Russian AK-47 Kalashnikov assault rifle.

In summary of dependence levels for small arms in the two periods, it appears that the decline of traditional arsenals in countries like Sweden, Denmark and Austria has been balanced by some lessening of dependence for the more developed of the developing nations.

Long Range Trends in Dependence

Despite some shifting in the dependence levels of some nations, and with some variation between weapons categories, the long-term situation has remained quite stable. Somewhat more nations appear to be more dependent in aircraft, somewhat fewer in naval and armored equipment, while a considerable number appear to have reduced their dependence in small arms. Perhaps developments in jet fighter aircraft have obscured a gradual overall trend in the opposite direction.

Technological development and increased costs have appeared to balance out the ongoing economic development of most of the world's nations. The slight trend toward greater dependence in some categories has mostly been the result of the tight bipolar alignment of the postwar period which has allowed a number of nations, mostly in Europe, to rely upon the hegemonic powers for their needs. This pattern appears gradually to be breaking down, abetted by the newer trend toward transnational codevelopment ventures.

The following list summarizes the basic changes in dependence between our two periods. Only a few nations have exhibited marked changes toward either greater dependence or independence. Most importantly, there have been few changes where it would count the most, that is, at Levels 1 and 2.

1.   Substantial Increase in Overall Independence: USSR, China, India, Australia, South Africa, Iran
2.   Moderate Increase in Overall Independence: Argentina, Bulgaria, Canada, Cuba, Dominican Republic, Egypt, Finland, Mexico, Portugal, Sweden, Switzerland, Yugoslavia, New Zealand, Belgium
3.   Moderate Decrease in Overall Independence: Chile, Czechoslovakia, Greece, United Kingdom, Japan, Thailand, Turkey
4.   Substantial Decrease in Overall Independence: Austria, Denmark, Germany, Italy, Norway, Romania, Netherlands

GNP, PER CAPITA GNP AND ARMS DEPENDENCE

One important question is the level of economic development or capacity necessary to sustain various degrees of arms independence. Both GNP and per capita GNP can be used here in conjunction with dependence levels, with the former being a measure of gross economic output and often used to measure national power and the latter a good measure of the level of economic development. We had speculated, in approaching the subject, that the level of per capita GNP, measuring technological development, might constitute a floor beneath which even a nation of huge population might be unable to maintain a viable arms industry.

In Tables 6-1 and 6-2 we listed both kinds of economic data with those for arms dependence levels. There is some incompatibility for the data from the two periods. GNP and per capita GNP figures were available for the postwar period at various junctures. For the interwar period we have national income and per capita income information for the year 1938 for most but not all nations for which we have arms production data. The national income data will, however, still afford a picture of relative economic capacity and development at that time.

It is clear that most or all nations in both periods high in both GNP and per capita GNP have been capable of developing and producing their own weapons, although in some cases maintaining a degree of dependence by choice.

On the other end of the continuum, those nations with both relatively low GNP and low per capita GNP have not been able to produce their own arms even with the aid of licensing or copying. There have been no significant exceptions to these generalizations in either period except Canada, which has consistently chosen to remain dependent on the United States and Britain in both periods, at least until very recently.[10]

Between the extremes where nations are either low or high on both counts, there has been a grey area of intermediate dependence. In the interwar period something like 20 nations with national incomes ranging between $1 billion and $10 billion exhibited dependence levels in various weapons systems between Levels 3 and 5, although with some cases of Levels 1, 2 or 6 dependence for individual systems. Only a few nations with smaller national incomes had Level 4 or 5 dependence in some categories. In the postwar period, below the rank of the major powers, degrees of arms-producing independence have been exhibited by a range of nations whose GNPs were between about $7 billion and $90 billion at 1965 figures. Below $7 billion there were only a few cases of intermediate level dependence, with Israel then somewhat of an anomaly at a GNP of about $4 billion.

Perhaps the most interesting cases are those nations high either on GNP or per capita GNP but low on the other. This raises the question of whether being low on one or the other is necessarily a bar to an independent arms base, and of which is the most crucial.

In the interwar period there were three nations—China, Japan and the USSR—which were in the top rank in national income, but very low in per capita income. None of these had, at that time, very much of an indigenous research and development capability, although both the Soviets and Japanese were able to produce most of their arms with borrowed or licensed technology. What is perhaps indicated here is that even with a large GNP, a nation with a relatively low level of economic development is not likely to have the scientific and technical infrastructure necessary to develop its own weapons, although perhaps it will have a higher production capability once the technology has been borrowed from elsewhere.

For the interwar period, the above generalization is somewhat belied by the case of Italy. It was then eighth in the world in GNP but only 23rd in per capita income. Still, it managed almost complete independence in arms development and production, although producing weapons which did not prove particularly effective during the Second World War.

For those developed nations with high per capita incomes but low GNPs because of meager populations, there are obvious bars to a comprehensive arms-producing industry. In the interwar period this was demonstrated with Canada, Switzerland, New Zealand, Norway and perhaps Sweden. Their efforts toward independence were presumably limited by shortfalls in industrial manpower and capital.

Similar conclusions can be derived from observation of the juxtaposition of economic and arms-dependence data in the postwar period. China and India, at least until recently in the case of the former, have both had trouble developing their own weapons systems, although both have been able to produce a good part of their weapons needs on license. The Soviet Union's per capita GNP is now sufficiently high to allow for independence, although only at the expense of development in other areas of its economy. Italy, oddly, has greatly improved its ranking in per capita income, while its dependence for arms has simultaneously increased, mostly because of its choice to become essentially a licensee of American products.

Among those nations on our list with GNPs of below $4 billion (1965 figures) only New Zealand and Israel rank relatively high in per capita GNP. The latter has achieved some independence, although at great cost in the distortion of its economy. At a higher level, Sweden has perhaps gone furthest in combining a rather modest GNP with high per capita GNP in building what is very close to an independent arms development and production base.

Gross National Product remains a fairly good indicator of the ability of nations to manufacture weapons. For indigenous development capability, however, reasonably high per capita GNP appears to be a prerequisite, although China may yet surprise by overcoming its handicaps.

Controls, Embargoes and Pariahs

We have demonstrated that the ability of lesser powers to develop an independent arms industry, even in small arms, is strongly circumscribed by limitations of economic and technological resources and of population, that is, by those factors which aggregate to GNP or per capita GNP. Fears about conventional arms proliferation have proved as unfounded thus far, on a somewhat less ominous level, as those about nuclear proliferation.

In the interwar period this was essentially a moot point, given the relative assuredness of arms supplies for most nations, most of the time. The absence of controls and the freewheeling activities of private arms traders found few, if any, nations being denied arms.[11] Now, a more complex situation has developed. Some nations, branded "aggressors" by some suppliers or by the "international community," find themselves not so automatically assured of outside supply. Some of these have been forced to make extensive efforts at independent arms-producing capacity. The successes and failures of these efforts to date may tell us something about the outside limits imposed by size or economic capacity on achieving autarky.

There have been a number of nations which have outdone themselves in arms production, beyond what might have been predicted from economic indicators. The most important have been Israel, South Africa, China and India, with recent indications that Iran may now be entering the lists. Enormous oil revenues may later allow for considerable arms production in some of the Arab countries. In each case, efforts toward independence have been encouraged by cutoffs of supply, although at least in the case of India this may have been secondary to considerations of prestige and of achieving independence in a broader sense. In this grouping we have two nations with low GNPs and high per capita GNPs (Israel and South Africa), and two with high GNPs and very low per capita GNPs (China and India), with Iran presently showing a rapid transition on both dimensions.

Israel, with a population of only 2.5 million, has carried out what is perhaps the most extensive effort at achieving autarky in the face of controls, embargoes, low leverage and the further prospect of a virtual cutoff if the threat to American oil interests should loom more starkly. Its efforts at overcoming these problems have been examined in some detail in a recent book by ex-Defense Minister Peres, and in the SIPRI volume.[1 2] The story is illustrative in a developmental sense.

In the early postwar period an elaborate clandestine system of scavenging weapons was developed, while an extensive small arms industry was built. Later, in the period of French generosity, some capacity for modifying major weapons systems was gradually developed. Old American Sherman tanks were refitted with larger caliber French and British cannon, and old American halftracks were similarly upgraded. In aircraft, extensive capability in over-hauling engines and producing spare parts was achieved, along with license-production of combat trainer aircraft.

Later, both before and after the imposition of the 1967 French embargo, there was movement toward a newer stage of self-sufficiency. Virtually complete independence in small arms production, including ammunition, was achieved and development was begun on still newer infantry weapons to supersede the UZI and Belgian models. Based on captured equipment, production was begun of the Soviet Katyusha rocket. In aircraft, a short-haul STOL transport was developed, while French licenses were obtained for engines usable with trainer aircraft and helicopters.

More recently, an almost fully indigenous jet fighter aircraft—copied from the French Mirage but powered by American engines—has been developed, and also an indigenous tank. A surface-to-surface missile, the Gabriel, has been developed for shipboard service, while a still more sophisticated missile, the Jericho, perhaps intended to be mounted with a nuclear warhead, has also entered production. There has also been indigenous development of a television-guided bomb reputed to be similar to those recently introduced by the United States in Vietnam, the Shafrir air-to-air missile and a home-produced naval patrol craft.[1 3]

Despite these achievements, however, it is clear that Israel's size does not allow for anything like Level 1 or 2 independence across the whole spectrum of weapons systems. Even with its defense budget stretched to the limit, now some 40 per cent of GNP, it is still critically dependent for jet aircraft, tanks, helicopters and some artillery. There is little prospect of its overcoming the lack of indigenously developed aircraft engines for jet fighters. And the Israelis' requirements for matching the arms acquisitions of their opponents are high and continuously increasing, as borne out by the 1973 war, with its lessons regarding a whole range of newer, conventional military equipment. Finally, the 1973 conflict did indicate that for Israel there are severe problems with respect to the quantity of production in addition to development of indigenous weaponry. Even in areas where Israel has its own production facilities, including infantry weapons and ammunition, resupply from the United States was necessary during the 1973 war to make up for heavy equipment losses, measured in billions of dollars. This case is a measure of the virtual insurmountability of such problems for a small nation.

Some recent press reports have indicated that the United States government has decided to help the Israelis build an indigenous arms manufacturing base.[14] One reason was said to be that of lowering the visibility of American exports. But also, American decisionmakers were said to have become fearful of losing all diplomatic influence in Tel Aviv if the Israelis should become independent on their own. This indicates that in some cases movement toward weapons-producing independence by a nation with initially low leverage may, if successful, paradoxically result in improving its leverage.

The case of South Africa, another nation with low leverage and under embargo, contains some similarities. There is one vast difference in that its requirements for sophistication in arms acquisition are lower, assuming the absence of big-power intervention in any future conflict.

In the mid-1960s, after the United Nations announced its embargo, the South Africans were cut off from American and British arms and have since relied on perhaps precarious deliveries from France and Italy. They, like the Israelis, have now begun to move toward self-sufficiency, and on a roughly equivalent economic base.[15]

South Africa has acquired numerous licenses which now allow it to produce all its small arms and ammunition, armored cars potentially useful for urban counterinsurgency and armed jet trainer aircraft. Also, there is a collaborative venture with the French said to have resulted in a superior surface-to-air missile, the Crotale, useful against low-flying tactical aircraft. South Africa still remains dependent for jet fighter aircraft, tanks, helicopters and most categories of naval craft. For the foreseeable future, however, and given its limited requirements, it would now appear to be very close to essential self-sufficiency.

India, having long licensed some British aircraft and tanks, is now slowly moving toward self-sufficiency with borrowed French, British and Soviet technology.[16] It already makes most of its own small arms. It has designed some indigenous aircraft and armored vehicles and produces several categories of naval craft. However, its essential dependence for arms is not likely to be mitigated for some time. Its failure to match the jet fighters of major powers with the HAL

Marut was an example of the difficulties faced by a nation with still limited technological capacity. On the other hand, India's recently successful explosion of a nuclear device may be anticipatory of significant future changes.

Pakistan's need for an indigenous arms base was recently made apparent, during the debacle of its war with India. Its supplies had become as precarious as those of Israel and South Africa, and as with Israel there was the necessity for matching vast stores of arms being supplied to an antagonist by outside powers. To date, though, Pakistan's efforts toward self-sufficiency have been quite meager. There has been some production of naval craft, and the licensing of a German antitank missile, in addition to considerable production of small arms. That is all. Essential dependence remains for most major systems.

China has made an effort toward self-sufficiency in the last decade which on a larger scale is even more impressive than that made by Israel.[17] Up to the early 1960s the Chinese were able to rely on a wide range of licensing agreements with the Soviets. Then there was a sudden cutoff. Fortunately for the Chinese the previously acquired licenses allowed for continued production of systems which remained usable, if gradually becoming obsolete. But a breathing spell was obtained in which no conflicts occurred which might have tested the efficiency of embryonic Chinese arms production.

Very recently, there have been numerous reports of the Chinese having developed indigenous systems over a wide range of weapons categories. Jet aircraft, missiles of all sorts, new tanks, nuclear submarines and advanced air-defense radars are all reported to be at or near the production stage. The disabilities associated with low per capita GNP are gradually being overcome. Still, there are questions of just how sound these weapons are and whether they would be a qualitative match for Soviet arms if a conventional conflict should occur. There is no indication yet of how China's new F-9 jet fighter would stand up against a Phantom, a MIG-21 or a Mirage, much less against the newer aircraft now about to be produced by each of the other major powers.

The Chinese case perhaps highlights the importance of the relative slowness of technological change in weaponry in the postwar period. If a nation had been cut off from all foreign weapons technology in the 1930s and forced to rely subsequently on previously concluded license agreements its air and armored equipment would have been hopelessly out of date within a few short years. The aircraft and tanks of 1930 were but primitive forebears of those of 1940. Nowadays, systems which were new technology in 1960 are still not at a terrible disadvantage in the early 1970s. China has had a breathing space which would not have been available in the earlier period. Still, for a nation suddenly cut off from outside supply the road to self-sufficiency is a long one.

Ironically, the embargoes and controls which have forced additional nations toward arms self-sufficiency may yet result in making future controls all the more difficult as these nations themselves become suppliers. Israel has already sold missiles to Iran and Singapore, jet trainers to Uganda and small arms to a number of nations, including several in Latin America.[18] China sells some weapons to Pakistan and to several African nations, as well as to North Vietnam. As its production capacity increases, it will no doubt become a more serious competitor to the other major powers in any number of recipient-nation markets. And, of course, a forced draft move toward arms self-sufficiency by Japan would have even more serious implications for controls.

Potential for Nuclear Proliferation

Analysis of the linkage between economic capacity and arms producing capability may be extended to problems of nuclear proliferation. There is a considerable literature on the "Nth country problem," with attempts to assess the capacity for certain nations to become additional members of the nuclear club.[19]

William Bader, among others, has noted that earlier fears prevalent a decade ago about the expansion of the nuclear club to 25 or 30 members have proved unfounded and are likely to continue to be unrealized.[20] As he and others have pointed out, the costs and technological requirements are exceedingly high, particularly if requirements for advanced delivery systems are taken into account. It turns out that there are now very few nations which would seem to have both a rational reason for acquiring nuclear weapons and the wherewithal to carry through a successful program to that end. To the contrary, however, India's 1974 explosion of a nuclear device appears to have triggered off long-dormant fears about widespread proliferation.

A few years ago a report was written under the aegis of the United Nations by a team of scholars representing various nations and disciplines in which the constraints imposed by limited economic capacity on nations wishing to go nuclear were analyzed in considerable detail.[21] Costs were estimated for the various major components of a nuclear program (fissile materials, warhead development and production, and delivery systems) and the overall costs for nuclear forces of various sizes were then computed. The latter figures were then in turn related to data on current defense expenditures in order to arrive at an estimate of the cutoff point below which it would not be likely that a nation could develop a nuclear force.

Certain assumptions were made, perhaps unrealistically, about proportions of defense budgets which could be allocated just to nuclear forces in competition with other defense requirements. And there was an assumed normalcy of an about 10 percent ratio of defense budgets to GNP, which ignored the possibilities for stretching which might have been obvious, if only on the basis of the wartime experiences of any number of nations. Worse yet, the United Nations report did not analyze the potential aggregate effect of stretching both of these factors to produce a combined effect.

The report concluded that it would cost a prospective nuclear power about $500 million per year for a small, high-quality nuclear force similar to those now possessed by France and Britain. There was also the possibility for a more moderate sized force, costing about $170 million per year, which might utilize 50 or so soft-emplaced missiles for delivery, an estimate which appears to have proved rather accurate in light of some of the figures published for the cost of the Indian program.

The upshot of the United Nations report was that it estimated, on the basis of these costs and of existing GNP's and defense budgets, that only a small number of additional nations beyond the then existing five nuclear powers would appear to have had the capacity for building a nuclear force. India, West Germany, Japan, Italy, Canada and perhaps a few others were considered to be possibilities. The cutoff for GNP was up near $20 billion, and for a defense budget, close to $2 billion.

Then, beginning in 1970, there were numerous reports in the press and elsewhere indicating that Israel either had, or was on the verge of having, nuclear weapons, along with a delivery system of surface-to-surface, solid-fueled missiles with ranges of about 280 miles.[22] In light of the United Nations report's analysis this was surprising, as Israel's GNP and defense expenditures were far beneath what was considered to be minimal for developing and maintaining a nuclear force.

Actually, a closer look at the specifics of the Israeli situation, along with an examination of the way they have availed themselves of a number of transfer modes, might have led the United Nations investigators to question their conclusions. First, the transfer of the Dimona reactor from France had saved the Israelis most of the costs of research and development which would had to have been borne in going it alone. Next, earlier collaboration with France on the surface-to-surface delivery missile appeared to have given Israel a technological windfall, enabling it to proceed with work on the missile even after the embargo.

Israel's ratio of defense budget to GNP is 40 percent, the highest in the world. Even with a low ratio of nuclear force costs to overall defense expenditures, this would appear to allow for something like $100-200 million per year to be spent on nuclear forces. The main point, however, is the low cost of delivery systems which are required to carry warheads no more than 300 miles. It had been demonstrated in the United Nations report that the bulk of the costs for a nuclear force are in the delivery system, and that these costs increase almost geometrically with increases in required ranges for delivery.[23] It is the delivery system, and not the bomb itself, which is the major impediment to nuclear proliferation, at least on a cost basis.

This case indicates just how far a given nation may go toward self-sufficiency in arms, given the prod of self-perceived extreme necessity. It is also a case of advanced weapons development on the basis of low GNP and high per capita GNP, in direct contrast to that of China and India. It is hard to say just what the Israeli experience indicates as a pattern for imitation by other nations, a large number of which have far higher economic capacity.

Further, Israel's apparent development of nuclear weapons may also be important for what it indicates about the tie-in between conventional arms control and nuclear proliferation. Its quest for a nuclear deterrent was critically impelled by insecurity about future supplies of conventional arms. It is ironic that it appears to have developed the capacity for building nuclear weapons before developing an equivalent capacity to build a tank or jet fighter aircraft.

Summary

We conclude that both in the past and at present there have been very firm operative restraints on the capacity for all but a few of the world's nations to develop or produce their own arms. The highly pyramidal structure of dependence remains intact and promises to remain so. As widespread proliferation has, until recently, remained a faint mirage in the context of nuclear developments, so has the prospect of a world without extreme dominance of arms supplies by a few major powers, with all that entails.

The few major arms suppliers have then, at least collectively, the power to enforce controls if they so wish. But that, of course, is not so simple, even if assumed desirable. On that note, we shall next look at both the history and the prospects for controls, and at the impact thereon of our diplomatic systems variables.

Chapter Seven

Controlling the Arms Trade

In the past several years, after a lengthy hiatus, there has been an increased sense of urgency in international forums about controlling the conventional arms trade. It had finally occurred to many observers that, while a tremendous amount of attention has been paid to the problems of strategic nuclear balance and nuclear proliferation, wars were still being fought with more prosaic weapons. Resolutions were offered in the United Nations, a literature flowered reminiscent of the 1930s and several research centers were set up to study the arms trade. The context was altered from several decades ago, but still there was a sense of deja vu as proposals were made which ranged from the palpably insufficient to the absurdly idealistic.

In this, our concluding chapter, we shall examine the implications for controlling the worldwide flow of arms which emerge from our comparative analysis of the two periods. We shall take a further look at the role of our systems variables and attempt to show how seemingly emerging trends may affect controls in the future.

Several topics will be handled in tandem here. First, we shall examine the history of attempts at controlling the conventional arms trade, disaggregating them into quasi-international, multilateral and unilateral measures. Along another dimension, we shall examine the problem from the differing perspectives of suppliers and recipients as aggregate groupings. We shall look at the successes achieved to date by embargoes, neutrality policies and government licensing, and the less visible impact of varying aggressiveness and/or passivity in selling arms by both public and private suppliers.

Next, we shall examine the history of a long-term ongoing debate over controls on the arms trade. We shall look at the rhetorical context of reformist efforts in both periods and, for the United States, at the skein of continuity running from the Nye Committee hearings to their recent successors in the Senate Foreign Relations and Banking and Currency Committees.

Finally, in concluding our analysis, we shall make use of the concepts of "levels of analysis" and "collective goods" in attempting to explain the seeming futility of all efforts at controlling the arms trade to date.

For an additional prefatory note, a truism. The long-term debate over controlling the arms trade has been merely a microcosm or subset of a broader, normatively based dialogue over the proper conduct of foreign policy itself and over the essential reality of international relations. Indeed, the failure to come to grips with this may have caused no little mischief, for at times suggestions for controls have seemed to be based on a forlorn hope of abstracting the arms trade from its overall context.

As in the broader context, there has been an identifiable dialogue between self-styled "realists" and "idealists." The debate has usually been over the very nature of man himself and has involved a dichotomization between essentially optimistic and pessimistic views on a variety of subjects ranging about conflict, war and the conduct of diplomacy. The essentials of this debate were set forth some time ago by E. H. Carr, in classic and almost enduring fashion.[1]

This writer has a confession of sorts to make. He is himself a self-styled "realist," at least on this subject. It will be clear that the remainder of this chapter will be written somewhat from a point of view, one hopefully based on the preceding analysis, and with an effort to see both sides. It is a point of view which runs strongly against the grain of the presently prevailing academic mood, on this as well as on related subjects.

THE HISTORY OF CONTROLS ON THE ARMS TRADE

Controls at the Quasi-International and Multilateral Levels

There have been various efforts at controls which may be described along a continuum running from multilateral to international. We will use the term quasi-international here at one end of the spectrum, for lack of a better term and to indicate that, in the fullest sense, no truly international effort has ever been undertaken. Although we shall simultaneously discuss multilateral and quasi-international measures because they blend into one another, there is perhaps one distinction between them. Quasi-international will denote those efforts which have been instituted by, or implemented through, the major international organizations of the two periods, namely, the League of Nations and the United Nations. Actually, as most measures promoted by these organizations have been respected by only some of their members, they have effectively devolved into what might more appropriately be called multilateral.

In earlier centuries, there were a few multilateral attempts at curtailing the arms traffic. Some writers, without advancing very much specific detail, have indicated that the Christian nations of Europe during the Middle

Ages had at least informal agreements on the impermissibility of selling arms to the much feared "infidel" Turks. There were cries of anguish when this agreement was periodically broken.[2] Then later, during the Reformation, Protestant nations led by Britain and Holland attempted to implement embargoes against Catholic Spain and its allies after a time in which laissez faire had been the norm in the arms trade.[3]

By and large, however, there appear to have been few significant attempts at multilateral controls before the period immediately preceding World War I. In broader context, this parallels the virtual absence of arms control arrangements in general and the effective absence of international organizations as control mechanisms.[4] And, as we have previously noted, the period between 1870 and 1914 was the zenith of laissez faire in arms trading, when the phrase "antinational trade in arms" was frequently used by critics of private arms dealers.

Nevertheless, one can date the modern beginnings of multilateral control efforts at about 1890. A number of multilateral agreements were effected between 1890 and 1914 by various combinations of colonial powers, each intended to regulate the importation of arms and ammunition into respective colonial spheres in Africa. Among these were the Brussels Act of 1890, the Anglo-French-Italian Agreement of 1906 on Ethiopia, the General Act of the Algeciras Conference of 1906 on Morocco and the Brussels Protocol of 1908 on Western Equatorial Africa.

The most important of these agreements was the Brussels Act of 1890, if for no other reason than that it raised some important issues which were to be echoed again and again and which have not subsided. Actually, the agreement on regulating arms transfers was part of a broader one on the repression of the African slave trade, signed by 13 European states and the United States, Iran, Zanzibar and the Congo Free State. The section on arms transfers prohibited the introduction of most arms and ammunition into a vast zone of Africa, except under some circumstances where there was to be publicity and supervision.[5]

The first major multilateral agreement, therefore, was essentially an attempt by the major powers to regulate arms flows into areas under their domination. It was inherently discriminatory, geared to preservation of the status quo.

The provisions of the Brussels Act dealing with the arms trade were never effectively implemented. At least one article on the arms trade in East Africa during that period indicates that the embargo was thwarted almost at will by rapacious European gun runners and their Arab accomplices.[6] As was later often to be the case, attempts at stanching small arms shipments, particularly to areas with lengthy coastlines, were essentially futile.

The next significant attempt at controls on an international level took place in the immediate aftermath of the First World War, embodied in the ill-starred St. Germain Convention of 1919. An attempt at comprehensive controls was given impetus at this juncture by the widely held belief that private arms trading activities had been among the main causes of the arms races preceding the war, and hence, of the war itself. The problem was cited in the Covenant of the League of Nations, which stated that:

> The Members of the League agree that the manufacture by private enterprise of munitions and implements of war is open to grave objection. The Council shall advise how the evil effects attendant upon such manufacture can be prevented, due regard being had to the necessities of those Members of the League, which are not able to manufacture the munitions and implements of war necessary for their safety.[7]

The subsequent Convention of St. Germain was an adjunct to the Versailles Peace Treaty and the covenant and was intended to provide for the general regulation of arms transfers under the supervision of the league. It envisaged a system of national licensing and publicity for the arms exports of each country, and further proposed to prohibit them except by the governments of contracting states. With an obviously short-term perspective, it was actually meant to control the large supplies of munitions on hand at the conclusion of the war, to prevent them from falling into hands considered undesirable by the victorious powers.

The Convention of St. Germain was a dead letter from its inception. Some nations, most significantly the United States, did not sign or ratify it. The United States felt that its provisions were so inextricably interwoven with the league as to make it impractical to sign. And the convention's provisions conflicted both with America's Monroe Doctrine and with its traditional laissez faire attitude toward the activities of private business.[8]

At any rate, the ill-fated agreement was generally perceived as a successor to the Brussels Act, advanced by Britain and France to prevent a flow of arms to their colonial holdings in Africa and the Middle East and hence to forestall anticolonial revolutions. Again, the issue of discrimination had arisen, although there could not yet be an effective complaining voice from those discriminated against.

The effect of this first quasi-international attempt at controls having been nugatory, there was subsequently an at least theoretical interest in supervising the arms trade, embodied in the Geneva Arms Traffic Convention of 1925.[9] Here, there was an attempt to revise the St. Germain agreement to make it more acceptable to the nonsignees, particularly the United States. It was part of a broader effort toward international disarmament at Geneva at that time which included the negotiations on chemical warfare and the protracted wrangles of the formal Geneva Disarmament Conferences.

The Geneva Arms Traffic Convention was to provide for systems of national licensing and, most importantly, for increased publicity on arms transfers. By not restricting arms exports to nonsignatory states, as entailed in the St. Germain agreement, it appeared to meet what had been one of the principle American objections to the earlier proposal. Also, there was to be no direct supervision by the league itself, which had been still another sticky point for the United States.

The Geneva convention never did come into force, although it was later ratified by the United States Senate in 1935, at the time of heightened concern over the arms trade demonstrated by the Nye Committee hearings and the neutrality legislation. The convention became a dead letter when it failed to get the number of signees required to bring it into being. By the mid-1930s the worsening world situation and the clear determination of the Axis powers to circumvent the provisions of the Geneva convention, as well as to ignore the league itself, had rendered both its spirit and letter rather irrelevant.

During the negotiations over the Geneva convention, the issue of discrimination had again arisen. The primary thrust of the agreement, watered down from the supervisory emphasis of St. Germain, was toward publicity as an implicit and partial measure of control. However, the nonproducers of arms objected, noting that their arms acquisitions, mostly from foreign sources, would be monitored while those of the producers would not. They pushed for an agreement which would cover production of arms as well and which would monitor state as well as private manufacture. The negotiations droned on amidst a welter of disagreement over these essential points.

One identifiable result of these attempts at international agreement was the initiation of the league's *Armaments Year Book*, begun in 1924. It was to become a prime source of information on the interwar arms trade, albeit with severe limitations, particularly those of underreporting by some nations and the omission of data on major weapons systems.

At the time, it was hoped that publication of arms trade data by the league would spotlight the activities of the major arms suppliers and thus help to limit their activities under the glare of international public opinion. This pathetic hope was raised in an era in which liberal and utopian reformers were more enamored of the practical value and moral infallibility of world public opinion than has since been the case.[10] But it was at least a first step. Some commentators on the contemporary arms trade have advocated a similar data-gathering and publicity role for the United Nations, seemingly undaunted by the almost complete impotence of these measures to achieve controls in an earlier period.[11]

During the 1930s, after the failure of the Geneva convention had become apparent, there were still other proposals made at the league in a similar vein. There was one by Spain on international supervision of both private and state manufacture of arms and another by Turkey which envisaged the actual internationalization of arms manufacture as a condition for abolishing private manufacture. These proposals were lost in the gathering storm of the period.[12]

At least until very recently, the postwar period has witnessed no really serious attempts at international agreements. The subject has seldom been raised at the United Nations, with the exceptions of a few resolutions, most notably those by Denmark and Malta in the 1960s, on increased publicity for arms transfers.[13] And the United Nations' data-gathering activities have been derisory at best.

The reasons for lack of activity are not difficult to comprehend. First, problems of conventional arms transfers have taken a back seat to those of controls over strategic weapons production and testing, and nuclear proliferation. Then, there has been the rather obvious futility of achieving any agreement among the major powers. For the league, at the outset, there was not as much division at the major power level. And as earlier had been the case, there has been strong resistance to control measures by the arms-dependent nations, which have perceived them as further attempts by the big powers at maintaining hegemony. There has been a parallel here with the negotiations over nuclear proliferation, where India and others have resisted signing and have carped at big-power monopoly and vertical proliferation.[14]

The problem of publicity seems essentially to have been solved outside the United Nations with the annual compilations of arms transfer data now undertaken by SIPRI and the Institute for Strategic Studies. The former has made a real effort at internationalizing its staff, and includes Soviet-bloc members to avoid the stigma of appearing to be tied to blocs or specific governments. Its obvious success would appear to have rendered a parallel effort by the United Nations superfluous, except as a perhaps more legitimate symbol of international concern.

More recently there has been some talk, and a few resolutions, pointing to regional agreements by recipient nations allegedly interested in reducing inflows of arms.[15] Most of this tentative activity has taken place in Latin America. First, there was a proposal by Costa Rica in 1958 which would have set regionwide ceilings on arms acquisitions, based on minimal internal security needs, and also envisioned maximum limits to air, sea and land forces for countries of the region. This proposal would also have involved an agreement among Latin American nations not to purchase arms outside the Western Hemisphere. Oddly, it seemed to reinforce the Monroe Doctrine, and is suspected of having originated at American behest.

In 1967 a similar proposal was made at the OAS gathering at Punta del Este. It, too, envisaged limits on various types of forces and on defense expenditures. Further, it was proposed that the nations of the region agree not to buy—or themselves manufacture—supersonic aircraft, naval vessels heavier than destroyers, tanks over 30 tons or missiles. The proposal was not accepted. Perhaps, however, it may serve as a model for more serious future efforts along the same lines.

Regional agreements of this sort would appear to have certain clear prerequisites. One is the relative absence of conflict or even of serious tension within the region and considerable trust among the participants—that is, the virtual achievement of what Deutsch has called "security communities."[16] Another, perhaps, is the absence of concern about future conflicts with outside powers, as the region's nations would be left relatively defenseless. These conditions are now closest to obtaining in Latin America, which may explain why matters got at least to the proposal stage there, although Soviet shipments to Peru, and rising tensions between it and the new conservative regime in Chile, may indicate some incipient breakdown of regional stability. To a much lesser degree, such a proposal might now make sense in sub-Saharan Africa. In the Middle East it would now appear out of the question. Of course, the participants to such agreements would have to ignore their prestige implications, as well as the formalizing of discrimination by larger powers whose arms superiority would be frozen. One might add here that the seeming impending change in the world balance of power to be wrought by rising prices for scarce raw materials may make such agreements less likely in the future, as many of the developing countries, sensing their growing power, are likely to be much less amenable to freezing the status quo as reflected in arms inventories.

Multilateral Embargoes

Aside from quasi-international or regional efforts at controls there have also been efforts at a more narrowly multilateral level. Mostly, these have involved the numerous embargoes undertaken in both periods. Here, too, there has been an almost unrelieved history of failure due to the lack of coordinated behavior by suppliers who have rarely achieved the perspective of a common interest.[17]

After World War I, and simultaneous with the negotiations over the St. Germain Convention, there was a concerted attempt by the major powers to embargo strife-ridden China. There had been a precedent with the short-lived prohibition of arms shipments to China during the Boxer Rebellion. In 1919, however, at the initiation of the United States, an agreement on a full embargo was reached by most of the major powers, including Japan, which was to be applied to the central authority in Peking as well as to the various warlord factions.[18]

The multilateral embargo upon China in the 1920s turned into a complete fiasco, so much so that it appears to have produced widespread cynicism which may in turn have affected subsequent attempts elsewhere. Arms found their way to China not only from the two major nonsignatories—the Soviet Union and supposedly restricted Germany—but also from France, the United States, Britain, Denmark, Norway and Japan. The agreement was marred by endless disputes over definitions of armaments and war materials, with military aircraft being transferred in the guise of commercial craft and explosives as industrial chemicals.

Evasions became so flagrant that the embargo was lifted in 1929, while the Civil War raged on unabated, albeit with a smaller number of recognizable viable factions. As Atwater commented: "All indications point to the conclusion that the reason for lifting the embargo was not the 'stability' of the situation in China, but rather the general ineffectiveness of the embargo agreement as a means of preventing arms and munitions of war from reaching that country."[19] In an era where the ability of private traders to evade embargoes by masked retransfers was unquestioned, the result was the familiar syndrome of "if we don't sell them arms, someone else will." Only later was it to become evident that state controls would mitigate, but by no means solve, the problem.

In China, confusion caused by the multiplicity of factions and the obscurity of the political issues involved, made it difficult to pin the label of aggressor on any party. Therefore, no issue arose over the merits of a policy applied, at least ostensibly, with an even hand to all parties. In subsequent cases, however, painful dilemmas would arise both over the practicality and morality of evenhanded approaches where distinctions might be made between aggressors and victims. The dilemma was particularly acute where an imbalance of armaments between belligerents existed at the initiation of the embargo, thereby freezing an advantage for one side. This conundrum has ever since dogged the efforts of well-meaning statesmen, complicating the desire for easy consistency in the application of moral standards.

The Chaco War between Bolivia and Paraguay was an important case in a number of respects and was commented upon at great length in the international legal journals of the mid-1930s.[20] The interplay between moral and pragmatic factors was highlighted and in the United States it was perhaps this case, more than anything else, which triggered the Nye Committee hearings, the neutrality laws, the setting up of formal licensing procedures and the erection of the Munitions Control Board. Similar reactions were inspired in Britain and France.

At the outset of the Chaco War in 1934, the United States and at least 30 other nations announced an embargo on both belligerents. It was bitterly denounced by Bolivia, because of Paraguay's alleged prior advantage in arms stores. As it turned out, there were wholesale violations of the embargo on both sides. Arms deals were consummated almost with impunity by international cartels which used transshipments through neighboring Latin American nations. There were blatant fabrications of consignment papers to hide intended destinations of arms. And, as later would happen with American shipments to Pakistan in 1971, there were questions about the continuation of arms deals contracted for before the embargo, allowing some governments to wink at transfers already "in the pipeline."

The Chaco embargo, like the one in China, was an almost total farce. Toward the end of the conflict, many of the ostensible adherents to the embargo lifted it with respect to Bolivia only, when it accepted—and Paraguay declined—the league's recommendation for a settlement. Though the embargo was by this time not very meaningful, something of a precedent was set in that there was a multilateral attempt at forcing cessation of conflict using the embargo as an instrument of coercion.

In the Italo-Ethiopian conflict of 1935, some 50 members of the league invoked a one-sided embargo on Italy. Switzerland and Luxembourg, along with the United States (which had just passed its neutrality laws), applied embargoes to both sides.[21] In this case, quasi-international or multilateral action was essentially futile from the outset, given Italy's virtual Level 1 independence in arms production and the one-sided nature of the war. A continuing trickle of arms to Ethiopia from some European nations, particularly France and Sweden, was unable to alter the outcome.

At the conclusion of this brief war, the league embargo against Italy was lifted with almost indecent haste at the behest of France and Britain. They were more interested in the appeasement policy toward Italy represented by the Hoare-Laval Pact.

Despite the merely cathartic nature of the league embargo against Italy, however, an important precedent was set, with an international organization having attempted to embargo an aggressor nation in what was a rather unambiguous case. The precedent was not to be followed until the postwar case of South Africa, where the issue involved essentially internal behavior.

One further attempt at a multilateral embargo took place during the Spanish Civil War.[22] Here, both the United States and Britain applied embargoes which effectively cut off their firms' arms shipments to the Loyalist side. The issue of the fairness of an evenhanded policy which appeared effectively to deny the victim of aggression weapons while the aggressor had an open pipeline to other sources arose here in bold relief.

Actually, the Loyalists were fairly well provisioned by France, Holland and the Soviet Union, although not well enough to match the vast inflow of German and Italian arms acquired by Franco's forces. Shipments to the Loyalists from France were only sporadic and became a matter of hot dispute among various factions of its governmental coalition.[23] Some American arms transshipped through Mexico and Canada by leftist supporters of the incumbent regime, also reached the Loyalists.

Thus, in the interwar period the looseness of controls, private activities and the breadth of the supplier market rendered attempts at controls ineffective and haphazard at best. And, the moral validity of policies which appeared to treat both aggressors and victims with cold impartiality was called into question. Just before World War II, the United States faced this latter question more squarely with its Lend-Lease agreements, after a period in which it had embargoed victims of aggression while routinely passing on arms licenses for aggressive nations which were imminently to be its enemies.[24]

In the postwar period there have been some few further attempts at multilateral embargoes and controls. Of course, in a period where arms sales have become a matter of continuous governmental policy and review, multilateral controls and embargoes have assumed a somewhat different meaning. Prior to 1940 an embargo had been a definitive act, interrupting what was normally an accepted policy of laissez faire. When all arms shipments had become a matter of positive governmental policy implementation, negative controls or embargoes came to represent merely an accentuation or highlighting of policy. The United States, for instance, doesn't need a formal arms embargo on Cuba. Over time, Israel has been embargoed by many potential suppliers, albeit without formal declarations.

However, some multilateral embargoes or controls have been put forth in the manner of announced policy, usually to dramatize a change. In the early 1950s the United States, Britain and France pronounced a tripartite arms control policy in the Middle East which was intended to forestall a heavy influx of arms in that contested region, to maintain a balance between the belligerents and to circumvent the policy dilemma presented by Israel for the West.[25] This was not a complete multilateral embargo, but rather an attempt at coordinating policy to effect a balance of arms at a relatively low level, that is, equivalent to what was later proposed by Latin American recipients at Punta del Este. The policy was initiated while Western influence in the Middle East was still dominant.

Hopes for the success of this effort were dashed in 1955 with the beginning of Soviet shipments to Nasser and later further exploded when coups in Iraq and Syria shifted their client relationships away from the West. This was a precursor of later situations in Nigeria and India where Soviet arms shipments in the face of Western recalcitrance were used as an opening wedge for the extension of overall influence. These cases have demonstrated that multilateral efforts at controls can be effective only when the objects of controls are wholly within the influence orbit of those seeking to implement them.

There were brief attempts at multilateral embargoes on both the Indo-Pakistan War of 1965 and the Arab-Israeli conflict of 1967. At the outset of the former conflict a coordinated embargo on both belligerents was announced by their erstwhile primary suppliers, the United States and Britain. Although the embargo was quickly lifted for both sides at the cessation of hostilities, the legacy of bitterness drove both into new client relationships, with Pakistan becoming primarily a client of China and India of the Soviet Union.

A similar embargo announcement by the United States and Britain greeted the opening of the Arab-Israeli conflict in 1967. It, too, was quickly lifted after a short war. However, no such formal embargoes were enunciated during the 1973 conflict, although Britain did cut off spare parts shipments to Israel for its Centurion tank force.

The rationale for this type of embargo seems almost incomprehensible. It appears to be merely a demonstration of disapproval and now seems to have become a traditional ritual of self-righteousness on the part of arms suppliers who feel compelled, for the benefit of world opinion, to act outraged when their arms are finally put to use. And, there may be the hope that cutoffs of further supplies and spare parts will serve to foreshorten a conflict once begun. Here again, the question of effective giving of advantage to one or another side may come into play. In the 1965 and 1967 conflicts, hostilities ended before these factors could have operated. In 1973 Israel was disadvantaged to some extent by what were effectively embargoes by Western European nations.

The United Nations-sponsored embargo on South Africa has previously been discussed. It was perhaps a milestone in that it was the first attempt by an international body to force compliant behavior on a nation for reasons other than external aggression.[26] The embargo on South Africa has not proved particularly effective, despite the adherence of the United States and Britain, its previous major suppliers. The refusal of France, Italy and Belgium to comply has negated the policies of the United States and Britain while, as we have seen, the South Africans have responded by building toward an indigenous arms-producing base.

It remains to be seen whether there will be additional embargoes in response to internal behavior deemed unacceptable by a majority of world opinion as measured in United Nations votes. Obviously, there would be numerous candidates for such action, aside from the question of the balance of voting strength in the United Nations.

In summary, the history of multilateral and quasi-international efforts at controls and embargoes has not been distinguished by any degree of success. In most cases, these actions have served merely as symbolic gestures of disapproval.

Controls at the Unilateral Level

Controls and embargoes at the unilateral level have, in the main, been the most significant ones. We will here merely summarize a subject which, at various junctures, has been touched upon before.

We know that the stringency with which unilateral controls have been applied has varied from period to period. An almost totally laissez faire emphasis in the Middle Ages gave way to some licensing in the period of the Reformation and in the Age of Mercantilism. Then, throughout the 19th century and on through most of the interwar period, controls on mostly private sales were minimal and used only in such rare instances as when the United States was interested in embargoing arms shipments to disapproved insurrectionists in Latin America. Here, controls were applied only to groups which lacked territorial sovereignty or legitimacy, although there was a pragmatic ideological coloring to this policy.[27]

In the mid-1930s most of the major arms producing nations began to utilize licensing as a control.[28] For the most part, these controls were only of a weakly negative sort. Applications for arms were normally denied only where embargoes had been declared on belligerents in conflict. Then, in the late 1930s, the United States and Britain began to apply some controls, however belatedly, on the Axis powers, although not in response to outright international aggression.[29] "Moral" embargoes were declared against expansionist or dictatorial regimes from whom aggression was expected.[30] What is most revealing here is the extent to which clear national interests still had to be papered over with the rhetoric of international morality.

In the postwar period all nations have effectively applied a system of continuous unilateral controls. Positive decisions are normally required for all arms sales, although the level of decision making may vary with the importance of the case.[31]

Some halting successes in unilateral control efforts have been achieved only in one of two types of cases. First, there have been those few cases of pariah nations with low leverage where no readily alternative supplier has existed. The leverage of the supplier is then high and it can coerce with the threat of discontinuing all shipments, thereby leaving the recipient with no supplier. The present relationship between the United States and Israel, utilized by the United States to force Israeli concessions, appears to be of this type as are, to a lesser degree, those between China and Pakistan, France and South Africa, and the United States and South Vietnam. Still, the lone supplier may not want to use its coercive power or may be inhibited from doing so by, for example, the kind of internal political pressure that is exerted in the United States on behalf of Israel.

The other general case in which unilateral measures may be effective is where the political, military and economic hegemony of the supplier over the recipient is such as to virtually preclude the use of alternative suppliers. Often, this will entail close geographical propinquity of the recipient to a major power, where other suppliers are reluctant to intrude on a clear sphere of influence. Thus, the United States was able to mute a conflict between Honduras and El Salvador, while the Soviet Union has applied what controls it wishes on some of its satellites.

A residual type of unilateral control is that enabled by end-use restrictions on retransfers. Here the control afforded the original supplier is quite high, because of the potential sanction of withholding further arms shipments. Circumventions of end-use restrictions in the postwar period appear to have been relatively rare.[32] There are no longer wholesale evasions of embargoes by this method, as in China and the Chaco in the interwar period. Here, at least, there has been some progress in controls.

Generally, there are severe limits to what can be accomplished unilaterally by any given supplier. The supplier market is simply too broad and is composed of too diverse a group of nations with varied interests. The optimism voiced by Thayer and others about what the United States could do on its own to stanch the worldwide flow of arms would appear unwarranted, as is amply portrayed by American failures in its efforts to control arms flows to Latin America, Greece and Portugal, efforts rendered ineffective by the arms sales of Western European competitors.

FROM THE NYE COMMITTEE TO THE EXIMBANK: IDEALISM VERSUS REALISM

We have seen that some of the systems characteristics which determine patterns of the arms trade have undergone changes over time, some relatively minor and others more extensive. Similarly, the focus of debate over what can be done to control the arms trade has both undergone some changes and retained a remarkable degree of continuity. It may be worthwhile to examine this long-term dialogue from the perspectives both of idealist reformers and their more pessimistic protagonists. In the process we may examine the historical phases of American policy in this area. Alternations of mood and policy toward arms shipments by the United States can easily be related to overall moods of idealism and realpolitik and to shifts between isolationism and interventionism or globalism.

      We can examine two separate but connected sources of commentary and policy suggestions. There is the critical literature on the arms trade in both periods. In both, most books and articles have been hortatory in tone, taking a strong adversary position. Most have been written from the perspective of left reformism, the usual thrust of which has been the excoriation of those forces deemed responsible for what is objectively considered both an evil and a correctable practice.

      For the United States at least, a second source of commentary has emerged from the congressional hearings and exposés which have peaked at two easily identifiable junctures in the past 40 years. In the mid-1930s there were the Nye Committee hearings and the neutrality laws. Then, between 1967 and 1970, America's military aid and trade programs came under the hot glare of congressional scrutiny to a degree not evidenced since the 1930s.

      The timing of these two surges of interest was not accidental. The Nye Committee hearings followed closely after the sensational and highly publicized scandals of the Chaco War, which followed similar revelations from the earlier Chinese situation. Also, at the same time, there was criticism of alleged attempts by armaments manufacturers to torpedo the Geneva Disarmament Conference.[33] All of this festered to a breaking point at around 1934 and 1935.

      The intensity of congressional concern over foreign arms sales, which built to crisis proportions in 1967, had its roots in the Vietnam conflict and in a growing overall concern over America's global role. Then, too, the revelations about the use of American military equipment on both sides of the Indo-Pakistani and Arab-Israeli wars had considerable impact. These events called into question the very rationale and doctrinal underpinnings of America's foreign military aid and sales programs. And, as in the mid 1930s, there was a mood of withdrawal and isolationism in the face of the seeming intractability of international problems.[34]

In examining the reports of the Nye Committee and the numerous books and articles of that period on the arms trade, one point stands out: the almost incredible extent to which private manufacture of arms and control over the arms trade were perceived as the root of the problem. The issue of nationalization, and the pros and cons of various forms of licensing controls, consumed almost all of the attention of the Nye Committee.[35] And for those who popularized the subject—Philip Noel-Baker, Hans Engelbrecht, Richard Lewinsohn, Otto Lehmann-Russbuldt and others—there was a similarly mono-causal emphasis.[36]

The indictment of private manufacturers by the reformists of the 1930s was serious and all-embracing. It began with the activities of arms firms in the period just preceding World War I, when they were charged with fomenting war scares and arms races. There was the almost symbolic case of the British "Dreadnought Gap."[37] There were also revelations of excessive profit taking during the Great War itself. Munitions makers were charged with later having sabotaged disarmament negotiations, with having deliberately evaded embargoes and with having instigated arms races among smaller nations, if not actual wars themselves. Bribery and all forms of corruption were seen everywhere.[38]

The problem of the arms firms themselves was not seen as altogether isolated. The later fixation on the bogey of the military-industrial complex was adumbrated by revelations that the tentacles of arms firms had spread into other institutions. Arms makers were alleged to have controlled a goodly proportion of the press in many countries.[39] Meanwhile, public opinion was said to have been rendered malleable to the entreaties of arms makers by the activities of various army and navy "leagues," the officials of which were demonstrated to have had ties to the arms industry.[40] And despite the main burden of charges against private manufacturers, the role of government was not considered to have been totally irrelevant. There were the baneful roles of military attachés as arms salesmen, and overseas diplomatic assistance to arms traders.[41]

In short, the critique of the "arms international" during the 1930s was different only in degree from the later onslaught on the military-industrial complex.[42] This was the case despite the relative absence of governmental controls over the arms industry and the then retarded nature of the contracting-out structure which was later to become the hallmark of military-industrial relations.

The arms trade literature of the 1930s and the Nye hearings seem to have had an almost obsessive morphological concern. Enormous energies were devoted to unraveling the seemingly endless skeins of personal and institutional connections which ran between the business, press, military and civil bureaucracies. There was repetitive hammering at interlocking directorates, interest group associations and the endless chains of subsidiaries and subsubsidiaries of world-spanning arms corporations. The connections thus made, an elite network was uncovered and a virtual conspiracy theory, with its easy assumptions about the roots of the arms trade, followed.[43]

Later, in the mid-1960s, there would be another flowering of organizational morphology with respect to the military-industrial complex and its adjuncts in the academies. There would be new unravelings of strands of influence, friendship and pecuniary connection running through the worlds of the corporations, government bureaucracies, foundations, universities and, of course, the Council on Foreign Relations.[44]

In the literature of the 1930s, there was scarce mention of the role of purely systemic factors operating to perpetuate the arms trade, factors which might well operate no matter what lines of influence might be found among various elite groupings in major supplier nations. There was a parallel absence of discussion of the self-perceived and sometimes real security needs of dependent nations, and a naive lack of fatalism about what some might claim must be the almost inevitable arming of most nations by some means. And, the arms-trading of the Soviet Union had not yet served as an object lesson to those who saw capitalism itself as a bête noire.

The root of the problem having been unmasked, recommendations for reform were easily forthcoming. Nationalization of arms industries was the optimal solution. Short of that, strict governmental licensing controls were thought to promise considerable mitigation. Removal of the profit motive from the sale of arms, supplemented by embargoes and "quarantines" of occasional aggressors were the hoped-for solutions in an age of utopian pacifism and lingering notions about the efficacy of collective security.

A few doubts were expressed by the unconvinced. Roosevelt and some of his supporters saw that the use of embargoes on all belligerents might effectively result in the rewarding and abetting of aggression. By 1939-1940 this realization led to the end of the neutrality policy in favor of allowing arms sales to Britain and France. Quarantine by embargo had ceased to make sense and gave way to Lend-Lease and "cash and carry."[45]

Concerning nationalization and state controls, only the prescient Quincy Wright among the commentators of the time was able to perceive that such measures were fraught with complexities. His comments, written during the Second World War, appear retrospectively to have demonstrated an admirable sense of premonition.

Their relative importance [the abuses of private manufacture] in the causation of modern war has probably been greatly exaggerated, and it is probable that some of the remedies proposed, especially those in a socialist direction, would aggravate the abuse.

Only ten states of the world have important arms manufacturers; regulation of the arms trade will not be effective unless accepted by all those states. Such regulation, if not .carefully drawn, might increase the imperial dominance of these powers in certain areas by controlling the internal policy of the governments dependent upon imported arms for police and defense. Governmental monopolies of arms production would move governments a long way toward state socialism, because modern arms, munitions and war materials constitute a large part of the national economy. Such monopolies would extend the imperial control of the present arms-producing states even more than would international regulation of the private industry. Control of the arms trade might stimulate all states to establish an arms industry and to increase the total quantity of the world's productive capacity devoted to this uneconomic activity.

Transfer of the arms industry from private to governmental hands would accentuate the national character of the industry and might make the balance of power less stable. When great international arms firms peddled their inventions among governments, each government knew what was available to the others. With national monopolies and secrecy of inventions, each state would continually be alarmed by rumors of new and devastating inventions by its rivals.

Neutral arms embargoes if equally applied to all belligerents actually favor the aggressor, who is usually better prepared than his victim. They tend to encourage economic self-sufficiency in defense materials even in time of peace and even among the most peaceful countries, because they threaten to deprive the victim of aggression of a source of defense materials when its life depends on them.

While private arms-trading, private international lending and private international investing have led to abuses, it seems probable that on the whole they have tended to stabilize the balance of power rather than to disturb it by equalizing the defensibility of states. Control of these activities by national governments would tend to increase international tensions.[46]

Wright seems to have anticipated how the hopes of reformers of his time would be dashed in the face of the basic intractability of the problem. He anticipated all of the dilemmas which later were to become all too familiar, and which would become the targets for a new crop of reformers. Aside from his somewhat exaggerated notion about the potential of smaller nations to develop their own arms industries, his analysis has held up well over time. And his pessimism about the baneful effects of the socialization of arms industries did not extend, as it might have, to a prediction about how governmental controls would be conducive to outright arms giveaways, thereby removing what at least had been a cost ceiling on arms imports.

In the postwar period, up to about the mid-1960s, we have indicated that the arms trade seems to have received little attention from scholars or publicists. With the exceptions of a few monographs published by the Institute or Strategic Studies there was almost no literature at all. In Congress, despite its authorization and appropriations powers, there appears to have been routine acceptance of arms sales and aid as an aspect of Cold War policy, with bipartisan backing. Considerable discretion was left to the Pentagon. Military aid was doled out lavishly up to 1961, and after that there was the newer emphasis on cash sales, which at first was also accepted with little criticism. Indeed, the relative laxity of congressional scrutiny seemed to feed the passions which later erupted when some legislators came to feel deceived about the full magnitude of activities and practices in this area.

Then, in the midst of the upsurge of recrimination against the military in the late 1960s, two separate Senate committees embarked upon probes of American arms sales and aid policies, and in both arenas there emerged full-fledged debates over the international arms trade.

The Senate Foreign Relations Committee, under Senator Fulbright's chairmanship, became one center of inquiry, being responsible for authorization of foreign military aid.[47] And the Senate Banking and Currency Committee became heavily engaged once it discovered the way the Export-Import Bank had become entangled in arms sales activities through its relationship with the Pentagon, financing "Country X" accounts.[48] In 1967, in the wake of the Middle Eastern war, these committees simultaneously wrangled over the basic issues of the arms trade, calling to testimony those executive branch personnel and outside experts most intimately concerned. The debates were to illuminate what changes in perspective had occurred since the Nye hearings.

Several major themes formed the pivots of controversy and advocacy in these hearings. There was considerable concern over trends in executive-legislative relations on this subject and over the alleged secrecy and circuitousness of arms sales operations. On a broader basis, there was the overall conflict between international security commitments and the desire for a reduction in armaments. There was increasing concern about weapons acquisitions by developing nations conflicting with goals of economic development, and about the morality of arms shipments to regimes of dubious character, usually those identified as right-wing military dictatorships. And encompassing all else there was general incredulity at the magnitude of human folly which maintained the need for armaments and the military itself.

Control of military sales and aid had become by 1967 one aspect of an attempt by the legislature to reassert some measure of influence over foreign policy making. The very susceptibility of policy in this area to clear-cut legislative acts made it a natural target for legislators bent on hamstringing what had come to be considered a runaway national security bureaucracy.

The hearings were suffused with congressional laments about how policy in this area had become the secretive arcane domain of almost invisible bureaucrats. There were charges of deliberate circumvention or bending of existing legislation, and a sense of being faced with a vast faceless bureaucracy, with its myriad levers for switching of funds and for utilization of different institutions for the same purposes.

These matters came to a head in the hearings of the Senate Banking and Currency Committee, once it concluded that the Eximbank's chartered purpose had been perverted to other channels.[49] It was discovered that the responsibility for funding and credit arrangements for arms purchases were scattered among a number of different agencies, not only in the Defense Department and Eximbank with their revolving credit funds but also in the intelligence services, whose ample budgets allowed for clandestine arms shipments. Ceilings on arms aid and credit arrangements for specific countries and regions had also been easily circumvented by selloffs of surplus military equipment which had already been amortized. Indeed, considerable discretion appeared to have been left to the military on whether to exact cash payments at all for surplus equipment. Surplus military equipment in Vietnam was allegedly being used to supply other nations in a manner altogether removed from congressional scrutiny.

The reformist onslaught of the late 1960s resulted in strong, harsh and specific legislation intended to cure the alleged abuses. Their spirit and purpose were reminiscent of the neutrality laws of the 1930s. There was a sense of urgency about curbing the worldwide flow of arms.

In a number of pieces of legislation, the Congress curtailed the power of the executive to supply arms.[50] There was repeal of the broad authority under which the Defense Department made credit sales to developing countries. The revolving fund used to finance those sales was done away with. With the Foreign Military Sales Act of 1968, a new system was instituted which required annual authorizations of ceilings for government-financed credit sales and annual appropriations to finance them.

Other legislation set definite ceilings on arms sales to Latin America and Africa.[51] The purpose was explicitly that of preventing arms purchases from seriously interfering with economic development. There was, of course, a presumption of the efficacy of unilateral American action.

There were provisions by which arms sales and guarantees would not be approved when they would have the effect of arming dictators who were "denying social progress to their people." Here was the institutionalization of a new policy of judging potential arms recipients by their internal political character. Additionally, ceilings were placed on sales of excess defense articles and there was a tightening up of restrictions on retransfers.

In a sense, these congressional activities represented new efforts at solving old problems. But they also represented the beginnings of a more purposeful use of arms sales as a policy weapon. The criteria for eligibility by recipients had been further narrowed. Recipients would now not only have to be nonbelligerents (1935-1940) or part of the American security commitment system (1945-1967) but also eligible on the basis of judgments on the character of the regime, including its use of budgetary resources. Ironically, as Britain and France moved toward a more commercial arms sales policy, the United States appeared at least temporarily to be moving from a hegemonic policy to the kind of restrictive policy usually associated with Sweden. Under the Nixon administration, however, policy has again been reversed, following recognition of the futility of a restrictive policy.[52]

A major theme, highlighted by the ceilings placed on sales to Latin America and Africa, was the tying of arms sales to economic development and resource allocation. In the earlier period of the Nye Committee hearings this question had been but dimly perceived and rarely articulated. With a less comprehensive state system and the fact of widespread colonial control the dichotomy of developed and underdeveloped had not yet really entered the consciousness and vocabulary of arms trade reformists.

Senator Fulbright, hinging his arguments for tighter controls primarily on the economic development problem, was fond of elaborate illustrations of how money being spent by developing countries on armaments could be translated into social expenditures. Sometimes his comparisons left his bureaucratic protagonists speechless, for on the face of it they were almost unanswerable. Citing a UNESCO source, he noted that the world spends 40 percent more on arms than on public education, with the arms expenditures soaring at the rate of 13 percent per year. It was also averred that "if one silver dollar coin was dropped every second, it would take 126,000 years to exhaust the amount of money that will be spent on world armaments in the next 10 years."[53]

Congress did, then, put ceilings on arms sales to some developing countries. It was also made clear that future foreign aid grants might be made contingent upon limiting arms acquisitions, since it was clear such payments were at least indirectly financing these arms.

The pressures from this new policy have not yet had the intended impact on recipients. Some nations—Brazil, Argentina and Peru among them— have reacted by switching some of their arms purchases to the United States' NATO allies who were not attaching political strings to such transactions. One observer even testified to Congress that at least one nation in Latin America had gotten so sick of wrangling with the United States over arms purchases that it would not do business there anymore on any terms.[54] Over several years, the American share in Latin American arms markets dropped precipitously from near 90 percent to slightly over 20 percent.

The use of arms sales as a reward or punishment for internal democratization or its absence was also quite new. A good part of recent congressional debates over the arms trade has centered on the advisability of continuing sales to nations such as Spain, Portugal and Greece, of whose regimes liberal critics were not particularly enamored.

Partial embargoes were placed on these countries by the use of ceilings on sales. And the result, parallel to what was happening with those nations laboring under ceilings intended to goad them into budgetary reallocations, was that the buyers simply went elsewhere. Greece, Spain and Portugal quickly became arms clients of France, which was only too happy to sell from its growing inventories of Mirages, Alouettes and Frelons.

Incidentally, amidst this change of policy, there was an absence of focused analysis of the impact on America's balance of payments. One might suspect that it was a part of the reason for America's worsening payments situation in the late 1960s and early 1970s. In fact, recognition of this problem, in conjunction with massive currency outflows associated with the oil crisis in 1973-74, appeared to have engendered new massive American arms sales to Iran, Saudi Arabia and others.

Aside from the specifics of the issues of economic development, the propping up of repressive military regimes and the minutiae of weapons inventories, there was the basic philosophical conflict between idealism and pragmatism, optimism and pessimism, moral politics and realpolitik. As this age-old dialogue was conducted anew in Congress there was a fascinating interplay of personalities and values. Some of the more interesting colloquies involved liberal-reformist Senators Fulbright and Church versus such contemporary archvillains as government arms supersalesman Henry Kuss and Interarmco chief Samuel Cummings.

The irony of this centerpiece confrontation in the 1967 hearings was poignant. For years critics of America's role in the arms trade had lamented, with no little nostalgia for the ghost of Sir Basil Zaharoff, the facelessness of a bureaucratic maze which seemed to make impossible a real confrontation with those making decisions. The Senate Foreign Relations Committee, with a good eye for publicity if not for the real heart of the matter, hauled before it two men who despite their lack of lofty government position had come to personify evil in an area where individuals were said no longer to count.

The tone of the debate was to illustrate, as well as anything could, the cruel dilemmas involved. Most significant, but often difficult to judge, was the kind of mock incredulity—or perhaps mock solemnity—of Fulbright and others who were still seeking solutions to an age-old problem. Consider the following typical dialogue between Fulbright and Cummings.

Mr. Cummings. Well, the press, of course, as you know, has a slight tendency to sensationalize the arms business.

Senator Fulbright. Yes, I have observed that myself.

Mr. Cummings. They probably have exaggerated Mr. Kuss's position just as they have exaggerated ours.

Really, the arms business in the era that we live in, in the Western world, is not a mystery, and it is certainly not sinister as every transaction has to be approved, in our case, by the United States or the United Kingdom.

We have no, in a sense, we ourselves, have no policy. We have to look to our government for that.

Senator Fulbright. I certainly have no quarrel with that. I question the judgment of our government's policies.

Mr. Cummings. Yes. Well, I find myself often mystified by that position.

Senator Fulbright. By their policy?

Mr. Cummings. Yes.

Senator Fulbright. This point you made about an arms balance a moment ago was very significant. There seems to be a continued escalation of this arms trade.

Mr. Cummings. Exactly.

Senator Fulbright. You think that is accurate?

Mr. Cummings. I do.

Senator Fulbright. This reflects on what we are told. Government officials tell us that this is all a means of trying to limit the increase of arms in the Middle East and other countries. But if what you say is correct, it does no such thing.

Mr. Cummings. Well, I can only observe from the reality of practical life.

Senator Fulbright. That is correct.

Mr. Cummings. I have not seen a diminution of arms anywhere in my lifetime.

Senator Fulbright. Neither have I.

Mr. Cummings. And I do not expect to see one as far as I can project in the future.

Senator Fulbright. You see no possibility, you have no idea of how it could be done or how it ought to be done?

Mr. Cummings. As long as we have the world situation the way it is, I think we can be positive it will not be done.

Senator Fulbright. That is a question of the hen and the egg. Does it exist because the world situation is the way it is, or did our actions contribute to making this situation?

Mr. Cummings. It is almost a perpetual motion machine. We all agree that the arms race is disaster, and we all agree that it could lead to an ultimate conflict which would more or less destroy the civilized world as we know it.

The old question is, who is going to make the first move to pull back?

Senator Fulbright. Yes.

Mr. Cummings. The Russians do not trust us any more than we, in essence, trust them.

Senator Fulbright. But ordinarily, it is the obligation of the most powerful nation to take the first step because it does not expose itself to the same kind of risk that a minor power does.

Mr. Cummings. That is right.

Senator Fulbright. Therefore, under present conditions, if anybody is going to take the first step, it ought to be the United States.

Mr. Cummings. We are more powerful in many ways and overall I consider that we are more powerful.

And later, as a finale.

Senator Fulbright. It seems to me that this country ought to be taking some kind of meaningful step in this direction. We are given a lot of propaganda up here that we all do not believe, but we do not know quite how to combat it. We are having hearings like this, because we do not know what do to about it.

Mr. Cummings. I agree.

Senator Fulbright. Thank you very much. I hope you realize we are very interested in this matter, and we are trying to understand a little bit.

Mr. Cummings. We try to understand it also, and we have as many doubts as you do.

Senator Fulbright. Our policies don't always seem to me to be very smart.

Mr. Cummings. It does not seem to me either, but I cannot resolve a practical solution.

Senator Fulbright. I do not have the answer; neither do you.[55]

If the dialogue between Fulbright and Cummings illustrates the despair, confusion and weltschmerz which surrounds these problems on a philosophical plane, the one which follows illustrates it with respect to a specific situation. Nowhere has the cruelty and even the absurdity of the problem facing American decisionmakers been better demonstrated than with arms sales to Latin America, all the more so because competition for influence with the Soviet Union has been favorably lacking, at least prior to recent events in Chile and Peru. But there remain the riddles posed by attempting to sort out policy goals variously based on alliance politics and national security, economic development, arms control for its own sake and balance of payments.

Here, Senator Fulbright exchanges views with an administration official, U. Alexis Johnson, on the effects of recent American attempts at applying more stringent restrictions on arms to Latin America. It is a policy which by then, and even more since, has resulted in many former American markets being taken over by West European competitors.

> *The Chairman.* Mr. Secretary, you said in your statement, "It is interesting to note in contrast to some $50 million in sales to Latin America, other NATO countries sell an estimated $343 million." Which NATO countries sell such a large amount?
>
> *Mr. Johnson.* The United Kingdom, France, and Canada are the first three in sales.
>
> *The Chairman.* What do the Germans have to sell?
>
> *Mr. Johnson.* They have a wide range of things.
>
> *The Chairman.* Do they?
>
> *Mr. Johnson.* Yes.
>
> *The Chairman.* F-104s, I guess.
>
> *Mr. Johnson.* No, no.
>
> (Laughter)
>
> *The Chairman.* What do the various countries sell?
>
> *Mr. Johnson.* Well, I would have to—I know both France and the United Kingdom sold aircraft, Germany has sold ground equipment, artillery, rifles, and things of that kind.
>
> *Mr. Chairman.* This is a very competitive business.
>
> *Mr. Johnson.* Very, very competitive.
>
> *Mr. Chairman.* Was the competitive aspect present in the sale of Mirages to Peru? Didn't we try to persuade them not to buy F-5s?
>
> *Mr. Johnson.* That is correct, and they did buy Mirages; Mirages are included in it.

> *The Chairman.* They could not afford F-5s. Did they buy Mirages?
>
> *Mr. Johnson.* Yes, they bought Mirages.
>
> *The Chairman.* Do you remember what they cost?
>
> *Mr. Johnson.* No.
>
> *The Chairman.* I would certainly approve of what I know of our attitude in that instance. Of course, that was a very clear case because we were at the very same time giving them substantial economic aid and to have them buy Mirages when they did not need them seems the grossest kind of improvidence. It did to me. I thought you were right about that in that case. I hoped you would do it more often.[56]

The unilateral application of controls was, therefore, not so simple a matter. The implication that American economic aid might actually be financing arms acquisitions from other sources was to arise again with the Indo-Pakistani conflict of 1971, when it was shown that heavy American economic aid to India was, in effect, financing arms purchases from the Soviet Union. Cynics were to observe which form of aid had gained the most influence, at least for the time being. A further question was whether the cutting back of foreign aid to countries like India would remove what appeared to be the one useful lever held by the United States in its quest to restrict arms flows.

Some of the most interesting discussion in these hearings was over the wisdom of continuing American arms sales or aid to nations such as Iran and Turkey. Both of these, as duly noted by Senator Fulbright, had established significant trading relations with the USSR, and in the case of Iran a low level arms client relationship as well. For the utopian, this had removed the last vestige of excuse for continuing arms sales to these nations, which were now considered no longer to need any arms because of their new trading relationships. Administration officials were forced to defend continuing sales to these countries with the seemingly outmoded rationale of retention of diplomatic influence and the forestalling of previous clients' moving still further into cross-bloc, multiple arms supplier relationships.

The debate was not always between a discouraged Congress and a jaded, cynical, interest-oriented administration. Former government luminary Chester Bowles gave one of the most impassioned appeals for slowing down American military sales, focusing on the guns and butter issue. With respect to further tank shipments to Pakistan, he asked: "Whose interests would be served by such decisions? Certainly not the interests of the American people in Asia. Or the cause of world peace. Or the welfare of the people of Pakistan, who need tractors, not tanks. A few military leaders in Pakistan would be helped and, perhaps, the American firms that manufacture the tanks."[57] Meanwhile, the Pakistanis were now going to China for their tanks, although some very recent reports indicated that the leverage thus achieved was beginning to reopen the American source.

On the other side, a more fatalistic perspective was offered by Defense Secretary McNamara near the end of his tenure. The context was American agonizing over arms transfers to Argentina, a nation which subsequently became fed up with dealing with the United States and began to shop elsewhere. McNamara said:

> I don't see any reason in the world why Argentina, for example, should not be allowed to procure military equipment from us if they are willing to do so. I think they are wealthy enough to undertake limited purchases of military equipment. They are going to do so anyhow. They will either buy it from us or from other nations. I see no reason why we should prohibit them from buying from us. There may be other countries in the same situation. I would suggest to you, however, that there is no evidence that I know of that this Government encourages a nation to divert needed resources from economic to military procurement.[58]

By the late 1960s, then, some policymakers were beginning to recognize the virtual intractability of the problem. The old bogey of private manufacture was dead, even if briefly exhumed by Mr. Bowles, and also by Professor Galbraith, who refused to concede the inherently systemic nature of the problem.[59]

There was some mutual recognition of the nature of the problem by idealists and pragmatists. But if arms control and economic development were altogether laudable goals, no one had yet found the levers by which to persuade the leaders of developing nations of the primacy of such goals over their self-perceived security needs.

If American security and maintenance of influence were increasingly perceived as independent of dominance in the arms markets, there still remained serious relative questions of just how far to go in risking the loss of all influence to those whose scruples were not so pure. The very structure of the arms supplier markets still left questions about whether the United States, or any other nation, could really have a significant unilateral impact on the acquisitions of smaller nations. If this were the case, and if the sole net effect of unilateral controls was to damage one's balance of payments position, one might easily expect a new swing of the pendulum—as had already occurred in France and Britain—when the full weight of reality dawned on decisionmakers. In fact, by 1974 it was clear that such a swing had occurred, as the Nixon administration, apparently no longer as harried by Congress as before, began to exhibit less inhibitions on arms sales, particulary in the Middle East and Latin America, in response to Western European competition and balance of payments pressures. Particularly marked were absolutely massive impending arms sales to Iran and

Saudi Arabia (in the former case including transfers of the brand-new F-14 and F-15 fighters), involving billions of dollars of long-term sales. An impasse had been reached, and no one had yet effectively countered the cynical Cummings' assertion that "it all comes down to who makes the sale."

Two decades ago Kenneth Waltz wrote an excellent general analysis of the causes of war in which he demonstrated that the bulk of writings on the subject could be divided into fairly distinct schools of thought corresponding to imagery at three levels: the individual, the state and the international system.[60]

At the first level, there is the allegedly inherent aggressiveness and combativeness of man, often related to the behavior of other species. War at this level is in the minds of men, or in their instincts.

On the second level, other theorists have located the impetus to war in the imperatives of certain internal state structures, variously classified as feudal, capitalist, fascist, socialist or whatever. Examples of focus on this level could be found in the analyses of imperialism by Lenin and Schumpeter, who respectively attributed international aggressiveness to the allegedly expansionist needs of capitalist economies and to the atavistic remnants of older, feudal, warrior classes.[61]

A third approach has focused on the international system qua system, the "billiard ball" approach. Much of modern writing on game theory appears to lean to this image, as does the power-national interest orientation of Morgenthau and others.

Waltz is not a partisan of any of these three approaches. Rather, he demonstrates the advantages and shortcomings of each, showing that excessive adherence to any approach would leave serious shortcomings in an analysis purporting to comprehensiveness.

In reviewing the literature on the arms trade, past and present, one can not help being struck by the extent to which various panaceas and reformist strictures have appeared to suffer from a lack of grasp of the levels of analysis problem, as outlined by Waltz. Risking an easy generalization, it would appear to me that most recommendations for reform have dwelled disproportionately on the nation-state level.

Perhaps it would be fruitless to discuss the problem on the first level of imagery, that of human personality and drives, even though the problem of arms control is a subset of those of war and conflict themselves.[62] In a sense, though, one supposes the cynicism of a Cummings is directed at this level. And there is the very human problem of avidity for profit as a force behind some arms transactions, as there is the individual imperative to bureaucratic empirebuilding which feeds into such activities.

Mostly, however, the problem for would-be reformers appears to be the difficulty of comprehending the clash between the nation-state and international system levels. Reformers have focused almost entirely on the former. In the interwar period most commentators seemed to assume the root of the problem was in the liberal-capitalist internal structure of states. The answer, then, was simple in a way—socialization of the arms industries themselves or, beyond that, full socialization of economies. The disappearance of the profit motive would do away with the arms traffic.

Analyses in the recent postwar period, such as those by Thayer and Senator Fulbright, also seem to have pointed the finger at the nation-state level. Amidst a zeitgeist of antimilitarism, and with private arms trading now a mere bagatelle, the onus has been put on allegedly furtive and overblown national security bureaucracies thought to have run amok and beyond public control. Here, we get the familiar themes of "military-industrial complexes," "garrison states," and "economies of death." The problem is at least usually conceded to be a worldwide one, although there is concomitantly some suspicion that there is more blame in Washington than elsewhere. The result has been almost morbid fixation on internal bureaucratic reorganizations, and legislative and public controls.

What seems to me amiss in these arguments is the failure to face the inherently world systemic nature of the problem, whereby the difficulties of controlling the arms trade become equivalent to those of eliminating conflicts of interest themselves.[63] By now it should be abundantly clear even to a casual analyst of these problems that the fault cannot lie with certain types of regimes, bureaucratic structures or internal control mechanisms. At best, this may account for marginal distinctions, for nuances. For in the recent past arms have been sold with equal insouciance by liberal-democratic, communist, fascist, monarchist and sometimes even avowedly neutralist and pacifist regimes.

As we have demonstrated, there may be some greater tendency for revisionist or expansionist regimes to push arms more aggressively than status quo or conservative ones. But that, too, is a nuance, and with little evidence that status quo regimes would not essentially match revisionist ones if the latter were not pushing them out of markets with more aggressive sales tactics. In short, reformists might do well to concede the validity of a remark by Cummings, who told the Senate Foreign Relations Committee that "there is no plumbing the depths of the arms trade, any more than there is plumbing the depths of human folly."[64]

Only recently, with the more sophisticated analyses of the MIT and SIPRI studies, has there appeared to be an awareness of the essentially systemic nature of the problem. Its root lay in the number of extant suppliers in conjunction with the demands and inherent bargaining positions of the recipients, most of which do have very real, or at least self-perceived, security needs.

What, then, can one add to mitigate a sense of pessimism? One theoretical handle on the problem may be provided by the notion of a "collective good." The essential question is how the collectivity of nations can be persuaded, or coerced, into cooperative behavior which would redound to the benefit of all.[65]

It is easy to speak of a collective good in this area for all nations. If one factors out prestige, fears for security and sheer machismo one is left with an obvious worldwide common interest, at least on an economic level.

Actually, it probably makes more sense here to disaggregate the notion of a collective good into constituent parts representing suppliers and recipients. The problem is a different one for the large and the small powers. Large powers are necessarily involved in the game of great power politics and there is no better way to extend and maintain influence than by selling arms. And sadly, there is money to be made, or at least exports to be achieved to balance imports.

On the recipient side, a collective good is, in a way, easier to perceive. Arms are costly, and the dependence relations resulting from arms client ties can be damaging to national pride. On the economic side, there are no real trade-offs as there are for suppliers, who can see both possible gains and losses from selling arms. For the recipients, however, there is the ever-present fear of the surrounding Hobbesian jungle, and more than a little concern with national status in which arms play an unfortunate but natural part. And then there is the problem of discrimination if the weak disarm while the strong remain armed.

Theoretically, one can speak of the collective good, but at a more specific level things become sticky. Even if the hegemonic drives of the superpowers are stilled, there are the problems of nations like Britain and France, who have now come to assume that they must pursue industrial arms sales policies if only to free themselves from dependence on what has for them become a hegemonic relationship with a still stronger power.

SUMMARY

We have demonstrated that patterns of the arms trade vary in response to changing systemic characteristics. Most importantly, we have tried to show the differential impact wrought by that combination of factors revolving about polarity, ideology and moods of totality. What, then, do we see emerging for the future?

All signs point to broadened arms supplier markets, in all weapons categories. China, Japan and the Western European consortia are now beginning increasingly to challenge the United States and the USSR in arms markets. In the future, Israel, India, Iran, South Africa, Brazil and perhaps others will enter the competition on a less significant level. Meanwhile, the movement of the world system toward multipolarity augurs more dependent nations being able to bargain with impunity among all of the suppliers for their arms. Simultaneously, there appear to be increasing pressures on suppliers to finance the spiralling costs of their domestic arms industries by exporting surpluses to the nonproducers. A new trend toward barter of arms for scarce raw materials has emerged, first with respect to Middle Eastern oil, but perhaps a harbinger of a significant new phenomenon as well as a reflection of what may be a significant reversal in the balance of power between the developed world and some resource-rich developing nations. In short, it is difficult to avoid the conclusion that emerging systemic factors would appear to point to exacerbation of present problems.

Even if some notion of a collective good could be agreed upon by the major powers, the gains made by their collective action might still be dissipated by more smaller nations moving toward independent arms production bases, thus in turn increasing the difficulty of achieving a notion of collective good among all the suppliers. What hope there is would appear to lie in collective agreements among groups of recipients. But that in turn requires a considerable degree of mutual trust or virtual absence of potential conflict—in short, the building of "security communities."

And so, one comes full circle to the ageless problem of world community and the elimination of conflict itself. Short of such a utopia, one fears the present level of arms trading will be difficult to reduce, much less eliminate.

Appendix A

Coding Instructions-Transfers

Card	Column	
1	1-2	Card Number
1	3-6	Transfer Number
1	7-8	Recipient
1	9-10	Date of Transfer (last 2 digits)
1	11	Accuracy of Date (1 = ± 1 years; 2 = ± 5 years)
1	12-13	Donor
1	14-19	System Name 1
1	20-25	System Name 2
1	26-31	System Name 3 Alphanumeric
1	32-37	System Name 4
1	38-43	First Modifier to Name
1	44-49	Second Modifier to Name
1	50-52	Quantity Transferred
1	53	System Classification
1	54	Is Transfer a License? (1 = yes)
1	55	Is Transfer for Assembly? (1 = yes)
1	56-57	Primary Role in Recipient Forces
1	58-59	Secondary Role in Recipient Forces
1	60-64	System Identification Number
1	65-66	Actual Date of Construction of System (last 2 digits)
1	67-68	Date Production of System Type Began (last 2 digits)
1	69-70	Date Production of System Ended (last 2 digits)
1	71-72	Original Manufacturer of System
1	73	Is System in Production in 1968? (1 = yes)
1	74	Is Donor a Licensee? (1 = yes)

*This is a reproduction of the MIT study coding sheet for transfers. We coded for the interwar period in the same columns, but omitted data in some categories, i.e., in columns 14-49. Additional information was coded for individual weapons systems, that is, for the performance characteristics of interwar aircraft, armor and naval types. The format was a constricted version of that in Appendix I of The MIT Study.

241

Appendix B

Military Intelligence Division Files-
Interwar Period, from Modern
Military Division, National Archives

Attache Report Files, by Weapons System

Country	Aircraft	Armor	Naval
Argentina	2076	2281-L	2720, 2789
Uruguay	2660	–	2787
Paraguay	2760	2657-N	–
Bolivia	2670	2281-N	–
Chile	2563	2281-O	2713
Brazil	2472	2281-K	2744
Peru	2459	–	2586
Venezuela	2564	2281-M	2739
Colombia	2538	2010	2777
Ecuador	–	2014	–
Nicaragua	2548	2281-P	–
Salvador	2548	2281-P	–
Honduras	2548	2281-P	–
Guatemala	2548	2281-P	–
Panama	2548	2281-P	–
Costa Rica	2548	2281-P	–
Cuba	2079	2281-Q	2725
Mexico	2537	2281-G	2764
Spain	2093	2657-S	2624
Portugal	2535	2281-J	2669
Turkey	2094	2281-T	2126
Bulgaria	2677	2281-V	2800
USSR	2090	2281-D	2503
Romania	2089	2281-V	2723
Persia (Iran)	2766	–	2788
Greece	2084	2281-V	2674
Iraq	2782	2281-HH	–
Egypt	2514	2281-AA	–
Albania	2779	–	–
Yugoslavia	2690	2281-V	2712
Hungary	2544	2281-GG	2294
Latvia	2775	2281-DD	2733
Lithuania	2731	–	–
Estonia	2737	–	2450-DD
Finland	2682	–	2729, 2657
Ethiopia	2791	–	–
Poland	2591	2281-DD	2699
Czechoslovakia	2726	2281-II	–
Sweden	2091	2281-U	2042
Hejaz (Saudi Arabia)	2724	–	–
Afghanistan	2563	–	–
Denmark	2080	–	2743

Appendix B—*Continued*

Country	Aircraft	Armor	Naval
Germany	2082	2281-B	–
Switzerland	2092	–	–
China	2078	2281-I	–
Netherlands	2087	2281-X	–
Norway	2088	–	–
Austria	2541	2281-FF	–
Belgium	2536	2281-Y	–
Italy	2086	2281-E	2125
Siam (Thailand)	2714	–	2716
India	2762	2281-HH	2784
France	2081	2281-C	2351, 2657-C
Eire	2767	–	–
Canada	2717	2281-A	–
Australia	2746	2281-MM	2740
New Zealand	2771	–	–
South Africa	2083	–	–
Japan	2085	2281-H	2342
Great Britain	2083	2281-A	2179

†Where dash indicates no file for a nation's air, armored or naval forces, intelligence information is usually available in attaché reports from neighboring countries (see subsequent listing of location of attachés). Much information on British Commonwealth nations is available in the files for Great Britain.

Combat Estimates

Country or Region	File 10641
Africa (Ethiopia and the Somalilands)	364
Argentina	328
Australia	329
Austria	311
Belgium	291 & 319
Bolivia	297
Brazil	273
Bulgaria	339*
Canada	330
Chile	282
China	275*
Colombia	308
Cuba	267
Czechoslovakia	309
Denmark	280
Estonia	333
Finland	316
France	295
Germany	315
Great Britain	337
Greece	331*
Hawaii	327
Hungary	313
India	332
Italy	294
Japan	281
Yugoslavia	310
Mexico	268
Netherlands	312
Panama	300
Peru	260
Poland	317
Portugal	278*
Russia	333
South Africa	334
Spain	278
Sweden	322*
Switzerland	314
Turkey	270
Venezuela	279

*Files apparently missing from Archives

Intelligence Surveys

Country or Region	File 10641
Argentina	261
Austria	271
British Empire	277
China	259
Far East	259
Japan	259
Russia	259 & 289
Brazil	362

Intelligence Digests

Argentina	303
Austria	287
Belgium	318
Chile	321
China	283
Cuba	336
Czechoslovakia	287
France	301 & 305
Hungary	288
Italy	293
Japan	272 & 281
Mexico	274
Paraguay	335
Russia	286
Uruguay	335
Germany	346
Philippine Islands	347
Mexico	351
Netherlands	353
Hawaii	360
Poland	375
Peru	385
Ecuador	388
Panama	365

Embassies with attachés in 1930s

Country	Country
Argentina	Paraguay
Austria	Peru
Belgium	Poland
Bolivia	Portugal
Brazil	Rumania
Bulgaria	Spain
Chile	Siam
China	Sweden
Colombia	Turkey
Costa Rica	Uruguay
Czechoslovakia	USSR
Denmark	Venezuela
Ecuador	Yugoslavia
Salvador	
Estonia	
Finland	
France	
Germany	
Great Britain	
Greece	
Guatemala	
Honduras	
Ireland	
Italy	
Japan	
Latvia	
Lithuania	
Luxembourg	
Mexico	
Netherlands	
Nicaragua	
Norway	
Panama	

Notes

Notes for Chapter One

1. See B. H. Liddell-Hart, *Strategy: The Indirect Approach* (New York: Praeger, 1954); J. F. C. Fuller, *A Military History of the Western World*, 3 vols. (New York: Minerva Press, 1955); Richard Preston and Sydney Wise, *Men in Arms* (New York: Praeger, 1956); Cyril Falls, *The Art of War: From the Age of Napoleon to the Present Day* (New York: Oxford University Press, 1961); Bernard L. Montgomery, *A History of Warfare* (London: Collins, 1968); Lynn Montross, *War Through the Ages*, 3rd ed. (New York: Harper, 1960); and G. B. Turner, ed., *A History of Military Affairs in Western Society since the Eighteenth Century* (New York: Harcourt Brace, 1953).

2. For analyses focusing on the interrelationship of war and society, see J. F. C. Fuller, *Armaments and History* (New York: C. Scribner's Sons, 1945); and Edward M. Earle, ed., *Makers of Modern Strategy* (Princeton: Princeton University Press, 1941).

3. The following books are devoted to histories of weaponry per se: Bernard Brodie and Fawn Brodie, *From Cross-Bow to H-Bomb* (New York: Dell, 1962); and T. H. Wintringham, *Weapons and Tactics* (London: Faber and Faber, 1940).

4. One notable exception to this gap is an excellent work on the Renaissance by Carlo Cipolla, *Guns and Sails in the Early Phase of European Expansion* (London: Collins, 1965). Cipolla's bibliography, in turn, lists a number of specialized historical sources on the arms trade and related topics, many of which are not generally available in the United States. His book has some fascinating material on the beginnings of the penetration of Western arms merchants into China, Japan and India during the latter stages of the Renaissance.

5. Stanley Hoffmann, *Contemporary Theory in International Relations* (Englewood Cliffs, N.J.: Prentice-Hall, 1960). He discusses, in tandem, the theories of Hans Morgenthau, Raymond Aron, Kenneth Thompson, Morton Kaplan, Jesse Bernard, George Liska and Richard Snyder, among others.

249

6. Morton Kaplan, *System and Process in International Politics* (New York: Wiley, 1957); and Richard N. Rosecrance, *Action and Reaction in World Politics: International Systems in Perspective* (Boston: Little, Brown, 1963).

7. J. David Singer and Melvin Small, *The Wages of War: 1816-1945* (New York: Wiley, 1972).

8. For discussions of the concepts of bipolarity and multipolarity, see, inter alia, Herbert S. Dinerstein, "The Transformation of Alliance Systems," *The American Political Science Review* LIX, no. 3 (September 1965): 589-601; Kenneth Waltz, "The Stability of a Bipolar World," *Daedalus*, 93, no. 3 (Summer 1964): 892-907; and Karl W. Deutsch and J. David Singer, "Multipolar Power Systems and International Stability," *World Politics* XVI, no. 3 (April 1964): 390-406.

9. The basic format is patterned, in somewhat altered form, after Amelia C. Leiss et al., *Arms Transfers to Less Developed Countries*, C/70-1 (Cambridge, Mass.: MIT Center for International Studies, 1970), hereinafter cited as The MIT Study.

10. The analogy with analyses of corporate market shares will be pursued further in Chapter Three. For the basic idea, I have drawn on Michael Gort, "Analyses of Stability and Change in Market Shares," in Bruce Russett, ed., *Economic Theories of International Politics* (Chicago: Markham Publishing Co., 1968), pp. 196-206. See also Russett's comments in same volume, pp. 171-172.

11. For an analysis of Sweden's policy regarding arms sales, see Stockholm International Peace Research Institute (SIPRI), *The Arms Trade and the Third World* (New York: Humanities Press, 1971), Chapter 11, Part III, hereinafter cited as The SIPRI Study, wherein this policy is characterized as one of "restrictiveness." However, there are recent indications that Swedish policy in this area is changing under economic pressures. See "Viggen Designed to Ease Pilot Workload," *Aviation Week and Space Technology*, May 20, 1974, p. 42, wherein recent Swedish efforts to expand aircraft sales outside of Scandinavia are discussed.

12. For a discussion of qualitative or modernity factors, see The MIT Study, Chapter IV.

13. U.S., Congress, House, Committee on Armed Services, *Report of the Special Subcommittee on the Middle East*, 93rd Cong., 1st sess., December 13, 1973, p. 3, reports that the United States was producing only 360 M-60 tanks per year, perhaps equivalent to about half of Israel's tank losses during the 1973 conflict.

14. This dilemma is discussed in an as yet unpublished manuscript by Barton Whaley on Soviet and Chinese clandestine arms transfers, which this author was privileged to examine.

15. For a brief discussion on the notions of "revisionist" and "status quo" powers, see William D. Coplin, *Introduction to International Politics* (Chicago: Markham Publishing Co., 1971), p. 130.

16. For an analysis of the importance of these factors to controls, see The SIPRI Study, Chapter 1, Part V.

17. For a discussion of various types of transfer modes, replete with definitions, see Lewis A. Frank, *The Arms Trade in International Relations* (New York: Praeger, 1969), Chapter 5, and The MIT Study, pp. 124-29.

18. This point will be elaborated more fully in Chapter Two. It was derived from a reading of Karl Polanyi, *The Great Transformation* (New York and Toronto: Farrar and Rinehart, Inc., 1944), and Herbert Feis, *Europe, the World's Banker: 1870-1914* (New York: Council on Foreign Relations, 1930).

19. See, for example, J. T. Walton Newbold, *The War Trust Exposed* (London: Blackfriars, 1916); George Herbert Perris, *The War Traders* (London: National Peace Council, 1914); and William Carey Morey, "The Sale of Munitions of War," *American Journal of International Law* X, No. 3 (1916): 467-491.

20. Among this prolific genre are: Joseph H. Baccus, *Arms and Munitions* (New York: Noble and Noble, 1935); Elton Atwater, *Administration of Export and Import Embargoes, 1935-36* (Geneva: Geneva Research Center, 1938); Fenner Brockway, *The Bloody Traffic* (London: Gollancz, 1933); George A. Drew, *Enemies of Peace: An Exposé of Armaments Manufacturers* (Toronto: Women's League of Nations Association, 1933); H. C. Engelbrecht and F. C. Hanighen, *Merchants of Death: A Study of the International Armaments Industry* (New York: Dodd, Mead & Company, 1934); H. C. Engelbrecht, *One Hell of a Business* (New York: R. M. McBride and Co., 1934); Julia Emily Johnsen, *International Traffic in Arms and Munitions* (New York: The H. W. Wilson Co., 1934); Cornelius D. Judd, *Traffic in Armaments* (Dallas: Southern Methodist University, 1934); Otto Lehmann-Russbuldt, *War for Profits* (New York: A. H. King, 1930); Richard Lewinsohn, *The Profits of War through the Ages* (London: G. Routledge and Sons, Ltd., 1936); Philip Noel-Baker, *The Private Manufacture of Armaments* (London: V. Gollancz, 1936); Thomas Andrew Rousse, *Nationalization of Munitions* (Austin: University of Texas Bulletin, 1936); George Seldes, *Iron, Blood, and Profits: An Exposé of the Worldwide Munitions Racket* (New York and London: Harper & Brothers, 1934); Eugene Staley, *Foreign Investment and War* (Chicago: University of Chicago Press, 1935); William T. Stone, "International Traffic in Arms and Ammunition," *Foreign Policy Reports* IX, no. 12, (August 16, 1933); Union of Democratic Control, *The Secret International: Armaments Firms at Work* (London: 1932); Seymour Waldman, *Death and Profits* (New York: Brewer, Warren and Putnam, 1932); Freda White, *Traffic in Arms* (London: League of Nations Union, 1932); and W. H. Williams, *Who's Who in Arms* (London: Labour Research Department, 1935). These works tend, in the aggregate, to be somewhat repetitive of the same themes and material and most are written from the same perspective. Like the Nye Committee reports, but usually far more polemical, they tend to focus on well-publicized scandals, incidents and personalities, but are lacking in really comprehensive analysis of data which would allow for an accurate picture of the patterns of the interwar arms trade. The works of Engelbrecht, Noel-Baker and Atwater are probably the most objective and informative.

21. Some examples are: Philip C. Jessup, "The New Neutrality Legislation," *American Journal of International Law* XXIX (1935): 665-70;

Charles G. Fenwick, "The Arms Embargo Against Bolivia and Paraguay," *American Journal of International Law* XXVIII, no. 3 (1934): 534-38; John Bassett Moore, "The New Isolation," *American Journal of International Law* XXVII (1933): 607-29; James Scott Brown, "Neutrality of the United States," *American Journal of International Law* XXIX (1935): 644-52; and Lester Hood Woolsey, "The Burton Resolution on Trade in Munitions of War," *American Journal of International Law* XXII (1928): 610-14.

      22. Nokhim M. Sloutzki, *The World Armaments Race, 1919-1939* (Geneva: Geneva Research Center, 1941).

      23. See the Institute for Strategic Studies' annual, *The Military Balance* (London), and John L. Sutton and Geoffrey Kemp, *Arms to Developing Countries; 1945-1965* (London: Institute for Strategic Studies, 1966). More recently, additional monographs have been published by the ISS in a series entitled Defence Technology and the Western Alliance, 1969. These include: John Calmann, *European Cooperation in Defense Technology: The Political Aspect*; C. J. E. Harlow, *The European Armaments Base: A Survey*; Arnold Kramish, *Atlantic Technological Imbalance: An American Perspective*; Kenneth Hunt, *The Requirements of Military Technology in the 1970s*; and Alastair Buchan, *The Implications of a European System for Defense Technology.*

      24. See, inter alia, Edgar C. Furniss, *Some Perspectives on American Military Assistance* (Princeton: Princeton University Press, 1957); Harold A. Hovey, *United States Military Assistance: A Study of Policies and Practices* (New York: Praeger, 1965); Charles Wolf, Jr., *Military Assistance Programs* (Santa Monica: Rand, 1965); Samuel Finer, *The Man on Horseback* (New York: Praeger, 1962); William Gutteridge, *Military Institutions and Power in the New States* (New York: Praeger, 1965); John J. Johnson, ed., *The Role of the Military in Underdeveloped Countries* (Princeton: Princeton University Press, 1962); and Edwin Lieuwen, *Arms and Politics in Latin America* (New York: Praeger, 1960).

      25. George Thayer, *The War Business* (New York: Simon and Schuster, 1969); and Frank, *Arms Trade.*

      26. The MIT Study.

      27. Lincoln P. Bloomfield and A. C. Leiss, *Controlling Small Wars: A Strategy for the 1970s* (New York: Knopf, 1969). This work utilizes a number of case studies on local conflict in which the arms acquisition process represents one problem among many.

      28. The SIPRI Study. Other recent additions to the growing arms trade literature are: John Stanley and Maurice Pearton, *The International Trade in Arms* (London: Chatto and Windus, 1972); Ulricht Albrecht, *Der Handel Mit Waffen* (Munich: C. Hanser, 1971); J. H. Hoagland and Erastus Corning, III, *The Diffusion of Combat Aircraft, Missiles and their Supporting Technologies* (Waltham, Mass.: Browne and Shaw Research Corporation, 1966); Catherine McArdle, *The Role of Military Assistance in the Problem of Arms Control: The Middle East, Latin America and Africa* (Cambridge, Mass.: MIT Center for International Studies, 1964); W. Joshua and S. Gibert, *Arms for the Third World: Soviet Military Aid Diplomacy* (Baltimore: Johns Hopkins, 1969); Laurence Martin, *Arms and Strategy* (New York: McKay, 1973) especially Part IV; and Uri Ra'anan, *The USSR Arms the Third World: Case Studies in Soviet*

Foreign Policy (Cambridge, Mass.: MIT Press, 1969). In addition, the arms transfer problem in the Middle East is handled in J. C. Hurewitz, *Middle East Politics: The Military Dimension* (New York: Praeger, 1969); and Nadav Safran, *From War to War: The Arab-Israeli Confrontation, 1948-1967* (New York: Pegasus, 1969). The SIPRI, ISS and MIT works are reviewed in Ulricht Albrecht, "The Study in International Trade in Arms and Peace Research," *Journal of Peace Research* 9, no. 2 (1972), which is followed by a rebuttal by Amelia C. Leiss.

      29. See the annex to *The MIT Study* by Jacob Refson, *U.S. Military Training and Advice: Implications for Arms Transfer Policies*, C/70-4 (Cambridge, Mass.: MIT Center for International Studies, 1970).

      30. For details of these situations, refer in Appendix B to the appropriate country index number in the Military Intelligence Division files (hereinafter referred to as The MID Files), wherein there is extensive analysis in military attaché reports.

      31. For a futuristic view of some upcoming battlefield weapons developments, see the articles by Drew Middleton in the *New York Times*, "Army is Developing Battlefield Computers and Detection Devices," October 27, 1970, p. 12, and "Futuristic Weapons Tested at Reservation on Coast," April 25, 1971, p. 47. For discussions of the battlefield impact of the various new weapons introduced in the 1973 Arab-Israeli conflict see, inter alia, "The Deadly New Weapons," *Time Magazine*, October 22, 1973, p. 37, "Technology of Armored War Makes for Intense Duels," *The New York Times*, October 21, 1973, p. 27, "Missiles Giving New Muscle to Infantry," *The New York Times*, November 2, 1973, p. 17, and U.S., Congress, House, Committee on Armed Services, *Report of the Special Subcommittee on the Middle East*, 93rd Cong., 1st sess., December 13, 1973, p. 3. Additionally, numerous articles in *Aviation Week and Space Technology* in the period following the October 1973 war provide additional analyses. See particularly, "Mideast War Spurs Renewed Interest in Standoff Weapons," December 10, 1973, p. 13.

      32. Engelbrecht and Hanighen, Chapter II; and Cipolla, Chapter I.

      33. See Frank, Appendix A, for the Battle Act lists, and for the interwar period see issues of the National Munitions Control Board, *Annual Report* (Washington, D.C.: Government Printing Office, annual).

      34. For the interconnection between the chemical industry and munitions production in the 1930s, see U.S., Congress, Senate, *Munitions Industry*, Report of the Special Committee on Investigation of the Munitions Industry, 73rd Cong., (Washington, D.C.: Government Printing Office, 1936), especially pp. 263-75. The Appendix entitled "Evidence Folder on Exhibits 1102 and 1103" enumerates hundreds of intercorporate relationships on a worldwide basis. See also Lewinsohn, *Profits of War*, pp. 168-71; and Brockway, *The Bloody Traffic*, p. 80 and p. 101.

      35. For example, DuPont owns Remington Rifles; Olin-Mathieson owns Winchester Rifles.

      36. See Fuller, *Armaments and History*, Chapters 6 and 7, for a discussion of the development of the role of oil as a key to military power in the 20th century.

      37. The inability of the Chinese Communists to obtain aircraft

during the 1930s is discussed in Richard Bueschel, *Chinese Communist Airpower* (New York: Praeger, 1968), pp. 8-9. I have nowhere found evidence of shipments of either armored or naval equipment to the Chinese Communists during this period, although it is possible that small shipments in the former category may have occurred.

38. Such a specialized capacity existed for Skoda (Czechoslovakia), FN (Belgium), Madsen (Denmark) and Bofors (Sweden) in the interwar period and now exists for Israel.

39. Sloutzki, especially pp. 60-71.

40. W. H. B. Smith, *Small Arms of the World* (Harrisburg, Pa.: Stackpole Books, 1966).

41. John H. Hoagland and Patricia A. Clapp. *Notes on Small Arms Traffic*, C/70-7 (Cambridge, Mass.: MIT Center for International Studies, 1970).

42. Thayer, Chapters II and III. This is about the only attempt at comprehensive coverage of the operations of private arms dealers in the postwar period. Another depiction of the small arms trader milieu, concerning events surrounding the Algerian War, is in Bernt Engelmann, *The Weapons Merchants* (New York: Crown Publishers, 1964).

43. Thayer, pp. 98-99, notes, humorously, this has led to rumors that the CIA was "buying" weapons from the Russians.

44. Ibid., p. 133, gives some examples of longevity and frequent changes of hands of certain weapons. In looking at the small arms inventories for a number of nations in the 1930s in The MID Files, it was apparent that many of these weapons had had a very long life, some exceeding 50 years.

45. See The MIT Study, pp. 29-32, for a full exposition of these arguments.

46. The MID Files for Greece in the late 1930s have extensive coverage of the extent to which that nation's arms-purchasing patterns were determined by its blocked currencies in Germany.

47. See Frank, pp. 26-27, for a summary of some representative costs of weapons systems produced by various nations in the postwar period. See also Geoffrey Kemp, *Arms Traffic and Third World Conflicts* (New York: Carnegie Endowment for International Peace, 1970), Appendix A.

48. See The MIT Study, Chapter II, for use of these categories and their application to data for countries in their sample.

49. For a good portrayal of the fantastic rise in costs of American weapons systems since World War II, see "Stopping the Incredible Rise in Weapons Costs," *Business Week*, February 19, 1972, p. 60, which is summarized in Table 2-3.

50. F. M. von Senger und Etterlin, *Die Kampfpanzer von 1916-1966* (Munich: J. F. Lehmanns Verlag, 1966); Ralph E. Jones, George E. Rarey, and Robert J. Icks, *The Fighting Tanks Since 1916* (Washington, D.C.: The National Service Publishing Company, 1933); Robert J. Icks, *Tanks and Armored Vehicles* (New York: Duell, Sloane and Pearce, 1945); and Richard Ogorkiewicz, *Armor* (New York: Praeger, 1960).

Notes for Chapter Two

1. See J. David Singer, "The Levels of Analysis Problem in International Relations," in Klaus Knorr and Sidney Verba, eds., *The International System: Theoretical Essays* (Princeton: Princeton University Press, 1961), pp. 77-92; and John Spanier, *Games Nations Play* (New York: Praeger, 1972), Chapter II.

2. Morton Kaplan, *System and Process in International Politics*, (New York: Wiley, 1957) especially Part I.

3. Ibid., pp. 22-43.

4. Richard Rosecrance, *Action and Reaction in World Politics: International Systems in Perspective* (Boston: Little, Brown, 1963).

5. William D. Coplin, *Introduction to International Politics*, (Chicago: Markham Publishing Co., 1971), Chapter 11.

6. For still another typology, geared to a longer range historical perspective, see Kenneth J. Holsti, *International Politics* (Englewood Cliffs, N.J.: Prentice-Hall, 1967), Chapters 2 and 3. He uses the following five classificatory desiderata: boundaries of the system, nature of the political units, structure of the system, major forms of interaction and major rules of the system.

7. For a discussion of the distinction between multipolarity and bimultipolarity, see Richard Rosecrance, "Bipolarity, Multipolarity and the Future," *The Journal of Conflict Resolution* X (1966): 314-27. See also Spanier, Part II, wherein the term bipolycentrism is defined and discussed.

8. The Chinese defection from the Soviet bloc in the 1960s might constitute a significant exception to this generalization.

9. Rosecrance, *Action and Reaction*, pp. 257-261.

10. Bruce Russett, *Trends in World Politics* (New York: MacMillan, 1965), p. 2.

11. For a discussion of the concepts of "balance of power," and "the balancer," see Ernst Haas, "The Balance of Power: Prescription, Concept or Propaganda," *World Politics* V, no. 4 (July 1953): 442-77.

12. For analysis of this period of diplomacy see, inter alia, Gordon Craig and Felix Gilbert, eds., *The Diplomats: 1919-1939*, vol. 2 (New York: Atheneum, 1963), especially Chapters XIII to XVII, and XX; E. H. Carr, *International Relations Between the Two World Wars, 1919-1939* (London: MacMillan, 1947); and C. M. Gathorne-Hardy, *A Short History of International Affairs, 1920-1934* (London: Oxford University Press, 1934).

13. See William Kaufmann, "Two American Ambassadors: Bullitt and Kennedy," in Craig and Gilbert, Chapter XXI.

14. For analysis of the waxing of the "peripheral" powers, see Ludwig Dehio, *The Precarious Balance: Four Centuries of European Power Struggle* (New York: Knopf, 1962); and Hajo Holborn, *The Political Collapse of Europe* (New York: Knopf, 1959).

15. Russett, *Trends in World Politics*, p. 4. For a lengthy analysis of measures of military power, see Klaus Knorr, *Military Power and Potential* (Lexington, Mass.: D. C. Heath, 1970).

16. For elaboration of the theme of existing or impending American

hegemony, see Jean-Jacques Servan-Schreiber, *The American Challenge* (New York: Atheneum, 1968).

17. There are numerous indications in The MID Files in the 1930s of the scorn held by Western military experts for the Soviet military and arms industry. This was despite Western military observers having been impressed with the performance of Soviet arms against German and Italian equipment in the Spanish Civil War, and with the performance of the Soviet Army against the Japanese in 1937-1938.

18. See Hans Morgenthau, *Politics Among Nations*, 4th ed. (New York: Knopf, 1967), Chapter 1; and Stanley Hoffmann's critique of Morgenthau in *Contemporary Theory in International Relations*, (Englewood Cliffs, N.J.: Prentice-Hall, 1960), pp. 54-73. See also Spanier, Chapter 2.

19. See Morgenthau, Chapter 7, for a typology of ideologies applicable to international politics.

20. For an excellent summary discussion of the ebbs and flows of ideological conflict and totality in warfare through time, see Robert E. Osgood, "The Expansion of Force," in Robert J. Art and Kenneth Waltz, eds., *The Use of Force* (Boston: Little, Brown, 1971).

21. For an analysis of the moral underpinnings of the conduct of warfare in the Middle Ages, see J. F. C. Fuller, *Armaments and History*, (New York: Charles Scribner's Sons, 1945), Chapters II and III.

22. See Carlo Cipolla, *Guns and Sails in the Early Period of European Expansion*, (London: Collins, 1965), Chapter I, on the introduction of weapons licensing by Elizabeth I in Britain and others during this period.

23. Osgood, "The Expansion of Force," in Art and Waltz. For a short summary of the diplomacy of this period, see Holborn, *The Political Collapse of Europe*.

24. An interesting portrayal of the ties between European elites even as late as the eve of World War I is rendered in Barbara Tuchman, *The Guns of August* (New York: Dell, 1962), introductory chapter.

25. Actually, Fuller sees the 18th century—the period of "enlightenment"—as a mere interlude between the period of ideological warfare of the 17th century and that inaugurated by the American and French Revolutions. See his *Armaments and History*, p. 108.

26. Raymond Aron, *The Century of Total War* (Garden City: Doubleday, 1954).

27. For extensive discussions of the "antinational" arms trade phenomenon, see H. C. Engelbrecht and F. C. Hanighen, *Merchants of Death: A Study of the International Armaments Industry* (New York: Dodd, Mead & Company, 1934); Phillip Noel-Baker, *The Private Manufacture of Armaments* (London: V. Gollancz, 1936); and George Seldes, *Iron, Blood and Profits: An Exposé of the Worldwide Munitions Racket* (New York and London: Harpers and Brothers, 1934).

28. In the MID files for Britain, for instance, there is considerable discussion in the early 1930s concerning Parliamentary debate over the sale of brand-new British tanks to the Soviets before the same tanks had been issued to the British army.

29. This atavism may be perceived as analogous to that discussed by Joseph Schumpeter in his analysis of the causes of imperialism, which he attributed to the time-lagged, anachronistic existence of a feudal-military class in Europe. See his *Imperialism* (Cleveland and New York: World Publishing Co. 1951).

30. For an excellent review of the development of international economic thought and practice, see John Fred Bell, *A History of Economic Thought*, 2nd ed. (New York: Ronald Press, 1967).

31. Samuel Huntington, "Arms Races: Prerequisites and Results," in Art and Waltz, pp. 369-72.

32. See Cipolla, pp. 67-71, for French developments under Colbert.

33. See Bell, Chapter 6, for the origins of classical economics, and pp. 305-10 for a discussion of List's critique from a German perspective.

34. See Richard Lewinsohn, *The Profits of War Through the Ages* (London: G. Routledge and Sons, Ltd., 1936), p. 118.

35. See Peter Batty, *The House of Krupp* (New York: Stein and Day, 1967); William Manchester, *The Arms of Krupp* (Boston: Little, Brown, 1968); J. D. Scott, *Vickers, A History* (London: Weidenfeld and Nicolson, 1962); and Alden Hatch, *Remington Arms in American History* (New York: Rinehart, 1956.)

36. The most famed and notorious arms merchant of them all, Sir Basil Zaharoff, is the subject of Richard Lewinsohn's biography, *The Mystery Man of Europe* (Philadelphia: J. B. Lippincott, 1929).

37. See Engelbrecht and Hanighen, pp. 74-79, for details on Krupp's dealings with Austria and France.

38. Ibid., p. 98, for details of this first submarine transaction.

39. Ibid., p. 75.

40. See J. T. Walton Newbold, *The War Trust Exposed* (London: Blackfriars, 1916), p. 22.

41. For an analysis of this mood, see E. H. Carr, *The Twenty Years Crisis, 1919-1939* (London: MacMillan, 1939).

42. The most celebrated case was that of the alleged effort by one W. Shearer at the 1927 Naval Disarmament Conference to "lobby" against the limitation of naval forces. Shearer was said to have been paid for these efforts by Bethlehem Steel and others. For details, see Noel-Baker, pp. 357-64.

43. An earlier exception was the partial nationalization of the Italian small arms industry in the 1920s. See Lewinsohn, *The Profits of War Through the Ages*, p. 177.

44. See Elton Atwater, "British Control over the Export of War Materials," *American Journal of International Law* XXXIII, No. 2 (1939); 292-317.

45. For analyses of the development of American policy on controls in this period, see Elton Atwater, *American Regulation of Arms Exports* (New York: Carnegie Endowment for International Peace, 1941); Manley O. Hudson, "The Chaco Arms Embargo," *International Conciliation* (New York: Carnegie Endowment for Peace, 1936); Philip C. Jessup, "The New Neutrality Legislation" *American Journal of International Law* XXIX (1935): 665-70; and

Murray S. Stedman, *Exporting Arms: The Federal Arms Export Administration, 1935-1945* (New York: Kings Crown Press, 1947). For a synopsis of the stated formal policies of the world's various nations as of 1937, see League of Nations Conference for the Reduction and Limitation of Armaments, *National Control of the Manufacture of and Trade in Arms*, Series of League of Nations Publications, IX, no. 1. Disarmament, 1938.

46. See Hugh Thomas, *The Spanish Civil War* (New York: Harper and Row, 1961) for materials on embargoes in this conflict and corresponding debates in interested countries. For an example of how arms sales can become a bitter political issue in a Western democracy, see "Leftist defies Wilson on arms sales," *Chicago Tribune*, April 16, 1974, Section 1, p. 10, wherein is discussed the recent controversy within the British Labour Party over arms sales to the new right-wing Chilean government.

47. For a discussion of the Swiss Oerlikon-Buehrle affair, as an example, see SIPRI, *The Arms Trade and the Third World* (New York: Humanities Press, 1971), pp. 356-58, hereinafter cited as The SIPRI Study.

48. Mira Wilkins, *The Emergence of Multinational Enterprise: American Business Abroad from the Colonial Era to 1914* (Cambridge, Mass.: Harvard University Press, 1970).

49. Otto Lehmann-Russbuldt, *War for Profits* (New York: A. H. King, 1930), pp. 27-28, quoting from a speech to the Reichstag by Deputy Erzberger on April 23, 1913.

50. Engelbrecht and Hanighen, pp. 142-43. Additional data on this subject are contained in Lewinsohn, *The Profits of War Through the Ages*, and in Williams, *Who's Who in Arms* (London: Labour Research Department, 1935).

51. U.S. Congress, Senate, *Munitions Industry*, Report of the Special Committee on Investigation of the Munitions Industry, 73rd Cong. (Washington, D.C.: Government Printing Office, 1936), p. 252; and Engelbrecht and Hanighen, p. 193.

52. Engelbrecht and Hanighen, pp. 203-4.

53. See a country-by-country analysis in C. J. E. Harlow, *The European Armaments Base: A Survey*, Defense Technology and the Western Alliance study series, no. 2 (London: Part II).

54. Thus, according to Lewinsohn, *The Profits of War Through the Ages*, p. 147: "The arms merchant sought to steal his rival's customers, but if competition got too keen for business to be profitable, then peace was made between the rivals and the market was shared between them. It was in the munitions trade that this process went furthest. After cut-throat competition during the long period of peace, the ammunition factories in 1897 formed a cartel which embraced practically the whole world. ... Production was controlled and markets delimited, and more important still, European and American manufacturers agreed to standardize their export prices. ... This of course was not a peculiarity of the arms trade. What was remarkable was that the arms manufacturers treated their business just exactly as if they were dealing in knitted woolen goods or mirrors. ... The financial alliance among armament firms did not necessarily correspond with the system of political alliances."

55. A. C. Engelbrecht, *One Hell of a Business* (New York: R. M. McBride and Co., 1934), gives the following example on p. 52: "The universal embargo gave way to the embargo against Bolivia and Paraguay in the Gran Chaco. DuPont gave official assurances that it would abide by the Presidential ruling, but there was an easy way round through I.C.I. [Imperial Chemical Industries]. When an inquiry came from Manuel Ferreira for TNT and other explosives, N. E. Bates, Jr., DuPont agent in South America, at once saw the way out. He wrote to the next I.C.I. office in South America, that 'we could not quote because of the embargo on munitions and military explosives promulgated by President Roosevelt on Paraguay and Bolivia. Since there is no embargo obtaining in England, we telegraphed I.C.I. in London to quote you direct so that you in turn may quote Ferreira.' In any case, DuPont made money on the sale and a way was found to evade the embargo."

56. Note this type of analysis is a subset of that used by Derek de Solla Price concerning exponential growth of science and technology, as discussed in Russett, *Trends in World Politics*, pp. 7-14.

57. Huntington, "Arms Races: Prerequisites and Results," in Art and Waltz, pp. 385-97.

Notes for Chapter Three

1. See *The Arms Trade and the Third World* (New York: Humanities Press, 1971), pp. 17-18, hereinafter cited as The SIPRI Study, for definitions of these categories and analysis in terms of individual Nations.

2. Both postwar France and interwar Czechoslovakia have had very high relative percentages of arms exports to overall exports. For data and accompanying discussion on the latter, see Sloutzki, *The World Armaments Race, 1919-1939* (Geneva: Geneva Research Center, 1941), pp. 68-69. For discussions of the contemporary nature of the problem, see John Stanley and Maurice Pearton, *The International Trade in Arms* (London: Chatto and Windus, 1972), Chapter 6, including analysis of the economies of scale problem, and Laurence Martin, *Arms and Strategy* (New York: McKay, 1973), chapter 14.

3. See The SIPRI Study, Chap. II, for an analysis of Sweden's policy and its arms industries.

4. If the theory of comparative advantage had any real relevance to arms production and trade, one might surmise that by now the United States military-industrial complex would have gone the way of some of America's other uncompetitive industries, and that offshore procurement would be more significant than it is. However, increasing trends towards codevelopment ventures with European partners may indicate that costs have begun to conflict seriously with the normal desire for autarky.

5. For a discussion of the relationship between oligopoly and controls, see Amelia C. Leiss et al., *Arms Transfers to Less Developed Countries* (Cambridge, Mass.: MIT Center for International Studies, 1970), pp. 60-61, hereinafter cited as The MIT Study.

6. For an analysis of the trend towards multipurpose systems

(commonality) see Charles L. Schultze et al., *Setting National Priorities: The 1973 Budget* (Washington: The Brookings Institution, 1972), pp. 132-139. For definitions of various types of combat aircraft, see Geoffrey Kemp, *Arms Traffic and Third World Conflicts* (New York: Carnegie Endowment for International Peace, 1970), Appendix A.

7. According to the *New York Times*, May 17, 1971, p. 1, the new Chinese fighter has been designated the Shenyang F-9 and is an advanced and improved copy of the Soviet MIG-19, with a top speed of about Mach 2. It is reportedly being produced in China at the rate of about ten per month, and by 1974, 300-400 were reported completed.

8. See The MIT Study, pp. 159-160, which indicates the new Mitsubishi aircraft will be powered by a Rolls-Royce-Turbomeca engine, indicating a degree of residual dependency for engines.

9. See the *New York Times*, September 15, 1971, p. 3 for details on the rumored attempt by the Israelis to develop their own fighter aircraft. More recent information is in Dale R. Tahtinen, *The Arab-Israeli Military Balance since October 1973* (Washington: American Enterprise Institute, 1974), pp. 10-15.

10. For projections on future developments in combat aircraft production on a country-by-country basis see The MIT Study, Chapter III.

11. For information on tank development and production during the interwar period, see F. M. von Senger und Etterlin *Die Kampfpanzer von 1916-1966* (Munich: J. F. Lehmanns Verlag, 1966); Robert J. Icks *Tanks and Armored Vehicles* (New York: Duell, Sloane and Pearce, 1945); and Richard Ogorkiewicz *Armor* (New York: Praeger, 1960).

12. A good summary of postwar tank developments, with data on combat characteristics, is in the Institute for Strategic Studies, *The Military Balance, 1971-1972* (London), p. 63.

13. For data on missile development and production, see the yearly issues of *Jane's All the World's Aircraft* (London: Sampson, Low, Marston and Co., annual); and "Specifications: Leading International Missiles," *Aviation Week*, March 8, 1971, pp. 72-73.

14. There have been small-scale transfers of the SS-11 antitank missile, the Crotale surface-to-air system, the Exocet surface-to-surface missile and some Alouette helicopters, and the codeveloped Roland missile is being considered for adoption by the United States Army.

15. The extent of recent French advances in aircraft markets can be gauged by examining the year-to-year compilations of the SIPRI and ISS annuals. See also *La France et le Commerce des Armes* (Toulon: Le Centre local d'information et de coordination de l'Action Non-Violente), 1972.

16. For analysis along these lines, see Geoffrey Kemp, *Classification of Weapons Systems and Air Force Designs in Less Developed Country Environments*, C/70-3 (Cambridge, Mass.: MIT Center for International Studies, 1970).

17. Considerable data on armored cars in both periods is scattered throughout the pages of K. Macksey and J. H. Batchelor, *Tank: A History of the Armoured Fighting Vehicle* (London: MacDonald, 1970).

18. More recently, the French have begun to make inroads with the

small Daphne submarine, paralleling market expansion in other categories. India and South Africa have been two recipients.

19. J. T. Walton Newbold, *The War Trust Exposed* (London: Blackfriars, 1916), p. 28, describes the British Navy going into a panic in 1884, worried about a "torpedo boat gap" after Russia had acquired 112 such vessels while Britain had none.

20. For an analysis of some possible future trends in naval weapons and warfare, see Paul Cohen, "The Erosion of Naval Power," *Foreign Affairs*, January 1971. See also "Gabriel Outmatches Soviet Styx in Mideast Engagements at Sea," *Aviation Week and Space Technology*, Dec. 10, 1973, p. 20.

21. For such definitions see William D. Coplin, *Introduction to International Politics* (Chicago: Markham Publishing Co., 1971), pp. 130-131; and Hans Morgenthau, *Politics Among Nations* 4th ed. (New York: Knopf, 1967), pp. 86-88.

22. Of course, some radical writers might characterize American postwar foreign policy as both expansionist-imperialist and essentially conservative. It is hard to say whether this is a paradox.

23. Recent data from ISS indicate significant British arms sales in Iran, Ceylon, India, Malaysia, Thailand, Argentina, Brazil, Kenya, South Africa and Uganda, among others. See Institute for Strategic Studies, *The Military Balance* (London: annual), 1971-1972, 1972-1973.

24. France's most significant recent arms deals, outside of NATO, have been in Spain, Libya, Lebanon, Saudi Arabia, Kuwait, Pakistan, Malaysia, Australia, Argentina, Brazil, Peru, Colombia, Ecuador, Zaire and Niger.

25. Given the generalization that arms trading was a less purposively used instrument of expanding influence in the 1930s, it might appear less valid to speak of aggressive arms sales policies on the part of revisionist powers in the interwar period. However, government direction of arms sales was well institutionalized in the late 1930s in Italy, Germany and Japan as well as the USSR. And even in the liberal democracies, laissez faire had waned by the late 1930s, at the time revisionist powers were taking markets away from the status quo powers.

26. Joseph Kraft, "In Search of Kissinger," *Harpers*, January 1971, p. 58.

27. Michael Gort, "Analysis of Stability and Change in Market Shares," in Bruce Russett, ed., *Economic Theories of International Politics* (Chicago: Markham Publishing Co., 1968).

28. Ibid., p. 195.

29. France has innovated with its Crotale, Exocet, Otomat and Roland missiles, and the Israelis with the Gabriel missile.

30. Klaus Knorr, *The War Potential of Nations* (Princeton: Princeton University Press, 1956), and Klaus Knorr, *Military Power and Potential* (Lexington, Mass.: D. C. Heath, 1970).

31. A. W. Marshall, *Problems of Estimating Military Power*, C/66-21. (Cambridge, Mass.: MIT Center for International Studies, 1968).

32. For the Middle Eastern arms race since 1950, this is graphically depicted—by weapons system—in the chart on p. 511 of The SIPRI Study.

33. Ibid., pp. 17-41.

34. The SIPRI authors note that some nations—West Germany, Italy, Japan and Britain—have mixed restrictive-industrial policy patterns, particularly with respect to the Middle East, Ibid pp. 32-41.

35. An analysis of prestige arms races and associated arms acquisitions is contained in Michael Mihalka, "Arms Races in the Third World" (Paper presented at Midwest Political Science Association meeting, Chicago, April 1972).

Notes for Chapter Four

1. Information for the following illustrations of recent arms deals was drawn from the recent annual editions of Institute for Strategic Studies, *The Military Balance* (London: annual), and the *SIPRI Yearbook of World Armaments and Disarmament* (New York, Humanities Press).

2. For information on the important recent Franco-Libyan arms deal, see "Israel Hits France on Jets for Libya," *Washington Evening Star*, Jan. 14, 1970, Section A. p. 3.

3. These definitions are taken, in somewhat altered form, from Amelia C. Leiss et al., *Arms Transfers to Less Developed Countries*, C/70-1 (Cambridge, Mass.: MIT Center for International Studies, 1970), p. 84, hereinafter cited as The MIT Study.

4. An excellent discussion of the tie-in between military training groups and arms transfers is contained in Jacob Refson, *U.S. Military Training and Advice: Implications for Arms Transfer Policies*, C/70-4 (Cambridge, Mass.: MIT Center for International Studies, 1970). For historical perspective, see George Liska, *The New Statecraft* (Chicago: Chicago University Press, 1960), pp. 54-58.

5. For a brief discussion of pre-World War I Turkey, see H. C. Engelbrecht and F. C. Hanighen, *Merchants of Death: A Study of the International Armaments Industry* (New York: Dodd, Mead & Company, 1934), pp. 148-149.

6. The gist of United States intelligence reports from the Spanish Civil War was that the earlier German emphasis on developing small but mobile armored equipment had proved a failure. German doctrine was reversed in time to build larger tanks for use in World War II.

7. The military intelligence reports from the Chaco conflict indicate that the performance of foreign tanks was closely monitored, as this was the first combat testing of the then greatly advanced armored systems being produced in the early 1930s.

8. This point is drawn from Barton Whaley's unpublished manuscript on clandestine Soviet arms shipments, which sheds new light on the Soviet policy towards the Spanish Civil War and on the distribution of Soviet priorities between Spain and the Far East in the late 1930s.

9. For a comparative analysis of the performance of American and Soviet military equipment in the 1973 war, see U.S., Congress, House, Committee on Armed Services, *Report of the Special Subcommittee on the Middle East*, 93rd Cong., 1st sess., December 13, 1973.

10. Syrian attempts at leveraging arms from the USSR by dealing with China are described in the *New York Times*, May 18, 1970, p. 5.

11. See "Sadat's Shopping List—'a lot' of U.S. missiles," *Chicago Tribune*, April 29, 1974, p. 3.

12. For discussion of the relenting of the British embargo on South Africa because of the latter's acquisitions from other sources, see "South Africans Heartened by Report of Naval Exercise with British," *New York Times*, July 27, 1970, p. 12.

13. Greece's use of leverage vis-à-vis the United States in purchasing arms from France is noted in "Greek-French Arms Deal Worries Turks," *Washington Post*, February 27, 1970, Section A, p. 14. For a general analysis of the United States dilemma in recent years, see "In a Seller's Market, the United States Sells," *The New York Times*, June 10, 1973, Section E, p. 5.

14. The Arab countries' leverage in the future will perhaps be much greater given the projections of increasing American, not to mention European, dependence on Middle Eastern oil. For an analysis including reference to the tie-in with arms shipments to Israel see "Western Nations Fret as Arabs Accumulate Massive Sums from Oil," *Wall Street Journal*, January 23, 1973, p. 1. See also "The Shah becomes a Traffic Cop," *Chicago Tribune*, March 23, 1974, Section 1, p. 10. For recent data on Middle Eastern arms purchases financed by increased oil revenues see "Oil Cutback Sparks Mideast Sales Battle," *Aviation Week and Space Technology*, February 4, 1974, p. 19.

15. For a detailed analysis of French success in pursuing an industrial arms supply policy in the face of political cross-pressures, see The SIPRI Study, Chapter 6; and George Thayer, *The War Business* (New York: Simon and Schuster, 1969), pp. 276-284.

16. France has not altogether avoided protests about its indiscriminate arms sales, particularly those to South Africa and Rhodesia. For a discussion of this, see *Le France et le Commerce des Armes* (Toulon: Le Centre Local d'information et de Coordination de l'Action Non-Violente, 1972), pp. 31-33.

17. See "Soccer Rivalry Leads to Salvador-Honduras Break," *New York Times*, June 28, 1969, p. 1.

18. Although Panama was one nation not acquiring major weapons systems in the 1930s, it is worth noting that it was one of two Latin American nations (the other was Peru) identified in the military intelligence files as having acquired small arms from Japan.

19. See Luigi Einaudi et al., *Arms Transfers to Latin America: Toward a Policy of Mutual Respect*, R-1173-DOS (Santa Monica: RAND Corporation, June 1973), Report Prepared for the Department of State.

20. For a discussion of Soviet arms supplies to Cyprus in the wake of British withdrawal, see SIPRI, *The Arms Trade and the Third World* (New York: Humanities Press, 1971), pp. 202-203 (hereinafter cited as The SIPRI Study).

21. See Thayer, p. 320, for a discussion of the unusual transaction between Colt Industries and Singapore involving M-16 rifles, in the face of the Pentagon's considerable apparent annoyance.

22. The orders of battle of the European neutrals, and their cross-bloc acquisitions, are indicated in the various recent editions of the Institute for Strategic Studies annual, *The Military Balance.*

23. See "Red Military Aides in Peru, United States Says," *Chicago Tribune,* February 26, 1974, Section 1, p. 3, wherein it is reported that Peru has already bought 200 tanks and considerable heavy artillery from the USSR, and is planning to purchase surface-to-air missiles.

24. Extensive trade data for 1938 and for various postwar years, on dyadic and regional bases, are contained in the annual, *Direction of International Trade* (New York), published jointly by the United Nations, International Monetary Fund and the International Bank for Reconstruction and Development. For a model analyzing transaction flows and indices of relative dyadic "acceptances," see I. Richard Savage and Karl W. Deutsch, "A Statistical Model of the Gross Analysis of Transaction Flows," *Econometrica, Journal of the Econometric Society* 28, no. 3. (July 1960).

25. France has apparently received special consideration from Iraq on this basis, having retained oil concessions while American and British assets have recently been nationalized. The final outcome of this situation was still somewhat in abeyance at this writing. Otherwise, it has recently engaged in massive deals with Saudi Arabia, Kuwait, Libya and Abu Dhabi, involving transfers of Mirage jets, various missiles, helicopters and tanks, with overtones of out and out, government-to-government barter arrangements. For details see "Oil Cutback Sparks Mideast Sales Battle," *Aviation Week and Space Technology,* February 1, 1974, p. 19.

26. See J. David Singer and Melvin Small, "Formal Alliances, 1815-1935," *Journal of Peace Research* 3, no. 1 (1966). For another typology used to compare alliances in the interwar and postwar periods, see Bruce M. Russett, "An Empirical Typology of International Military Alliances," *Midwest Journal of Political Science* XV, no. 2 (May 1971). For analysis of the differing impact of various systems' attributes on alliance formation and maintenance, see John D. Sullivan, "National and International Sources of Alliance Maintenance" (dissertation, Stanford University, 1969). This work deals with comparisons of the interwar and pre-World War I periods. For additional commentary on the changing nature of alliances, see Herbert S. Dinerstein, "The Transformation of Alliance Systems," *The American Political Science Review* LIX, no. 3 (September 1965); and George Liska, *Nations in Alliance* (Baltimore: The Johns Hopkins Press, 1962).

27. See Russett, "Empirical Typology," pp. 286-287, for discussion of the greater tendency in the interwar period for smaller powers to band together in alliances not headed by a hegemonic power. A more "feudal" system existing in the earlier postwar period is indicated now to be breaking down.

28. For a discussion of German-Soviet military cooperation in this period, see inter alia, Gustav Hilger and Alfred G. Meyer, *The Incompatible Allies: A Memoir-History of German-Soviet Relations, 1918-1941* (New York: Hafner, 1971), pp. 187-208.

29. Postwar alliance data have been drawn from Russett, "Empirical

Typology," the Yale World Data Analysis Program and various recent editions of ISS, *The Military Balance*.

Notes for Chapter Five

    1. For definitions and descriptions of various types of transfer modes, see Amelia C. Leiss et al., *Arms Transfers to Less Developed Countries,* C/70-1 (Cambridge, Mass.: MIT Center for International Studies, 1970), pp. 124-129, hereinafter cited as The MIT Study; and Lewis A. Frank, *The Arms Trade in International Relations* (New York: Praeger, 1969), Chapter 5.

    2. See Carlo Cipolla, *Guns and Sails in the Early Phase of European Expansion* (London: Collins, 1965), pp. 46-47.

    3. See George Thayer, *The War Business* (New York: Simon and Schuster, 1969), pp. 206-218.

    4. For an analogous discussion of various kinds of economic aid in different diplomatic periods, see George Liska, *The New Statecraft* (Chicago: Chicago University Press, 1960), Chapter II. He discusses the use of subsidies in the age of dynastic statecraft (17th and 18th centuries), some of which were used to finance arms purchases. This was in the Age of Mercantilism, with considerable national control over arms industries. See also John M. Sherwig, *Guineas and Gunpowder; British Foreign Aid in the Wars with France, 1793-1815* (Cambridge, Mass.: Harvard University Press, 1969), for a review of British military aid to Continental allies during the Napoleonic Wars, preceding the period of private dominance of arms transfers.

    5. An exception was the gift of a few Soviet tanks to Afghanistan around 1930, which transaction worsened Soviet-Afghan relations when the tanks proved inoperable.

    6. For a discussion of this policy watershed in the early 1960s, see Thayer, pp. 179-201.

    7. For an overview of Soviet postwar policy on arms sales and aid, see W. Joshua and S. Gibert, *Arms for the Third World: Soviet Military Aid Diplomacy,* (Baltimore: Johns Hopkins, 1969); and SIPRI, *The Arms Trade and The Third World* (New York: Humanities Press, 1971), Chapter 4, hereinafter cited as The SIPRI Study.

    8. This is pointed out in, "Soviet Union's Entire Foreign Aid Program Undergoing Major Shift in Emphasis," *Kalamazoo Gazette*, December 7, 1971 (Newsweek Service dispatch). Here, it is indicated that while in the past, the ratio of Soviet economic to military aid had been about 1:1, now the ratio was approximately 1:4. The Soviets were estimated to have spent about $1.5 billion in achieving influence with military aid in India, in contrast to the $9 billion of economic aid lavished upon India by the United States.

    9. For discussions of British and French arms-trading policies, and anatomies of the bureaucracies which implement them, see Thayer, Chapter 6; The SIPRI Study, Chapters 5 and 6; Frank, pp. 171-172, and John Stanley and Maurice Pearton, *The International Trade in Arms* (London: Chatto and Windus, 1972), Part III.

10. In one Congressional hearing, Samuel Cummings, head of Interarmco, cited Argentina's recent move towards Europeanization of its weaponry, which originally had been almost entirely American. Cummings had tried to sell Argentina some tanks for one-fifth the price being asked by the French for their modern AMX-30s, but the Argentinians bought from the French, telling Cummings, "We are sick of the United States." Similar manifestations were reported on for Brazil and Peru. For details, see U.S., Congress, Senate, *Foreign Military Sales Act Amendment: 1970, 1971*, Hearings before the Committee on Foreign Relations, 91st Cong. (Washington, D.C.: Government Printing Office, 1970), p. 42. For recent trends in Latin American arms purchases, see Luigi Einaudi et al., *Arms Transfers to Latin America: Toward a Policy of Mutual Respect*, R-1173-DOS, Report prepared for the Department of State (Santa Monica: RAND Corporation, June 1973).

11. For a brief analysis of the licensing mechanism, see Frank, p. 173. For a general discussion of the use of licensing and also of joint ventures, see Wolfgang Friedmann and George Kalmanoff, *Joint International Business Ventures* (New York: Columbia University Press, 1961), Chapters VI and VII. See, as well, *Aviation Week and Space Technology*, May 13, 1974, p. 53, wherein it is reported that licensing was becoming an "artifact of another era," and that American firms were becoming increasingly reluctant to license because, despite the royalty income, competition with licensed producers abroad was being created. Many companies were said increasingly to be moving towards equity participation and coproduction ventures.

12. For an analysis of the growing indigenous Indian and Israeli arms industries, see The SIPRI Study, Chapter 22.

13. See, inter alia, Robert Rhodes James, *Standardization and Common Production of Weapons in NATO*, Defense Technology and the Western Alliance Study series, no. 3 (London: Institute for Strategic Studies, 1967).

14. For analysis of France's buildup of scientific and technological infrastructure, and its military implications, see Robert Gilpin, *France in the Age of the Scientific State* (Princeton: Princeton University Press, 1968), especially Chapter 9.

15. France has licensed whole weapons systems to Israel (Fouga Magister aircraft), as well as Turbomeca jet engines. The United States, to date, has licensed only subsystemic components to Israel.

16. For a discussion of Sino-Pakistani relations with respect to arms transfers, see The SIPRI Study, pp. 496-498.

17. Considerable data on licensing agreements among the developed nations of the two major blocs can be gleaned from Frank, Chapters 3 and 4; from the ISS monograph by James; from C. J. E. Harlow, *The European Arms Base: A Survey*, Defense Technology and the Western Alliance Study Series, no. 2 (London: Institute for Strategic Studies, 1967); and from the annual arms trade registers of SIPRI and ISS.

18. Information on licensing and assembly agreements are here combined. As previously noted, these categories are often difficult to distinguish.

19. For a listing of postwar licensing agreements to developing nations, see The MIT Study, p. 42. It should be noted, however, that this list will have been expanded somewhat in recent years. Argentina and Brazil, for instance, are now assembling and licensing an expanded range of military equipment. Iran is also moving towards considerable license production, as outlined in Dale R. Tahtinen, *Arms in The Persian Gulf* (Washington: American Enterprise Institute, 1974), p. 18.

20. See *Aviation Week and Space Technology*, May 13, 1974, for a discussion of possible licensing of Rapier by Norden.

21. For an analysis of Japan's arms acquisition policy and its burgeoning indigenous arms industry, see The SIPRI Study, Chapter 10; and "Japan Arms Makers Push Buildup," *Washington Post*, November 6, 1970.

22. Frank, pp. 174-175.

23. James, p. 17.

24. Ibid., pp. 1-6.

25. See Jean-Jacques Servan-Schreiber, *The American Challenge* (New York: Atheneum, 1968). This is a much criticized book, and increasingly so in recent years, as the flaws in American society and economy have become all too apparent. Nevertheless, it affords psychological insight into European fears of American dominance which have translated into increased strivings for independence in arms production.

26. For analysis and discussion of some of these codevelopment ventures, see the ISS monograph by Harlow, where extensive material is contained amidst a country-by-country review of West European arms industries.

27. For an analysis of the politics of this, particularly with respect to Franco-American rivalry, see inter alia, "Europeans Shaping Up Group to Build U.S.-Licensed Fighter," *Aviation Week and Space Technology*, February 4, 1974, p. 16.

28. For projections of future developments within NATO and elsewhere in combat aircraft, see The MIT Study, pp. 149-165.

29. See Thayer, pp. 114-115. Here it is indicated that two British private arms trading firms—Cogswell and Harrison, and Parker-Hale Ltd.—have actually acted as sales outlets for Omnipol products in the noncommunist world. It is hinted that Omnipol is allowed to act somewhat independently from the Czech government, which appreciates its role in earning foreign currency.

30. For details of this situation, see J. H. Hoagland and Erastus Corning III, *The Diffusion of Combat Aircraft, Missiles and Their Supporting Technologies* (Waltham, Mass.: Browne and Shaw Research Corp., 1966), Appendix F.

31. The case of Israel's acquisition of Mirage secrets from Switzerland through the espionage efforts of a Swiss collaborator, Mr. Frauenknecht, was detailed in the *New York Times*, April 23, 1971, p. 1.

32. For a portrayal of the stark inferiority of American aircraft as late as the Battle of Midway in 1942, see inter alia, John Toland, *The Rising Sun*, vol. I (New York: Random House, 1970), Chapter 13.

33. See the National Munitions Control Board, *Annual Report* (Washington, D.C.: Government Printing Office) for 1937 and 1938. For

analyses of American arms sales policy during this period, see Murray S. Stedman, *Exporting Arms: The Federal Arms Exports Administration, 1935-1945* (New York: Kings Crown Press, 1947); and Elton Atwater, *American Regulation of Arms Exports* (New York: Carnegie Endowment for International Peace, 1941), Chapters III-V.

34. The Christie transaction with the USSR is discussed in K. Macksey and J. H. Batchelor, *Tank: A History of the Armoured Fighting Vehicle* (London: MacDonald, 1970), p. 128; and Richard M. Ogorkiewicz, *Armored Forces* (New York: Arco Publishing Co., 1960), p. 225.

35. For discussions of China's arms production problems after the break with the Soviets, see the *New York Times*, May 17, 1971, and February 1, 1972, p. 6.

36. The brokerage function of private or quasi-private arms traders in secondary deals is discussed in Thayer, Part II.

37. The activities of these offshore German aircraft subsidiaries were noted in the various editions of *Jane's All the World's Aircraft* (London: Sampson, Low, Marston and Co., annual) in the early 1930s.

38. This point about the contrast between increased transnational transactions and lessened migration or emigration is made by William D. Coplin, *Introduction to International Politics* (Chicago: Markham Publishing Co., 1971), pp. 192-194.

39. See Cipolla, pp. 103-131.

40. Information on the peregrinations of Hotchkiss and Maxim is contained in Richard Lewinsohn, *The Profits of War Through the Ages* (London: G. Routledge and Sons, Ltd., 1936), pp. 136, 141.

41. See Hoagland and Corning, Appendix F, F-1.

42. For a concise charting of the differential policies of various major powers on retransfer policy, see The SIPRI Study, pp. 37-40.

43. See The MIT Study, pp. 125-126.

44. A discussion of the Arab-Israeli-West German triangle in the context of Germany's arms sales to Israel in the mid-1960s at the behest of the United States government is contained in Thayer, pp. 223-225.

45. Ibid., pp. 203-204.

46. Italy's role as a sales outlet for surplus United States tanks is discussed in The SIPRI Study, p. 271.

47. United States policy on loans of military equipment is discussed in the report of the Senate, Foreign Relations Committee, *Foreign Military Sales Act Amendment: 1970, 1971*, pp. 31, 44-46.

Notes for Chapter Six

1. For a related type of analysis, see Laurence Martin, *Arms and Strategy* (New York: McKay, 1973), p. 254, where capabilities for weapons production and design are charted for a number of nations.

2. For a listing of indigenous aircraft developments by developing countries, see SIPRI *The Arms Trade and the Third World* (New York:

Humanities Press, 1971), Table 22.3, pp. 727-728, hereinafter cited as The SIPRI Study.

3. See "Barak in Combat," *Aviation Week and Space Technology*, October 15, 1973, p. 12.

4. For a listing of indigenous programs in combat naval vessels, see The SIPRI Study, Table 22.8, p. 734.

5. For an excellent and amusing analysis of the lingering hold of horse cavalry doctrine beyond its time, see Edward L. Katzenbach, "The Horse Cavalry in the Twentieth Century," in Robert J. Art and Kenneth Waltz, eds., *The Use of Force* (Boston: Little, Brown, 1971), pp. 277-297. The debate between cavalry and armor exponents was also aired in any number of articles in American and British military journals in the 1930s.

6. For a listing of indigenous programs in developing countries for armored fighting vehicles, see The SIPRI Study, Table 22.2, p. 726.

7. This is discussed in George Thayer, *The War Business* (New York: Simon and Schuster, 1969), pp. 285-286, with a listing of the various destinations of F.N. exports and licenses. Similar ground is covered in Lewis A. Frank, *The Arms Trade in International Relations* (New York: Praeger, 1969), pp. 51-52.

8. For data on postwar small arms production programs, see The SIPRI Study, Table 22.1, p. 725. A good general source for small arms information, past and present, is W. H. B. Smith, *Small Arms of the World* (Harrisburg, Pa.: Stackpole Books, 1966).

9. These developments in Israeli small arms are discussed in the *New York Times*, Sept. 15, 1971, p. 3.

10. Canadian plans to move toward an independent aircraft industry are noted in "Canada to buy aircraft plants from foreign firms," *Chicago Tribune*, May 28, 1974, Section 3, p. 7, seemingly a reflection of an obvious recent surge of Canadian nationalism.

11. Despite the laissez faire nature of the arms trade in that period, some nations may have feared arms cutoffs in the future and thus were impelled towards independence. It is this, and perhaps strivings for the trappings of world power status, which explains the extensive efforts towards arms independence by Japan, Italy and the USSR during the 1930s.

12. Shimon Peres, *David's Sling* (New York: Random House, 1970). This is a fascinating, anecdotal account of Israel's efforts at arming itself since the 1940s, in the larger context of its diplomatic relations with the major powers. For a rundown of Israel's present arms-producing efforts, see The SIPRI Study, pp. 768-782, wherein there is a particularly interesting account of Israel's efforts at producing a jet engine for fighter aircraft.

13. For recent information on Israel's efforts at building an indigenous conventional arms industry, see the following articles in the *New York Times*: "Israeli Industry Easing Dependence on Foreign Arms," January 16, 1969, p. 4; "Israel Opens Plant to Manufacture French-Designed Jet Engine," April 23, 1971, p. 1; "Aircraft Was Made Right Here," September 15, 1971, Section IV, p. 6; and "Israel Building a Prototype for a Jet Fighter-

Bomber," September 19, 1971, p. 3. See also Dale R. Tahtinen, *The Arab-Israeli Military Balance Today* (Washington, D.C.: American Enterprise Institute, 1974).

14. See "U.S. Said to Plan to Help Israelis Make Own Arms," *New York Times*, January 14, 1972, p. 1. Mentioned here are components for tank transmissions, nose wheel steering mechanisms for aircraft and the J-79 jet aircraft engine, presumably meant to be fit to Israeli-built Mirages.

15. For details on the South African arms industry, see The SIPRI Study, Chapter 20. See also the *New York Times*, October 3, 1971, p. 17, and July 27, 1970, p. 12.

16. India's burgeoning armaments industry is analyzed in The SIPRI Study, pp. 741-758.

17. For analyses of China's growing self-sufficiency in arms, see the *New York Times*, "China Producing Jet of Own Design," May 17, 1971, p. 1; and "China Said to Install Improved Missile," February 1, 1972, p. 1. There have been some indications of the possibility of American arms sales to China to make up for shortfalls in indigenous development. See "Chinese Seeking U.S. Copter Deal," *Chicago Tribune*, January 16, 1974.

18. See "Report Israeli arms sale," *Chicago Tribune*, September 22, 1973, p. 1, wherein Israeli arms sales to Latin America are discussed, including aircraft transfers to El Salvador and Mexico.

19. See, inter alia, C. F. Barnaby, ed., *Preventing the Spread of Nuclear Weapons* (London: Souvenir Press for the Pugwash Movement, 1969); Alastair Buchan, ed., *A World of Nuclear Powers?* (Englewood Cliffs, N.J.: Prentice-Hall, 1966); Leonard Beaton, *Must the Bomb Spread?* (Harmondsworth: Penguin, 1968); Leonard Beaton and John Maddox, *The Spread of Nuclear Weapons* (London: Chatto and Windus, 1962); Richard Rosecrance, ed., *The Future of the International Strategic System* (San Francisco: Chandler, 1972), Part I; and George H. Quester, *The Politics of Nuclear Proliferation* (Baltimore: Johns Hopkins University Press, 1973).

20. William Bader, *The United States and the Spread of Nuclear Weapons* (New York: Pegasus, 1968), especially Chapters I and III.

21. United Nations, Department of Political and Security Council Affairs, *Effects of the Possible Use of Nuclear Weapons and the Security and Economic Implications for States of the Acquisition and Further Development of These Weapons* (New York: United Nations, 1968), hereinafter cited as The UN Report. In Annex IV, there is a detailed analysis of the costs for various aspects of nuclear programs.

22. See the *New York Times*, "U.S. Assumes the Israelis Have A-Bomb or its Parts," July 18, 1970, p. 1; and "Israel Believed Producing Missile of Atom Capability," October 5, 1971, p. 1. Also see George Quester, "Israel and the Nuclear Non-Proliferation Treaty," *Bulletin of the Atomic Scientists,* June 1969. For a recently written and fairly comprehensive analysis, see Fuad Jabber, *Israel and Nuclear Weapons* (London: Chatto and Windus, 1971).

23. The UN Report, Annex IV, p. 22.

Notes for Chapter Seven

1. E. H. Carr, *The Twenty Years Crisis, 1919-1939* (New York: MacMillan, 1939), especially Chapters 3-6. Carr saw a fundamental antithesis between utopia and reality—with a balance swinging towards and away from equilibrium without ever attaining it—which reveals itself in many forms of thought, including theorizing in international relations.

2. This is discussed in Richard Lewinsohn, *The Profits of War Through the Ages* (London: G. Routledge and Sons, Ltd., 1936), pp. 116-117. He describes the activities of the great metal dealers, Jacques Coeur and Jacob Fugger, as purveyors of arms and raw materials to the Turks, with Fugger having been supplier to both sides of the Turko-Venetian War.

3. Carlo Cipolla, *Guns and Sails in The Early Phase of European Expansion* (London: Collins, 1965), pp. 47-50.

4. See Richard Rosecrance, *Action and Reaction in World Politics: International Systems in Perspective* (Boston: Little, Brown, 1963), p. 229, for a discussion of the regulative forces in the international system, which as he notes may range from the formal or institutional to the informal.

5. The Brussels Treaty is briefly discussed in SIPRI, *The Arms Trade and the Third World* (New York: Humanities Press, 1971), p. 90, hereinafter cited as The SIPRI Study.

6. R. W. Beachey, "The Arms Trade in East Africa in the Late Nineteenth Century," *Journal of African History* III, no. 3 (1962).

7. Quoted in The SIPRI Study, p. 91, amidst a brief discussion of the St. Germain Convention. Additional coverage of the latter is in Lynn H. Miller, "The Reporting of International Arms Transfers," ACDA/WEC-126, prepared for the United States Arms Control and Disarmament Agency at the Security Studies Project (Los Angeles: University of California, June 1968) pp. 3-5.

8. The SIPRI Study, p. 92.

9. The Geneva Convention is discussed in The SIPRI Study, pp. 95-98; Miller, pp. 9-15; and Elton Atwater, *American Regulation of Arms Exports* (New York: Carnegie Endowment for International Peace, 1941), pp. 175-176.

10. See Carr, *The Twenty Years Crisis*, pp. 31-40, for a discussion of the "apotheosis of public opinion," in the interwar context. The older faith in the efficacy of world public opinion as applied to achieving peace is also discussed in Walter Lippmann, *The Public Philosophy* (New York: Mentor, 1955), especially Chapter 2.

11. George Thayer, *The War Business* (New York: Simon and Schuster, 1969), in Chapter IX, ends his book with a plea for an enhanced role for the United Nations.

12. These proposals are listed and briefly described in The SIPRI Study, Table 2.1, pp. 87-89.

13. Ibid., pp. 100-109, summarizes postwar proposals and resolutions.

14. See William Bader, *The United States and the Spread of Nuclear*

Weapons (New York: Pegasus, 1968), especially Chapters III and IV, for one perspective on the alleged myopia of the nuclear "haves" when it comes to the sensibilities and interests of the "have nots."

15. Regional proposals are discussed in The SIPRI Study, pp. 110-114.

16. For an explication of this concept, see Karl Deutsch et al., *Political Community and the North Atlantic Area* (Princeton: Princeton University Press, 1957), Chapter 1.

17. Little has been written of a general or theoretical nature on the history of embargoes and the extent of—and reasons for—their accustomed failures. For some interesting data and analysis of the record for the application of economic sanctions, see Peter Wallensteen, "Characteristics of Economic Sanctions," in William D. Coplin and Charles W. Kegley, eds., *A Multi-Method Introduction to International Politics* (Chicago: Markham Publishing Co., 1971), pp. 128-154.

18. A lengthy analysis of the ill-fated China embargo is in Atwater, *American Regulation of Arms Exports*, Chapter IV.

19. Ibid., p. 139.

20. See, inter alia, Atwater, *American Regulation of Arms Exports*, pp. 193-202; Manley O. Hudson, "The Chaco Arms Embargo," *International Conciliation* (New York: Carnegie Endowment for International Peace, 1936), no. 320, pp. 217-246; and Charles G. Fenwick, "The Arms Embargo against Bolivia and Paraguay," *American Journal of International Law* XXVIII, no. 3 (1934), pp. 534-538.

21. See Atwater, *American Regulation of Arms Exports*, pp. 219-221.

22. Ibid., pp. 221-225.

23. See Hugh Thomas, *The Spanish Civil War* (New York: Harper and Row, 1963), Book III.

24. See Atwater, *American Regulation of Arms Exports*, pp. 235-257, for analysis of the reversal of American arms sales policy in the late 1930s.

25. See Thayer, p. 236; Lewis A. Frank, *The Arms Trade in International Relations* (New York: Praeger, 1969), p. 205; and The SIPRI Study, p. 47.

26. The SIPRI Study, pp. 679-682.

27. *American Regulation of Arms Exports*, devotes considerable emphasis to past American arms sales policy in Latin America in revolutionary situations. He discusses situations in the Dominican Republic after 1905 (pp. 37-49), in Mexico from 1912-1929 (pp. 50-121), in Cuba after 1900 (pp. 144-148), in Honduras and Nicaragua in the 1920s (pp. 149-156) and in Brazil from 1930-1932 (pp. 157-168).

28. For a country-by-country survey of the development of arms export controls in the interwar period, see League of Nations Conference for the Reduction and Limitation of Armaments, *National Control of the Manufacture of and Trade in Arms*, League of Nations Publications, IX, no. 1, Disarmament (Geneva: 1938).

29. See Murray S. Stedman, *Exporting Arms: The Federal Arms Exports Administration, 1935-1945* (New York: Kings Crown Press, 1947); and Elton Atwater, "British Controls Over the Export of War Materials," *American Journal of International Law* XXXIII, no. 2 (1939), pp. 292-317.

30. See *American Regulation of Arms Exports,* pp. 214-229, for discussion of the policy of "moral embargoes" during this period. Russia, in 1939-1940, was on the receiving end of an embargo labeled in this manner along with Germany and Japan.

31. See Thayer, Chapter IV, for an analysis of downward devolvement of American decision making for various types of arms transactions.

32. The one major publicized exception for the United States was a case involving a shipment of F-86 fighters from West Germany to Pakistan via Iran. This case is discussed in, inter alia, Thayer, pp. 203-204.

33. Philip Noel-Baker, *The Private Manufacture of Armaments* (London: V. Gollancz, 1936), Chapter IX.

34. One excellent general work on American foreign policy, which analyzes varying perspectives along a continuum from traditionalist to limitationist to revisionist, is Howard Bliss and M. Glen Johnson, *Consensus at the Crossroads* (New York: Dodd Mead, 1972).

35. Perhaps the best secondary source on the Nye Committee hearings is John Edward Wiltz, *In Search of Peace: The Senate Munitions Inquiry, 1934-1936* (Baton Rouge: Louisiana State University Press, 1963).

36. The pros and cons of the nationalization issue are discussed in greatest detail in Noel-Baker, *The Private Manufacture of Armaments.*

37. Ibid., pp. 403-429.
38. Ibid., Chapter II.
39. Ibid., Chapter VII.
40. Ibid., Chapter VIII.
41. Ibid., Chapter III.

42. For the military-industrial complex see, inter alia, Seymour Melman, *Pentagon Capitalism* (New York: McGraw-Hill, 1970); Adam Yarmolinsky, *The Military Establishment: Its Impacts on American Society* (New York: Harper and Row, 1971); Sam C. Sarkesian and Charles C. Moskos, Jr., eds., *The Military-Industrial Complex: a Reassessment* (Beverly Hills: Sage, 1972); and Harold Nieburg, *In the Name of Science* (Chicago: Quadrangle Books, 1966).

43. See, for instance, W. H. Williams, *Who's Who in Arms* (London: Labor Research Department, 1935).

44. See, inter alia, James Ridgway, *The Closed Corporation: American Universities in Crisis* (New York: Random House, 1968); Seymour Hersh, *Chemical and Biological Warfare* (Garden City, N.Y.: Doubleday, 1969); Richard Barnet, *The Roots of War* (New York: Atheneum, 1972); and David Horowitz, *Corporations and the Cold War* (New York: Monthly Review Press, 1969), especially article by William Domhoff, "Who Made American Foreign Policy, 1945-1963?"

45. A good source for the dialogue between FDR and his antagonists on this point is the collection of Jerome Frank's private papers,

located in the Library of Congress. Also, see *American Regulation of Arms Exports*, pp. 208-257.

46. Quincy Wright, *A Study of War*, Volume II (Chicago: University of Chicago Press, 1942), pp. 1175-1176.

47. The activities of the Senate Foreign Relations Committee are illuminated in the following documents: U.S., Congress, Senate, *Foreign Military Sales Act Amendment: 1970, 1971*, Hearings before the Foreign Relations Committee, 91st Cong., 2nd sess., March 24 and May 11, 1970 (Washington, D.C.: Government Printing Office, 1970); U.S., Congress, Senate, *Arms Sales to Near East and South Asian Countries*, Hearings before the Foreign Relations Committee, 90th Cong., 1st sess., March 14, April 13, 20, 25, and June 22, 1967 (Washington, D.C.: Government Printing Office, 1967); and U.S., Congress, Senate, *United States Economic and Military Foreign Assistance Programs*, Hearings before the Foreign Relations Committee, 90th Cong., 1st sess., March 29, 1971 (Washington, D.C.: Government Printing Office, 1971).

48. U.S., Congress, Senate, *Export-Import Bank Participation and Financing in Credit Sales of Defense Articles*, Hearing Before the Committee on Banking and Currency, 90th Cong., 1st sess., July 25, 1967 (Washington, D.C.: Government Printing Office, 1967); and U.S., Congress, House, *To Amend the Export-Import Bank Act of 1945—Supplemental Hearings*, Hearings before the Committee on Banking and Currency, 90th Cong., 1st sess., September 12 and 13, 1967 (Washington, D.C.: Government Printing Office, 1967).

49. The Eximbank's activities are analyzed in Thayer, pp. 210-218, and in The SIPRI Study, p. 176, wherein it is indicated that approximately one-quarter of the bank's business before 1967 had been financing arms transfers.

50. These legislative restrictions are summarized in The SIPRI Study, pp. 175-179.

51. Ibid., p. 177. The ceilings on arms sales to Latin America and Africa were set at $75 and $40 million, respectively. Clearly, the United States could no longer be a dominant, or even a major, factor in those markets at that level of sales. Later, the ceiling for Latin America was raised to $150 million. Still, it was reported that for the year ending June 30, 1972 that Latin American nations had purchased over $1 billion in arms, the bulk of it from France and Britain. British naval sales for the past few years were estimated between $500 million and $600 million. See "Weapons Big Business," *Kalamazoo Gazette*, March 1, 1973, section B, p. 8. For more detail on shifting Latin American arms purchasing patterns, see Luigi Einaudi et al., esp. Part II. *Arms Transfers to Latin America: Toward a Policy of Mutual Respect* R-1173-DOS, report prepared for Department of State. (Santa Monica: RAND Corporation, June 1973).

52. See "In a Seller's Market, the United States Sells," *The New York Times*, June 10, 1973, Section E, p. 6, where it is stated that "it had been American policy in recent years to bar the sale of sophisticated weapons in areas of the world where, in Washington's judgment, they were not needed or would contribute to an arms race. This policy has now been declared a failure. Governments denied American equipment have been buying it from other suppliers."

53. Senator Fulbright was here reading into the record and citing from "Arms Costs Called Gigantic," *Christian Science Monitor*, March 4, 1970, reproduced in the *Foreign Military Sales Act Amendment: 1970, 1971*, p. 33.

54. See the *New York Times* article by John Hess, "Poor Nations Spend Fortune on Arms Purchases," August 18, 1969, entered into the record in Ibid., p. 42. John Stanley of the Institute for Strategic Studies is here quoted as saying that "You don't make friends by delivering arms, but you certainly make enemies by stopping."

55. *Arms Sales to Near East and South Asian Countries*, pp. 44-45.

56. *Foreign Military Sales Act Amendment: 1970, 1971*, pp. 30-31.

57. Chester Bowles, "Will We Ever Learn in Asia?" *New York Times*, March 21, 1970, read into the record of the *Foreign Military Sales Act Amendment.*, pp. 16-17.

58. See *Export-Import Bank Participation and Financing*, p. 6.

59. Galbraith is quoted as having suggested that "all companies whose business comes mainly from the government be nationalized," in the *New York Times* article by John Hess, quoted in *Foreign Military Sales Act Amendment*, p. 43.

60. Kenneth Waltz, *Man, the State and War* (New York: Columbia University Press, 1954). See also John Spanier, *Games Nations Play* (New York: Praeger, 1972), Chapter 2.

61. V. I. Lenin, *Imperialism. The Highest Stage of Capitalism* (New York: International Publishers Co., Inc., 1939); and Joseph Schumpeter, *Imperialism and Social Classes* (Cleveland and New York: The World Publishing Co., 1951).

62. For various perspectives on the applicability of this level of analysis to the causes of war see the interdisciplinary mix of selections in Leon Bramsted and George Goethals, ed., *War: Studies from Psychology, Sociology and Anthropology* (New York: Basic Books, 1964).

63. An opposite opinion to mine can be read in Ulricht Albrecht, "The Study of International Trade in Arms and Peace Research," *Journal of Peace Research* 9, no. 2 (1972). See also Amelia C. Leiss' following rebuttal to Albrecht.

64. *Foreign Military Sales Act Amendment*, p. 44.

65. For definitions and discussions of this concept, see Mancur Olson, *The Logic of Collective Action* (Cambridge, Mass.: Harvard University Press, 1965); and Bruce Russett and John D. Sullivan, "Collective Goods and International Organization," *International Organization* XXV, no. 4 (1971).

Bibliography

Postwar Arms Trade and Military Assistance

Albrecht, Ulricht. *Der Handel Mit Waffen.* Munich: C. Hanser, 1971.

Bakal, Carl. *The Right to Bear Arms.* New York: McGraw-Hill, 1966.

Barnaby, G. F., ed. *Preventing the Spread of Nuclear Weapons.* London: Souvenir Press for the Pugwash Movement, 1969.

Beaton, Leonard. *Must the Bomb Spread?* Harmondsworth: Penguin, 1968.

Beaton, Leonard and Maddox, John. *The Spread of Nuclear Weapons.* London: Chatto and Windus, 1962.

Bell, M. J. V. *Army and Nation in Sub-Saharan Africa.* Adelphi Paper no. 21. London: Institute for Strategic Studies, August 1965.

————. *Military Assistance to Independent African States.* Adelphi Paper no. 15. London: Institute for Strategic Studies, December 1964.

Bloomfield, Lincoln P. and Leiss, A. C. *Controlling Small Wars: A Strategy for the 1970s.* New York: Knopf, 1969.

Buchan, Alastair, ed. *A World of Nuclear Powers?* Englewood Cliffs, N.J.: Prentice-Hall, 1966.

Buchan, Alastair. *The Implications of a European System for Defense Technology.* Defense Technology and the Western Alliance study series, no. 6. London: Institute for Strategic Studies, 1967.

Bueschel, Richard. *Chinese Communist Airpower.* New York: Praeger, 1968.

Calmann, John. *European Cooperation in Defense Technology: The Political Aspect.* Defense Technology and the Western Alliance study series, no. 1. London: Institute for Strategic Studies, 1967.

Center for International Studies. *Regional Arms Control Arrangements for Developing Countries.* Report prepared for ACDA. Cambridge, Mass.: 1964.

277

Cohen, Paul. "The Erosion of Naval Power." *Foreign Affairs,* January 1971.

Coward, H. Roberts. *Military Technology in Developing Countries.* Cambridge, Mass.: MIT Center for International Studies, 1964.

Department of Defense. *Military Assistance and Foreign Military Sales Facts.* Pamphlet. Washington, D.C.: Government Printing Office, May 1967.

————. *Military Assistance Facts.* Pamphlet. Washington, D.C.: Government Printing Office, March 1966.

Department of State. *International Traffic in Arms.* Federal Register, vol. XXXI, no. 233, December 2, 1966, Part II (Revisions of Rules and Regulations).

Einaudi, Luigi; Heymann, Hans Jr.; Ronfeldt, David; and Sereseres, Cesar, "Arms Transfers to Latin America: Toward a Policy of Mutual Respect." R-1173-DOS, report prepared for the Department of State. Santa Monica: RAND Corporation, June 1973.

Engelmann, Bernt. *The Weapons Merchants.* New York: Crown Publishers, 1964.

Ewing, Laurence L. and Sellers, Robert C. *1966 Reference Handbook of the Armed Forces of the World.* Washington: Robert C. Sellers Associates, 1966.

Finer, Samuel. *The Man on Horseback.* New York: Praeger, 1962.

Frank, Lewis A. *The Arms Trade in International Relations.* New York: Praeger, 1969.

Furniss, Edgar C. *Some Perspectives on American Military Assistance.* Princeton: Princeton University Press, 1957.

Georgetown Research Project. *The Soviet Military Aid Program as a Reflection of Soviet Objectives.* Washington, D.C.: Atlantic Research Corporation, 1965.

Green, William. *The World's Fighting Planes.* Rev. ed. Garden City, N.Y.: Doubleday, 1965.

Gutteridge, William. *Armed Forces in the New States.* New York: Oxford University Press, 1962.

————. *Military Institutions and Power in the New States.* New York: Praeger, 1965.

Harlow, C. J. E. *The European Armaments Base: A Survey.* Defense Technology and the Western Alliance study series, no. 2. London: Institute for Strategic Studies, 1967.

Haas, Ernest. "The Balance of Power: Prescription, Concept or Propaganda." *World Politics* V, no. 4 (July 1953): 442–77.

Hess, John. "Poor Nations Spend Fortune on Arms Purchases." *The New York Times,* August 18, 1969.

Hoagland, John H. "Arms in the Developing World." *Orbis* XIII (Spring 1969).

Hoagland, John H. and Clapp, Patricia A. *Notes on Small Arms*

Traffic. C/70-7. Cambridge, Mass.: MIT Center for International Studies, 1970.

Hoagland, J. H. and Corning, Erastus, III. *The Diffusion of Combat Aircraft, Missiles and their Supporting Technologies.* Report prepared for the Office of the Assistant Secretary of Defense (International Security Affairs). Waltham, Mass.: Browne and Shaw Research Corporation, 1966.

Hoagland, John H. and Teeple, John B. *Arms Control and Weapons Transfer: The Middle Eastern Case.* Ann Arbor, Mich.: Bendix Systems Division, Bendix Corporation, August 1965.

————. "Regional Stability and Weapons Transfer: The Middle Eastern Case." *Orbis* IX (Fall 1965).

Hovey, Harold A. *United States Military Assistance: A Study of Policies and Practices.* New York: Praeger, 1965.

Hunt, Kenneth. *The Requirements of Military Technology in the 1970s.* Defense Technology and the Western Alliance study series, no. 5. London: Institute for Strategic Studies, 1967.

Hurewitz, J. C. *Soviet-American Rivalry in the Middle East.* New York: Praeger, 1969.

————. *Middle East Politics: The Military Dimension.* New York: Praeger, 1969.

Institute for Strategic Studies. *The Military Balance.* London: Yearly publication, earliest titles vary slightly.

Institute of International Education. *Military Assistance Training Programs of the U.S. Government.* New York: Institute of International Education, 1964.

James, Robert Rhodes. *Standardization and Common Production of Weapons in NATO.* Defense Technology and the Western Alliance study series, no. 3. London: Institute for Strategic Studies, 1967.

Janowitz, Morris. *The Military in the Political Development of New Nations.* Chicago: University of Chicago Press, 1964.

Johnson, John J., ed. *The Role of the Military in Underdeveloped Countries.* Princeton: Princeton University Press, 1962.

Joshua, W. and Gibert, S. *Arms for the Third World: Soviet Military Aid Diplomacy.* Baltimore: Johns Hopkins Press, 1969.

Kemp, Geoffrey. *Arms and Security: The Egypt-Israel Case.* Adelphi Papers, no. 52. London: Institute for Strategic Studies, 1968.

————. *Classification of Weapons Systems and Force Designs in Less Developed Country Environments.* C/70-3. Cambridge, Mass.: MIT Center for International Studies, 1970.

Kramish, Arnold. *Atlantic Technological Imbalance: An American Perspective.* Defense Technology and the Western Alliance study series, no. 4. London: Institute for Strategic Studies, 1967.

Le France et le Commerce des Armes. Toulon: Le Centre Local d'information et de coordination de l'Action Non-Violente, 1972.

Leiss, Amelia C., et al. *Arms Transfers to Less Developed Countries.* C/70-1. Cambridge, Mass.: MIT Center for International Studies, 1970.

Lieuwen, Edwin. *Arms and Politics in Latin America.* New York: Praeger, 1960.

Martin, Laurence. *Arms and Strategy.* New York: McKay, 1973.

McArdle, Catherine. *The Role of Military Assistance in the Problem of Arms Control: The Middle East, Latin America and Africa.* Report prepared for ACDA. Cambridge, Mass.: MIT Center for International Studies, 1964.

Miller, Lynn H. "The Reporting of International Arms Transfers. ACDA/WEC-126. Prepared for United States ACDA at the Security Studies Project. Los Angeles: University of California, June 1968.

Peres, Shimon. *David's Sling.* New York: Random House, 1970.

Quester, George H. *The Politics of Nuclear Proliferation.* Baltimore: Johns Hopkins University Press, 1973.

————. "Israel and the Nuclear Non-Proliferation Treaty." *Bulletin of the Atomic Scientists,* June 1969.

Ra'anan, Uri. *The USSR Arms the Third World: Case Studies in Soviet Foreign Policy.* Cambridge, Mass.: MIT Press, 1969.

Refson, Jacob. *U.S. Military Training and Advice: Implications for Arms Transfer Policies.* C/70-4. Cambridge, Mass.: MIT Center for International Studies, 1970.

Rogers, Hugh C. B. *Weapons of the British Soldier.* London: Seeley Service, 1960.

Safran, Nadav. *From War to War: The Arab-Israeli Confrontation, 1948-1967.* New York: Pegasus, 1969.

Select Committee on Estimates. *Sale of Military Equipment Abroad.* Second Report. Session 1958-1959. London: HMSO.

Sherwig, John M. *Guineas and Gunpowder: British Foreign Aid in the Wars with France, 1793-1815.* Cambridge, Mass.: Harvard, 1969.

Stanley, John and Pearton, Maurice. *The International Trade in Arms.* London: Chatto and Windus, 1972.

Stockholm International Peace Research Institute (SIPRI). *The Arms Trade and the Third World.* New York: Humanities Press, 1971.

"Stopping the Incredible Rise in Weapons Costs." *Business Week,* February 19, 1972.

Sutton, John L. and Kemp, Geoffrey. *Arms to Developing Countries; 1945-1965.* Adelphi Paper no. 28. London: Institute for Strategic Studies, October 1966.

Tahtinen, Dale R. *The Arab-Israeli Military Balance Since October 1973.* Washington, D.C.: American Enterprise Institute, 1974.

————. *Arms in The Persian Gulf.* Washington, D.C.: American Enterprise Institute, 1974.

Thayer, George. *The War Business.* New York: Simon and Schuster, 1969.

Tompkins, John S. *The Weapons of World War III—The Long Road Back from the Bomb.* Garden City, N.Y.: Doubleday, 1966.

Tunis, Edwin. *Weapons, a Pictorial History.* Cleveland, Ohio: World Publishing Co., 1954.

U.S., Congress, House, Committee on Banking and Currency. *To*

Amend the Export-Import Bank Act of 1945—Supplemental Hearings. 90th Cong., 1st Sess., 1967, September 12 & 13, 1967. Washington, D.C.: Government Printing Office, 1967.

U.S., Congress, House, Committee on Armed Services. *Report of the Special Subcommittee on the Middle East,* 93rd Cong., 1st Sess., December 13, 1973.

U.S., Congress, Senate, Banking and Currency Committee. *Export-Import Bank Participation and Financing in Credit Sales of Defense Articles.* 90th Cong., 1st Sess., 1967. July 25, 1967. Washington, D.C.: Government Printing Office, 1967.

U.S., Congress, Senate, Foreign Relations Committee. *Arms Sales and Foreign Policy.* Staff study pamphlet, 1967.

U.S., Congress, Senate. *Arms Sales to Near East and South Asian Countries.* Hearings before the Foreign Relations Committee, 90th Cong., 1st Sess., March 14, April 13, 20, 25 and June 22, 1967 (Washington, D.C.: Government Printing Office, 1967).

U.S., Congress, Senate. *Foreign Military Sales Act Amendment: 1970, 1971.* Hearings before the Foreign Relations Committee, 91st Cong., 2nd sess. March 24 and May 11, 1970 (Washington, D.C.: Government Printing Office, 1970).

U.S., Congress, Senate. *United States Economic and Military Assistance Programs.* Hearings before the Foreign Relations Committee, 90th Cong., 1st Sess., March 29, 1967 (Washington, D.C.: Government Printing Office, 1967).

Washburn, Alan V. *Compendium of U.S. Laws on Controlling Arms Exports.* USACDA Research Report 66-2. Washington, D.C.: 1966.

Wolf, Charles, Jr. *Military Assistance Programs.* Santa Monica: Rand, 1965.

Wood, David. *Armed Forces in Central and Latin America.* Adelphi Paper no. 35. London: Institute for Strategic Studies, April 1967.

————. *The Armed Forces of the African States.* Adelphi Paper no. 27. London: Institute for Strategic Studies, April 1966.

————. *The Middle East and the Arab World: The Military Context.* Adelphi Paper no. 20. London: Institute for Strategic Studies, July 1965.

Pre-World War II Arms Trade
and Military Assistance

Abad, C. H. "The Munitions Industry in World Affairs." *Scribners,* September 1933, pp. 176-181.

Atwater, Elton. *Administration of Export and Import Embargoes, 1935-36.* Geneva: Geneva Research Center, 1938.

————. *American Regulation of Arms Exports.* New York: Carnegie Endowment for International Peace, 1941.

————. "British Control over the Export of War Materials." *American Journal of International Law* XXXIII, no. 2 (1939): 292-317.

Baccus, Joseph H. *Arms and Munitions.* New York: Noble and Noble, 1935.

Baldwin, Hanson. *The Caissons Roll—A Military Survey of Europe.* New York: Alfred A. Knopf, 1938.

Barnes, Gladeon Marcus. *Weapons of World War II.* New York: D. Van Nostrand, 1947.

Batty, Peter. *The House of Krupp.* New York: Stein and Day, 1967.

Beachey, R. W. "The Arms Trade in East Africa in the Late Nineteenth Century." *Journal of African History* III, no. 3 (1962).

Berdrow, Wilhelm. *Alfred Krupp.* 2 Vols. Berlin: Reimar Hobbing, 1927.

Borchard, Edwin M. "The Arms Embargo and Neutrality." *American Journal of International Law* XXXVII (1933): 293-298.

Brockway, Fenner. *The Bloody Traffic.* London: Gollancz, 1933.
——————. *Death Pays a Dividend.* London: Gollancz, 1941.

Brown, James Scott. "Neutrality of the United States." *American Journal of International Law* XXIX (1935): 644-652.

Chamberlain, Joseph P. "The Embargo Resolutions and Neutrality; Text of the Resolutions, the Treaty of St. Germain and the Trade in Arms Convention." *International Conciliation,* no. 251, June 1929.

Cole, Wayne S. *Senator Gerald P. Nye and American Foreign Relations.* Minneapolis: University of Minnesota Press, 1962.

"Convention for the Control of the Trade in Arms and Ammunition and Protocol Signed at St. Germain-en-laye, September 10, 1919." *International Conciliation,* no. 164, July 21, 1921.

Crowell, Benedict. *The Armies of Industry—Our Nation's Manufacture of Munitions for a World in Arms, 1917-1918.* New Haven, Conn.: Yale University Press, 1921.

Drew, George A. *Enemies of Peace: An Exposé of Armaments Manufacturers.* Toronto: Women's League of Nations Association, 1933.

DuPont de Nemours and Co. *The DuPont Company and Munitions.* Wilmington, Del.: E. I. DuPont de Nemours and Co., 1934.

Drexel, Constance. *Armament Manufacture and Trade.* New York: Carnegie Endowment for International Peace, 1933.

Einzig, Paul. *The Economics of Rearmament.* London: K. Paul, Trench, Trubner, and Co., Ltd., 1934.

Engelbrecht, H. C. *One Hell of a Business.* New York: R. M. McBride and Co., 1934.

Engelbrecht, H. C. and Hanighen, F. C. *Merchants of Death: A Study of the International Armaments Industry.* New York: Dodd, Mead & Co., 1934.

Fenwick, Charles G. "The Arms Embargo against Bolivia and Paraguay." *American Journal of International Law* XXVIII, no. 3 (1934): 534-538.

Geering, Traugott. *Handel und Industrie der Schweiz unter dem Einfluss des Weltkrieges.* Basel: B. Schwabe, 1928.

Gregory, Charles Noble. "Neutrality and the Sale of Arms." *American Journal of International Law* X (1916): 543-555.

Hatch, Alden. *Remington Arms in American History.* New York: Rinehart, 1956.

Hilger, Gustav and Meyer, Alfred. *The Incompatible Allies: A Memoir-History of German-Soviet Relations, 1918-1941.* New York: Hafner, 1971.

Hudson, Manley O. "The Chaco Arms Embargo." *International Conciliation.* New York: Carnegie Endowment for International Peace, 1936.

Jessup, Philip C. "The New Neutrality Legislation." *American Journal of International Law* XXIX (1935): 665-670.

Johnsen, Julia Emily. *International Traffic in Arms and Munitions.* New York: The H. W. Wilson Co., 1934.

Judd, Cornelius D. *Traffic in Armaments.* Dallas: Southern Methodist University, 1934.

Kobayashi, Ushisaburo. *War and Armament Taxes of Japan.* New York: Oxford University Press, 1923.

League of Nations Conference for the Reduction and Limitation of Armaments. *National Control of the Manufacture of and Trade in Arms.* League of Nations Publications, IX, no. 1, Disarmament (Geneva: 1938).

League of Nations Secretariat; Economics, Financial and Transit Department, *Raw Materials Policies.* Geneva: League of Nations, 1940.

Lehmann-Russbuldt, Otto. *War for Profits.* New York: A. H. King, 1930.

Lewinsohn, Richard. *The Mystery Man of Europe.* Philadelphia: J. B. Lippincott, 1929.

————. *The Profits of War through the Ages.* London: G. Routledge and Sons, Ltd., 1936.

Low, Archibald M. *Modern Armaments.* London: J. Gifford, Ltd., 1940.

Manchester, William. *The Arms of Krupp.* Boston: Little, Brown, 1968.

McCormick, Donald. *Peddlar of Death.* London: MacDonald, 1965.

Moore, John Bassett. "The New Isolation." *American Journal of International Law* XXVII (1933): 607-629.

Morey, William Carey. "The Sale of Munitions of War." *American Journal of International Law* X, no. 3 (1916): 467-491.

Morgan, Laura P. "Armaments and Measures of Enforcement," in *World Organization, A Balance Sheet of the First Great Experiment.* Washington, D.C.: American Council on Public Affairs, 1942.

National Munitions Control Board. *Annual Report.* Washington, D.C.: Government Printing Office, 1936, 1937, 1938, 1939.

Newbold, J. T. Walton. *The War Trust Exposed.* London: Blackfriars, 1916.

Newman, James Roy. *The Tools of War.* Garden City, N.Y.: Doubleday, Doran and Co., 1942.

Noel-Baker, Philip. *Hawkers of Death; the Private Manufacture of Armaments.* Pamphlet. London: The Labour Party, 1934.

————. *The Private Manufacture of Armaments.* London: V. Gollancz, 1936.

Noyes, Alexander. *The War Period of American Finance, 1908-1925.* New York: Putnam, 1926.

Perris, George Herbert. *The War Traders.* London: National Peace Council, 1914.

Rauschenbush, Stephen. *War Madness.* Washington, D.C.: National Home Library Foundation, 1937.

Robertson, H. Murray. *Krupp's and the International Armaments Ring, The Scandal of Modern Civilization.* London: Holden and Hardingham, 1915.

Rousse, Thomas Andrew. *Nationalization of Munitions.* Austin: University of Texas Bulletin, 1936.

Scott, James Brown. "Neutrality of the United States." *American Journal of International Law* XXXIX, no. 4 (1935): 644-652.

Scott, J. D. *Vickers, A History.* London: Weidenfeld and Nicolson, 1962.

Seldes, George. *Iron, Blood, and Profits: an Exposé of the Worldwide Munitions Racket.* New York and London: Harper and Brothers, 1934.

Sloutzki, Nokhim. *The World Armaments Race, 1919-1939.* Geneva: Geneva Research Center, 1941.

Staley, Eugene. *Foreign Investment and War.* Chicago: University of Chicago Press, 1935.

Stedman, Murray S. *Exporting Arms: The Federal Arms Exports Administration, 1935-1945.* New York: Kings Crown Press, 1947.

Stone, William T. "International Traffic in Arms and Ammunition." *Foreign Policy Reports* IX, no. 12 (August 16, 1933).

Thomas, Hugh. *The Spanish Civil War.* New York: Harper and Row, 1963.

Union of Democratic Control. *The Secret International: Armaments Firms at Work.* London: 1932.

U.S., Congress, Senate. *Munitions Industry.* Report of the Special Committee on Investigation of the Munitions Industry, 73rd Cong. Washington, D.C.: Government Printing Office, 1936.

Van Gelder, A. P. and Schlatter, Hugo. *History of the Explosives Industry in America.* New York: Columbia University Press, 1927.

Waldman, Seymour. *Death and Profits.* New York: Brewer, Warren and Putnam, 1932.

White, Freda. *Traffic in Arms.* London: League of Nations Union, 1932.

Williams, W. H. *Who's Who in Arms.* London: Labour Research Department, 1935.

Wiltz, John Edward. *In Search of Peace: The Senate Munitions Inquiry, 1934-1936.* Baton Rouge: Louisiana State University Press, 1963.

Woolsey, Lester Hood. "The Burton Resolution on the Trade in Munitions of War." *American Journal of International Law* XXII (1928): 610-614.

Miscellaneous Sources

Albrecht-Carrie, René. *A Diplomatic History of Europe Since the Congress of Vienna.* New York: Harper and Row, 1958.

Aron, Raymond. *The Century of Total War.* Garden City: Doubleday, 1954.

Art, Robert J. and Waltz, Kenneth, eds. *The Use of Force.* Boston: Little, Brown 1971.

Bader, William. *The United States and the Spread of Nuclear Weapons.* New York: Pegasus, 1968.

Bell, John Fred. *A History of Economic Thought.* 2nd Ed. New York: Ronald Press, 1967.

Black, Cyril E. and Helmreich, E. C. *Twentieth Century Europe.* 3rd Ed. New York: Knopf, 1966.

Blackstock, Paul W. *The Strategy of Subversion.* Chicago: Quadrangle, 1964.

Bliss, Howard and Johnson, M. Glen. *Consensus at the Crossroads.* New York: Dodd Mead, 1972.

Bramsted, Leon and Goethals, George, eds. *War: Studies from Psychology, Sociology and Anthropology.* New York: Basic Books, 1964.

Brodie, Bernard and Brodie, Fawn. *From Cross-Bow to H-Bomb.* New York: Dell, 1962.

Carr, E. H. *International Relations Between the Two World Wars, 1919-1939.* London: MacMillan, 1947.

————. *The Twenty Years Crisis, 1919-1939.* London: MacMillan, 1939.

Cipolla, Carlo. *Guns and Sails in the Early Phase of European Expansion.* London: Collins, 1965.

Coplin, William D. *Introduction to International Politics.* Chicago: Markham Publishing Co., 1971.

Craig, Gordon and Gilbert, Felix, eds. *The Diplomats: 1919-1939.* Vol. 2. New York: Atheneum, 1963.

Dehio, Ludwig. *The Precarious Balance; Four Centuries of the European Power Struggle.* New York: Knopf, 1962.

Deutsch, Karl W. and Singer, J. David. "Multipolar Power Systems and International Stability." *World Politics* XVI, no. 3 (April 1964): 390-406.

Deutsch, Karl W., et al. *Political Community and the North Atlantic Area.* Princeton: Princeton University Press, 1957.

Dinerstein, Herbert S. "The Transformation of Alliance Systems." *The American Political Science Review* LIX, no. 3 (September 1965): 589-601.

Earle, Edward M., ed. *Makers of Modern Strategy.* Princeton: Princeton University Press, 1941.

Falls, Cyril. *The Art of War: From the Age of Napoleon to the Present Day.* New York: Oxford University Press, 1961.

Feis, Herbert. *Europe, the World's Banker: 1870-1914.* New York: Council on Foreign Relations, 1930.

Friedmann, Wolfgang and Kalmanoff, George. *Joint International Business Ventures.* New York: Columbia University Press, 1961.

Fuller, J. F. C. *Armaments and History.* New York: C. Scribner's Sons, 1945.

————. *A Military History of the Western World.* 3 Vols. New York: Minerva Press, 1955.

Gathorne-Hardy, C. M. *A Short History of International Affairs, 1920-1934.* London: Oxford University Press, 1934.

Gilpin, Robert. *France in the Age of the Scientific State.* Princeton: Princeton University Press, 1968.

Hersh, Seymour. *Chemical and Biological Warfare.* Garden City, N.Y.. Doubleday, 1969.

Horowitz, David. *Corporations and the Cold War.* New York: Monthly Review Press, 1969.

Hoffmann, Stanley. *Contemporary Theory in International Relations.* Englewood Cliffs, N.J.: Prentice-Hall, 1960.

Holborn, Hajo. *The Political Collapse of Europe.* New York: Knopf, 1959.

Holsti, Kenneth J. *International Politics.* Englewood Cliffs, N.J.: Prentice-Hall, 1967.

Icks, Robert J. *Tanks and Armored Vehicles.* New York: Duell, Sloane and Pearce, 1945.

Jabber, Fuad. *Israel and Nuclear Weapons.* London: Chatto and Windus, 1971.

Jane's All the World's Aircraft. London: Sampson, Low, Marston and Co., annual.

Jane's Fighting Ships. London: Sampson, Low, Marston and Co., annual.

Johnson, George B. and Lockhoven, Hans Bert. *International Armament.* 2 Vols. Cologne, Germany: International Small Arms Publishers, 1965.

Jones, Ralph E.; Rarey, George E.; and Icks, Robert J. *The Fighting Tanks Since 1916.* Washington: The National Service Publishing Co., 1933.

Kaplan, Morton. *System and Process in International Politics.* New York: Wiley, 1957.

Knorr, Klaus. *Military Power and Potential.* Lexington, Mass.: D. C. Heath, 1970.

————. *The War Potential of Nations.* Princeton: Princeton University Press, 1956.

Knorr, Klaus and Verba, Sidney, eds. *The International System: Theoretical Essays.* Princeton: Princeton University Press, 1961.

Liddell-Hart, B. H. *Strategy: The Indirect Approach.* New York: Praeger, 1954.

Lippmann, Walter. *The Public Philosophy.* New York: Mentor, 1955.

Liska, George. *Nations in Alliance.* Baltimore: The Johns Hopkins Press, 1962.

————. *The New Statecraft.* Chicago: Chicago University Press, 1960.

Lusar, Rudolf. *German Secret Weapons of the Second World War.* New York: Philosophical Library, 1959.

Macksey, K., and Batchelor, J. H. *Tank: A History of the Armoured Fighting Vehicle.* London: MacDonald, 1970.

Marshall, A. W. *Problems of Estimating Military Power.* C/66-21. Cambridge, Mass.: MIT Center for International Studies, 1968.

Marshall, S. L. A. *Battle at Best.* New York: Morrow, 1963.

Melman, Seymour. *Pentagon Capitalism.* New York: McGraw-Hill, 1970.

Millis, Walter. *Arms and Men.* New York: Putnam, 1956.

Montgomery, Bernard L. *A History of Warfare.* London: Collins, 1968.

Montross, Lynn. *War Through the Ages.* 3rd Ed. New York: Harper, 1960.

Morgenthau, Hans. *Politics Among Nations.* 4th Ed. New York: Knopf, 1967.

Nieburg, Harold. *In the Name of Science.* Chicago: Quadrangle Books, 1966.

Ogorkiewicz, Richard M. *Armor, A History of Mechanized Forces.* New York: Praeger, 1960.

————. *Armored Vehicles.* New York: Arco Publishing Co., 1960.

Olson, Mancur. *The Logic of Collective Action.* Cambridge, Mass.: Harvard University Press, 1965.

Oman, Charles. *A History of the Art of War in the Middle Ages.* London: Methuen, 1900.

Polanyi, Karl. *The Great Transformation.* New York and Toronto: Farrar and Rinehart, Inc., 1944.

Preston, Richard and Wise, Sydney. *Men in Arms.* New York: Praeger, 1956.

Ridgway, James. *The Closed Corporation: American Universities in Crisis.* New York: Random House, 1968.

Rosecrance, Richard. *Action and Reaction in World Politics: International Systems in Perspective.* Boston: Little, Brown, 1963.

————. "Bipolarity, Multipolarity, and the Future." *The Journal of Conflict Resolution* X (1966): 314-327.

————. ed. *The Future of the International Strategic System.* San Francisco: Chandler, 1972.

Russett, Bruce, ed. *Economic Theories of International Politics.* Chicago: Markham Publishing Co., 1968.

————. *Trends in World Politics.* New York: MacMillan, 1965.

Russett, Bruce and Sullivan, John D. "Collective Goods and International Organization." *International Organization* XXV, no. 4 (1971).

Sarkesian, Sam C. and Moskos, Charles C. Jr., eds. *The Military-Industrial Complex: A Reassessment.* Beverly Hills: Sage, 1972.

Schumpeter, Joseph. *Imperialism.* Cleveland and New York: World Publishing Co., 1951.

Servan-Schreiber, Jean-Jacques. *The American Challenge.* New York: Atheneum, 1968.

Singer, J. David and Small, Melvin. "Formal Alliances, 1815-1939." *Journal of Peace Research* 3, no. 1 (1966).

————. *The Wages of War: 1816-1965.* New York: Wiley, 1972.

Smith, W. H. B. *Small Arms of the World.* Harrisburg, Pa.: Stackpole Books, 1966.

Spanier, John. *Games Nations Play.* New York: Praeger, 1972.

Toland, John. *The Rising Sun.* 2 Vols. New York: Random House, 1970.

Tuchman, Barbara. *The Guns of August.* New York: Dell, 1962.

Turner, G. B., ed. *A History of Military Affairs in Western Society since the Eighteenth Century.* New York: Harcourt Brace, 1953.

United Nations, Department of Political and Security Council Affairs. *Effects of the Possible Use of Nuclear Weapons and the Security and Economic Implications for States of the Acquisition and Further Development of these Weapons.* New York: United Nations, 1968.

von Senger und Etterlin, F. M. *Die Kampfpanzer von 1916-1966.* Munich: J. F. Lehmanns Verlag, 1966.

Wallensteen, Peter. "Characteristics of Economic Sanctions," in William D. Coplin and Charles W. Kegley, eds., *A Multi-Method Introduction to International Politics.* Chicago: Markham Publishing Co., 1971.

Waltz, Kenneth. *Man, the State and War.* New York: Columbia University Press, 1954.

————. "The Stability of a Bipolar World." *Daedalus* 93, no. 3 (Summer 1964): 892-907.

Weller, Jac. *Weapons and Tactics, Hastings to Berlin.* London: Nicholas Vane, 1966.

Wilkins, Mira. *The Emergence of Multinational Enterprise: American Business Abroad from the Colonial Era to 1914.* Cambridge, Mass.: Harvard University Press, 1970.

Wintringham, T. H. *Weapons and Tactics.* London: Faber and Faber, 1940.

Wright, Quincy. *A Study of War.* Volume II. Chicago: University of Chicago Press, 1942.

Yarmolinsky, Adam. *The Military Establishment: Its Impacts on American Society.* New York: Harper and Row, 1971.

Index

aircraft: autarky, 192
Algeria, 20
alliance patterns, 29, 30; and arms acquisition, 132; arms pattern and controls, 215; arms flow, 38; arms trade, 8; with China and Japan, 28; cross-bloc acquirers, 139; licensing, 149; multipolarity, 169; by region, 134–140; and suppliers, 123
ANZAM (Anglo-Malaysian Defense Agreement), 139
Arabs, 97, 109; arms transfer, 102; League, 138
Argentina, 22
arms industry: acquisition pattern, 101; control, 88; definition of trade, 19; embargoes and control, 217; history of trade, 2; joint efforts, 145; models of trade, 11; multinationalization, 172; nationalization, 36; navy, 58; privatization, 35; tanks, 68
Aron, R., 3, 32
artillery, 19
Atwater, E., 218
autarky: analysis of, 184; concept of, 2; dependence for components, 16; economic data, 204; interwar period, 53; leverage, 108; licensing, 152; by weapon, 196–199

Bader, William, 208
Biafra, 29
bipolarity: definition, 29
Bowles, Chester, 234
Brazil, 22

Cambodia, 129
Canada: warships, 72

Caplin, W., 26
Carr, E.H., 212
CENTO, 134
Chaco War, 15; as weapon proving ground, 106
Chapultepec Agreement, 137
China, 12; acquisitions, 129; autarky, 207; missiles, 59
Church, Senator, 230
Cipolla, C., 177
codevelopment, 167
coproduction: concept of, 162
Convention of St. Germain, 214
Council on Foreign Relations, 225
counterinsurgency, 56; trainer aircraft, 65
Cuba, 20, 113
Cummings, Samuel, 230
Czechoslovakia, 46, 80

data: methodology problems, 112; sources, 23
Defense Department, 228
Deutsch, K., 217
diplomacy: and acquisition, 105; alliances and arms, 134; and arms supply, 106; control of arms trade, 213; Japan, 29; leverage, 108; polorization in 1930s, 33; and warfare, 31

economies of scales exports, 5
embargoes: and arms control, 219; and spare parts, 16
Engelbrecht, Hans, 224; –Hanighen, F., 39
Ethiopia, 12
Eximbank, 228

fighter aircraft, 52–55; and coproduction,

About the Author

Robert E. Harkavy, presently an Assistant Professor at Kalamazoo College, received a Ph.D. in International Relations from Yale in 1973. Earlier, he had obtained degrees at Berkeley and Cornell, having majored in chemistry as an undergraduate. Mr. Harkavy has worked as an administrative assistant in the Secretariat of the U.S. Atomic Energy Commission, and also as a Wall Street investment analyst.

Aside from his work on the arms trade, Mr. Harkavy has recently been engaged in additional research on Middle Eastern military affairs. He has completed a manuscript on the Israeli nuclear weapons program, and is working on another dealing with pre-emption in conventional warfare.

Mr. Harkavy is married and the father of one child.